THE WONDERFUL TRUTH ABOUT OUR HEAVENLY FATHER

OTHER BOOKS BY MICHAEL F. CLUTE

Does God Kill People?	1977	$4.95
The Final Absolute-Ultimate Truth About God	1979	$6.95
Into The Father's Heart	1982	$2.95

PAMPHLETS

The Sign of God's Power To Save and Seal His People	1967
God Does Not Kill	1980

The author also publishes a monthly newspaper and newsletter, copies of which will be sent to anyone free upon request.

THE WONDERFUL TRUTH ABOUT OUR HEAVENLY FATHER

MICHAEL F. CLUTE

THE TRUTH THAT GOD DESTROYS NO MAN

A Study of the Character of God

Published by

God's Last Call Ministries

GOD'S LAST CALL MINISTRIES
P.O. BOX 1170
NEWBERG, OR 97132
1-503-538-1255

Scripture quotations in this book are from the King James Version (KJV) of the Holy Bible, unless otherwise noted.

All bold and/or italic emphasis given to Scripture or Ellen G. White quotations is supplied by the author.

Library of Congress Catalog Number: 86-080851

1st printing, April, 1986
Published by God's Last Call Ministries
ISBN 0-9608682-1-6

TO:

The thousands of dedicated, open-hearted, and open-minded people who have prayed for me and supported me through the years. May this book provide you with some of the answers you have been searching for, so you can reach the millions of precious souls who still don't know the depths of God's eternal love.

CONTENTS

v

PART III

PREFACE

After *"INTO THE FATHER'S HEART," (IFH)* was published in the summer of 1982, I had no further plans to write anymore on this subject. I was living in West Virginia then and believed it was time to go to the "Gentiles" with the message most of God's professed people either did not want to hear or only wished to argue about. Very few wished to sincerely pray and study over it. Little did I realize that in just 12 short months I would be back in Oregon, out here on the West coast where most of the SDAs in the USA live.

The Lord spoke to me very clearly about returning to Oregon. He said, "Son, your work here is finished. I want you to return to the West coast, to Oregon. *My time is near.* You must tell the people *my true character,* for the plagues will soon begin and probation will soon close." Sharon had been wanting to return all along, but I would not go until the Lord gave the word to go back. Now, He had spoken and so in August of 1983, we moved back. The Lord sold the farm the same day we advertised it and He provided a place for our family and the ministry as well.

But the idea of writing another book was not in my mind at all. People kept asking me to print up some of the additional light and concepts I presented in my meetings on cassette tape, so I had one of my complete lectures I gave at College Place, Wash., in late 1983, transcribed. This covers the first five chapters of this book. I had planned to combine that with my second manuscript or book, but the Lord impressed me to just make a whole new book. Chapters six through ten is all new material and chapters eleven and twelve deal mainly with the *"TWO LORDS"* concept and how this relates to many of the questionable and violent acts in the Old Testament. So, the book has **three distinct parts** to it, plus the additional thoughts. I have quoted liberally from the pen of Ellen G. White (EGW) throughout to show that she supports, confirms and re-inforces the concept of a loving God in her writings, even though there are a few quotations in which she seems to indicate that she believed God was justified in acts of destruction. However, you will find very few of these quotations. I would estimate that 80 to 90 percent of Ellen White's writings vindicate God's character and prove that *"God destroys no man."* COL 84. If the Old Testament prophets, John the Baptist, the disciples and even the angels themselves did not fully comprehend the nature and Character of Satan until *"the death of Christ,"* DA 758, then I think it is safe to say that they didn't understand the character of Christ either. Why then should we demand that EGW be the final authority on the character of God when she died in 1915? The understanding of God's character is a progressive revelation just as all truth is unfolding progressively.

Because *"God is love,"* He has chosen to solve the problems connected with the Great Controversy without force or violence, for these principles are contrary to both His nature, government and character. *"Rebellion was not to be overcome by force.* Compelling power is found only under Satan's government. *The Lord's principles are not of this order.* His authority rests upon *goodness, mercy, and love;* and the presentation of these principles is the means to be used. God's government is moral, and *truth and love are to be the prevailing power.* It was God's purpose to place things on an eternal basis of security, *and in the councils of heaven it was decided that time must be given for Satan to develop the principles which were the foundation of his system of government.* He had claimed that these were superior to God's principles. Time was given for the working of Satan's principles, that they might be seen by the heavenly universe."* DA 759.

An English historian, First Baron, John Emerich Edward Dalberg-Acton (1834-1902) stated one of the greatest truths of all time when he said: "POWER TENDS TO CORRUPT AND ABSOLUTE POWER CORRUPTS ABSOLUTELY." Letter in Life of Mandell Creighton (1904). The carnal nature of man has proved this true over and over again throughout the centuries. But why does man desire power over his fellow man? The answer is that man is **afraid.** His heart is filled with **fear.** Ferrero, the Italian historian, in his book "The Principles of Power," points out that the basic human (carnal) trait underlying all illegitimate governments is that of **fear.** He proved that this fear is obsessive within man, controlling both the ruled and rulers alike in its Satanic clutches. The ruler is afraid of the people and people's hearts are filled with terror because they are being ruled. This has been fully demonstrated in countries such as Germany and Italy with rulers like Hitler and Mussolini. But mankind has often overlooked, what perhaps is, the greatest demonstration of this fear principle in organized religion itself. Innocent men and women, from the cradle to the grave, are kept in an absolute bondage of fear that God will punish them, not only in this life, but all through eternity, in an ever-burning hell fire. Some are more benevolent and say that He will only burn them up for a little while, until they are completely consumed.

Well, take courage, dear heart. I have **GOOD NEWS** for you. **God is not the kind of person you thought He was.** You are about to be delivered from the **fear tactics** of man and given your freedom to worship the **beautiful God** we see in the face of Jesus Christ, whose wonderful and eternal love will **"cast out all fear."** I John 4:18.

Truly your friend and servant in Christ,

Evang. Mike Clute

INTRODUCTION

The Apostle Paul wrote the following admonition to the believers at Philippi about A.D. 64. *"Let this mind be in you, which was also in Christ Jesus:"* Philippians 2:5.

Jesus had a mind that was in tune with His Father's mind in heaven. That is, He was on the same wave length or frequency as His Father and always heard His voice and was always in harmony with Him. He had a light connection with His Father on the throne and that connection always kept Him in His Father's perfect peace and love no matter what situation Jesus might find Himself in on earth.

Adam had that same light connection in his mind when he was first created, but lost it through disobedience. Jesus came down to this dark earth to restore that light connection. He came to plug us back in, back into the main power source.

John the beloved said Jesus was the *"true light, which lighteth every man that cometh into the world."* John 1:9. Paul met this "Light" (Jesus) on the Damascus road about A.D. 34, sometime after the death of Stephen. Acts 9. He became a blazing infernal for Christ, setting people on fire with the love of God everywhere he went throughout the then known world. In fact, he and his contemporaries were accused of turning the world "upside down."

Most people don't realize they are going through life upside down until they come face to face with Jesus. But as soon as they submit to Him, as Paul did, they are turned right side up. That is, they are converted or "born again," and plugged into the main power line, even God's eternal throne of light. This immediately sets them in opposition to the majority of people in society who are still upside down, but think they are right side up. Those who have been born again and turned right side up look upside down to them. Secular society and organized religion continually war against anyone who is different than themselves. They do everything they can to turn them back the way they were, upside down, so they will fit into their plans and programs.

Doctor Luke records the opposition Paul and his cohorts received from both Romans as well as the envious and unbelieving Jews who followed Paul from city to city assaulting the believers and complaining to the *"rulers of the city, ... These that have turned the world upside down are come hither also;"* Acts 17:6.

The same thing is happening again today. Whenever the character of God message is preached, the people become aroused. Some are happily enlightened, but others are enraged and go into deeper Laodicean darkness and apostasy as they blindly strike out against and attack those who wish to study and share the "good news" that Jesus is a "harmless" life-God, who shed His blood as a witness or proof that He will never strike back at us no matter what we do to Him. But He is always and only seeking to protect and save the sinner from destruction, no matter what the cost to Himself may be.

The servant of the Lord tells how Jesus encountered this same kind of unbelief and persecution from His own people. *"Jesus told them plainly, 'There are some of you that believe not;' adding 'Therefore said I unto you, that no man can come unto Me, except it were given unto Him of My Father.' He wished them to understand that if they were not drawn to Him it was because their hearts were not open to the Holy Spirit. 'The natural man receiveth not the things of the spirit of God: for they are foolishness unto him: neither can he know them, because they are spiritually discerned.'* I Cor. 2:14. *IT IS BY FAITH THAT THE SOUL BEHOLDS*

THE GLORY OF JESUS. THIS GLORY IS HIDDEN, UNTIL, THROUGH THE HOLY SPIRIT, FAITH IS KINDLED IN THE SOUL." DA 391, 392.

Jesus was rejected by His generation because He would not take up the sword and lead His people in battle against the Romans. Today Christ is again being rejected by His own people because they desire a God who will destroy their enemies now and at the end of the world. But they are only creating a "god" after their own carnal minds. Paul tells us, *"to be carnally minded is death; but to be spiritually minded is life and peace. Because the carnal mind is enmity against God: for it is not subject to the law of God, neither indeed can be. So then they that are in the flesh cannot please God."* Romans 8:6-8.

There is a spiritual warfare we must fight in this life if we are to overcome and receive the character of Christ. Listen to this beautiful statement as to how Christ's character was formed while on earth.

> "We are forming characters for heaven. No character can be complete without trial and suffering. We must be tested, we must be tried. Christ bore the test of character in our behalf that we might bear this test in our own behalf through the divine strength He has brought to us. Christ is our example in patience, in forbearance, in meekness and lowliness of mind. *He was at variance and at war with the whole ungodly world, yet He did not give way to passion and violence manifested in words and actions, although receiving shameful abuse in return for good works.* He was afflicted, He was rejected and despitefully treated, yet He retaliated not. He possessed self-control, dignity, and majesty. He suffered with calmness and for abuse gave only compassion, pity, and love.
>
> Imitate your Redeemer in these things. Do not get excited when things go wrong. Do not let self arise, and lose your self-control because you fancy things are not as they should be. Because others are wrong is no

excuse for you to do wrong. Two wrongs will not make one right. You have victories to gain in order to overcome as Christ overcame.

Christ never murmured, never uttered discontent, displeasure, or resentment. He was never disheartened, discouraged, ruffled, or fretted. He was patient, calm, and self-possessed under the most exciting and trying circumstances. All His works were performed with a quiet dignity and ease, whatever commotion was around Him. Applause did not elate Him. He feared not the threats of His enemies. He moved amid the world of excitement, of violence and crime, as the sun moves above the clouds. Human passions and commotions and trials were beneath Him. He sailed like the sun above them all. Yet He was not indifferent to the woes of men. His heart was ever touched with the sufferings and necessities of His brethren, as though He Himself was the one afflicted. He had a calm inward joy, a peace which was serene. His will was ever swallowed up in the will of His Father. Not My will but Thine be done, was heard from His pale and quivering lips.

We long and pray that the grace of God may come into your hearts. We want you to make an entire surrender to God .... May God help you all to walk humbly and carefully is our prayer."

—Letter 51a, 1874.
By Ellen G. White

And so we see that the war Jesus fought while on this earth was a spiritual battle, not a literal war. In fact, the Greek word for war, as used in Rev. 12:7 is "polemikos," from which we derive the English word "polemics," which simply means "a controversy or argument." It refers more specifically to a war of words ... a debate, not a physical battle with carnal weapons as used in this earth.

And so, the purpose of this book is to encourage you, the reader, to learn the truth about God's true character of love. I wish that I could share with you all the wonderful letters I have received thanking me for writing my last book, *"INTO THE FATHER'S HEART."* If you haven't read it yet, I hope you will. I have written this book you are now holding to show that EGW taught the concept that God does not kill. If you will read it prayerfully and with an open mind, I am confident you will learn the real truth on this most important subject. This is the sincere hope and prayer of the author.

PART
I

"The more we know of God, the higher will be our ideal of character and the more earnest our longing to reflect His likeness."

MB 19, by Ellen G. White.

CHAPTER 1

CHRIST'S EFFORTS TO SAVE JUDAS

"When Mary annointed the Saviour's feet, Judas manifested his covetous disposition. At the reproof from Jesus his very spirit seemed turned to gall. Wounded pride and desire for revenge broke down the barriers, and the greed so long indulged held him in control. **This will be the experience of everyone who persists in tampering with sin. The elements of depravity that are not resisted and overcome respond to Satan's temptation, and the soul is led captive at his will.**

But Judas was not yet wholly hardened. Even after he had twice pledged himself to betray the Saviour there was opportunity for repentance. At the Passover supper Jesus proved His divinity by revealing the traitor's purpose. He tenderly included Judas in the ministry to the disciples. But the last appeal of love was unheeded. **Then the case of Judas was decided, and the feet that Jesus had washed went forth to the betrayer's work.**"

"DESIRE OF AGES"—P. 720—
By Ellen G. White

JUDAS WAS CONTROLLED
BY LUCIFER

"Lucifer's mind is revealed through Judas. Judas figured that he would bring Jesus of Nazareth to the acid test. If Jesus were really the Messiah He would act as he believed the Messiah should act and would be able to act under the circumstances Judas was going to set up with the priests. The Jewish leaders would also have to accept Him and Judas would receive all the credit for having carried out such a brilliant scheme to its successful conclusion. In either case, he would be thirty pieces of silver richer no matter what happened. He was sure he couldn't lose. His plan was fail safe. Such is the mind of man."

"INTO THE FATHER'S HEART"—P. 273—
By Michael F. Clute

JESUS AND JUDAS
AT THE LAST SUPPER

I hope all of you will stay for the whole swith very simple concepts. I am going to start tonight with the last program because the development of the character message is progressive. So we supper and will take you step-by-step through Christ's last meal and show you how Jesus tried to save Judas from destroying himself, at least 10 times. Then we will go into the wrath of God. What is the wrath of God? And does God change?

I want to share with you one other statement that I feel is very significant. But first, let's read this text. *"Behold,"* says the scripture, *"the darkness shall cover the earth, and gross darkness the people; but the Lord shall arise upon thee, and His glory shall be seen upon thee."* Isa. 60:2. The word "glory" means character. His character will be seen upon God's people when the moral darkness of the earth, in the last days, is at its peak, which will be parallel to the peak reached at the time of Christ's first coming. And then this significant statement, *"It is the darkness of misapprehension of God that is enshrouding the world. Men are losing their knowledge of His character. It has been misunderstood and misinterpreted. At this time (the very time that this darkness shall be the greatest) a message from God is to be proclaimed, a message illuminating in its influence and saving in its power. His character is to be made known. Into the darkness of the world is to be shed the light of His glory, the light of His goodness, mercy and truth . . . the last rays of merciful light, the last message of mercy to be given to the world, is a revelation of His character of love."* COL 415. Beloved, we have almost reached the darkest hour. It is time for this message to be understood by God's people and proclaimed to the world.

Tonight, I am going to talk to you about the theological aspect of this message. I have been preaching about this for nearly seven years and I have found out something very interesting. A person can talk about the theological aspects of anything and fail to live it. I talked about the theological aspects of God's character, and how He does not destroy and how wonderful He is, etc., years before I realized that I wasn't really living up to all aspects of it myself. And that really shocked me. It is in the home, the relationship between the husband and the wife, where, as they say in the world, the real test comes—the rubber or tire meets the road. Do we really know our weaknesses until we get married? I've heard some men say, "I didn't know I had a temper until I got married." So it is in the marriage relationship that you really are tested and tried. And it is through this relationship that God many times brings to our knowledge and our understanding the defects of our character. So as I began to talk about the theological concepts and aspects of God's character, people would say to me, "That is a wonderful message; it will really be great when you start living it." So, I was challenged by these people who believed in what I was saying but didn't see a corresponding action in my life. Tonight we will talk about the theological concepts. That is the first thing we must understand, and then as we go along, I will bring in the deeper spiritual applications of the message.

First, let's go to John 6, and then we will go to John 13. *"From that time many of his disciples went back, and walked no more with Him. Then Jesus said unto the twelve, Will ye also go away? Then Simon Peter answered him, Lord, to whom shall we go? Thou hast the words of eternal life. And we believe and are sure that thou art that Christ, the Son of the Living God. Jesus answered them, Have not I chosen you twelve, and one of you is a devil."* John 6:66-70. If we would go back to the statement He made before, in vs. 53, He is bringing a very, very severe test upon them. He said, *"except ye eat the flesh of the Son of Man, and drink His blood, ye have no life in you."* As a result of saying this almost everyone deserted Him. Evidently, the only ones left were the twelve disciples, so He said *"are you going away too?"* Peter said, *"No, you are the only one who has the words of eternal life. After all, we believe you are the Christ, the Son of the Living God."* A lot of people in Jerusalem and Judea believed Jesus was a wonderful teacher, even a prophet, but they weren't so ready to say He was the Messiah. But Peter believed and said, *"Yes, you are the Messiah, the very Son of God."*

Then Jesus makes his first reference to Judas. I have a tape, #729, called "Jesus and Judas," which I preached a number of years ago. In this sermon, I parallel how Jesus Christ treated Judas and I use that to show how He treated Lucifer in the beginning, because God never changes. If we will notice here how He treated Judas, I think we will then know how He treats all of His creatures, because God never changes. *"Jesus answered them, (the twelve), Have not I chosen you twelve, and one of you is a devil?"* That is a pretty strong statement to make. *"He spake of Judas Iscariot the son of Simon: for he it was that should betray him, being one of the twelve."* John 6:70,71.

Chapter 13, *"Now before the feast of the Passover, when Jesus knew that his hour was come that he should depart out of this world unto the Father, having loved his own which were in the world, he loved them unto the end. And supper being ended, the devil having now put into the heart of Judas Iscariot, Simon's son, to betray him; Jesus knowing that the Father had given all things into his hands, and that he was come from God, and went to God; He riseth from supper, and laid aside his garments; and took a towel and girded himself. After that he poureth water into a basin, and began to wash the disciples' feet."*

If you read *Desire of Ages*, 644, 645, you will find Christ started with Judas, went around in a circle and ended up with John. *Then cometh he to Simon Peter: and Peter saith unto him, Lord, dost thou wash my feet? Jesus answered and said unto him, What I do thou knowest not now; but thou shalt know hereafter."* Peter, of course, protests and says, *"Thou shalt never wash my feet."* Because Peter believed the Messiah would never do such a thing; He would never lower Himself like this. Simon Peter said unto Him. *"Lord, not my feet only, but also my hands and my head."* John 13:9. There is a little play on the two Greek words. The Greek word which means to take a bath and be washed completely is *"luo"* and the word that means to wash in part is *"nipto."* Dr. Litke, who still lives here in College Place, taught us that in Greek class back in 1956-57. So he says, *"Peter you have already been baptized and washed completely and you don't have to have that done again because you are clean."* *"He that is washed needeth not save to wash his feet, but is clean every whit: and ye are clean, but not all."* John 13:10. *"One of you is not clean,"* and he is referring to Judas. *"For he knew who should betray him; therefore said he, Ye are not all clean. So after he had washed their feet, and had taken his garments, and was set down again, he said unto them, Know ye what I have done to you? Ye call me Master and Lord: and ye say well; for so I am. If I then, your Lord and Master, have washed your feet; ye also ought to wash one another's feet: For I have given you an example, that ye should do as I have done to you."* John 13:11-15.

Now, this is a very clear statement. I have always taken this literally. But most churches take it symbolically and don't believe in the feet washing. However, the Seventh-day Adventist church does believe in this. I think it is a service that really should be taken seriously because it can help take care of a lot of problems between people.

"Verily, verily, I say unto you, The servant is not greater than his lord; neither he that is sent greater than he that sent him. If ye know these things, happy are ye if ye do them. I speak not of you all: I know whom I have chosen: but that the scripture may be fulfilled, He that eateth bread with me hath lifted up his heel against me." John 13:16-18.

Many times through Jesus' ministry He uses this expression *"that the scripture may be fulfilled,"* and the writers say that too, as if they are doing these things for the very purpose of fulfilling scripture. But, of course, that is not the way it is. Just look at your own life and see how God has led you. Today you probably understand many events in your past life which were a great mystery at the time they happened to you. But Jesus, being so close to God, could immediately know when something was happening that was fulfilling scripture, because He knew the Bible so well, and because He was in touch with His Father. But we have the same opportunity, friends, to experience that. Notice He is making an appeal here. Do you think that Judas knew what He was talking about? Oh, yes, he did, but Judas' heart is hardening, it is getting harder and harder. In fact *Desire of Ages* 645, says, he made up his mind when Jesus washed his feet and that was it. He had a strong impression to confess right there, that he was in the process of selling his Lord to the priests and rabble, but he didn't do it. He hardened his heart and said *"No, I could never do that, because the true Messiah would never humble Himself like that."*

"Now I tell you before it come, that, when it is come to pass, you may believe that I am he. Verily, verily, I say unto you, He that receiveth whomsoever I send receiveth me; and he that receiveth me receiveth him that sent me." John 13:19, 20. I want you to notice the progression here as Christ comes closer to the point a little bit more each time. And now He is really going to zero in, but His heart is breaking, not only for Judas, but for all the disciples. *"When Jesus had thus said, he was troubled in spirit, and testified, and said, Verily, verily, I say unto you, that one of you shall betray me."* Jesus was hoping He wouldn't have to bring this up. He was hoping that these other appeals would lead to repentance, a conversion for Judas, but all these had failed.

You know, God does that in every life. He will progressively come closer and closer to you until you make the decision or go completely away from Him, and He doesn't want you to go away, that breaks His heart. He can't stand to just let you go, so He is really caught between a rock and a hard place. If He draws closer and closer and you choose to go away from Him, you are going to destroy yourself but, if He doesn't make the appeal you are going to destroy yourself anyway. And that is what Judas was doing. So, Jesus was making every appeal He could to save him. Then He said, *"One of you shall betray me. Then the disciples looked one on another, doubting of whom he spake."* vs. 22. They were not at all aware that Judas was going to do this; no inkling at all. *"Now there was leaning on Jesus'*

bosom one of his disciples, whom Jesus loved." vs. 23.
He loved them all, but John was more receptive to His love
than any of the other ones. Some scholars teach that this is
in the "Present Indicative," and Dr. Litke taught us about
the "Present Indicative." It is not used very much because
the 1611 version of the Bible was translated by classical
Greek scholars commissioned by the King of England, King
James. So they were not so familiar with the Biblical
Greek, but they were familiar with the Classical Greek, in
which the continuous action is not emphasized. But this
could be translated *"whom Jesus kept on loving."* It
doesn't mean John was the special one He loved the most.
No, it means in spite of what John was, Jesus never gave up
on him. He kept on loving him even though John was one of
the sons of thunder with his brother James. They wanted to
bring fire down from heaven, Luke 9:51-54. They wanted to
destroy the Samaritans, because they were tough headed
and hard-hearted people. Jesus kept on loving him, and
John is telling about how Jesus' wonderful love toward him
finally softened his heart.

Vs. 24. *"Simon Peter therefore beckoned to him,
that he should ask who it should be of whom he spake.
He then lying on Jesus' breast saith unto him, Lord
who is it?"* We believe that Judas is on the left and John on
the right leaning on Christ's breast. D.A. 644. *"Jesus
answered, He it is to whom I shall give a sop, when I
have dipped it."* vs. 26. I always thought, and most people
have always believed, that when Jesus answered this question everyone heard what He was saying, but I don't think
this was the case. Even if Jesus said it loud enough for them
to hear, they did not understand, which was not unusual, for
they did not understand much of what He said anyway,
until after His death and resurrection. The Holy Spirit
brought it back to their minds. At this time, many of the
things He said were just a puzzle to them. So He answered,
but how loud He answered, or if He only spoke it to one
person, John, and John kept it quiet or John himself did not

understand what it meant, we don't know. We do know from the rest of the verses here that the other disciples did not have any idea that Judas was going to do this. *"And when he had dipped the sop, he gave it to Judas Iscariot, the son of Simon."* vs. 26. Some people have suggested that He said this only to Judas, loud enough for only Judas to hear it. Perhaps He turned to Judas and whispered to him alone, something like this: *"Judas, I know what you are doing, please don't do this to yourself and to Me." "When he had dipped the sop, he gave it to Judas Iscariot, the son of Simon."* vs. 26. This was an act of honor for Him to dip a piece of crusty bread into some jelly-like substance and give it to the person either on His right or left. That was a sign of honor, that He really liked that person. This was not a sign that this was the dirty rat that was going to betray Him. No, it was nothing like that. So there was no reason at all for the disciples to think that He was fingering Judas. *"And after the sop Satan entered into him."* His heart is becoming more hardened each time. This is the seventh appeal. *"Then said Jesus unto him, That thou doest, do quickly."* In other words, Jesus was saying to Judas, "If you are going to do it, go ahead, I can't stop you. You have a free will, I cannot stop you from betraying me and destroying yourself. So, if that is what you are going to do, do it as quickly as possible, and get it over with so the pain of your act will be over with as soon as possible."

Vs. 28 gives a strong clue that no one knew what was going on. *"Now no man at the table knew for what intent he spake this unto him."* That is amazing. No one here knew what was going on. Just for a little added information and emphasis, do you really think that Peter would have remained calm if he had known? I doubt it. For example, we know the disciples had swords. At least two, for earlier they had said, *"Lord here are two swords."* Luke 22:38. Do you think these rough and tough disciples, with their swords, and whatever weapons they had besides would have let Judas leave that place if he was indeed going to go

out and betray him? I don't think so. They probably would
have grabbed Judas and slammed him up against the wall
and given him a real talking to or maybe they would have
killed him. We don't know what they would have done. But
Christ did not expose him.

*"For some of them thought, that because Judas
had the bag, that Jesus had said unto him, Buy those
things that we have need of against the feast; or, that
he should give something to the poor. He then having
received the sop went immediately out: and it was
night."* John 13:29, 30. And it was night in Judas' heart, as
we know. John 18. This is the actual act of betrayal when
Jesus is out in the garden praying and He knows they are
going to come and get Him. Next, the Jewish leaders come
with the mob and He asks them, *"Who are you looking
for?"* *"They answered him, 'Jesus of Nazareth,' Jesus
saith unto them, I am he."* This is very significant. I have
read that many times and didn't understand what Christ
was doing. Do you realize He was trying to save Judas from
going through with his betrayal? He was saying, *"Judas
you don't have to come and kiss me to identify me, you
don't have to do that. I will identify myself."* No doubt
the disciples circled themselves around Christ to protect
Him. Why would the mob say *"which one of you is Jesus
of Nazareth?"* If they had known they would have just gone
up and said, *"you are under arrest"* and taken Him. But
they did not know. They were probably all dressed the same
and it was night, and they were probably trying to protect
Him. They had their swords ready. So Jesus identified himself. No fear was in His heart. *"Jesus saith unto them, I
am he. And Judas also, which betrayed him, stood
with them. As soon then as he has said unto them, I am
he, they went backward, and fell to the ground."* John
18:5, 6. We read on pages 694 and 695 of *Desire of Ages*
that an angel came; Gabriel, probably. This was a supernatural act to show this mob and Judas that what they were
doing was not blessed or approved of by Heaven. Yet that did

not stop them. It was a sign. This is a glorious angel, and they all fall down, but the light of this glorious angel does not knock them out like it did the soldiers at the time of the resurrection. *"Then asked he them again, Whom seek ye? And they said, Jesus of Nazareth."* John 18:7. He never takes away their free will. No, He never does anything to stop them. *"And he that betrayed him had given them a token, saying Whomsoever I shall kiss, that same is he; take him, and lead him away safely. And as soon as he was come he went straight away to him and saith, Master, Master; and kissed him."* Mark 14:44, 45. But Jesus said unto him, *"Judas, betrayest thou the son of man with a kiss?"* Luke 22:48. I take that as an appeal. *"Judas what are you doing? What are you doing to yourself and to me? And why are you doing this?"* (I Cor. 13:7). I see this as Jesus never giving up. When did Judas close his probation? According to *Desire of Ages* 645, 720, it was at the time when Jesus washed his feet. That is when Judas made up his mind, and yet Christ kept making all these appeals. So what is probationary time? I've decided that probation is not an act of God against man, it is an act of man against God. Just reverse it and you have the truth of the matter. God never closes anyone's probation. We close probation upon Him. We tempt Him. Spit in his face, crucify Him, and He just keeps forgiving us and taking the blame. It is the hardest thing for people to understand how the Bible is written, even Ellen White's writings. God takes the blame upon Himself and then people say that God is a liar; because the Bible says one thing and you are saying it means something else. No, God does not lie. The Bible says God does not lie. But what right does He have to take the blame? He is the Creator. He created Lucifer and everything stems from Lucifer's actions and choices and, therefore, He is responsible because Lucifer is the cause of it all. Yet, Lucifer is the greatest victim of his own rebellion. Probation is something we need to understand. We need to study it more and we will talk about it more here, but God is always taking the blame. When Jesus got up on the cross, He said, *"put all the blame on me."* In my study of the Old Testament, I have found one really good example of this principle, when Judah was willing to take the blame. *"For thy servant became surety for the lad unto my father, saying, If I bring him not unto thee, then I shall bear the blame to my father forever."* Gen. 44:32. So Judah became a type of Christ in this instance. See also Gen. 43:9.

CHAPTER 2

THE WRATH OF GOD

"To remain free and unafraid of God, the universe must learn the truth about the results of sin. They must be helped to understand that the sinner's death is not execution at the hands of a vengeful God.

But does not the Bible make frequent mention of the awesome wrath of God? The third angel of Revelation 14 warns that in the end the wrath of God, unmixed with mercy, will be poured out on the heads of unrepentant sinners, and they will be consumed with unquenchable fire (Revelation 14:9-11).

What is this wrath of God? Is it like our human anger?

In the first chapter of Romans, Paul describes how the wrath of God is poured out on those who reject and suppress the truth. Three times he explains that God gives up such people and turns them over to the results of their rebelliousness."

"CAN GOD BE TRUSTED?"—P. 82, 83—
By A. Graham Maxwell

We are going to talk now about the *"wrath of God."* I have already read from *"Can God be Trusted?"* where Dr. Maxwell makes a very good explanation of what the wrath of God is. Now, we will read it and develop it from Paul's writings. I think Paul understood God's character better than any other Bible writer. *"For the wrath of God is revealed from heaven against all ungodliness and unrighteousness of men, who hold the truth in unrighteousness; . . . Because that, when they knew God, they glorified him not as God, neither were thankful; but became vain in their imaginations, and their foolish heart was darkened. Professing themselves to be wise, they became fools, and changed the glory of the incorruptible God into an image made like to corruptible man, and to birds, and four-footed beasts, and creeping things."* Rom. 1:18, 21-23. Paul develops this from vs. 18 and he talks on and on like preachers sometimes do, and we finally find in vs. 24 that he gets to the point in defining what he started out in vs. 18 of Roman 1 to define, which is the wrath of God. He finally says, *"Wherefore God also gave them up"* (that phrase 'gave them up' is very significant, it is used over and over throughout the entire Bible), *"God gives up, he gave them up, He gave them over."* This idea is used repeatedly throughout the scriptures and Paul is using it here. That is why I like the KJV best, because these expressions are very consistent and are easy to spot throughout the Bible. *"Wherefore God also gave them up to uncleanness through the lusts of their own hearts, to dishonor their own bodies between themselves: perversion, homosexuality, etc."* vs. 28, *"God gave them over to a reprobate mind."* Then we find the *"the wrath of God"* again mentioned in Chapter 5. *"But God commendeth his love toward us, in that while we were yet sinners, Christ died for us. Much more then, being now justified by his blood, we shall be saved from wrath through him."* Rom. 5:8-9. Jesus Christ is not the one who is bringing the wrath. He is the one who is saving us from the wrath. *"For if, when we were enemies, we were reconciled to God by the death of his Son, much more, being reconciled, we shall be saved by his life."*

vs. 10. A lot of people tell me that we are saved by his death, but Paul says we are saved by His life, and reconciled by His death. The cross is what reconciles us but it is His life that saves us. This is an important distinction we should make. *"And to wait for God's son from heaven, whom he raised from the dead, even Jesus, which delivered us from the wrath to come."* I Thess. 1:10. This could be defined as the wrath that was going to come upon Jerusalem later on, and the wrath that would come upon us all at the end of the world, upon those who have not received God's mark of deliverance, the seal of God.

This could also be referring to the seven last plagues which fill up the wrath of God, *"for God hath not appointed us to wrath, but to obtain salvation by our Lord Jesus Christ."* I Thess. 5:9. *And the anger of the Lord* (the word anger is synonymous with wrath in the Bible, and always means the same thing) *was kindled against them and he departed.* Numbers 12:9. This is when Miriam got the leprosy, *"and the cloud departed from off the tabernacle and Miriam became leprous, white as snow."* One of the clearest *Spirit of Prophecy* concepts is that God never brings disease or sickness. Satan is the destroyer and author of all disease and sickness. So, since leprosy is a disease, we know that God did not bring it. In fact, it says that He departed and Miriam did not get the leprosy until after He had left, showing that when God separates Himself from us, then Satan attacks us with disease or whatever disaster he is allowed to bring upon us. Whatever tragedy happens takes place as a result of God taking his hands off. Sometimes we overindulge and bring sickness upon ourselves. But Satan and his forces of evil are around us all the time. If God's protection is removed because we push him out of our lives, then, at that point, sin has its natural result.

Psalm 78:18, 19, 27: *"And they (Israel) tempted God in their heart by asking meat for their lust. Yea, they spake against God; they said, can God furnish a table in the wilderness? . . . He rained flesh also upon them as dust, and feathered fowls like as the sand of the sea. So they did eat, and were well filled; for he gave them their own desire."* Here is another definition of what God's wrath is: "**God's wrath is when He is forced to give up and let us have and go our own way and do our own thing, and the Bible then calls it God's anger and God's wrath.**" *"They were not estranged from their lust. But while their meat was yet in their mouths, the wrath of God (which is their own desire) came upon them, and slew the fattest (or healthiest) of them, and smote down the chosen men of Israel. For all this they sinned still, and believed not for his wondrous works."* Psalm 78:30-32. They gorged themselves until it came out their nostrils, the Bible says. Numbers 11:16-20. Yet God claims to be destroying them. Sickness and death was only the natural result of what they themselves did to their own bodies, and yet God says; it is HIS WRATH. Whatever we do to ourselves, whatever God allows us to do to ourselves or to anyone else, He says this is MY WRATH. And wrath is defined as the natural result of disobedience.

   "He gave up." Here is this expression again, Ps. 78:40-49. When I first studied this, I didn't realize the importance of these other verses that precede 49. The Psalmist builds up and he is talking about all the things that happened in Egypt during the ten plagues that came upon Egypt. Now, he is going to tell you how and why or the means by which the ten plagues came upon Egypt. Notice, *"He gave up their cattle also to the hail, and their flocks to hot thunderbolts. He cast upon them the fierceness of his anger, wrath, and indignation, and trouble, by sending evil angels among them."* Please notice that it is the evil angels who are destroying; not our wonderful God. All these words are synonymous with wrath; they mean the same thing. But even here God takes the blame by saying He "sent" them. He claims to be sending plagues, because anything that God allows to happen

He says that He sent it. He did it. When Saul fell on his sword and killed Himself, I Chron. 10:4-5 says very clearly that Saul killed himself and he died. Yet, vs. 13-14 distinctly state that God killed him. So whatever God allows us to do to ourselves or to someone else, He says that He did it. If you can understand that God is almost always taking the blame, you will save yourself a lot of misunderstanding when you read the scriptures.

In the Hebrew language, the word for evil is *'ra'* which is used about 424 times, *'roa'* is used 8 times, and *'raa'* once. *'Raa'* according to the ***Britannica World Language Dictionary,*** 1959, defines *'raa'* thusly: ***"The supreme Egyptian deity, the sun-god, usually represented as a hawk-headed man crowned with a solar disc and uraeus: also spelled 're'. The uraeus is the emblem of the sacred serpent (Haje) in the headdress of Egyptian divinities and kings. A symbol of sovereignty."*** This *'raa'* of Egypt is really Lucifer or Satan, the same as the prince of Tyre, Ezek. 28:2, Lucifer-Satan. In Isa. 45:7 we read, ***"I form the light, and create darkness: I make peace, and create evil: I the Lord do all these things."*** Here God is taking the blame for everything that goes wrong in the world. He says He alone is responsible. The word ***"create"*** is bara in Hebrew and means to ***"form, prepare and fashion."*** And God says that raa is something that he fashioned and created. He made Lucifer and therefore He takes the blame for all of Lucifer's actions. Ezek. 28:15 tells us that Lucifer was created ***"perfect"*** but that ***"iniquity"*** was found in him.

It is very interesting that this word 'raa' in the actual Hebrew means ***"harmful."*** ***"Raa"*** is translated harmful. In Heb. 7:26, it says that Jesus Christ is harmless, the very opposite of Satan. ***"Holy, harmless, undefiled."*** Isn't that amazing.

Now we will go a little deeper into the subject of God's character. We are going to talk about the law of God, His covenant, which is the 10 commandments. That is very clear in the scriptures. God says His *"covenant will he not break nor alter the thing that has gone out of his lips."* Ps. 89:34. I hear preachers and people saying, the Bible says *"thou shalt not kill,"* and that God is allowed to kill but he is not allowed to murder. I talked to some Hebrew scholars on this. They say there is no distinction between kill and murder, per se. The word for kill and murder is the same word, only it becomes more intense, intensified to the grossness of it or the intent, or how that murder is committed and how terrible the action is; going from an accidental death, something that happened accidentally, no one premeditated it or did it on purpose, to a murder that is done with vengeance, premeditated and they carried it out because of a lot of anger and hatred in their hearts. So the Hebrew only intensifies the word kill and many times the words kill and murder are used interchangeably. See *"murder"* in the Old Testament—"Ratsach" meaning "to kill or murder"—strongs (Hebrew section 7521). Strongs 5407—Phonevo meaning *"kill, do murder, slay."* See Greek section. So when it says *"thou shalt not kill,"* God is saying *MY COVENANT I WILL NOT BREAK. I WILL NOT BREAK MY OWN LAW.* You can go through the 10 commandments and ask *"Does God keep His Sabbath? Does God lie or bear false witness? The 9th commandment. Does God break that commandment? No, the Bible says that God does not. Does he commit adultery? or worship other idols?"* No. You can go through all nine of the ten commandments and people will say, *"yes, God keeps his commandments."* But when you go to the sixth one, *"does God kill?"* they will say *"Yes, God kills."* It is amazing how they come to that conclusion. So you see when you think of this subject with a carnal mind, (I don't want to condemn someone or put a guilt trip on you), but if we think about God on our level, in our carnal mind, we will end up making God just like ourselves; But, God says He is not like us. *"My thoughts are higher than your thoughts, my ways are higher than your ways."* Isa. 55:9.

"My covenant will I not break nor alter the thing that has gone out of my lips." Ps. 89:34. *"God is not a man, that he should lie; neither the son of man, that he should repent: Hath he said, and shall he not do it? or hath he spoken, and shall he not make it good?" "Behold, I have received commandment to bless: and He hath blessed; and I cannot reverse it."* Num. 23:19-20. We will see more later on, as I talk about the old and the new covenant, the covenant that Israel entered into at Sinai, and the one that Jesus said, *"I will make a new covenant with you."* What is the real distinction? We are going to talk about the animal sacrifice system. That is a very controversial subject. We are going to go through it. Stay with me for that is the most interesting part.

"For I am the Lord, I change not; therefore ye sons of Jacob are not consumed." Mal. 3:6. *"Jesus Christ, the same yesterday, and today and forever."* Heb. 13:8. *"Forever, O Lord, thy word is settled in heaven. Thy faithfulness is unto all generations."* Ps. 119:89. *"Thy word* (the Bible and Jesus) *is true from the beginning: and everyone of thy righteous judgments endureth forever."* Ps. 119:160. *"Every good gift and every perfect gift is from above, and cometh down from the Father of lights, with whom is no variableness, neither shadow of turning."* James 1:17.

The Jews in Christ's day believed in a Messiah of violence who would come and destroy all their enemies. Jesus told them they should love their enemies; He healed and helped people. They said He did miracles by the power of Satan, but He told them, *"ye do the deeds of your father."* Then said they to Him, *"we be not born of fornication, we have one father even God."* Jesus said unto them. *"if God were your father you would love me: for I proceedeth forth and came from God; Neither came I of myself, but He sent me."* Then this interesting and shocking statement, and I don't think He is saying it with any kind of anger or hatred like we think we might. *"Ye are of*

your father the devil." We each have a father. We either
have a heavenly Father up in heaven or we have a father
here on earth, and it is the devil. Jesus said the Jewish
nation had Satan as their father. That is an amazing thing
to say, isn't it! Certainly they did not agree with Him. If you
read John 8:48, you all will be absolutely shocked at their
crudeness and anger. I don't know if "Samaritan! and For-
eigner!" were curse words, but they were extremely angry
and enraged that He would say that Satan was their father.
They thought their father was Jehovah-God, but their ideas
of what Jehovah was like, were of course, the very characteristics that Satan had. *"Ye are of your father the devil,
and the lusts of your father you will do. He was a murderer from the beginning and abode not in the truth,*
(and Jesus is the truth, so they abode not in Jesus) *because
there is no truth in him. When he speaketh a lie, he
speaketh of his own: For he is a liar, and the father of
it."* John 8:41-44. I want to ask you a logical question. What
right would Jesus Christ have to identify Lucifer as a murderer and liar, if in fact Jesus himself murders and lies?
Wouldn't He be a supreme hypocrite? What right would He
have to say that?

   **JESUS AND HIS FATHER NEVER KICKED
SATAN OUT OF HEAVEN.** *"And the angels which kept
not their first estate,* (principality) *but left* (and notice the
little word, left) *their own habitation, he hath reserved
in everlasting chains under darkness unto the judgment of the great day."* Jude 6. It simply says that the evil
angels still believe the original lie that Satan told them
about the Father and the Son. *"The Father and Son are
tyrants, despots,"* Satan and his angels say, *"And we will
never serve them."*

   "And his (Satan's) *tail drew the third part of the
stars of heaven and did cast them to the earth."* Who
was it that cast the evil angels to the earth? Why it was
Satan who caused them to leave heaven. He *"drew"* them
with him. Rev. 12:4. Rev. 1:20, proves that stars represent

angels, *"when the morning stars sang together."* Job 38:7. This makes it crystal clear that Satan is the one who cast one-third of the angels down to this earth. *"There was war in heaven and Michael and his angels fought against the dragon and the dragon fought and his angels prevailed not, neither was their place found anymore in heaven."* Why? Because they left, Jude 6, *"and the great dragon was cast out, that old serpent called the Devil and Satan, which deceiveth the whole world. He was cast out and his angels were cast out with him."* Rev. 12:7-9.* We have always read those scriptures and the Ellen White quotes about Satan being *"cast out"* and *"expelled"* and other strong words like that, but EGW is only saying basically what the Bible says. We have always assumed that it was God who used force and cast Satan out by some forceful means or other. EGW makes it clear in *Desire of Ages*, Pg. 759, that God never uses force. Light never attacks Darkness. But Darkness has to flee when the Light appears. Satan, the Prince of Darkness could not remain in the presence of God's Eternal Light and Love. *In some places I paraphrase the text.

Now, I want to show you how the word *"cast down or out"* is used in the Bible. *"Destroy thou them, O God; let them fall by their own counsels;"* Ps. 5:10. God's word is a sword. *"Out of His* (Christ's) *mouth* (this is Jesus riding on a white horse) *goeth a sharp sword* (the word of God) *that with it, he* (Jesus, through his people) *should smite the nations."* *"For the word of God is quick and powerful and sharper than any two-edged sword piercing even to the dividing asunder of soul and spirit and of the joints and marrow as a discerner of the thoughts and intents of the heart."* Rev. 19:15, Heb. 4:12. This is a little example of how the Bible uses these symbols.

CHAPTER 3

Twenty Reasons

TWENTY REASONS
FOR BELIEVING THAT
JESUS DOES NOT DESTROY

"What is this Good News about which Paul felt so sure and which through the centuries has provoked such opposition and been so misunderstood? And what did Paul consider so serious a contradiction and perversion of the Good News that he could be moved to express himself so strongly to the Galatian believers?

I have asked many Christians to state what they understand to be the essence of the Good News. The varied replies have included much of the content of the Christian faith, from grace and the Atonement to the Second Coming and eternal life.

But one reply that I believe comes especially close to the heart of the matter is this: *The Good News is that God is not the kind of person Satan has made Him out to be.*

That the Good News should be related to the issues in the great controversy between Christ and Satan is perhaps suggested by Paul's bold assertion that if even an angel from heaven dared to teach a different gospel, he should be held outcast. At first this seems incredibly presumptuous and dogmatic. But was it not an angel who began the circulation of misinformation about God and who still masquerades 'as an angel of Light?' (2 Corinthians 11:14) as he seeks to deceive men into rejecting the Good News?"

"CAN GOD BE TRUSTED?"—P. 30—
By A. Graham Maxwell

No. 1, The life of Jesus Christ is the fullest revelation of God's character of love. Our precious Lord Jesus never once hurt or killed anyone, thus proving what God is like. God does not kill, He is a life God. Neither God the Father, God the Son, nor God the Holy Spirit have ever once killed an evil angel, including Satan himself, the chief of the devils. Why then should we blame the God family for the death of any human being?

No. 2, Are you willing to indict God for murder on the basis of circumstantial evidence? Satan and his angels are much more guilty than we and therefore by all rights should be killed, not us. No. 3, the sixth commandment says *"thou shalt not kill."* The lawgiver cannot break His own law or He Himself will come under His own condemnation. He would be untrue to His own character which is a transcript of the very law itself. He must be true to Himself in His own law and character. No. 4, God never changes. If Jesus never killed anyone on earth, and we know He never did, then Jesus' life was the fullest demonstration of God's character. The Father then, is just what Jesus showed Him to be like, a life God not a death God. Heb. 13:8, and Mal. 3:6. These scriptures say, *"Jesus Christ the same yesterday, today and forever."* Mal. 3:6 says, *"I am the Lord, I change not, therefore ye sons of Jacob are not consumed."* No. 5, it is an irreconcilable, self-negating statement to say that the life giver takes life. The Creator cannot be both a life God and a death God. The Hindu God, Shiva, has both light and darkness in him. When we say that God kills, we are making Him both good and evil, and we are attributing human characteristics to the Creator, carnal characteristics. *"God is light and in Him is no darkness at all."* I John 1:5. Satan is a death god and the sign of his power is Sun(day) worship. No. 6, The Sabbath is the final proof that God is a life God; the proof that He gives life and sustains life. It is the central theme of the final message. No. 7, God destroys no man, *Christ's Object Lessons*, pg. 84. *Every good gift and every perfect gift cometh down from the Father of lights, with whom is no variableness, neither shadow of turning."* James 1:17. If you go back to James 1:13 and the verses preceding, you will find in vs. 13, *"God tempts no man,"* and it goes on through and says, *"don't be deceived friends, don't err on this point, for only good comes from God. Bad comes from another source."* No. 8, the cross of Christ answers every question in the great controversy. The cross is the greatest demonstration of God's love. It proves that God was willing to die so that we might live. Instead of killing us or letting us die, He came and died in our place that we might live forever with Him.

No. 9, the book of Job, chapters 1-3 especially prove that Satan is the destroyer. No. 10, Satan is the one who causes floods, hurricanes, tornadoes, pestilences, and all the abberations of nature. *Great Controversy*, 589, 590. God does not execute anyone, but leaves the sinner to reap what he has sown, *Great Controversy,* 35-36. No. 11, Ps. 103:20, proves that God's angels hold back evil, they do not bring it. God's angels are called destroying angels, only because they withdraw and permit evil to come. Notice I Kings 22, where God's angels are said to lie. No. 12, Angels sent from the heavenly courts. This is a very good statement because it answers *Great Controversy*, 614, where they quote Ellen White and try to prove a point, but they don't understand what she is saying. This statement makes it very clear. I don't think the spirit of prophecy contradicts itself anymore than the Bible does. *"Angels are sent from the heavenly courts not to destroy,* (a very clear statement) *but to watch over and guard imperiled souls, to save the lost, to bring the straying ones back to the fold." Review and Herald,* May 10, 1906. And here is one more that says approximately the same thing about the angels not killing. Ps. 103:20 says that God's angels keep his 10 commandment law. No. 13, The instrument of death for the wicked is the law of God. *"Against every evil doer God's law utters condemnation. He may disregard that voice. He may seek to drown its warning, but in vain. It follows him. It makes itself heard. It destroys his peace. If unheeded, it pursues him to the grave. It bears witness against him at the judgment. A quenchless fire, it consumes at last soul and body." Education,* pg. 144-145.

This is talking about the law of God, a transcript of His character. If you read *Great Controversy,* 666 in the regular edition, you will find that the servant of the Lord says that the eye of Jesus rests upon all sinners and they become aware or remember every sin they ever committed. Jesus says in John 12:47, 48 that He did not come to condemn us. That it is the word that He is speaking, and has spoken all through the centuries, through the prophets, that will condemn us in the last days. So all this information is stored in our minds. After the 1000 years the panoramic view will be shown in the sky, which is the love of God. *"Look how I've fed you and given you meat and drink."* Prov. 21:25. *"When your enemy is hungry give him food and when he is thirsty, give him drink,"* God does that everyday. *"He makes the sun to shine on the good and the bad,"* and He takes care of His enemies all the time. Look what He is doing with Lucifer; taking care of him and his angels . . . the angels that rebelled against Him. He has always taken care of them, saving Lucifer and his angels from destroying each other. They would all kill each other if He didn't protect them from each other. So this is all going to come out in this panoramic view. This will be the symbolic part of the *"Fire of God"* (which is His fiery love) which is the first phase of the fire of God. This will be the *"truth"* or *"fire"* in the sky; that movie in the sky. God says, *"Look what I have done for you. Look how I have loved you."* And even Lucifer bows down and says, *"You are right, God! You are right! I don't deserve to live."* And he pronounces the death sentence upon himself as all of them do. Then all the wicked will turn upon Lucifer and each other, physically, and begin destroying each other with all the nuclear weapons they have built to take the city. This is the second phase of the fire of God, which is the physical or literal part.

No. 14, The rod of Moses represented God's power which He had put into man and nature from creation. God held and controlled those powers as long as Moses held the rod in his hand, but when the rod left the prophet's hand, it changed into a snake or serpent which represents Satan, the destroyer. That is what he was trying to show Pharaoh. *"Pharaoh, I have control of the god that rules you, the snake god, and this rod represents that snake god."* But when he dropped it and let it fall, God said, *"When I let go, that snake will take over your country and he will destroy you."* Then He said, *"It is not too late, Pharaoh."* And He picked up the serpent by the tail after it had eaten the other snakes to show that the chief snake kills all the lesser snakes, proving Satan destroys his own. Anyway, the point is that God says, *"I am still in control. I still rule over your gods so they will not kill you. I am greater than all your gods. Serve me and live."* I think Pharaoh saw the symbolism but he didn't accept it. He wanted to think he was in charge. Satan makes us think that we are in charge of our own lives. He tells us that we can become a god. *"Ye shall become as gods knowing good and evil."* Gen. 3:5. So if he can get us to become the arbiter of our own destiny and think that we are in charge of our own life and other people too, then he has us where he wants us. Then he rules over us. And he made Pharaoh think, *"You are a god, you really are a great god and you have a right to rule over these people."* And he deceived him until Pharaoh's own first born was dead and his whole army was killed in the Red Sea.

No. 15, The *Westminster Confession* (1645-1647) says, *"When God revealed His attributes to people, the attributes are not only true to people but true to God. That is, when God tells people what He is like, what He says is not just relatively true, but absolutely true. As finite beings, people do not have exhaustive truth about God, but they can have truth about God; and they can know, therefore, truth about that which is the ultimate universal. And the Bible speaks to men and women concerning meaning, morals, and values."* This is from Francis A. Schaeffer, *How Should We then Live?* pages 84-86.

No. 16, *"Had the head of Christ been touched, the hope of the human race would have perished. Divine wrath would have come upon Christ as it came upon Adam."* SDA Bible Commentary, Vol. 5, age 1131.

Did Jesus kill Adam? No, He has never killed any human being. But wrath has been upon us all. When we reject God's protection and His love, that is when the wrath comes upon us. And God says it is "His wrath," because wrath represents the results of breaking the law. He takes that upon Himself, on the cross especially, but all through the ages too. He has taken all the results of that broken law upon Himself to save us, so we won't hurt, because God can't stand for us to hurt. When we hurt, He hurts, and it hurts Him terribly. And He is hurting more today than He ever has before. So He takes all this wrath upon Himself and He says, *"Oh, please, don't do that, because I have to give it back to you. If you demand this wrath, I have to give it to you."* And that is when we get hurt and are destroyed. Of course, there are times when God allows destruction, like in the time of Job. But Job said, *"The thing that I feared came upon me."* Do you realize what a privilege we have? Read *Desire of Ages, A Night on the Lake,* and also *Peace Be Still.* In those chapters you will find where Jesus turned to the disciples and asked, *"Why were you afraid?"* When I read that, I thought, *"That is really too much to expect from us Lord. These disciples had a right to be afraid, for they were about to sink in the ship and there was a terrible storm out there. Why didn't you at least let them have their fears over that?"* But the servant of the Lord tells us that it was because of unbelief that they were afraid. Because of unbelief, Israel failed and so God says if you believe in Me and trust in Me you will never be afraid. What a challenge that is! If you want to be perfect, friends, get to the place where you are not afraid of anything and you will know that you are perfect. People talk about becoming holy and undefiled by monitoring their behavior. But that is not the way to do it. The only way you can become perfect in God's eyes is not to offend in deed and word. James 3:2. Become harmless . . . and when you become harmless in word and deed, you will be unafraid. That is what Jesus says He is. Heb. 7:26. And *Great Controversy*, pg. 636, says, *"They come, they come, holy, harmless and undefiled."* Everyone who goes in those gates up there will be harmless. *"They shall not hurt nor destroy in all my holy mountain."* Isa. 11:9.

No. 17, Psalms 78:49 proves Satan's angels destroy. *"He cast upon them the fierceness of his anger, wrath, and indignation, and trouble by sending evil angels among them."* God always takes the blame.

No. 18, Satan is destroyed by people, not God. You can read this yourself. This is a shocking scripture. The terrible of the nations refer to both evil men and evil angels who rule the nations. You see this world is divided up very systematically by evil angels, and they rule over nations under Satan's control. *"The terrible of the nations shall draw their swords against the beauty of thy wisdom, and they shall bring thee down to the pit."* Ezek. 28:7. When these evil angels and all the wicked who come up in the resurrection find out that it was the devil who has been deceiving them all the time, they are going to turn against him. That is what it is talking about. *"They shall bring thee down to the pit."* The word *'pit'* means the grave most of the time in the Bible. *"Will you then say, 'I am god,' in the presence of those who kill you? You will be but a man, not a god, in the hands of those who slay you."* Ezek. 28:9. NIV. *"Lucifer, don't you realize you won't be a 'god' to these people anymore? No, you will only be a man and they are going to kill you." "Thou shalt die the deaths of the uncircumcised by the hand of strangers."* There are not going to be any friends out there. Only enemies. Satan's only power over the human race is that he is able to deceive them and at that point he can no longer deceive them. Satan suffers much longer than the people, but they initiate the fires that destroy both him and themselves. People ask, *"How could the people kill Lucifer when he is the last to die?"* That is simple, because they initiate it and they give him the death blow but they die before he does. He is only a *"created being"*

It is also clear from Ezek. 28:18 that the fire that destroys Satan comes from within Satan himself and not from any outside source. So it is from his own followers and his own sin and his own rebellion and hatred within his own heart that will destroy him. This is not the literal sword or fire that people start but the fire of hatred, remorse and regret for all the rebellion which comes back to his mind with full force and causes him terrible pain, mental anguish and torture. That is the second part of the torture that comes to his mind, but at the point when he bows down and admits that God is right and he is wrong, he is bowing down as a result of his remembering the good times he had with God, all the love that God has shown to him.

When Satan sees this panoramic view in the sky he is led to bow down, because Romans 2:4 says that it is the goodness of God that leads us to repentance. You will never get anyone to repent on the basis of condemning them.

Believe me, it doesn't work. Only when God's love is presented do people repent and really, truly turn away from their sins. So God shows his love in the panoramic view and all bow down and admit that they are not worthy of eternal life. But even here their repentance is not genuine.

The worm of sin that is spoken of in Mark 9 is explained with this concept and explained in *Early Writings,* pg. 294-295. Remember that the scapegoat was not killed but left in the wilderness to die. The Lord's goat representing Jesus died but the scapegoat was left alive, representing Satan, showing that God doesn't even kill Satan. The Sanctuary proves that.

No. 19, The creation belongs to God. The Lord could, by neglecting man, stop his breath at once. *Manuscript 36, 1890.* He could do this just by neglecting man. But God never even neglects us. Even in the plagues it says He has power over the plagues. In the seven last plagues God is still regulating them because if they were allowed to go full force the whole world would be destroyed.

No. 20, Jesus never brought disease in the Old Testament or the New. He only healed. *"God anointed Jesus of Nazareth with the Holy Ghost and with power who went about doing good and healing all that were oppressed of the devil, for God was with him."* Acts 10:38. The devil is the oppressor, but Jesus is the healer, and that principle never changes, because God never changes. Satan's character never changes either.

Sister White says as the scroll is unrolled we will understand the prophecies if we are reading the scriptures, and if we are praying and keeping in touch with God. 6T 17; DA 17; EV 19; GW 470. Today it is a battle to stay in touch with God because there are so many forces in the world, in the church, and in the family that are against a person who is trying to stay in touch and keep that communion with Jesus Christ. There are so many things calling for attention, so many things trying to wrench us away from what God would have us to do.

Father in Heaven, thank you for the time we've had together so far tonight. We pray we will be able to answer the questions that are on the hearts of some of these people and pray that you will bless us as we continue to talk about your wonderful, loving, character, Father. We know that the end of the world is coming. We see all the forces of evil lining up but we also see the forces that are on your side too, Father, and we praise your name for your great power that is stronger than Satan. We pray that we will be on your side and understand your true character so we might become like you, that we might have your character to survive the time of trouble and be found with you in your eternal Kingdom. In Jesus' Holy name. Amen.

CHAPTER 4

THE FIRE OF GOD

"The Lord knows the thought and purposes of man, and how easily He can melt us! How His Spirit, like a fire, can subdue the flinty heart! How He can fill the soul with love and tenderness! How He can give us the graces of His Holy Spirit, and fit us to go in and out, in laboring for souls!" — MS., *"Consecrated Efforts to Reach Unbelievers,"* June 5, 1914.

"CHRISTIAN SERVICE"—P. 169—
By Ellen G. White

"Against every evildoer God's law utters condemnation. He may disregard that voice, he may seek to drown its warning, but in vain. It follows him. It makes itself heard. It destroys his peace. If unheeded, it pursues him to the grave. It bears witness against him at the judgment. A quenchless fire, it consumes at last soul and body."

"EDUCATION"—P. 144,145—By Ellen G. White

"Again the piercing look of Jesus swept over the desecrated court of the temple. All eyes were turned toward Him. Priest and ruler, Pharisee and Gentile, *looked with astonishment and awe upon Him who stood before them with the majesty of heaven's King. Divinity flashed through humanity, investing Christ with a dignity and glory He had never manifested before.* Those standing nearest Him drew as far away as the crowd would permit. Except for a few of His disciples, the Saviour stood alone. Every sound was hushed. The deep silence seemed unbearable. Christ spoke with a power that swayed the people like a mighty tempest: *'It is written, My house shall be called the house of prayer; but ye have made it a den of thieves.'* His voice sounded like a trumpet through the temple. *The displeasure of His countenance seemed like consuming fire. With authority He commanded, 'Take these things hence'." John 2:16.*

"DESIRE OF AGES"—P. 590, 591—
By Ellen G. White

THE FIRE OF GOD

The words of Jesus are like a fire in the soul, enlightening the mind. As we go through these transparencies tonight, some of the words that Christ has spoken, that maybe you have not understood before, will become clear. Christ says, *"I am come to send fire on the earth; and what will I, if it be already kindled?"*Luke 12:49. What is He talking about? He didn't come and set any fires; He didn't blow the world up or set fires around anywhere. So what is He talking about? *"I've come to cast fire on the earth and how I wish it were already kindled."* Ibid. *"I have a baptism to be baptized with."* "Modern Language

Version". In the original Hebrew, the first meaning is usually symbolic or figurative. The second, literal. Then there is the positive vs. negative. So, actually, there are four aspects of fire. But fire in its basic meaning in the Bible represents God's love and the first manifestation I will refer to is the burning bush on Mt. Sinai; it was not a literal fire but a revelation of God's presence. There the I AM was revealed to Moses. Then on the day of Pentecost, the fire came on their heads representing the Holy Spirit, the presence of God, and that was His love. Look what it did to the disciples. It changed their whole lives. Jesus came to reveal the true meaning of this fire—of His eternal love.

"Suppose ye that I am come to give peace on earth? I tell you nay; but rather division:" Luke 12:51. And in Matt. 10:34 He said He has come to bring *"a sword"*. It is not God's intent that His love would bring a sword, but it is the effect. God's intent is to bring love, to bring peace and healing, but because man rejects His love, then division and strife come. *"Suppose ye that I have come to give peace, no I have come to bring a sword."* What is He doing? He is taking the blame for it. Jesus blames Himself for everything. Yet, He kept on showing and telling them of His love. But they said to Him, *"We hate you, false messiah. We are going to put you on a cross and get rid of you."* But in this crime they destroyed themselves. Jesus, the Prince of Peace, did not cause strife, war and bloodshed; but here, true to His eternal and unchanging character, He takes the blame for it. Jesus is the way, the truth and life; therefore, it is not Jesus who brings the sword, but it is the rejection of Him and His message of truth that leaves the rejecter of truth to himself to kill himself and others. The sword, strife and division are called fire. Fear, anger and hatred are fiery experiences. *But truth and righteousness are also called fire, "for our God is a consuming fire."* Heb. 12:29. God's presence is fire. God manifested Himself to Moses as a burning bush, but it was not literal fire. *Israel was guided in the wil-*

derness by a cloud by day and a pillar of fire by night, and that fire was Jesus Christ. Neh. 9:9-15. But that fire was not literal. It was a symbol of the presence of God.

"And when the day of Pentecost was fully come, they were all with one accord in one place. And there appeared unto them cloven tongues like as a fire, and it sat upon each of them. And they were all filled with the Holy Ghost." This was the presence of God, Acts 2:1-4. *"Like as a fire."* It didn't say it was fire, but it looked like fire. God's fire represents His eternal love for us. *"And their eyes were opened and they knew him."* Luke 24:31. The word *'knew'* is very important. *"I never knew you,"* Matt. 7:23. *"Adam knew his wife."* Gen. 4:1. It has a sexual connotation, but it is always in a spiritual sense. God wants to get married to us; He wants us to become His bride; He wants to make love to us. God is a very romantic person, He just can't stop loving. God never stops loving and Satan never stops hating. *"They knew him; and he vanished out of their sight."* This means that they recognized him. This is Jesus, the Messiah. *"And they said one to another, did not our hearts burn,"* (symbolical word for fire) *"within us, while he talked with us by the way, and while he opened to us the scriptures?"* Opened ... God always starts these fires in our hearts through the scriptures. Luke 24:31-32. *"Then I said, I will not make mention of him, nor speak anymore in his name. But his word was in mine heart as a burning fire shut up in my bones, and I was weary with forebearing, and I could not stay."* Jere. 20:9. He means that He could not remain silent very long.

"Thy word is a lamp unto my feet and a light unto my path." Ps. 119:105. This is a Hebrew parallelism. Hebrew poetry in this instance is making a statement in one way and saying it again without using the same word twice. It is using different words to make it clear. *"In Him,* (Christ) *was life and the life was light,* the fire *of men."* Jesus Christ came to set us on fire for Him. Isn't that won-

derful! John 1:4. *"Then said Jesus unto them again say-ing, I am the light* (the fire) *of the world."* If Christ abides in us we also are lights unto the world. Matt. 5:14.

Gen. 15:17, God appeared to Abraham as a smoking furnace and a burning lamp. The smoking furnace was Satan and the burning lamp was Jesus and they were both there and went between the pieces of animal that had been slaughtered, representing what they would do to Jesus. See Ex. 20:18; Isa. 42:3; Rev. 9:2. *"And they went up on the breadth of the earth, and compassed the camp of the saints (round) about, and the beloved city: (New Jeru-salem) and fire came down from God out of heaven, and devoured them."* Rev. 20:9.

We have already referred to the fire of God in this instance, but people always ask, *"What is this fire that comes down out of heaven that God sends at the end of the world?"* The first aspect of this fire is the panoramic view in the sky. Sister White says, *"as letters of fire."* G.C. 666. She makes it very clear what it is. It is the fire of His love saying, *"Look how I have loved you! Look how I have fed you, and given you drink! You are my ene-mies, and yet I have done all this for you. How can you resist my love?"* And He is making His last appeal. He is very romantic and He is saying, *"You have resisted my love. Oh, how I love you. I can't stand to go into eter-nity without you."* And they all bow down and worship the Lord. But they will bow down because they realize how stu-pid they have been. They realize that His love is so great; it is because of this, that they realize they are wrong, and their stubborn blindness is revealed, and they bow down. But they don't bow down because they have submitted and are sorry for their sins. They are only sorry for the results. Their hearts are filled with fear. By the way, that is the first category mentioned of those who will go in the lake of fire, *"the fearful." "They went up on the breadth of the earth and compassed the camp of the saints, and the beloved city and fire came down from God out of*

heaven and devoured them. Rev. 20:9. Then they get up
off their knees and start blowing each other up. *"Our God
shall come and a fire shall devour before him."*
*"Gather my saints together unto me; those that have
made a covenant with me by sacrifice."* Ps. 50:3-5. That
is His sacrifice; and as a brother said, "It is a sacrifice or
covenant of love based on the Ten Commandments!" *"And
the heavens shall declare his righteousness."* Not our
righteousness, but His. *"Upon the wicked he shall rain
snares, fire and brimstone, and a horrible tempest."* Ps.
11:6. God is going to let people blow themselves up and yet
He says He is doing it to them. *"This will be the portion
of their cup."* Ibid. *"If thine enemy be hungry, give him
bread to eat; and if he be thirsty, give him water to
drink: For thou shalt heap coals of fire upon his head,
and the Lord shall reward thee."* Prov. 25:21, 22; Quoted
in Rom. 12:20.

THE FIERY DESTRUCTION
OF THE WICKED

The word of God is an unquenchable fire that will burn
in a man's soul and will give him life or death. Jesus said
that He came as a light or a fire into the world that *"Whosoever believeth on me shall not abide in darkness.
And if any man hear my words, and believe not, I
judge him not: for I came not to judge the world, but to
save the world. He that rejecteth me, and receiveth not
my words, hath one that judgeth him: the word that I
have spoken, the same shall judge him in the last day."*
John 12:46-48. These are the words that Jesus spoke. His
words of love. And that love is what will be revealed and
that is why they all will bow down and judge themselves. I
will throw this in right here. Susan Atkins, a lover and

follower of Charles Manson, said that Helter-Skelter is
when every man will judge himself and then that revelation
of himself will cause him to go out and kill the first man he
comes to; and she says "what a day it will be when every
man judges himself and then goes out and takes it out upon
every other man." That is exactly what Ezek. 38:21 and
Zech. 14:13 say will happen in the endtime when every
man's sword shall be against his brother. This earth is
going to be a vast graveyard as a result of people killing
each other. The *Great Controversy*, 655-657, brings this
out. That is what God is trying to save us from—universal
slaughter, the suicide of the nations.

Christ speaking to the Jewish leaders said, *"Ye shall
die in your sins for if you believe not that I am he, the
Messiah, you shall die in your sins."* He didn't say "if you
don't believe in me I am going to kill you." No, He said "if
you don't believe me, you shall die in your sins." John 8:24.
God does not destroy the wicked; it is sin that destroys
them. *"The wages of sin is death,"* not the wages of God
killing us. Rom. 6:23. *"Every man's work shall be made
manifest: for the day* (of Christ's return) *shall declare it,
because it shall be revealed by fire;"* I Cor. 3:13. This has
two aspects, for fire has a dual meaning. First, it means
truth and righteousness, or light which uncovers or destroys
darkness. The light of God's truth in the last days will
destroy all dark dealings and this will bring a trial upon
those who profess but do not live up to God's truth. The
mental suffering and torment of the wicked, as described in
Rev. 14 is the second part of the fire, a fire of anger, remorse
and regret. Rev. 1:14. "His hairs were white like wool, as
white as snow, and his eyes were as a flame of fire;" Can you
imagine Jesus having a hateful look? Jesus Christ never
had a hateful look for anyone. He only had love. So this fire
coming out of His eyes, this flame of fire, is not literal fire,
it is the *fire of His love*. Jesus' eyes reveal love, truth and
righteousness. This will burn in the souls of the wicked.
One endtime writer said, *"As soon as the books of*

record are opened and the eye of Jesus looks upon the wicked, they are conscious of every sin which they have ever committed." Great Controversy, pg. 666. Isn't that amazing that happened to be on that page? You see, the number 6 represents the number of man, in his incomplete state, because he was created on the sixth day; and God was never able to finish His creation because man ran off and has had a 6000 year affair with Satan and left Jesus standing at the altar, stood Him up, and Jesus still has never gotten married. Isn't that terrible? And three 6's represent eternal death.

Every single sin that was ever committed by the lost will come to their minds, and that will cause them to bow down, but they will get up and then destroy each other. *"For the day of the Lord* (the end of the world) *is near upon all the heathen: as thou hast done, it shall be done unto thee: thy reward shall return upon thy own head. And the house of Jacob shall be a fire, and the house of Joseph a flame, and the house of Esau for stubble, and they shall kindle in them, and devour them: and there shall not be any remaining of the house of Esau; for the Lord hath spoken it."* Obadiah 1:15, 18. Here are the righteous, Jacob and Joseph, representing all of the righteous inside the city, and all the Esaus outside. That is really going to burn them up. Have you ever heard the expressions, *"That really burns me up"* or *"I did a slow burn"*? These expressions are still used today to represent hatred and anger inside the human heart. Don't you realize what they are going to do? They are going to come out there and say, "what are all those goody goodies doing inside while I am out here?" They are going to get very angry about that and they are going to debate with God. You know what is going to happen? Satan is going to eventually appear and say to the wicked outside, *"You know what? You are not lost; you are saved! I am the prince of this world, and I have come to save you. They have wrested the kingdom from me, and I am really the prince of that kingdom; and if you join me, we will get it back."* And the people will say, *"Wow, you mean I am not lost? I thought I was lost, but you tell me I am saved. Praise the Lord! I am not lost, I am saved. If I join you I am saved and we'll take this kingdom and get our rightful inheritance, our birthright."* You see Jacob got the inheritance and Esau was mad. Here Esau gets cheated again. He says, *"He went and stole the birthright from me again. We are going to get him now. We are going to regain our lost inheritance and make them pay for cheating us."* So they say, *"Praise the Lord, we are not lost. Pass the ammunition; we will go get them."* So they join Satan's army, and they assault the city. That is how it will happen. You can read it in the *Great Controversy*. 662-666. It is very clear.

"And it shall come to pass in that day, (the end of the world) *that a great tumult from the Lord* (God always takes the blame when His righteousness and love is revealed from heaven) *shall be among them; and they shall lay hold everyone on the hand of his neighbor, and his hand shall rise up against the hand of his neighbor."* Zech. 14:13. That will be *"Helter-Skelter."* Satan is the one who dreamed up the idea of Helter-Skelter. And that is what it will be like when every man will go out and kill someone. Maybe a lot of people.

"A noise shall come even to the ends of the earth; for the Lord hath a controversy with the nations, he will plead with all flesh;" Jer. 25:31. Here God is pleading, begging them, He's in love with them and they hate Him, but He is pleading with all flesh to accept his salvation. *"He will give them that are wicked to the sword."* He has to let them go, give them up. Says the Lord, *". . . Evil shall go forth from nation to nation, . . . and the slain of the Lord shall be at that day from one end of the earth even unto the other end of the earth."* Jere. 25:33. They are lying dead all over the earth. They have killed themselves because they can't stand the brightness of His glory. The above Scriptures from Jer. 25 are referring to

events which transpire at the Second Coming of Christ. But the following Scriptures from Ezek. 28 are referring to the events that will transpire after the 1,000 years are expired, at which time Satan will lead the wicked to surround the holy city, New Jerusalem. But after God allows everyone to see the entire history of the great controversy in the form of the panoramic "movie in the sky," as I call it, all the wicked will turn upon Satan. The inspired writer's comment on Zech. 5:1-4, says, *"Against every evildoer God's law utters condemnation. He may disregard that voice, he may seek to drown its warning, but in vain. It follows him. It makes itself heard. It destroys his peace. If unheeded, it pursues him to the grave. It bears witness against him at the judgment. A quenchless fire, it consumes at last soul and body." Education*, pg. 144-45. I already went over that. But it is good to repeat it. *"The terrible of the nations: shall draw their swords* (instruments of death like bombs, guns, etc.) *against the beauty of thy wisdom,* (Satan's wisdom)... *They shall defile thy brightness. They shall bring thee down to the pit,* (grave) *and thou shalt die the deaths of them that are slain in the midst of the seas."* Ez. 28:7,8 (peoples or nations who rejected God). (See Rev. 17:15.) *"Wilt thou yet say before him that slayeth thee, I am God? but thou shalt be a man, and no God, in the hand of him that slayeth thee... therefore will I bring,* (permit to come) *forth a fire from the midst of thee, it shall devour thee, and I will bring thee to ashes upon the earth in the sight of all them that behold thee."* Ezek. 28:7-9, 18.

ELIJAH DID NOT
FULLY UNDERSTAND
GOD'S CHARACTER

But Elijah replied, *"If I am a man of God, let fire come down from heaven and destroy you and your 50 men!" "Then lightning or fire struck them and killed them all."* 2 Kings 1:12 LB. So Elijah did this. Did Elijah fully understand the character of God? I don't think so. Jesus said to James and John, *"You don't know what spirit you are of, because you want to do what Elijah did and Elijah took the sword and killed all those prophets of Baal and called down destructive fire."* So evidently, according to Jesus, Elijah didn't fully understand God's character of love for the truth about God is progressive. *"And when his disciples James and John saw this, they said, Lord, wilt thou that we command fire to come down from heaven, and consume them, even as Elias* (Elijah) *did? But he turned, and rebuked them, and said, ye know not what manner of spirit you are of. For the son of man is not come to destroy men's lives, but to save them."* Luke 9:54-56. Jesus came to save us, not to hurt us or destroy us. *"I am come that they might have life, and that they might have it more abundantly."* John 10:10. That is the true message of the Sabbath, friends . . . that God is a life God. He is the Creator, He is not a death God. Satan is the death god and Sunday is his sign. But the Sabbath is the sign of the life God and that is the importance of the Sabbath. And that is why everyone is going to give it up, because their character is the character of Satan, and they are only in tune with death. They have made a covenant with death, and they don't know anything about life. They think they do, because Satan has a counterfeit *"life"* program that leads to death. *"The sinners in Zion,* (God's professed people) *are afraid; fearfulness hath surprised the hypocrites. Who among us shall dwell with the devouring fire?"* Here God is called a devouring fire. But this fire gives us life. *"Who among us shall dwell with everlasting burnings? He that walketh righteously, and speaketh uprightly;"* Isa. 33:14-15. *"Thine eyes shall see the king in his beauty:"* Isa. 33:17. *"The Lord has redeemed Jacob and glorified himself in Israel."* He has put His glory, His character on Israel. Isa.

44:23. *"Christ in you, the hope of glory."* The character
that Christ came to reveal. Col. 1:27. That is Christ in you.
What is this business that Christ never does anything in us,
it is all from the outside? That is not what the Bible says; it
says, *"Christ in you,"* the hope, the character that Jesus
revealed about His Father. The Hebrew word for glorified in
Isa. 44:23, means to *"beautify"* oneself which shows that
glory and beauty can be used synonymously and interchangeably as a Hebrew parallel. *"The son of man shall
come in the glory of the character of His Father with
his angels and then,* (or at that time) *he shall reward
every man according to his works."* Matt. 16:27. *"When
the Lord Jesus shall be revealed from heaven with his
mighty angels, in flaming fire taking vengeance,* (same
as wrath) *on them that know not God and that obey not
the gospel of our Lord Jesus Christ: Who shall be punished with everlasting destruction from the presence
of the Lord, and from the glory of his power; When he
shall come to be glorified in his saints."* 2 Thess. 1:7-10.
We will talk about the brightness of His coming and what
that fully means in a little while.

   "God came from Teman, and the Holy one, (Jesus)
*from Mt. Paran. His glory covered the heavens, and
the earth was full of his praise. And His brightness,*
(His glory) *was as the light;* (fire) *He had horns,* (bright
beams) *coming out of his hand; and there was the hiding of his power."* That is the cross. It is the central revelation of God's character. *"Before him went the pestilence,
and burning coals* (diseases) *went forth at his feet. He
stood, and measured the earth: He beheld, and drove
asunder the nations, and the everlasting mountains
were scattered."* Habakuk 3:3-6. *"Thine hand shall find
out all thine enemies; thy right hand shall find out
those that hate thee."* (do not prefer thee). The word
"hate" usually means *"to not prefer"* in the Bible. Jesus
holds out His hands, and says, *"I love you, I love you, I
died for you. Look at the nail prints in my hand. It is*

proof that I love you. Come to me . . ." and it says, *"thy right hand shall find out those that hate thee,"* Psalm 21:8, because they hate God when they see the nail prints in His hands, they can't stand it. *"Thou shalt make them as a fiery oven in the time of thine anger:"* Ps. 21:9. How does an oven burn? It says that the people are going to become like ovens, like fiery ovens, in fact. How does an oven burn? It burns on the inside. These people are going to be burning up with remorse and regret and hatred, and they are going to take it out and judge themselves and say, *"How stupid I've been. I am lost,"* and they are going to pronounce the death sentence upon themselves and they are going to start taking it out on everybody else, blaming everyone else. No one wants to take the blame, they always want to blame everyone else. *"As a fiery oven in the time of thine anger:* (the same as wrath). *"The Lord shall swallow them up in his wrath,* (He is going to take His hands off them) *and the fire* (brightness) *shall devour them.* Ps. 21:9. *For they intended evil against thee."* Ps. 21:11. Here they are, surrounding the city to kill God and the saints. (See Rev. 20:9.) They *"imagine"* this mischievous device. (To take the holy city) *"which they are not able to perform. Therefore shalt thou make them turn their back,* (the shoulder)." Ps. 21:9-11, 12. They look back over their shoulders and say, *"I can't do it"* and start running away. *"And the stars of heaven fell . . . and the heaven departed as a scroll . . . and every mountain and island* (mountain also represents governments) *were moved out of their places."* Rev. 6:13, 14. *Then people of every nation hid themselves in the dens, rocks and mountains and said to the rocks and mountains, "Fall on us and hide us from the face of him who sitteth on the throne, and from the Wrath of the Lamb. For the great day of his wrath has come; and who shall be able to stand?"* Rev. 6:16, 17. Remember, wrath is when God removes His protection and withdraws His restraint. *"And all the men that are upon the face of the earth shall shake at my presence,* (second coming of Christ) *and the mountains (governments) shall be thrown down . . . and I will call for a sword against him throughout all my mountains,"* (governments throughout the world which God claims to control even though Satan rules them. Satan rules them but with God's permission.) *saith the Lord God:"* Ezek. 38:20, 21. What is the result of this sword? His sword is His word, His love, and the reaction against it. They reject the character message and the Sabbath message and they select Sunday. I can show you in the Psalms that the Sunday law will cause the cities of the earth to be destroyed. See Psalm 9:6. Sr. White says that national apostasy, when they accept Sunday worship, will lead to the destruction of the United States.[1] That is the next thing that is going to happen in this world. When they accept the national Sunday law, this will lead to destruction of this country. Satan knows that and this is the way he is going to destroy this United States, through Sunday worship. And it is all because they have rejected God's true character.

Remember that wrath is when God is forced to withdraw His restraint. *Satan rules them by God's permission, "Saith the Lord. Every man's sword shall be against his brother."* Ez. 38:21. There you have Helter-Skelter, the final destruction of man against man, the wrath of God; the brightness of His coming. I want you to really pray as we study now on the "brightness of His coming," for this will be a great revelation to your mind. *"And then shall that Wicked be revealed, whom the Lord shall consume with the spirit of his mouth, and shall destroy with the brightness of his coming:"* II Thess. 2:8. *"And I saw heaven opened, and behold a white horse; and he that sat upon him was called Faithful and True, and with righteousness he doth judge and make war. His eyes were as a flame of fire, and on his head were many crowns; and out of his mouth goeth a*

[1] 5T-541, 2SM373, 2TT 151, 7BC977, Evang. 235

sharp sword, that with it he should smite the nations: and he shall rule them with a rod of iron; and He treadeth the winepress of the fierceness and wrath of Almighty God." Rev. 19, 11, 12, 15. *And finally I will deliver King Zedekiah himself and all the remnant left in the city into the hands of King Nebuchadnezzar of Babylon, to slaughter them without mercy or pity.* (See Jer. 21:7.) LB. Remember whatever God permits He claims to be doing Himself. It is a very important concept. You must understand it.

A Christian writer with much insight (EGW) has written the following comment on our first text, 2 Thess. 2:8. The Lord led her to make this comment about it. *"Then shall they that obey not the gospel be consumed with the spirit of his mouth and be destroyed with the brightness of his coming."* Here is the comment from the servant of the Lord. *"Like Israel of old,* (and what is she always saying—that we are repeating the history of Israel) *the wicked destroy themselves. They fall by their iniquity. By a life of sin, they have placed themselves so out of harmony with God, their natures have become so debased with evil that the manifestation of His glory* (His character) *is to them a consuming fire."* G.C. 37. This is a progressive experience. And we are learning about it right now. So this business of God's glory destroying the wicked doesn't happen in 15 minutes, it is a progressive experience. I think that is the main thing people misunderstand about the second coming; that it has an endtime point, when it will be consummated, but there is a build-up to it. The Bible's Hebrew writers never spoke about time, they always spoke about the events. The time factor was just ignored, as it were, and they spoke of three comings in the Old Testament, first, second, and third coming; but they are all spoken of as one event. The writers never separated them, so it gets very confusing. What the Jewish nation expected, the kind of coming they thought He should enact is coming in our day. But they thought it would happen in their day. But they misunderstood. And we misunderstand today.

Again the same writer tells us, ***"The swords which were to slay God's people are now employed to destroy their enemies. Everywhere there is strife and bloodshed." Great Controversy***, pg. 656. ***"Destroy them O God, let them fall by their own counsels."*** Ps. 5:10. ***"God destroys no man." Christ's Object Lessons***, pg. 84. ***"Whatsoever a man soweth, that shall he also reap."*** Gal. 6:7. ***"The wages of sin is death."*** Romans 6:23. Jesus destroyed the Jews with the brightness of His character, glory, at His first advent. There is a parallel between His first coming and the second coming. A very definite parallel. Jesus Christ destroyed the Jewish nation and all the people there with His first coming, the same as the wicked will die at His second coming. ***Christ declared that he had come to send fire on the earth.*** Luke 12:49. It was a fire, or the light of truth and righteousness, the fire of His glorious character. The Holy Spirit came as tongues of fire on the day of Pentecost. Notice the sequence of events that destroyed the Jews:

1. The Jews were in a state of apostasy. 2. Jesus revealed His true character to the Jews, His glory, by deeds of mercy and words of love.

3. And what is the final message supposed to be? It is medical missionary work. They resisted and rejected this revelation of love and became separated from Him, the source of all life. 4. By rejecting Him, they forfeited His divine protection and came under the power of the Roman eagle and its legion of Roman soldiers. I want to tell you something. Most people don't understand what the Roman eagle represents. It represents the ancient phoenix and the ancient phoenix represents sun worship. That is what you have all over the United States: in every post office you have the eagle. On all our coins we have the eagle. I will tell you something else. There is one animal throughout the world, one symbol that is the same, and that is the eagle. Every

country in the world has the eagle, the Russians have it, the Americans have it, Hitler had it, and ancient Roman legions had it. The eagle represents the ancient phoenix and it represents sun worship. Every 500 years, legend says, the phoenix would burn itself up on a funeral pyre and then out of the ashes would arise a new phoenix and he would carry the ashes, his father's ashes, to Heliopolis, city of the sun. Do you know what Phoenix, Arizona represents? Phoenix, is a bird; sun worship. If you ever fly into Phoenix, go into the front door of the airport and you will see a great big beautiful phoenix in tile. Someone did a terrific job making a big beautiful bird, a phoenix. That is what the American eagle represents, an ancient phoenix, representing sun worship.

So they came under the power of the Roman eagle, sun worship and his legion of Roman soldiers, and that is where sun worship came from. 5. Their city was surrounded and they began hating each other inside the city and when the Romans finally did break down the walls, they slaughtered the remaining Jews without mercy. In exactly the same way, the wicked will be destroyed in this our day. Notice, 1. The world is in a deep state of rebellion, apostasy against God today. The world is in darkness about God's love and His true character and glory. 2. The brightness of His coming glory will be revealed to them in the final message of the loud cry of the third angel's message, which will be preached throughout the world through the Sabbath truth. That is, *"God is a life God, not a death God."* 3. The church world, most of the Sunday-keeping churches, will reject this revelation of His character, (His glory) and pass Sunday laws against God's people for preaching the Sabbath, and finally a death decree. The secular world, like Rome of old, will use the sword to enforce it and instead of killing Christians, they will end up killing themselves. The wild passions within them and nature gone wild outside of them—the result will be the seven last plagues. Can you see the parallel?

CHAPTER 5

THE CEREMONIAL LAW AND ANIMAL SLAUGHTER SYSTEM

"As Jesus came into the temple, He took in the whole scene. He saw the unfair transactions. He saw the distress of the poor, who thought that without shedding of blood there would be no forgiveness for their sins. He saw the outer court of His temple converted into a place of unholy traffic."

"DESIRE OF AGES"—P. 157—
By Ellen G. White.

"Jesus looked upon the innocent victims of sacrifice and saw how the Jews had made these great convocations scenes of bloodshed and cruelty. In place of humble repentance of sin, they had multiplied the sacrifice of beasts, as if God could be honored by a heartless service. The priests and rulers had hardened their hearts through selfishness and avarice. The very symbols pointing to the Lamb of God they had made a means of getting gain. Thus in the eyes of the people the sacredness of the sacrificial service had been in a great measure destroyed. The indignation of Jesus was stirred; He knew that His blood, so soon to be shed for the sins of the world, would be as little appreciated by the priests and elders as was the blood of beasts which they kept incessantly flowing.

"Against these practices Christ had spoken through the prophets. Samuel had said, 'Hath the Lord as great delight

(51)

in burnt offerings and sacrifices, as in obeying the voice of the Lord? Behold, to obey is better than sacrifice, and to hearken than the fat of rams.' And Isaiah, seeing in prophetic vision the apostasy of the Jews, addressed them as rulers of Sodom and Gomorrah: 'Hear the word of the Lord, ye rulers of Sodom; give ear unto the law of our God, ye people of Gomorrah. To what purpose is the multitude of your sacrifices unto Me? saith the Lord: I am full of the burnt offerings of rams, and the fat of fed beasts; and I delight not in the blood of bullocks, or of lambs, or of he-goats. When ye come to appear before Me, who hath required this at your hand, to tread My courts?' Wash you, make you clean; put away the evil of your doings from before Mine eyes; cease to do evil; learn to do well; seek judgment, relieve the oppressed, judge the fatherless, plead for the widow.' I Sam. 15:22; Isa. 1:10-12, 16, 17.

"He who had Himself given these prophecies now for the last time repeated the warning. In fulfillment of prophecy the people had proclaimed Jesus king of Israel. He had received their homage, and accepted the office of king. In this character He must act. He knew that His efforts to reform a corrupt priesthood would be in vain; nevertheless, His work must be done; to an unbelieving people the evidence of His divine mission must be given."

"DESIRE OF AGES"—P. 590—
By Ellen G. White

THE PRICE HE PAID

In the Holy Bible, God tells us through Paul that we *"are bought with a price; therefore glorify God in your body and in your spirit, which are God's."* I Cor. 6:20. The price Paul is talking about refers to the death of Jesus Christ upon the cruel cross. We need to study and pray so we may more fully understand what this means. If we think that Jesus' death on the cross satisfied God the Father's anger toward us, so He would not have a legal right to kill us, we need to pray and study more. Jesus told us that His Father loves us too, *for the Father Himself loveth you.* You see Jesus came to get the record straight about the Father. The Father is a loving, kind person, just like Him. That was His message. Jesus tells us that the Father's love toward Him is the same or just as great as Christ's love toward us. Therefore, the Father loves us just as much as the Son does, for God the Father was in Christ reconciling the world unto Himself. John 16:27; 2 Cor. 5:19.

The animal sacrifices in the Old Testament were thought to appease the wrath of God. Sin had so blinded the minds of men that they could not see that the death of animals hurt God. We today do not realize that God has deep feelings and emotions, the same as we do, much more though. Even the death of a little sparrow grieves Him. God attends the funeral of every sparrow the Bible says in Matt 10:29. The fact is that the sacrificial system was God's permissive will, not His perfect will, for it was not the Father's perfect will that His Son be nailed to a tree, but it was His will that all men be saved, and the price that He paid to draw us back to Him was the cross, which was prefigured in the animal sacrifice. *"For thou desirest not sacrifice."* Ps. 51:16.

God put up with all this blood and slaughter for four thousand years, but the reason He did was because it was the only way He could reach our hardened hearts. It was an object lesson of what sin will do, even to God's only Son. Chapter 28 of my book (IFH) goes through the animal sacrifice in much greater detail.

The story or the parable of the prodigal son proves that God does not consider us in debt to Him. When this lost boy returned home, *there was no debt to pay.* The Father freely forgave him as if he had never sinned and treated him as if he had never left. Read it all in Luke 15. Jesus' death on the cross was not to pay a debt to the Father, but it was the price He and His only Son had to pay to win our hearts back to Him. It took the cross to break our hearts and open our eyes to the horrible, horrifying and ghastly results of sin. Jesus said, *"And I, if I be lifted up from the earth, will draw all men unto me."* The word *'men'* is supplied. It is not in the original. *"I will draw all."* All the evil angels were drawn to the cross. John 12:32. Yes, it is the cross which has demonstrated both the love of God and the hideous truth about sin. God's true character is revealed and Satan's true character is revealed at the cross. Every mystery in the great controversy is solved at the cross. *Great Controversy,* pg. 652.

Not once did Jesus ever hint or insinuate that a human being should go to the temple and sacrifice an innocent animal to wash away his or her sin. Jesus never told anyone to go to the temple and kill an animal. The only time He ever told anyone to go and make an offering, according to Moses' law, was for the leprosy being cleansed. And that was only to reach the priest so that he would rule that the Leper was now clean in accordance with the Law of Moses.

In fact, He cleansed the temple precincts twice before His death proving once and for all that the whole system was man-made, not even His original idea, let alone His perfect will. Man's carnal mind could not be awakened to the results of sin without the shedding of blood, even the blood of God's dear Son. But the killing of animals was offensive to Him; it hurt and grieved Him. He, Jesus, saw this, *Desire of Ages,* pg. 157. Sr. White says this: *"He saw the distress of the poor, who thought that without the shedding of blood there could be no forgiveness for their sin."* Ah, but they were wrong. After the money changers fled from His holy presence, Jesus began healing the people. Tears were in His eyes as He forgave and delivered them. *"Oh, Jesus, deliver us and cleanse us today from our own idea of how to gain salvation by our own works."* Because sacrifice of animals is a human work, something you do, putting the blame on an animal, one of God's creation, it becomes a work. *"Sacrifice and offering thou didst not desire."* Ps. 40:6. Look it up in the Hebrew, (the word desire) and see what God means by that word. It is really a heavy meaning. *"Mine ears hast thou opened; burnt offering and sin offering hast thou not required."* Ps. 40:6. God said He didn't desire it or require it. *"Lo, I come; in the volume of the book it is written of me, I delight to do thy will, O my God. Yea, thy law* (or character) *is within my heart."* Ps. 40:8. Here is another scripture from Ps. 50. *". . . It isn't sacrificial bullocks and goats that I really want from you. For all the animals of field and forest are mine! The cattle on a thousand hills! And all the birds upon the mountains."* Ps. 50:9-11. He says, *"I love these, they are my own creation, why should I want you to kill them?"* *"No, I don't need your sacrifices of flesh and blood. What I want from you is your true thanks;* (to be grateful). *I want your promises fulfilled. I want you to trust me in your times of trouble, so I can rescue you and you can give me glory."* "Glory" means character and God wants us to reveal His true character in our lives. But killing animals doesn't do that. Ps. 50:15 LB. *"Therefore have I hewed them with the prophets; I have slain them by the words of my mouth and thy judgments* (decisions) *are as the light that goeth forth. For I desired mercy and not sacrifice; and the knowledge of God more than burnt offerings."* Hosea 6:5, 6. Jesus quotes that very verse in Matt. 9 and also Matt. 12. *"The Lord of Hosts, the God of Israel says, away with your offerings and sacrifices. It wasn't offerings and sacrifices I wanted from your fathers when I led them out of Egypt. That was not the point of my command. But what I told them was: Obey me and I will be your God and you shall be my people.*

Only do as I say and all shall be well! But they wouldn't listen; they kept on doing what they wanted to, following their own stubborn, and evil thoughts. They went backward instead of forward." This is the Living Bible. If you read it in the King James it is much stronger. God said that He never commanded, never even gave the word to kill animals at Mt. Sinai. See Jere. 7:22-26.

RULERS

"Hear the word of the Lord, ye Rulers of Sodom; give ear unto the law of our God, ye people of Gomorrah. To what purpose is the multitude of your sacrifices unto me? saith the Lord: I am full of the burnt offerings of rams, and the fat of fed beasts; and I delight not in the blood of bullocks or of lambs or of he goats. . . . When you come to appear before me, who hath required this?" Not me, I didn't require it. Isa. 1:10-12, and He is addressing them as Sodom and Gomorrah. It is a heavy indictment against them.

We are now going to contrast Jesus and Satan. Jesus is the prince of light and life, and Satan is the prince of death and darkness. The Bible is very, very clear. Two princes of the Bible, two Lords, two Gods, two Saviours, all the way through and they are in absolute total contrast. *"For such a high priest became us, who is holy, harmless, undefiled,"* Heb. 7:26 (and underline the word *harmless*), . . . talk about the importance of the sanctuary service . . . beloved, have you ever heard anyone talk about God being holy? Yes, you have heard lots of sermons about God's holiness. And God is undefiled? Yes, God is undefiled. I have heard lots of sermons about God being undefiled. But have you ever heard a preacher preach even one single time about God being harmless? No, you have never heard that, because that would set the people free, and that is one thing that organized religion cannot afford to do. Organized religion, many times, is the greatest enemy of God, because it puts fear in people's hearts. Look at the Catholic church, how they rule their people. They rule the people by fear. If you told the people in the Catholic church or any Protestant church or any church at all, as far as that goes, that God is harmless, He won't hurt you, that would be a shocking revelation. *"For such a high priest became us, who is holy, harmless, undefiled, separate from sinners, and made higher than the heavens."* Heb. 7:26. *"In Him* (Christ Jesus) *was life; and the life was the light of men."* John 1:4. *"God is light and in Him is no darkness at all, for we wrestle not against flesh and blood, but against principalities and powers, against the rulers of darkness of this world."* I John 1:5, Eph. 6:12. Speaking of Lucifer, Isaiah says, *"How hath the oppressor ceased! The Golden city ceased!* Isa. 14:4. (or the exacters of gold)" That is very interesting in light of what is happening to the banking world. The Lord will break the staff of the wicked and the staff of the rulers. *"He who smote the people in wrath with a continual stroke, he that ruled the nations in anger, is persecuted, and none hindereth."* Isa. 14:5, 6. He is talking about Lucifer. *"The whole earth is at rest, and is quiet:* (during the thousand years). *They break forth into singing. Yea, the fir trees rejoice at thee, and the cedars of Lebanon, saying, Since thou art laid down,* (Lucifer) *no feller is come up against us."* Now, God starts appealing to His first created being, *"How are thou fallen from Heaven, O Lucifer, son of the morning!"* Isa. 14:7, 8, 12. (day star). "How art thou cut down to the ground, which didst weaken the nations! For thou has said in thine heart, (I am going to tell you what your thoughts are, I know what your thoughts are, Lucifer) *I will ascend into heaven, I will exalt my throne above the stars of God; I will sit also upon the mount of the congregation, in the sides of the north: I will ascend above the heights of the clouds; I will be like the most high. Yet thou shalt be brought down to hell."* Isa. 14:13-15. "This is what is going to happen to you, please don't let this happen to you, Lucifer, please." *"To the sides of the pit* (grave). *They that see thee shall narrowly look upon thee, they will squint their eyes and say, 'really, is this him?' They will consider thee, saying, 'Is this the man'* ("I can't believe it," the people will say.) *Is this the man that made the earth to tremble?"* Isa. 14:16. (Who makes the earth to tremble, friends? Is it God? It doesn't say so in the Bible. It says that the devil is the one that makes the earth to tremble. Let's stop blaming God for making everybody afraid and for making the earth to quake and to tremble. That is the kind of God that Satan has convinced the world is the Saviour of mankind.) *"Is this the man who made the earth to tremble, that did shake kingdoms?"* Who shakes the kingdoms? It is the devil that does that, *"That makes the world as a wilderness?"* Isa. 14:7. Who is it that is destroying nature and wrecking this world? Is it God? No, the Bible says it is the devil. *"And destroyed the cities thereof?"* Isa. 14:17. Who is it that destroys the cities? Wait a minute! All these cities that are destroyed by the brightness of his coming were not done by God? No, it says that it was the devil that did it, and the people recognized it finally. *They looked narrowly upon him after seeing the revelation in the sky. They look upon him and see and consider Satan, saying, "Is this the man that destroyed the cities thereof, that opened not the house of his prisoners?" They exclaim, "He did all this? He is the one who did it!" And they finally find out, after a thousand years. The movie in the sky reveals it, and then they find out the truth. He is the one who made the earth to tremble, he is the one who destroyed the cities, and he is the one who put everyone in the grave and wouldn't let them come out.* Isa. 14:5-17.

*Who then made Mt. Sinai to tremble and smoke?
Think about it, who was responsible for doing that?*
Exod. 19:18. The actual word is *"quake"* but the same
Hebrew word is used in vs. 16, *"sharade." "All the people
that were in the camp trembled." Who is it that makes
people to tremble? It says right here that it is Satan
who makes the people to tremble. So who is the one
who actually brought all the abberations of nature at
Mt. Sinai? Who brought the smoke? Let's read it in
Revelation. "And the fifth angel sounded, and I saw a
star fall* (Satan) *from heaven unto the earth; and to him
was given the key to the bottomless pit."* Rev. 9:1. The
pit represents the grave. This angel that fell is Satan, and
all the people that he has used through the ages. It says
that Satan has the key and he kept all these prisoners
locked up in the grave. Jesus Christ got that key when He
died and when He came up from the grave. Rev. 1:18 says
He, Jesus Christ, has the *"keys"* to hell and death. Praise
the Lord! *"And he opened the bottomless pit;* (the endless graves upon the earth) *and there arose a smoke out
of the pit, as the smoke of a great furnace."* Who
brought the smoke? You find the phrase *"of a furnace"*
used at Mt. Sinai, and here it is again, *"the smoke of a
great furnace."* Rev. 9:1-2. Compare this text with Exod.
19:18. *"And Mt. Sinai was altogether on a smoke,
because the Lord descended upon it in fire; and the
smoke thereof ascended as the smoke of a furnace."*
Who makes the earth to tremble and quake? That Hebrew
word tells you it is Satan.

Jesus' fire is not a literal fire. The burning bush did
not oxidize or burn up, therefore it did not give off any
smoke. When the Holy Spirit came at Pentecost, the fire
that came and appeared on the top of the disciples' heads
was not a literal fire. Literal fire did not even exist until
after sin entered the world. Do you realize that? *"The lion
has come up from his thicket, and the destroyer of the*

Gentiles is on his way." Who is that? It is Satan. *"He is gone forth from his place to make thy land desolate; and thy cities shall be laid waste without an inhabitant."* Jere. 4:7. Who is it that destroys cities? It is the destroyer of the Gentiles, and the Bible never calls God a destroyer, except that He takes the blame for it, because He let Satan do it. But He is not the one who is doing it.

Jesus has the keys to the bottomless pit and will open it for the righteous at the first resurrection. Satan and all the wicked will remain on this earth for 1,000 years, but all the wicked will still be dead. Only Satan will remain alive with his unholy angels. And that is when they will suffer a lot of mental suffering.

We are going to hit the high points in Exodus 19, and get an idea of what is happening. Here is where the Israelites reach Sinai; they have just come through the Red Sea, and God is going to reveal to them His law. I will tell you, friends, we've never understood the law of God; and Sr. White says that there are deep, deep truths in the law of God that we have never understood. We definitely didn't understand it in 1844 and 1888, 1901, and all the way through. We have never understood it like we should. *"In the third month, when the children of Israel were gone forth out of Egypt, the same day came they into the wilderness at Sinai. For they were departed from Rephidim and were come to the desert of Sinai, and had pitched in the wilderness; and there Israel camped before the mount. And Moses went up unto God, and the Lord called unto him out of the mountain, saying, Thus shalt thou say unto the House of Jacob, and tell the children of Israel."* Ex. 19:1-3. It goes on and talks more about this. Let's skip over to where God tells him, warns him about a lot of things, then vs. 14, *"And Moses went down from the mount unto the people, and sanctified the people; and they washed their clothes. And he said unto the people, Be ready against the third day: come not at your wives. And it came to*

pass on the third day in the morning, that there were thunders and lightnings, and a thick cloud upon the mount, and the voice of the trumpet exceeding loud; so that all the people that was in the camp trembled." Ex. 19:14-16. Now, all the people came out of the camp to meet God. And they stood at the nether part, that means the base of the mount. **"And Mt. Sinai was altogether on a smoke, because the Lord descended upon it in fire."** Ex. 19:18. Jesus comes down with His fire of love, truth, and righteousness, the fire of His love and law and Satan says, **"Here he comes. He is going to take the people away from us unless we deceive the people. We've got to put on a big show to make them afraid of God."** You see, the devil always wants to make you afraid of God. As long as he can make you afraid of God, you will never understand what God is like, and you will never get Him in your heart and you will never get married to Jesus. Do you want to get married and kiss someone that you are afraid of? No, you will never do it.

So the people were afraid. **"The smoke thereof ascended as the smoke of a furnace, and the whole mountain quaked greatly. And when the voice of the trumpet sounded long, and waxed louder and louder, Moses spake, and God answered him by a voice."** Ex. 19:18, 19. I believe that is a still small voice. Vs. 20, **"And the Lord came down upon Mt. Sinai on the top of the mount; and the Lord called Moses up to the top of the Mount and Moses went up."** Remember, this is very important. The top of the mount. That is where Jesus is, in the top of the mount. **"And the Lord said unto Moses, Go down, and charge the people, lest they break through unto the Lord to gaze, and many of them perish. And let the priests also which come near unto the Lord, sanctify themselves, lest the Lord break forth upon them. And Moses said unto the Lord, the people cannot come up to Mt. Sinai; for thou chargest us, saying, Set bounds about the mount and sanctify it. And the**

Lord said unto him, Away, get thee down, and thou shalt come up, thou, and Aaron with thee: but let not the priests and the people break through to come up unto the Lord, lest he break forth upon them. So Moses went down unto the people and spake unto them." Ex. 19:21-25.

I want to go through this again, because I want to show you how God speaks about Himself. It is extremely important to understand this. Notice how God talks about Himself. God never talks about Himself in the third person. He talks about Himself in the first person. Watch this, **"And God spake all these words, saying, I am the Lord thy God, which have brought thee out of the land of Egypt, out of the house of bondage. Thou shalt have no other gods before Me."** Ex. 20:1-3. See that. He didn't say **"thou shalt have no other gods before the Lord."** He said, **"thou shalt have no other gods before Me."** It is very important to understand. I am going to define the two lords and make it very clear to you so you will understand what I am talking about. When it is the Lord Jesus, I will say the Lord Jesus, but when it is lord Satan, I will say lord Satan and you can make up your mind if it is right or not. If you don't come to the same conclusion that I do, that is OK, I still love you anyway.

Vs. 20, **"And the Lord** (Jesus) **came down upon mount Sinai, on the top of the mount; and the Lord** (Jesus) **called Moses up to the top of the mount; and Moses went up. And the Lord** (Jesus) **said unto Moses, Go down, charge the people, lest they break through unto the lord** (Satan) **to gaze, and many of them perish. And let the priests also, which come near to the lord,** (Satan) **sanctify themselves, lest the lord** (Satan) **break forth upon them. And Moses said unto the Lord,** (Jesus) **The people cannot come up to mount Sinai; for thou charged us, saying, Set bounds about the mount, and sanctify it."** Moses is arguing with Jesus because he doesn't understand what he is talking about. Vs. 24, **"And**

the Lord (Jesus) **said unto him, Away, get thee down, and thou shalt come up, thou, and Aaron with thee; but let not the priests and the people break through to come up unto the lord** (Satan), **lest he break forth upon them."** And so Moses finally goes down there and speaks to the people, because going up and down that mountain got tiresome and he said, **"Why do I have to go back down there? I already told them once"** Jesus is so concerned; He doesn't want anyone to get hurt, so He says, **"Go down and tell them again."**

Now I want to show you a couple more. First we will read Exod. 32:7-10, then we will read Exod. 24:9-12. Let's just read the first verse of Exod. 32 to give you an idea what it is about. **"And when the people saw that Moses delayed to come down out of the mount, the people gathered themselves together unto Aaron, and said unto him, Up, make us gods, which shall go before us:"** You see, Israel was part of the Canaanite society; they lived in a polytheistic society where they worshipped many gods. In Genesis, it says, **"In the beginning God,** (in the plural) **created the heavens and the earth."** But when Jesus was talking about another lord, that didn't mean anything to Moses. There were many gods, and there was the chief one at the top, then there were lesser ones down the mountain. **"And the Lord said unto Moses, Go, get thee down; for thy people, which thou broughtest out of the land of Egypt, have corrupted themselves. They have turned aside quickly out of the way which I commanded them: they have made them a molten calf, and have worshipped it, and have sacrificed thereunto, and said, These be thy gods, O Israel, which have brought thee up out of the land of Egypt. And the Lord said unto Moses, I have seen this people, and behold, it is a stiffnecked people: Now therefore let me alone, that my wrath may wax hot against them, and that I may consume them: and I will make of thee a great nation."** Isn't that amazing? You read this and say, **"Wow, God is** *really getting mad there. He is sure different than I thought God would be."* Let's examine this, going back to vs. 7 and go through it. *"And the Lord said unto Moses, Go, get thee down: for thy people, which thou broughtest out of the land of Egypt, have corrupted themselves."* Who is this voice claiming to be the Lord? He is condemning Israel. God never condemned Israel. *"They have turned aside quickly out of the way which I commanded them: they have made them a molten calf, and have worshipped it, and have sacrificed thereunto, and said, These be thy gods, O Israel, which have brought thee up out of the land of Egypt."* Now He is building up, and is saying, *"Look how bad these people are. Just let me alone, Moses, that my wrath may wax hot against them that I may consume them and make thee a great nation."* This is similar to the temptation that Satan brought to Jesus when he said, *"Bow down before me and worship me and I will give you all the kingdoms of the world."* Matt. 4:9.

I am suggesting, beloved, that this voice here claiming to be the Lord is not the Lord Jesus, but is really lord Satan. It is a temptation that came to Moses by Satan, because God doesn't tempt anyone. James 1:13. This is not Jesus, it is Satan tempting Moses and this gives him away.

"Now therefore let me alone, . . ." Friends, I challenge you to search the scriptures through and find one place in the entire Bible where God ever says, *"Let me alone."* God never talks like that. It is not His character. But this is a very familiar phrase in the New Testament when the evil angels are speaking. They say, *"Let us alone."* Mark 1:24. That gives him away right there. *"Now therefore let me alone."* . . . you see that is the way the devil talks. *"That my wrath may wax hot against them that I may consume them."* Get out of the way, Moses, so I can kill them, and I will make of thee a great nation. What

WHO TEMPTED MOSES IN EXODUS 32?

Moses does not realize that it is Satan who is tempting him to step aside so Satan can destroy the people, so Moses pleads with God not to destroy His own people. "Lord, you must not do this evil thing . . . you must not destroy your own people, for it will make you look bad." Exodus 32:11, 12. Paraphrased by author.

Satan, claiming to be God, tempts Moses to let him destroy Israel. "Let me alone, that my wrath may wax hot against them, and that I may consume them: and I will make of thee a great nation." Ex. 32:10.

Satan successfully tempts the people to put pressure on Aaron to make them a golden calf to worship. Once they have broken the first and second commandments, Satan then goes to Moses, posing as God, and tries to get Moses' permission to destroy the people. But Moses' love for the people is so great that he stands in the breach and offers his own eternal salvation, so they will not be lost. By doing this, Moses became a type of Christ. Exodus 32:7-14, 32.

a motive! Is that the way God talks? The way He operates? If you think that about God, that is the kind of God that will be in your heart. See also IFH 180, 181.

Remember the true God was on the top of the mountain, the people at the bottom, and Satan was halfway up the middle as an angel of light claiming to be God himself. *"Then went up Moses, and Aaron, Nadab, and Abihu, and seventy of the elders of Israel; and they saw the God of Israel: and there was under his feet as it were a paved work of a sapphire stone, and as it were the body of heaven in his clearness. And upon the nobles of the children of Israel he laid not his hand: also they saw God, and did eat and drink."* Exodus 24:9-11. Beloved, I want you to think about these verses. What does the Bible say? *"No one has ever seen God at anytime."* Ex. 33:20; John 1:18; I Tim. 6:16; I John 4:12. So who was this that they saw? It wasn't the true God. They thought it was, but it was Satan pretending to be God, as an angel of light.

Now, you will see how this understanding of the two Lords will open up the whole Old Testament so it will make a lot more sense. For example, what this does for us in the Old Testament, is it answers a very familiar question that people bring up. I Sam. 15, for example, vs. 1-2, *"Samuel also said unto Saul, The Lord sent me to anoint thee to be king over his people, over Israel: now therefore hearken thou unto the voice of the words of the Lord. Thus saith the Lord of hosts, I remember that which Amalek did to Israel, how he laid wait for him in the way, when he came up from Egypt."* Now we are going to get even. *"Now go and smite Amalek, and utterly destroy all that they have, and spare them not; but slay both man and woman, infant and suckling, ox and sheep, camel and ass."* What a motive! What a command! And people, many atheists, who don't even believe in the Bible, say, *"If that is what God is like, I don't want to have anything to do with Him."* You know that many people reject God on that basis. This opens up the whole Bible; there are two lords in the Bible. There are two princes, two gods in this Bible. What a book we have. God Himself revealed the truth about Satan here. He acknowledges Satan as a god. He says he is the god of this world; he is the prince of the power of the air. He acknowledges Satan as a god who had control of us; and Jesus Christ had to come to this dark earth and give His life a ransom for us . . . let us bloody Him up, put Him on a cross so we could see the difference between the two. You say, "Wait a minute, you mean that even the angels didn't understand?" No, they didn't understand either.

Listen: *"Not until the death of Christ was the character of Satan clearly revealed to the angels or to the unfallen worlds. The archapostate had so clothed himself with deception that even holy beings had not understood his principles. They had not clearly seen the nature of his rebellion. It was a being of wonderful power and glory that had set himself against God. Of Lucifer the Lord says, 'Thou sealest up the sum, full of wisdom, and perfect in beauty.' (Ez. 28:12) Lucifer had been the covering cherub. He had stood in the light of God's presence. He had been the highest of all created beings, and had been foremost in revealing God's purposes to the universe. After he had sinned, his power to deceive was the more deceptive, and the unveiling of his character was the more difficult because of the exalted position he had held with the Father." Desire of Ages,* pages 758, 759.

So, at Mount Sinai, the holy angels did not understand or realize the character of Satan anymore than Moses did; and they were all there together. So what I do, I show, for example, Matt. 5. This is when Jesus began His first sermon. Sr. White says He did not attack error, but revealed truth. Look what He did. On the Mount of Olives He gave them what He had wanted to give them at Mount Sinai, but wasn't able to because of the darkness of their minds. Matt. 5:17. *"Think not that I am come to destroy the law, or the prophets: I am not come to destroy, but to fulfill."* Then He proceeds with the rest of the chapter to destroy everything they believe. He took away everything they believed in, point by point. Can you imagine why they hated

Him. The priests never invited Him to preach in their temples. But the people wanted to hear Him. Notice what He said, Vs. 21, *"Ye have heard that it was said by them of old time, Thou shalt not kill; and whosoever shall kill shall be in danger of the judgment: but I say unto you, That whosoever is angry with his brother without a cause shall be in danger of the judgment."* If you get angry with someone you have already killed them. What is He doing? He is making the law spiritual. The Jews kept the legal letter of the law. Christ made the law spiritual. He goes on in vs. 27, *"Ye have heard that it was said by them of old time, Thou shalt not commit adultery; but I say unto you, That whosoever looketh on a woman to lust after her hath committed adultery with her already in his heart."* The Pharisees prided themselves in keeping the law, but Jesus said, *"You are not even keeping the law. Everyone of you are sinners."* What do you think that did to the Pharisees? It just blew their minds away.

Vs. 38, *"Ye have heard that it hath been said, An eye for an eye, and a tooth for a tooth: but I say unto you, That whosoever shall smite thee on thy right cheek, turn to him the other also. And if any man will sue thee at the law, and take away thy coat, let him have thy cloak also."* "Beloved, if the Roman soldiers want you to walk a mile, go two." How did the Jews relate themselves to these statements? They thought the man was totally insane. This man is absolutely of the devil. That is the way they related themselves to Jesus. But Jesus Christ came and said, *"You have heard all these things from your past teachers and theologians, but I say unto you . . ."* Jesus put Himself above the law by saying, *"You have a beautiful temple, but there is one here that is greater than the temple."* What was He doing to the Jewish nation? As far as the Pharisees and the Scribes were concerned, He was destroying it. Do you realize that today we have an exact parallel. This message of God's love will cause the same kind of reaction by church leaders today. *"We can't believe this. We can't accept this. It will destroy the church, and everything we believe in."* And that is the actual truth, because we are repeating the history of Israel step by step. Everything the Jews believed was leading them to death, and Jesus was trying to tell them they were going the wrong way. You are going to destroy yourself. Jeremiah said in his day, *"The answer is surrender to the Chaldeans, the Babylonians, and you will live."* Jeremiah 38:1-4. And they said, *"You are crazy. We can't surrender. We have to fight."* Jeremiah says, *"No, you must surrender. Let the Lord's punishment come. Accept it, it will be 70 years, and then you can come back and everything will be okay."* And they said, *"Jeremiah, you are absolutely insane. Get out of here Jeremiah, you are against us."* But the very opposite was true and what they were saying was false. The same thing applies to Christ's day, as well as to our day. It repeats itself throughout history, because we don't want to surrender; we want to do it ourselves. This is righteousness by works.

Let us go on with the Sermon on the Mount. *"An eye for an eye and a tooth for a tooth, but I say unto you"* . . . wait a minute, Jesus, you mean you didn't give that law, which demands that for every eye that is punched or gouged out another eye must be punched or gouged out?" *No, I didn't give that law."* Well, who gave it then? That is the question. I will give you a little hint. Turn to Job 2:3. *"And the Lord said unto Satan, Hast thou considered my servant Job, that there is none like him in the earth, a perfect and an upright man, one that feareth God, and escheweth* (hates) *evil? and still he holdeth fast his integrity, although thou movedst me against him, to destroy him without cause."* God is taking the blame, here, and He is saying this before the entire heavenly council. I estimate there was a representative from every planet in the entire universe. How many people could that be? I don't know how many planets there are. Millions, perhaps billions. And Jesus is covering up for Lucifer because He loved him so much. He is covering up for him in front of all the representatives of the worlds, and before all the holy, unfallen, angels. He doesn't want to expose His beloved first creation, Lucifer, because He loves him so much and says, *"It is all my fault. Look what you have made me do to Job."* Vs. 4, *"And Satan answered the Lord, and said, Skin for skin, yea, all that a man hath will he give for his life."* Eye for eye, tooth for tooth, skin for skin ... a voice from the past is identified, Satan, the author of the animal sacrifices.

Now, let's go to Deut. 5:22. Moses has just reiterated the ten commandments and then in Vs. 22, He says, *"These words the Lord spake unto all your assembly in the mount out of the midst of the fire, of the cloud, and of the thick darkness, with a great voice: and he added no more. And he wrote them in two tables of stone, and delivered them unto me."* All that God spoke and all that God wrote on Mount Sinai were the Ten Commandments, and that was it. No more. That is Deut. 5:22.

Now, let's go to Jere. 7:21-22. *"Thus saith the Lord of hosts, the God of Israel; Put your burnt offerings unto your sacrifices and eat flesh."* He is saying, *"I know you want to do it, so go ahead and do it all you want."* Vs. 22, *"For I spake not unto your fathers, nor commanded them in the day that I brought them out of the land of Egypt, concerning burnt offerings or sacrifices:"* I never spoke a word about it. *"But this thing commanded I them, saying, Obey my voice, and I will be your God, and ye shall be my people: and walk ye in all the ways that I have commanded you, that it may be well unto you. But they harkened not, nor inclined their ear, but walked in the counsels and in the imagination of their evil heart, and went backward, and not forward. Since the day that your fathers came forth out of the land of Egypt unto this day ..."* Evil and sin never go forward. It always progresses worse and worse. So, every year it got worse until Jesus came; and if Christ had not come when He did, the world would have been destroyed in a short time. And in our day, if Jesus doesn't come again soon to this earth, our world is going to blow up and there will be no one left. Christ must soon come, or we are all going to be dead. Isn't that clear? What do you think the *"Day After"* was about? The bankers want to put fear on the people. Did you see the news recently? Twenty-one percent boost in defense. They are getting a defense budget. The bankers loaned them more money. They are getting rich. Everyone is getting rich off the fear of the people. And where does it end? The rich people of the earth who are in control . . . Satan has lied to them too, saying, *"Just go ahead and get all the money and blow all the people up. They are no good. They are stupid. Just get rid of all the people, then you will be the Kings of the earth."* That is the same thing he said to Moses, *"Get out of the way, Moses, I will kill them all, and I will make you the king."* That is what he is saying to the leaders of the earth today. *"All these people are no good, just get rid of them, then you will be king."* Satan always lies to people. But that is the motive he is giving them.

But we have a parallel to Jeremiah 7:21, 22 in the writings of Sr. White, Vol. 2, pgs. 441-442. She makes a very strong indictment and says (this is a rough paraphrase), like ancient Israel, the Church, our own church, the Seventh-Day Adventist church, has left her God, has gone into darkness away from God's light and Satan is inside the church working side by side with professed Christians. And they don't even know it. Satan is inside running the show. She wrote these words about 1868. Evil never stops once it gets going. She called us Laodicea as early as 1857. Has Laodicea ever gotten better? No, it's only gotten worse. Laodicea has never gotten any different, it has only gotten more Laodiceaean. Laodicea is blind, for they can't see, they don't realize what they are. Beloved, we are repeating the history of Israel step by step.

Isa. 66:3, 4 says this, *"He that killeth an ox is as if he slew a man; he that sacrificeth a lamb, as if he cut off a dog's neck; he that offereth an oblation, as if he offered swine's blood; he that burneth incense, as if he blessed an idol. Yea, they have chosen their own ways, and their soul delighteth in their abominations."* What is he talking about? Animal sacrifices. *"I also will choose their delusions, and will bring their fears upon them; because when I called, none did answer; when I spake, they did not hear: but they did evil before mine eyes, and chose that in which I delighted not."* How many times have we already read that God says he didn't delight in the killing of animals? Many, many times, and here it is again.

Now Paul talks about this in I Cor. 10. He says animal sacrifice is devil worship, plain and simple. Isn't that amazing? Vs. 14, *"Wherefore, my dearly beloved, flee from idolatry. I speak as to wise men; judge ye what I say. The cup of blessing which we bless, is it not the communion of the blood of Christ? The bread which we break, is it not the communion of the body of Christ? For we being many are one bread, and one body: for we are all partakers of that one bread. Behold Israel after the flesh,* (notice, after the flesh, not spiritual Israel, but literal Israel) *are not they which eat of the sacrifices partakers of the altar? What say I then? that the idol is anything, or that which is offered in sacrifice to idols is anything? But I say, that the things which the Gentiles sacrifice, they sacrifice to devils, and not to God: and I would not that ye should have fellowship with devils."* I Cor. 10:14-20. See also Acts 7:41-43; Amos 5:25.

Now go to Galatians 3:19. He talks a little more about this. Paul talks about the added laws in vs. 19. *"Wherefore then serveth the law? It was added because of transgressions, till the seed should come to whom the promise was made; and it was ordained by angels in the hand of a mediator."* Here he talks about angels, at Mt.

Sinai. Where in the scripture does God say angels ever "ordained" anything? How could these be God's angels if Jesus abolished this law? Satan and his angels were allowed to give Moses this law which Christ abolished at Mt. Olivet and Mt. Calvary. They wanted to kill animals. They wanted an eye for an eye and tooth for tooth. That is the kind of society they lived in. It was the only thing God could do. It is just like the death decree today, and all the laws we have in society. It is the only thing God can do. It is like Laodicea, the way the churches are organized, even the Seventh-Day Adventist. It is the only thing God can do with us. Can't you understand? . . . we are all so blind and so stubborn and self-willed. It is the only thing God can do with us. But we are coming to the end and he is saying, *"Look, you have to wake up."* What have we spoken of . . . Every text I am giving you tonight is in Ch. 28 of my book (IFH). I can go over these with you later on if you have questions. But let us go on.

"Now a mediator is not a mediator of one, but God is one." This is what I believe this means. This is what I understand happened at Mt. Sinai. Jesus came down on the top of the mount. The people were at the bottom, and Satan was halfway up in the middle and everything that God did for Israel, He had to go through Lucifer, because Lucifer had control of the whole world, including Israel. Isn't that exactly what happens with Laodicea? God has to speak through the Laodicean preachers who are just as blind, in most cases, as the people. And what does Sr. White say will happen in the last days? That eventually the only kind of preacher that will be in the pulpit would be the kind of preacher like Hazael, the one that destroyed Israel. See I Kings 19, 2 Kings 8-10. The false torch of prophecy and torch of Satan from the pulpits would be a scourge to God's people. These would be the kind of preachers who would be a scourge to God's people in the last days, because the people reject God's messages and the only kind of preachers that would be left will be Hazaels. 5T 79. Elijah was sent to

anoint Hazael just before he was translated. He tells him to go annoint these people, Hazaels. The only kind of preachers that would be left in the last days in the Seventh-Day Adventist church would be Hazaels, which would be a scourge to the people and they would teach the people the wrong thing, and it would lead Modern Israel to destruction. That is the same thing that happened to Ancient Israel. And that is what we've come to. I'm not saying all ministers are like that yet, but that is the prediction. The people themselves don't want to hear the truth; and if a preacher gets up and starts preaching the truth, some people make such a stink that the conference moves him somewhere else. This happens all the time. It is unfortunate, but that is the way it goes. It is not only in our church, but in all churches. I have heard stories about Baptist preachers who got up to preach revival and the people rebelled. Look what they did when Moses was up in the mount. They rebelled and Aaron gave them the golden calf. That is our nature, not to have confrontations, not to have controversy, just give the people what they want, and it makes everyone happy. Let's not have any controversy, let's have peace. But compromise never brings lasting peace.

Now to the point I am trying to make in Galatians 3:20. *"Now a mediator is not a mediator of one, but God is one."* Satan was the mediator. He was the one who was presenting this law. But God was there to edit it to save the people from as many ill effects of this evil law as possible. Paul says it was *"against us"* and *"contrary"* to us. COL. 2:14. Does God ever give us anything that is against us or contrary to us? And where else in the Bible does it say God "ordained" anything by angels that was carnal, weak, unprofitable and later abolished? God's holy angels would never ordain such a law. No. He only gives us *"good"* gifts. James 1:17. Moses wrote all this down in a book, and where was this law put? The law that we call The Law of Moses, where was that put? It was put on the outside of the Ark.

Where were the Ten Commandments put? Yes, on the inside of the Ark. Why was there a difference between the Ten Commandments and the law of Moses? God wrote the Ten Commandments with His own finger. That is all He wrote and that was put inside the Ark. The Ark represented the mind or conscience of the believer. And all that God will allow to come into our experience and our mind is His own law, His own character; because the law is a transcript of His very character. See the importance of the law of God? And God says that the only thing that He allows inside your mind, your heart and conscience is what He spoke. He didn't speak the other law. That is on the outside of the outside of the Ark. It was the people's idea. That is what they wanted and Satan gave them what they wanted; the eye for an eye and the killing of animals. Because that had come from Eden, outside the gates of Eden. Adam was the one who started the animal sacrifices, and Hosea 6:7 says that Adam *"dealt treacherously"* with God because Satan had control of Adam's mind. Adam's mind was taken over by Satan after he sinned and he was separated from God. Outside the Garden of Eden, Satan put it in Adam's mind to kill the animals, and God took the dead animals and made skins out of them and clothed them. That is where that came in. God didn't kill the animals. EGW said that God *"ordained"* the animal sacrifice system. What does that mean? It is the same thing as God ordaining the first divorce law. God ordained the first king of Israel. God ordained the sword. He let them have flesh food to eat. He let them have anything they wanted, right? Because He wanted it? No, because they wanted it. Do you realize that if a person wants something bad enough, Satan will put it in his mind and say, *"I am God speaking."* And the deceived person responds, *"Oh, yes, God, what do you want me to do?"* One thinks that it is God putting it in his mind when it is really Satan. Then the Lord has to let him have what he wants. Why do you think people get married to the wrong people? Because they think God wanted them to get married, and it is not God, but God is allowing it, and the Lord has to work through these kind of terrible predicaments people get themselves into because they can't tell the difference between the voice of Jesus and the voice of Satan. Yet, God always stays with us to save us from the worst effects of our wrong choices. Let me give you an explanation here. God claims that all these laws are His . . . God says He gave them. Ezek. 20:24-25. *"Because they had not executed my judgments, but had despised my statutes, and polluted my sabbaths, and their eyes were after their fathers' idols. Wherefore, I gave them also statutes that were not good, and judgments whereby they should not live;"* And Jesus died on the cross; and what did He nail to the cross? Does God ever do away with anything that He gave? No, He doesn't do away with His laws because every law God gives is perfect and never has to be changed or abolished. Paul says that the law of animal sacrifice was a *"carnal"* law. Read it in Heb. 7:16. It was a carnal law. Does God ever give anything that is carnal? No, God is spiritual. He only gives holy, spiritual laws. Rom. 7:12, 14.

Eph. 2:14-15, *"For he is our peace, who hath made both one, and hath broken down the middle wall of partition between us; Having abolished in his flesh the enmity, even the law of commandments contained in ordinances. . . ."* It says He abolished that. Col. 2:14 says He nailed it to the cross. Of course, the Protestants, the Sunday-keepers, say this is the Ten Commandments that He nailed to the cross. Col. 2:14-15. *"Blotting out the handwriting of ordinances that was against us."* Does God ever give any law that is against us? No, His laws are only for us—*"Which was contrary to us, and took it out of the way, nailing it to his cross;"* Don't we always say it was the ceremonial law that was abolished? Always! And so

God, through His Son, got rid of it because it was against us; it was hurting and killing innocent animals. And it was polluting our conscience. Heb. 9:14.

Who put it in their minds to eat flesh food? Was it God's idea or Satan's that put it in the people's minds? We know Satan put it in their minds to eat flesh food and God says, ***"Alright, if you are going to eat flesh foods, here are the flesh foods you are allowed to eat."*** In other words, whenever they chose to do something, God says, "alright, if this is what you choose to do, here is how you do it. If you want a king, I'll get you a king, but here are the rules of the kingdom." **"God never leaves his people. He never forsakes them."** He stays with them to save them from the worst effects of their wrong choice.

Here is a young girl and she wants to get married to this guy; and her father says, "Honey, don't marry that guy. He is a bum and he will break your heart." She says, "But, Daddy, I love him and he is a wonderful person, and I know that we are going to be happy." "No, I tell you, he is a bum; don't get mixed up with him." So time goes on. She dates him and she comes home and says, "Daddy, we are going to get married, and we will elope if you don't give us your blessing." And he says, "Alright, Honey, if that is your decision." So he sees there is no use to argue anymore and he goes downtown the next day, gets the announcements ready, and helps her pick out a wedding dress. While he is down there, he meets his friend, Joe, in the street. And Joe says, "What are you doing down here, John? Nice to see you and your lovely daughter here." "Well, Joe, we are getting ready for Susan's wedding." "That is wonderful. Who is she getting married to?" "Pete." "I thought you didn't want her to marry Pete." "I don't." "Well, what are you doing this for?" "Because I love my daughter and I don't want to break communication with her because she is really going to need me one of these days." So the wedding goes through. A few weeks later what happens? "Daddy," she calls up in the middle of the night, and says, "Daddy, you are right; he's a bum and he has broken my heart. What am I going to do?" "You stay right there, Honey, and I will be right over and pick you up." But if he had rejected his daughter and kicked her out of the house, what would have happened? She probably would not have called him for help in her time of need. And that is the same reason we know God will always help us in our time of need.

What about the son that says, "Dad, I want to go out and kill animals," and the father says, "No, son, I don't want you to do that." But the son says, "But, Daddy, I want to do it." And he says, "But, son, you can't do it. It is not the right thing to do. God made the animals and He loves them. Son, I used to be a killer myself; I was an expert hunter and marksman. I don't want you to do this." Next year, the boy says, "Dad, all my friends are going hunting this year, and I am going to go hunting, too. I have saved all my money and I am going to go out and buy a gun, and I am going to do it whether you want me to or not. You can kick me out, Dad, but I am going hunting this year. My friends are all going and they are making fun of me. They think I am a sissy." "Son, don't do anything. We will go downtown tomorrow and we will get you the best gun money can buy." So they go down the next day, buy a gun, and he goes out on the range, with his son and teaches him how to become an expert marksman. He teaches him how to do everything a good hunter needs to know. Now, someone sees him teaching his son all this and says, "I thought you didn't want your son to be a killer?" "I don't." "Why are you doing it then?" "To save him from the worst effects of his wrong choice." God never leaves us. Don't you realize that? God never leaves us. He always stays with us to save us from the worst effects of our wrong choices. What a wonderful God we have. It wasn't God's idea for them to kill animals, but when they chose to do that right outside the Garden of Eden, God says, "All right, if you want to kill animals, I will **license** you to kill them and even which ones to kill. You can only kill birds, cattle, sheep, and goats, only those four categories, because they represent what you are going to do to my Son." Do you think it was God's will for the people to put His Son on a cross? Do you think it was God's idea? God gave His Son to us as a gift. We took that gift and turned it into a human sacrifice that is what we thought God wanted. We thought that the Father demanded blood, and we thought that God the Father demanded this kind of sacrifice. We thought the Father said, "Son, forget about those stupid people down there on planet earth. They are no good; let them die." The son said, "Oh, please, Daddy, don't kill them yet, let me go down and I will try and straighten things out." "All right, Son, if you have to do it, go do it. If you have to pay for it, go ahead, and I'll let them put you on the cross so their sins will be taken away." That is the people's view of God, right? That is man's view, the carnal view.

I know some of these concepts are difficult to grasp. You may have to struggle with them awhile. When people first hear about the Sabbath don't they always have a struggle? They say "I always thought Sunday was the Sabbath," and they have all these arguments in their minds and it takes a while for them to get it straight. The same is true of the state of the dead. *"I always thought that you went up when you died and went to heaven or down to hell?"* How long does it take to get people's minds straight on that? Sometimes a long time. So, as you read the Word, I think you will understand it more, and the Bible especially. Sr. White's writings are filled with all kinds of statements about the love of God and how wonderful He is. You will find a progression in her writings. In the early years of her life and writings, especially, she didn't understand certain things. But as she grew older she understood more. The same is true for us today. The Lord is giving us more light on His wonderful character of Love.

This loving father seems to be instructing his son how to be a hunter, whereas, in fact he is advising the lad, who has elected to be a killer again his father's wishes, how to avoid the worst effects of his wrong choice and thereby be safe and just in his use of this lethal weapon.

GOD SAYS THERE IS MORE LIGHT FOR HIS PEOPLE AND HE COUNSELS US TO INVESTIGATE IT

But someone may protest by saying, *"We have all the light we will ever need."* Let me share with you what EGW has said about *"new light."* *"God intends that, even*

in this life, truth shall be ever unfolding." 5T 703.
*"There is no excuse for anyone taking the position that
there is no more truth to be revealed, and that all our
expositions are without error. The fact that certain
doctrines have been held as truth for many years by
our people, is not a proof that our ideas are infallible."*
(R. & H., Dec. 20, 1892, C.W.E. 35).

*"We must not think, 'Well, we have all the truth,
we understand the main pillars of our faith, and we
may rest on this knowledge.' Truth is an advancing
truth, and we must walk in the increasing light."*
Evang. 296, 297. *"New light will ever be revealed on the
word of God to him who is in living connection with
the Son of Righteousness. Let no one come to the conclusion that there is no more truth to be revealed. The
diligent, prayerful seeker for truth will find precious
rays of light yet to shine forth from the word of God.
Many gems are yet scattered that are to be gathered
together to become the property of the remnant people
of God." COUNSELS TO WRITERS AND EDITORS,*
page 35.

*"No matter by whom light is sent, we should open
our hearts to receive it with the meekness of Christ.
But many do not do this . . . when a doctrine is presented that does not meet our minds, we should go to
the word of God, seek the Lord in prayer, and give no
place for the enemy to come in with suspicion and
prejudice. We should never permit the spirit to be manifested that arraigned the priests and rulers against
the Redeemer of the world." GOSPEL WORKERS,* 301.

*"Precious light is to shine forth from the word of
God, and let no one presume to dictate what shall or
what shall not be brought before the people in the messages of enlightenment that He shall send, and so
quench the Spirit of God. Whatever may be his position of authority, no one has a right to shut away the*

light from the people. WHEN A MESSAGE COMES IN THE NAME OF THE LORD TO HIS PEOPLE, NO ONE MAY EXCUSE HIMSELF FROM AN INVESTI-GATION OF ITS CLAIMS. No one can afford to stand back in an attitude of indifference and self-confidence, and say: 'I know what is truth. I am satisfied with my position. I have set my stakes, and I will not be moved away from my position, whatever may come. I will not listen to the message of this messenger; for I know that it cannot be truth.' It is from pursuing this very course that the popular churches were left in partial dark-ness, and that is why the messages of heaven have not reached them." COUNSELS ON SABBATH SCHOOL WORK, p. 28.

When most SDAs think of the Sanctuary, they envision a structure of some kind, similar to Solomon's temple or the tent sanctuary Moses built in the wilderness. Most people think God dwells in these man-made structures, but He doesn't. Paul tells us, *"God that made the world ... dwelleth not in temples made with hands;"* Acts 17:24. And in Psalm 114:1-2 we read: *"When Israel went out of Egypt, ... Judah was his sanctuary, and Israel his dominion."* And in Psalm 132:13 we read, *"For the Lord hath chosen Zion; he hath desired it for his habitation. This is my rest for ever: here will I dwell; for I have desired it."*

And in John 14:17, Jesus promised us that through His own Spirit of truth He would be in us. *"Even the Spirit of truth; whom the world cannot receive, because it seeth him not, neither knoweth him: but ye know him; for He dwelleth with you, AND SHALL BE IN YOU."*

Then in John 17:21, Jesus prayed that all of us might be together with Him in His Father's heart. *"That they all may be one; as thou, Father, art in me, and I in thee, that they also may be one in us: that the world may believe that thou hast sent me."*

The mystery of God is to be solved in this last hour of earth's history. Paul reveals the secret of understanding this mystery in Col. 1:27. *"To whom God would make known what is the riches of the glory of this mystery among the Gentiles; which is CHRIST IN YOU, THE HOPE OF GLORY."* And Rev. 10:7 indicates that the *"mystery of God"* would be finished in the days of the *"voice of the seventh angel."* In Eph. 6:19 Paul prayed that the proper words might be given to him, so he could open his mouth *"boldly, to make known the mystery of the gospel,* (good news)." And that is my prayer here in this book, as I write these words.

The first point I want to make is this: God's original plan was to dwell in man Himself. Whenever He was able to do this with a human being, it did not take God very long to bring that person to perfection. Enoch is an example of this. Gen. 5:21-27. Paul tells us more about Enoch in Heb. 11:5. *"By faith Enoch was translated that he should not see death; and was not found, because God had translated him: for before his translation he had this testimony, that he pleased God."* There are a few others mentioned in the Bible who allowed the Holy Spirit to completely control them and bring them to such a state of perfection that nothing is recorded in Holy Writ against their names. Joseph and Daniel are two such individuals. And yet, even these men never realized the fullest depths of God's eternal love that Christ revealed when He walked upon this earth and when He suffered in dark, Gethsamane . . . alone . . . and then was crucified between two thieves on the cruel cross, breaking history in two.

But the vast majority of mankind never allowed God the privilege of dwelling in their hearts. Even His own people, Israel, kept Him at arms length when He tried to get close to them. Because their minds were so full of darkness and fear at Mt. Sinai they entered into a false covenant of works. But God even used this ceremonial system to illustrate His ultimate goal of having them dwell in Him and He in them. Through the slaughter of innocent animals God pointed them forward in time when He would come Himself in a body of flesh, called the *"Son of God"* and would die on the cross, shedding His own blood for their sins. And then, through the apostle Paul, God explained that Jesus had taken His shed blood back up to heaven to continue making complete and final at-one-ment for them. Why? It was obviously because He had not yet been able to help even his closest disciples to comprehend that when He shed His very own blood He was saying, *"look, I am letting you kill me, and yet I am not hurting you back. I am not retaliating against you even though you are being so cruel and heartless. I do not deserve this treatment, but if this is what it takes for you to see what kind of a person I really am, then I WILL LET YOU KEEP ON DOING THIS TO ME UNTIL IT BREAKS YOUR HEART AND OPENS YOUR EYES TO THE FACT THAT I LOVE YOU WITH AN EVERLASTING LOVE THAT WILL NEVER REJECT YOU OR LET YOU GO. Oh, please come to Me so I can heal you and make you perfect so we can be together always and never part again."*

But instead of comprehending this glorious truth, men once again became bogged down in the ceremonies and rituals of the medieval church during the dark ages. And then in the 1830's a man named William Miller began preaching about the sanctuary message. He said the time was near when Christ would return. The date of Oct. 22, 1844 was set by some of Miller's followers, but time passed and Jesus did not return. The joy that many had known during the Great Advent movement died away. But then the scattered believers came together, prayed, wept and asked God for more light. As a result, the Lord gave them the truths of the Sabbath, non-immortality of the soul, (state of the dead), and the Sanctuary message that Jesus is our great high priest in the most holy place of the heavenly sanctuary, making final atonement for His people. This humble little group of believers were very happy and began sharing this new light with others. They realized now that Christ did not come in 1844 to cleanse the earthly sanctuary (with the fires of destruction upon the wicked), for they believed that this earth was the sanctuary that needed cleansing, and Jesus' return would fulfill Dan. 8:14, *"Unto two thousand and three hundred days; then shall the sanctuary be cleansed* (or justified)." This is what Wm. Miller taught, and this is what most of them believed. The majority of them continued to believe in almost everything they had believed in before. Even Miller rejected the Sabbath and state of the dead truths. Only a few would believe in the new understanding of the sanctuary truth, let alone the prophetic gift of Ellen G. White. But time went along and even these new believers began to become Laodicean. Their numbers grew and they formed into an organization known as the Seventh-day Adventist Church. They believed in and preached the doctrines, but most of them did not know Jesus as their Saviour, let alone as Lord. Very few went into the most holy place of the heavenly sanctuary; into a deeper and more intimate relationship with Jesus. Sister White said that not even one in twenty were ready to meet their Lord. 1T 504: MYP384.

And even though the sanctuary message has been preached and debated all of these years, most people still do not understand what it really is all about. And many others have just thrown it out the window as so much extra, unneeded baggage. I would like to share with you what the Lord has revealed to my mind about the deeper and really important meaning of the sanctuary.

We have already quoted Dan. 8:14 regarding a time when the sanctuary would be *"cleansed, justified or made right."* When you think of anything that needs to be cleaned up or cleansed, your mind immediately pictures something that is dirty. For example, if someone said your suit or your car needed to be cleaned, you would automatically know that they thought your suit or car was dirty. Right? Right. Well, when Daniel tells us that in 2300 days the sanctuary would be *"cleansed"* you would naturally believe that it was dirty. Wouldn't you? Yes, of course, you would.

But, we have a very large problem here. If this sanctuary, that is needing to be *"cleaned up or cleansed"* after 2300 days, is up in heaven, and if the sanctuary is where Jesus and His Father live and dwell, then how could the place possibly be called a *"dirty place"* in need of cleansing? Heaven is a very clean place and God and His Son are perfect and spotless. We all must agree upon these two points. So, the cleansing of the sanctuary has to have some very special meaning that we have not yet comprehended.

The SDA Bible Commentary Vol. 4, pages 844, 845 give much insight. I hope you will study this yourself. It is pointed out that the phrase, *"be cleansed,"* from Dan. 8:14 is from the Hebrew word, *"SADAQ"* meaning *"to be just,"* or *"to be righteous."* They also point out that the *"verb occurs in the form here found (niphal) only this once in the OT, which may suggest that a specialized meaning of the term is indicated. Lexicographers and translators suggest various meanings, such as 'be put right,' or 'be put in a rightful condition,' 'be righted,' 'be declared right,' 'be justified,' 'be vindicated.'"*

When you read Dan. 7:9, 10, it describes a court scene with God as the judge on His throne, books being opened and *"ten thousand times ten thousand"* standing before him, and *"a thousand thousand"* ministering to Him. We presume these are angels and other angelic beings. It would take another book or two in order to go over all that has already been written about the judgment, the 2300 years, and all of the hundreds of quotations by EGW describing how God is continually keeping records of every thought and deed of every person who has ever lived on this earth. In her book, *"THE GREAT CONTROVERSY,"* she says, *"As the books of record are opened in the judgment, the lives of all who have believed on Jesus come in review before God. Beginning with those who first lived upon the earth, our Advocate presents the cases of each successive generation, and closes with the living. Every name is mentioned, every case closely investigated. Names are accepted, names are rejected. When any have sins remaining upon the books of record, unrepented of and unforgiven, their names will be blotted out of the book of life, and the record of the good deed will be erased from the book of God's remembrance."* GC 483.

This is known as the *"investigative judgment,"* which takes place before Christ returns. GC 485. EGW compares this judgment to an earthly *"tribunal"* in *"the heavenly courts."* There are times in EGW's writing when her descriptions of the judgment remind one of the old, hell-fire and damnation preachers, except she does not teach that the sinner burns forever and ever in hell. But there are also quotations in which she presents the presence of the Father as a wonderful place to come to for forgiveness, love and help. GC 489. And yet in other places she speaks of the frightening experience of the righteous who will have to live *"in the sight of a holy God without an intercessor,"* after probationary time has ended or closed. GC 425, GC 614, EW 71, 280, PK 691. Because Ellen G. White's writings span a time period of about 70 years you have a great mass of literature to sort through. Although I can find a consistency in her writings, I also can find an emphasis in her earlier writings that would tend to picture God in a more legalistic setting than she does in her later writings. Because of this, you can find zealous and determined laymen through the years, who have made compilations on the same subject, but who came up with opposite and conflicting conclusions. Why? Because one compiler selected all the quotes he wanted to prove his point and the other compiler picked out other quotes that seemed to contradict the man he wished to prove wrong. Of course, the same thing has been done with the Bible. But beyond that we have the additional problem of recognizing the limitations of EGW's writings. Many, sincere, but ultra-conservative Adventists have tried to make Ellen White's writings the final test and criterion, even placing her writings above the Bible itself. Sister White, herself, rebuked this practice. She said her writings were a *"lesser light,"* (CM 125), and never to be placed ahead of the Bible. Ev. 256. She said her writings were given *"FOR THE PEOPLE OF GOD ... THE SINS THEY ARE TO SHUN ARE POINTED OUT ... THE WRITTEN TESTIMONIES ARE NOT TO GIVE NEW LIGHT, BUT TO IMPRESS VIVIDLY UPON THE HEART THE TRUTHS OF INSPIRATION ALREADY REVEALED."* 2T 605. When I was in pastoral work I found that less than 50% of the members had the nine volume set of Testimonies to the Church. And fewer read them and even fewer believed them, if they ever did read them. I found a very small percentage of God's professed people who took her writings seriously. It was an eye-opening and most disheartening situation, to say the least. But the most shocking experience I had later on in my life, after the Lord called me into this ministry, was to find that many leaders of the SDA Church upheld the writings of EGW, but did not really believe them. They only used them to keep the people in bondage to their interpretation of her writings, by quoting her out of context. This is what the Jewish leaders did in Christ's day, leading the people to reject Christ as their Messiah. And that is the same problem we face today. But let us not dwell on that or let it in any way discourage us or detract from our study. We will be able to learn the way into the most holy in spite of all these problems.

The first and most important truth we must learn is that *"There is no fear in love; but perfect love casteth out fear: because fear hath torment. He that feareth is not made perfect in love."* I John 4:18. So, any teaching about the most holy place that makes you fearful or afraid is not from God, and is, in fact, a false teaching from Satan. The wonderful truth that we will be able to *"dwell in the sight of a holy God without an intercessor,"* is not a fearful thought, if that God is Jesus, our Wonderful Saviour! To live and abide in His presence is the most ecstatic and joyous experience one can have in life. *"He that dwelleth in the secret place of the most High* (Jesus) *shall abide under the shadow of the Almighty."* Psalm 91:1. Jesus and the Father are one. They are the same; and so we do not need to be afraid of our Heavenly Father any more than we need to be afraid of Jesus. The only ones who were afraid of Jesus when He was upon earth, were those who wanted to continue in their sins. These were mainly the leaders of the church; the ones who rejected His teachings, spied on Him daily and finally used trickery and deceit to have him crucified. But, we must remember that Paul the faithful apostle, was once one of them and that he repented when Jesus appeared to him. So, let us remember that Jesus loves everyone and so should we. But, let us *"Beware of the leaven of the Pharisees, which is hypocrisy, For there is nothing covered, that shall not be revealed; neither hid, that shall not be known."* Luke 12:1, 2.

Some very godly men were used of the Lord to put some most insightful comments in the SDA Bible Commentary, published in 1955, before a lot of the present apostasy took place within the SDA Church. We notice one of their comments in BC 4 p. 845, comments on Dan. 8:14, *"Be cleansed." "A significant feature of the final judgment is the vindication of God's character before all the intelligences of the universe. The false charges that Satan has lodged against the government of God must be demonstrated as utterly groundless ... The final acts of God will evoke from men the confessions, 'Just and true are thy ways'* (Rev. 15:3), *'Thou are righteous, O Lord' Rev.* (Rev. 16:5), *and, 'True and righteous are thy judgments'* (Rev. 16:7). *Satan himself will be led to acknowledge God's justice* (see GC 670, 671)."

This brings us to a second and most important point. If the vindication of God is what the court scene is mainly about, then it must be that it is God Himself who is on trial because of the false charges Satan has made against Him, even before Satan left heaven. Jude 6. And it is God's dealings with both the wicked, and the righteous here on planet earth that are being investigated in this heavenly court scene pictured by the prophet Daniel. Our Wonderful, heavenly Father is on trial and Satan is the prosecuting attorney. But Jesus is the advocate or lawyer in defense of His Father, as well, as our advocate and lawyer. This, of course, means that everyone who sides in with our Heavenly Father is on trial too. Because Jesus has taken up our case, to prove us innocent, and worthy of a place in heaven with the Father, Satan bends all of his genius to tempt us to sin so his charges against both the Father, Jesus and us will be proved true. Notice: *"While Jesus is pleading for the subjects of His grace, Satan accuses them before God as transgressors. The great deceiver has sought to lead them into skepticism, to cause them to lose confidence in God, TO SEPARATE THEMSELVES FROM HIS LOVE, and to break His law. (NOTICE THAT SATAN HAS TO FIRST BREAK YOU AWAY FROM GOD'S LOVE BEFORE HE CAN GET YOU TO BREAK THE LAW) Now he points to the record of their lives, to the defects of character, the unlikeness to Christ, which has dishonored their Redeemer, to all the sins that he has tempted them to committ, and because of these he claims them as his subjects. Jesus does not excuse their sins, but shows their penitence and faith, and, claiming for them forgiveness, He lifts His wounded hands before the father and the holy angels, saying: I know them by name. I have graven them on the palms of My hands."* GC 484.

And so we see that in this judgment, court scene, God is not judging or condemning anyone, but is in fact, being condemned Himself, for trying to help His subjects come to Him so they will know Him, whom to know is eternal life. Why is it then that we have read Rev. 14:6, 7, in the sense that God is judging or condemning the world, *WHEN IN*

REALITY, GOD HIMSELF IS ON TRIAL? Is it not because our minds are carnal? We are born upside down, inside out and cross-eyed, as it were. The *"sanctuary"* that needs to be cleansed is our minds. We need to be *"born again,"* turned right side up (Acts 17:6) and our eye-sight healed so we will not have it backwards anymore and help others see it too. So, let's read these verses again. *"And I saw another angel fly in the midst of heaven, having the everlasting gospel to preach unto them that dwell on the earth, and to every nation, and kindred, and tongue, and people, Saying with a loud voice, Fear God, and give glory to him; FOR THE HOUR OF HIS JUDGMENT IS COME: and worship him that made heaven, and earth, and the sea, and the fountains of waters."* Rev. 14:6, 7.

In the original Greek the word for *"judgment"* is *"krisews."* The phrase is *"e wra tes krisews autou,"* which literally reads, *"THE HOUR OF THE JUDG-MENT OF HIM."* The noun *"judgment"* is in the genitive case which is the specifying case, expressed in English by the possessive or the objective with *"of."* The noun *"judg-ment"* here is in the *"objective"* case, and its relative pro-noun, *"him"* is also in the genitive case. Their endings are both in the objective case. This means that *"him,"* (refer-ring to God) is receiving the action. In other words, it is impossible for *"him"* in this sentence to be judging anyone, for he is, in fact, the one who is being judged! *HE IS THE ONE WHO IS ON TRIAL.* I looked up the word for judg-ment in my Greek-English lexicon and found the Greek word for judgment. It says, *"Krisis, ews, distinction; dis-crimination; judgment, decision, sentence, TRIAL."* When the word judgment is in the *"nominative"* (subjec-tive) case it is spelled *"Krisis."* But when it is in the *"gene-tive"* (objective case in English) it is spelled *"Krisews."* The *"ews"* is the ending denoting a different case. In Greek there are 8 cases, whereas, in English there are only two, namely, subjective (meaning the noun is the subject of the sentence) and objective (meaning that the noun is the object of the sentence and receiving the action). When a noun is in the objective case, as it is in Rev. 14:7 *"Judgment of Him* (God)" it means the noun (Him or God) is receiving the action. And that is exactly what is happening in Rev. 14:7. God is on trial. He is the recipient of the action. When God (Jesus) came to earth the first time, in the person of His Son, He was on trial from the moment of His birth until the moment of His death. He proved His case before the universe, as far as His own character, but now God is on trial before the universe because of us . . . His people. He claims that we can develop the same character as He displayed while here on earth in a body of flesh. Satan claims that we cannot. And so court is in session and every thought, word and action is being carefully weighed before the heavenly tribunal. Meanwhile, down here on planet earth, Satan is very busy sending his agents throughout the length and breadth of this earth with the *"good news?"* saying, that we can never be like Jesus, so just relax and wait til He comes again and He will **MAKE YOU PERFECT AT THAT TIME.** Meanwhile, He has just **DECLARED YOU PERFECT,** and that is all that is necessary for now. These same religious agents are also preaching, along with the rest of the religious world, that God destroys people and everyone who does not *"do his best,"* and *"try his utmost,"* will not be accounted worthy to be made perfect when Christ comes. They are involved in a *"do-it-yourself"* works program similar to the Jews of old. Those who don't make it will, of course, be destroyed by God Himself. Of course, there are also those, from the old school of thought, that still teach that it is possible to be perfect by perfectly keeping the law of God. Their idea is that when you have become perfect like Christ, you will then be able to go into the most holy place without being struck dead, so you can live in the sight of a holy God without an intercessor, when probation closes. Actually, the exact opposite is true. We go into His presence in the most holy place, even into His very heart and mind, so He can **MAKE US PERFECT,** like Himself. Both of these groups have one thing in common. They are motivated by their *"fear"* of being lost, which more simply put, means, that they are afraid of being destroyed by God if they do not keep all of His rules and regulations.

Now, beloved, which motivation is it that will bring us to perfection? Is it fear? or is it love? **WHY, IT IS LOVE, OF COURSE. WE LOVE HIM BECAUSE HE FIRST LOVED US.** And we do not have to stand outside of the most holy place until we are *"good"* enough. Otherwise we would never go in. No, we go *"boldly"* into the most holy place, as Paul tells us. *"For we have not an high priest which cannot be touched with the feeling of our infirmities; but was in all points tempted like as we are, yet without sin. Let us therefore come boldly unto the throne of grace* (in the most holy place) *that we may obtain mercy, and find grace to help in time of need."* Heb. 4:15, 16. On page 255 of *"Early Writings,"* Sister White tells that *"the people of God"* . . . were shown . . . *"the way to the holiest of the heavenly sanctuary. As they by faith enter the most holy, they find Jesus, and hope and joy spring up anew."* She goes on to tell about how Jesus shows them the true beauty of the Sabbath. God's true Remnant will not keep the Sabbath like the Jews, but as Jesus kept it. Going into the most holy place simply means walking with Jesus . . . going all the way with Him, wherever He leads. It doesn't mean observing a man-made list of do's and don'ts written up by some committee of men or some organized religion whose leaders don't even keep the laws themselves, let alone believe them to be inspired. **ORGANIZED RELIGION IS GOD'S WORST ENEMY. ORGANIZED RELIGION IS WHAT PUT JESUS ON THE CROSS.** On page 55 of *"Early Writings,"* Sister White describes the Father going into the *"holy of holies"* (most holy) in a *"flaming chariot."* Then she saw Jesus rise *"up from the throne, and the most of* *those who were bowed down arose with Him."* Then He told all those who were following Him to *"Wait here; I am going to My Father to receive the kingdom; . . ."* She then explains how Jesus went into the holiest with His Father and how those *"who rose up with Jesus would send up their faith to Him in the holiest, and pray, 'My Father, give us Thy Spirit.' Then Jesus would breath upon them the Holy Ghost. In that breath was light, power, and much love, joy, and peace. I turned to look at the company who were still bowed before the throne; they did not know that Jesus had left it. Satan appeared to be by the throne, trying to carry on the work of God."* She then tells how Satan answered their prayers by giving them his power. *"Satan would then breath upon them an unholy influence; in it there was light and much power, but no sweet love, joy, and peace. Satan's object was to keep them deceived and to draw back and deceive God's children."* EW 56. Beloved, this is a perfect description of what is happening in most of organized religion today, including God's professed people. They think they are worshipping God when they are worshipping Satan. See 2T 441, 442. It is time for God's true people to arise and go into the most holy place with Jesus who will accept you just as you are. He is not keeping a record of all of your sins so He can condemn you in the final day of judgment. No, that is Satan who does that. Yes, it is true that records are being kept for the purpose of carrying on the court trial currently being conducted in heaven for the benefit of the unfallen worlds, and the angels who are watching with intense interest, to see if God's people are truly going to vindicate their Creator and the faith He has placed in them. That is what this great court scene in heaven is all about, and every bit of evidence available is being presented. Jesus is presenting all of the good He can find and Satan is keeping track of all the bad he can find, and presenting that as proof that God is a liar and unworthy of anyone's faith or trust. **WHY WOULD GOD NEED**

A RECORD OF YOUR LIFE WHEN HE CAN READ YOUR MIND? Jesus even knows our thoughts before we know them. Psalm 139:4. LB. God is never identified in His word as an *"accuser"* of anyone, but Satan is in Rev. 12:9-12. In these verses Satan is pictured as a dragon and serpent who was *"cast out"* and *"cast down,"* in the eyes of the universe as a liar and accuser of the brethren, *"which accused them before our God day and night."* But God's people are pictured as overcomers *"by the blood of the Lamb, and by the word of their testimony; and they loved not their lives unto the death."* In GC 618 EGW recounts the experience of Jacob when Esau was coming to destroy him. She tells how Satan accused Jacob of being unworthy of God's protection. And so, it will be, in our day, in the final court scene in heaven, and the last battle between Christ and Satan on the battle fields of planet earth, as Satan strives to tempt God's people to sin. She tells how Satan *"infers that their sins have been pardoned; but he does not know that their cases have been decided in the sanctuary above."* By this statement we can see that the heavenly jury has already cast their verdict of acquital for God and His people. But Satan doesn't know this and so he continues to accuse God's elect who have been sealed into the Father's heart of eternal love. *"He* (Satan) *has an accurate knowledge of the sins which he has tempted them to commit, and he presents these before God in the most exaggerated light, representing this people to be just as deserving as himself of exclusion from the favor of God. He declares that the Lord cannot in justice forgive their sins and yet destroy him and his angels. He claims them as his prey and demands that they be given into his hands to destroy."* GC 618. When you read GC 666 you will find that the record of sins of the wicked are recorded in their minds. *"As soon as the books of record are opened, and the eye of Jesus looks upon the wicked, they are conscious of every sin which they have ever committed.*" GC 666. Is it possible that the word *"book"* and *"books"* are actually symbols for our own memory banks or *"sanctuaries"* for either God's love and forgiveness or Satan's lies about God which lead us to be afraid of God and go into all kinds of sinning? It would seem that the wicked are simply people whose minds or *"sanctuaries"* have not been cleansed of all the filthiness of the flesh, wrong attitudes, and lies about God, His truth and His people. As a result, they all end up destroying each other.

And so we see at last, that God's real sanctuary, His very own people, are finally *"cleansed," "justified"* and *"made right or righteous and just"* in the eyes of the heavenly jury or council who at long last cast a verdict of *"not-guilty"* for God and His people. One wonders if Enoch and Elijah, whom God translated, and Moses whom he raised from the dead and took to heaven, gave their witness and testimony before the heavenly tribunal while God and His people were on trial before the universe. And what about the *"saints"* who arose at the time of Christ's resurrection (Matt. 27:52, 53) that Paul is no doubt referring to in Eph. 4:8, *"When he ascended up on high, he led captivity captive,"?* Is it possible that their testimony had some bearing in this long trial? There are no doubt many things we will learn during the 1,000 years. But, for right now we can know that the *"cleansing of the sanctuary,"* is referring to a process whereby God is cleansing our hearts and minds from the dirty and filthy lies Satan and men have told about Jesus, our *"Wonderful, Counselor, ... Mighty God,"* and ... *"Everlasting Father"* Isa. 9:6. And so, the cleansing of the *"sanctuary,"* is a clearing away of the tradition of false teaching about God's character that has filled our hearts with fear, and made us afraid to go into His glorious presence so we could be healed and made whole like unto Jesus. And once our hearts and minds have been *"cleansed"* of these falsehoods and God is vindicated and justified in our eyes, we will rush into His waiting arms of love and get married to our Wonderful Redeemer.

THE INCREDIBLE POWER OF HIS BLOOD

There are many theories among religious groups about the blood of Christ. But, what does the Holy Bible say? Is the blood a "magical formula or potion" that washes all of our sins away? Or did the Father demand so many quarts of blood to be spilled before He could forgive us? Did the Father demand some kind of "price" to be paid?

Jesus made it extremely clear that the Father Himself loves us just as much as He does. John 16:27 says, "For the Father Himself loveth you." In fact, Paul tells us, "God was in Christ, reconciling the world unto himself, not imputing (charging) their trespasses unto them: and hath committed unto us the word of reconciliation." 2 Cor. 5:19.

We must remember that man deserted God—broke the covenant and "Dealt treacherously against Me (God)." Hosea 6:7. Yet God never left man. He never did anything to hurt man, but has always been trying to bring him back to Himself. God's love as manifested in Christ has always been just as strong as it was at the cross. This is the supreme demonstration of the Father and Son's eternal love for the human race.

Paul tells us, "and, having made peace through the blood of His cross, by Him to reconcile all things unto Himself; by Him, I say, whether they be things in earth, or things in heaven. And you, that were sometime alienated and enemies IN YOUR MIND by wicked works, yet now hath He reconciled." Col. 1:20, 21.

Jesus knew that man's heart had become so hardened against His Father's love that it would be impossible to win them back unless He allowed wicked men to slaughter Him just as they slaughtered a helpless animal. Man was afraid of God. Through the centuries Satan had erected so many barriers that man could only think of God as a harsh, cruel and vindictive God who demanded that blood be shed for every sin, no matter how small. In his heart, man feared God. He was afraid of Him. A few souls tuned into His Spirit and realized God was a loving Father, but the majority of people served God out of fear.

Jesus predicted how He would win the human race back to Himself. *"And I, if I be lifted up from the earth, will draw all men unto me. This he said, signifying what death he should die."* John 12:32, 33.

When Jesus died, the curtain separating the holy place from the most holy place was ripped open from top to bottom, Matt. 27:51. "having therefore, brethren, boldness (confidence) to enter into the holiest by the blood of Jesus. By a new and living way ... Let us draw near with a true heart in full assurance of faith, having our hearts sprinkled from an evil conscience, and our bodies washed with pure water." Heb. 10:19-22.

Now, beloved, what was it that was removed from our minds by the shedding of Christ's dear and precious blood? *"Having abolished in his flesh the enmity, even the law of commandments contained in ordinances;"* Eph. 2:15. *"Blotting out the handwriting of ordinances that was against us, which was contrary to us, and took it out of the way, nailing it to his cross."* Col. 2:14. Rom. 8:31 tells us that *"God is for us."* He is never against us. He never does anything or gives anything that is against us. He only gives "good" gifts, James 1:17-Psalm 84:11. He is against the "wickedness" of the wicked, their sin, but not against them per se ... just their wrong doing. Now, the point is this: If God never gives anything that is "against" us and this law of ceremonies and sacrifices was against us, is it not logical that God never gave these laws in the first place? He only allowed them because man's carnal mind, under Satan's influence thought God wanted him to kill animals and go through endless ceremonies and rituals before he could be forgiven. But Christ's death "spoiled" the "principalities and powers ..." Col. 2:15, that had originally set up the whole "unprofitable, weak, and carnal" system which could never help anyone to be well or "PERFECT." HEB 7:16-19. WHY? BECAUSE IT WOULD NEVER ALLOW THE SINNER TO COME INTO THE presence of his Creator and Saviour. Man was filled with "fear," "anger" and "resentment," toward God for allowing Satan to lead him into sin and be cast out of paradise. It is God's fault because He created Lucifer who turned into Satan and why did God create me in the first place? How did I get into this mess anyway? And if Satan is the cause of all of our miseries why doesn't God kill him and get it over with? And on it goes . . . endless questions, doubts and perplexities.

But the final message of God's eternal love is going to answer every one of those questions . . . if not now, at least in the future and certainly during and after the 1,000 years. The Bible declares that "God is love." I John 4:8, 16. And v. 18 says that "perfect love casts out fear." Therefore, when we go into the most holy place, into the very presence of God, we have all fear cast out. But what was it that gave us the courage to go in? It is the "blood" of Jesus. But what is there about the blood that gives us this boldness?

Paul tells us in Heb. 7:26. "For such an high Priest became us, who is holy harmless, undefiled . . ." There is the key word—"HARMLESS." God is *harmless*; He will not hurt you in any way, shape or form. Jesus' entire ministry demonstrated how kind, gentle and loving God the Father really is. And when we see Him slaughtered like an innocent lamb with no anger or retaliation . . . but only total forgiveness toward His enemies the Holy Spirit whispers to us . . . "See, God is harmless. He won't hurt you even though you kill Him. You can go to Him in confidence and boldness and assurance that He will only love you and will only forgive you no matter what you have done." Beloved, that is the power of the blood. That is the great lesson of calvary.

The Prophet Daniel predicted that the Messiah would "make an end of sins." Dan. 9:24. Paul says Christ fulfilled this prophecy. "But now once in the end of the world hath

He appeared to put away sin by the sacrifice of Himself."
Heb. 9:26. It was not until 1844 that God's people began to
see that the way was truly open to go into the very presence
of God without being struck dead. This was when the great
truths of the Adventist movement were given to the early
pioneers . . . such as the Sabbath, state of the dead and the
sanctuary truths. But it is mainly the Sabbath that proves
that God is the life-giving Creator and sustainer. He only
gives life . . . He never takes it. *The Sabbath proves He is
a life-God*.

God's perfect love gives us perfect faith and trust. Listen: *"If we have perfect love, we shall know that God is
not seeking to injure us, but that in the midst of trials,
and griefs, and pains. He is seeking to make us perfect,
and to test the quality of our faith."* S.D. 193.

HOW IS SIN EXPELLED FROM THE HEART?

"With untold love our God has loved us, and our love
awakens toward him as we comprehend something of the
length and breadth and depth and height of this love that
passeth knowledge. By the revelation of the attractive love-
liness of Christ, by the knowledge of His love expressed to
us while we were yet sinners, the stubborn heart is melted
and subdued, and the sinner is transformed and becomes a
child of heaven. God does not employ compulsory measures;
LOVE IS THE AGENT WHICH HE USES TO EXPEL SIN
FROM THE HEART. By it (that is by Love) He changes
pride into humility, and enmity and unbelief into love and
faith." Love Unlimited 207, MB77.

AND SO THE POWER OF HIS LOVE IS THAT IT
DRAWS US TO HIM BECAUSE IT CONVINCES US THAT
HE TRULY IS A LOVING GOD THAT WILL NEVER
HURT US, BUT ONLY HELP US. 'His very life is the out-
flow of unselfish love." Ibid. " 'I will that they also, whom
Thou hast given Me, be with Me where I am.' Jn. 17:24.
Again a voice, musical and triumphant, is heard, saying:
'They come! They come! Holy, *harmless*, and undefiled."
GREAT CONTROVERSY, PAGE 636.

PART
II

"Man's mind—stretched by a new idea—never goes back to its original dimensions."

Oliver Wendell Holmes.

CHAPTER 6

A LETTER TO PASTOR CLUTE

The Scripture declares, *"These things ... are written for our admonition, upon whom the ends of the world are come"* (I Cor. 10:11). And if men and women who have the knowledge of the truth are so far separated from their great Leader that they will take the great leader of apostasy and name him Christ our Righteousness, it is because they have not sunk deep into the mines of the truth. They are not able to distinguish the precious ore from the base material.

2 SM 393
Book 2 By Ellen G. White

Dear Pastor Clute,

I have been impressed that I should write to you and share the story of my husband's and my experience in coming to understand the truth about God's loving character. For many years I have been impressed with the importance of sharing the testimony of one's own experience in the knowledge and unfolding of heavenly things, by this statement in *"Ministry of Healing."*

"Our confession of His faithfulness is Heaven's chosen agency for revealing Christ to the world. We are to acknowledge His grace as made known through the holy men of old; but that which will be most effectual is the testimony of our own experience." M. H. 100.

Since we are also exhorted in the Scriptures that His is the only way we overcome the powers of darkness (as well as the condition for being confessed by our Saviour before the Father), it is most expedient that I do this very thing. (See Rev. 12:11 and Luke 12:8.) It is both a joy and a privilege!

About two years ago, my husband and I went to work in a tract-publishing work with a fellow-Adventist laborer. I was given many pages of material to typeset about the destruction of the wicked in the Old Testament, all the way to the final annihilation of the "lost" (including Satan and his angels) after the Millenium. The evidence seemed so conclusive that it was GOD who was directly responsible for punishing the wicked, that I made comment to a co-worker at the close of the day's typing, *"How could anyone not see that God destroys?!"*

Her reply was, *"Millie, please don't make up your mind until you've examined both sides of the argument."* I was amazed even to think there could be another side!

Just previous to the work of preparing twelve tracts on this subject (which have since been published), I had put together the material for a five-tract study on the nature of Christ. I had experienced great blessing in the daily compilation of these blessed truths, and could not but contrast the terrible gloom and depression I experienced as I worked on the material depicting a *"killer"* God! My husband noticed the effect it had on me!

A short time later we had to leave our work there and, as we parted from our co-laborers, they felt they should offer us your two manuscripts concerning the character of God. We believed it was our duty to examine them, being aware of the admonitions in *Christ's Object Lessons,* page 112 (concerning preconceived opinions) and *I Selected Messages* 411, *"Those who cannot impartially examine the evidences of a position that differs from theirs, are not fit to teach in any department of God's cause."*

At the time we began a perusal of your books, brother Mike, we just happened to be reading two volumes of the **Spirit of Prophecy** which helped us find some of our own answers to the questions posed by your studies. Don was reading **I Selected Messages,** and I was reading my favorite volume, *"Desire of Ages."* This seems to have been very providential! We found so MUCH in confirmation of your views, especially in *"Desire of Ages!"*

Somehow I was impressed to write to you (I don't remember why) and you sent us a little pamphlet by Keith Gilbertson entitled, *"Has God Ever Killed Anyone During the 6,000 Years of the Great Controversy?"* The fact that it was put together as a research project for a Master of Arts degree in religion at Andrews University enticed us to examine it. Somehow his brevity posed a clearer exposition of the subject, and my husband and I felt inspired to take a very careful look into all the evidence presented.

The ONE THING that kept us looking into a subject we really felt was a foregone conclusion in favor of a destructive God, was that many statements in Ellen White's writings clearly stated that God's law was *"a transcript of His character."* We well knew that something had to be reconciled in order for that to apply to the sixth commandment, *"Thou shalt not kill!"*

I had just begun reading *"Desire of Ages,"* so I decided to make a compilation of references bearing on the subject in a fly leaf. I soon ran out of space! The evidence was overwhelming! Don began having a similar experience in **I Selected Messages**! I began to put these statements in questionnaire form in the front of the Keith Gilbertson tracts we received from you, and began sending these out to family and friends. We could not really have anticipated the result! We have come to realize that those who have a wrong conception of God's character react exactly as they believe God would behave! We began to see the real issues of *"the great controversy"* for the first time to our utter amazement! *"The truth as it is in Jesus"*; how little that had meant to us before we began to take a really intense look at both His life and His sacrifice on Calvary! Paul's statement that he refused to know anything outside of *"Jesus Christ, and Him crucified,"* began to take shape in our minds! We became even more aware that it is GOD who is on trial!

Both my husband and I had been raised by fathers who did not represent the character of God in any way. Neither were they practicing Christians. The manner in which we were reared in no way taught us the truth about our heavenly Father!

The following simple statement my husband shared with me from 1 SM has become the pivotal reference in our understanding of the conflict of the ages.

"The understanding of the people of God has been blinded, for Satan has misrepresented the character of God. Our good and gracious Lord has been presented before the people clothed in the attributes of Satan, and men and women who have been seeking for truth, have so long regarded God in a false light that it is difficult to dispel the cloud that obscures His glory from their view." 1 Selected Messages 355.

Several key phrases stand out in that paragraph. God's glory is His character, as Exodus 33:18, 19; 34:5, 6 show clearly. (Also COL 414, etc.) Of course, the usual observation of how God's character has been clothed with the attributes of Satan could be limited to the fact that most Christians, including most early Adventists in Sr. White's day, thought that God would burn sinners forever and ever. But this has to go much deeper in order to meet and answer James 2:10 and give understanding to the comment made in *"Desire of Ages"* regarding the principle posed thereby:

"This do and thou shalt live, Jesus said. He presented the law as a divine unity, and in this lesson taught that IT IS NOT POSSIBLE to keep one precept, and break another; for the same principle runs through them all." Desire of Ages 498.

We have seen some pretty fancy intellectual *"foot-work"* (by those who have not candidly examined the evidence) as to how God can destroy and not be guilty of violating His own law! This is not a matter of spiritual semantics, it is the issue of the great controversy itself! Amazed, and deeply humbled, we now saw how many years we have studied the Bible and *Spirit of Prophecy* oblivious to these truths! My husband studied theology as his major in academy and two years of college. We had both read the Bible for the first time when we were 15 years of age. Yet the very fundamental truth of God's character and the meaning of the cross of Calvary had but barely dawned upon our minds!

There were many apparent contradictions which we saw had to be reconciled for us to understand and share what we were beginning to realize. It was like seeing a small light at the end of a very dark tunnel. Isaiah 60:1-3 began to open our understanding as this text was explained in *Christ's Object Lessons,* page 415.

"It is the darkness of misapprehension of God that is enshrouding the world. Men are losing their knowledge of His character. It has been misrepresented and misunderstood. At this time, a message from God is to be proclaimed, a message illuminating in its influence and saving in its power. HIS CHARAC-TER is to be made known . . . Those who wait for the Bridegroom's coming are to say to the people, 'Behold Your God'. The last rays of merciful light, THE LAST MESSAGE OF MERCY to be given to the world, is a revelation of His character of love." COL 415.

Does this indicate that the message of that other angel which is to lighten the earth with His glory (Rev. 18:1) is concerning a misrepresented God? Did this indicate that we who thought we knew Him, did not? John 17:3 began to take an enlarged proportion! *"This is life eternal, that they might know thee, the only true God, and Jesus Christ, whom thou has sent."*

This gave answer to another question which had perplexed my mind for many years in regard to the foolish virgins and why they were shut out of the marriage supper, after being so long in company with those who love and practice the truth! On p. 411 of COL, it says, *"they are not hypocrites,"* but goes on to state, *"they did not know God. They had not studied His character."*

Baal worship took on a more solemn, and modern-day meaning! The Lord says that we just as verily worship a false god, as ancient Israel worshipped Baal, if we give Him false attributes of character! (P.K. 177).

"But turning from all lesser representations, we behold God in Jesus. Looking unto Jesus we see that it is the glory of our God to give. (John 8:28; 6:57; 7:18) ... In these words is set forth the great principle which is the law of life for the universe. All things Christ received from God, but He took to give ... Through the beloved Son, the Father's life flows to all; through the Son it returns, in praise and joyous service, a tide of love, to the great Source of all. And thus through Christ the circuit of beneficence is complete, REPRESENTING THE CHARACTER of the great Giver, the law of life.

"In heaven itself this law was broken. Sin originated in self-seeking ... Therefore, he (Lucifer) misrepresented God, ATTRIBUTING TO HIM the desire for self-exaltation. With his OWN evil characteristics he sought to invest the loving Creator. Thus he deceived angels. Thus he deceived men ....

"The earth was dark through misapprehension of God. That the gloomy shadows might be lightened, that the world might be brought back to God, Satan's deceptive power was to be broken. THIS COULD NOT BE DONE BY FORCE. The exercise of force is CONTRARY to the principles of God's government; He desires only the service of love; and love cannot be commanded; it cannot be won by force or authority. Only by love is love awakened. To know God is to love

Him; His character must be manifested in CONTRAST to the character of Satan. This work only one Being in all the universe could do. Only He who knew the height and depth of the love of God could make it known." D.A. 21, 22.

"... no other light ever has shown or ever will shine so clearly upon fallen man as that which emanated from the teaching and example of Jesus." D.A. 220. THIS is the truth as it is in Jesus! This is where we must look to know God!

"What speech is to thought, so is Christ to the invisible Father. He is the manifestation of the Father, and is called the Word of God ... He made known in His works, His character, His power and majesty, the NATURE AND ATTRIBUTES OF GOD. Divinity flashed through humanity in softening, subduing light. He was the embodiment of the law of God, which is the TRANSCRIPT OF HIS CHARACTER." 5 BC 1131.

We often pass by such sublime statements without attempting to define what we have read! If God's character is to be **contrasted** to the character of Satan, it stands by definition alone that there are NO similarities! How easily we are taken in by Satan's artifice and we know not that it is he!! (We are even told that we are in danger of taking the enemy of souls, Satan, and naming him *"Christ our righteousness."* 2SM 393.)

We most desperately need a more humble opinion of our opinion!

A Scripture which has given much assistance in resolving the seeming contradictions posed by the investigation of this most precious truth is Isaiah 55:8, 9. *"For my thoughts are not your thoughts, neither are your ways my ways, saith the Lord. For as the heavens are higher than the earth, so are my ways higher than your ways, and my thoughts than your thoughts."*

One does not have to get very high off the earth to use the threatening tactics we have ascribed to the Ruler of the universe! The Mafia is a perfect representation of these principles, but a more accurate example would be found in those who use persecution techniques to force their version of religion upon others! We *decry* these methods of proscription on the part of human beings, while *ascribing* them to our Creator! We understand that religious liberty originated with God, but have set false limits to the exercise thereof! On p. 22 of *"Desire of Ages"* it says plainly that *"force and authority"* cannot win love. Many state that it is God's perogative to use force, but that is not the issue. He says it is contrary to His nature, character, and government! This plainly indicates that He does not use it, though He has every power and right to do as He will!

Does this limit God? Is He thereby unable to deal with rebellion and bring it to an end? We found that it is only *because* of the way He deals with transgression that He can, in fact, bring it to an end! If God used any manner, whatever, which could be defined as force, or threat of force, He would thereby lose the great controversy! Read DA p. 22 again, very carefully. Satan has attributed to God his own evil characteristics. Force and fear are two of Satan's weapons. Does God use either?

"There is no fear in love; but perfect love casteth out fear; because fear hath torment. He that feareth is not made perfect in love." I John 4:18.

"For God hath not given us the spirit of fear; but the power of love and of a sound mind." 2 Timothy 1:7.

"That which alone can effectually restrain from sin in this world of darkness, will prevent sin in heaven. The significance of the death of Christ will be seen by saints and angels." 5 BC 1132.

"Kneeling at the cross, he has reached the highest place to which man can attain. The light of the knowledge of the glory of God is revealed in the face of Jesus Christ ... The cross is in direct line with the shining of the divine countenance, so that by beholding the cross men may see and know God and Jesus Christ, whom He hath sent ... In beholding the cross the view is

extended to God ... To the world the cross is the incontrovertible argument that God is truth and light and love." 5 BC 1133.

"It will be seen that the glory shining in the face of Jesus is the glory of self-sacrificing love. In the light from Calvary it will be seen that the law of self-renouncing love is the law of life for earth and heaven; that love which 'seeketh not her own' has its source in the heart of God; and that in the meek and lowly One is manifested the character of Him who dwelleth in the light which no man can approach unto." DA p. 20.

We have a different role to play in the great controversy than we had thought! It is not to secure salvation as much as it is to defend the character of God and exemplify the principles of the government of heaven, the same as Jesus did while walking this earth as a man and as God with us, *"Emmanuel."* This IS the loud cry of Rev. 18 as described in COL 414 and 415! This is the very meaning of Col. 1:27, *"... the glory of this mystery ... which is Christ in you, the hope of glory."*

What manner of character did Jesus display?

"It is no part of Christ's mission to compel men to receive Him. It is Satan, and men actuated by his spirit, that seek to compel the conscience. Under a pretense of zeal for righteousness, men who are confederate with evil angels bring suffering upon their fellow men, in order to convert them to their ideas of religion ... There can be no more conclusive evidence that we possess the spirit of Satan than the disposition to hurt and DESTROY those who do not appreciate our work, or who act contrary to our ideas." DA 487.

Does the title *"destroyer"* belong to both Christ and Satan? Does He merit the ascription given to Him, as joining with Satan to destroy the wicked, as has been attributed to Him by some who have even put in print that the trumpets of Revelation 8 and 9 are the acts of Satan, while the seven last plagues of Rev. 16 are acts of God in conjunction?

Is God in partnership with the great adversary to heap punishment upon the wicked whom Satan has deluded? Is this not the blasphemy spoken of in Rev. 16:9-11?!

Scientists perfectly describe the effects of nuclear war to coincide with the very descriptions of the seven last plagues. We have only to understand what God means when He says HE does something, and HOW He does it. Remember Isaiah 55:8, 9, *"His ways are not our ways."* This will enable us to unravel the most difficult of all the statements in the *Spirit of Prophecy* on this subject:

"The same destructive power exercised by holy angels when God commands, will be exercised by evil angels when He permits." Great Controversy, p. 614. Be careful to observe that it is the same POWER, but not necessarily exercised in the same manner! The whole paragraph prior to this statement states unequivocally that it is Satan who brings devastation when God releases control.

"The wicked have passed the boundary of their probation; the Spirit of God, persistently resisted, has at last been withdrawn. Unsheltered by divine grace, they have no protection from the wicked one. SATAN will then plunge the inhabitants of the earth into one great, final trouble. As the angels of God cease to hold in check the fierce winds of human passion, all the elements of strife will be let loose. The whole world will be involved in a ruin more terrible than that which came upon Jerusalem of old." GC 614.

Notice the descriptions here. The *"winds"* are designated to be *"human passion"* which create strife. These are the winds which Rev. 7 declare are now being held by the four angels. (We conjecture that the *"four angels"* could represent the messages that have yet to go out to the world to harvest the earth. The restraint is upon the elements of evil until the truth has been proclaimed with a loud voice.)

It would be well for us to examine the destruction of Jerusalem as the *"type"* of the destruction at the end of time, and then the description of what happens at the coming of Jesus.

"Says the prophet: 'Oh, Israel, thou hast destroyed thyself;' 'for thou has fallen by thine iniquity.' Hosea 13:9, 14:1. Their sufferings are often represented as a punishment visited upon them by the direct decree of God. It is thus that the great deceiver seeks to conceal his own work. By stubborn rejection of divine love and mercy, the Jews had caused the protection of God to be withdrawn from them, and Satan was permitted to rule them according to his will." GC 35. Consider the play and counterplay of words as in the case with Job. The language is always Satan blaming God, God taking the blame by permitting Satan to work the destruction, yet God restraining him from taking Job's life. This is an encapsulated version of the experience of the people of God during the time of trouble. It is their work to establish that there was no excuse for sin in a perfect Heaven, nor in a perfect earth on the part of perfect creatures brought into existence by a perfect God! Their fidelity, as the last of a weakened race, under the worst imaginable circumstances, wholly cut off from human support, ends the great controversy forever!

"The disobedient and unthankful have great reason for gratitude for God's mercy and long-suffering in holding in check the cruel, malignant power of the evil one. But when men pass the limits of divine forbearance, that restraint is removed. GOD DOES NOT STAND TOWARD THE SINNER AS AN EXECUTIONER of the sentence against transgression; but He leaves the rejecters of His mercy to themselves, to reap that which they have sown." GC 36.

Jerusalem was destroyed by Roman soldiers, but at Christ's second coming the whole world will be involved in ruin. After the millenium this destruction will include the evil angels. Does God have to alter His principles of dealing with sin and sinners ultimately? Let us take a careful look at both times as described by inspiration.

"The multitudes are filled with fury. 'We are lost!' they cry, 'and you are the cause of our ruin;' and they turn upon the false shepherds. The very ones that once admired them most will pronounce the most dreadful curses upon them. The very hands that once crowned them with laurels will be raised FOR THEIR DESTRUCTION. The swords that were to slay God's people are now employed to destroy their enemies. Everywhere is strife and bloodshed." GC 656. This is "how" God destroys! God's methods have never changed. In 2 Chron. 20:15-23 is described how God has always worked.

"And this shall be the plague wherewith the Lord will smite the people that have fought against Jerusalem; their flesh shall consume away while they stand upon their feet, and their eyes shall consume away in their holes, and their tongue shall consume away in their mouth. And it shall come to pass in that day, that a great tumult from the Lord shall be among them, AND THEY SHALL LAY HOLD EVERYONE ON THE HAND OF HIS NEIGHBOR, AND HIS HAND SHALL RISE UP AGAINST THE HAND OF HIS NEIGHBOR. Zech. 14:12, 13. *In the mad strife of their own fierce passions, and the awful outpouring of God's unmingled wrath, fall the wicked inhabitants of the earth."* GC 657. Compare Ezek. 38:21.

Is this a description of TWO manners of destruction, or ONE described in two ways? What IS the Bible and *Spirit of Prophecy* definition of *"the wrath of God"*? The wrath that Jesus suffered for fallen man, as his substitute, is a description of the wrath of God that every last soul will finally suffer. We must look at this through the cross, *"the mystery that explains all other mysteries."*

"The mystery of the cross explains all other mysteries. In the light that streams from Calvary, the attributes of God which have filled us with fear and awe appear beautiful and attractive. Mercy, tenderness, and parental love are seen to blend with holiness,

justice, and power. While we behold the majesty of His throne, high and lifted up, WE SEE HIS CHARACTER in its gracious manifestations, and comprehend, as never before, the significance of that endearing title, 'Our Father'. GC 652.

"All that man needs to know or CAN know of God has been revealed in the life and character of His Son." 8T 286.

Let us take a careful look at the only time in the earthly life of Christ where He performed an *"act"* of destruction.

"Christ's act in cursing the fig tree had astonished the disciples. It seemed to them unlike His ways and works. Often they had heard Him declare that He came not to condemn the world, but that the world through Him might be saved. They remembered His words, 'The Son of man IS NOT COME TO DESTROY men's lives, but to save them.' Luke 9:56. His wonderful works had been done to restore, NEVER TO DESTROY... This act stood alone. What was its purpose? they questioned... To Him the work of destruction is a 'strange work.' Isa. 28:21. But it is in mercy that He lifts the veil from the future, and reveals the results of a course of sin. The cursing of the fig tree was an acted parable... a symbol of the Jewish nation. The Saviour desired to make plain to His disciples the CAUSE and certainty of Israel's doom." DA 582.

"They brought ruin upon themselves by refusing to minister to others... In the barren fig tree they might read BOTH their sin and its punishment... the fig tree showed what the Jewish people would be when the grace of God WAS REMOVED from them. Refusing to impart blessing, they would no longer receive it." DA 583 (Please see also SC p. 80, 81.)

Does this not plainly declare that the *"curse of God,"* *"His wrath,"* His *"strange act,"* is the withdrawal of His life-support from those who choose to separate from Him, the Source of all life? Is this not *"suicide"* rather than *"Homicide"*?! Psalm 78:49; Rom. 1:18, 24, 26.

"The WRATH OF GOD against sin, the terrible manifestation of His displeasure because of iniquity, filled the soul of His Son with consternation ... He cannot see the Father's reconciling face. THE WITHDRAWAL of the divine countenance from the Saviour in this hour of supreme anguish pierced His heart with a sorrow that can never be fully understood by man ... He feared that sin was so offensive to God that THEIR SEPARATION was to be eternal. CHRIST FELT THE ANGUISH WHICH EVERY SINNER WILL FEEL when mercy no longer pleads for the guilty race. It was the sense of sin, bringing the FATHER'S WRATH upon Him as man's substitute, that made the cup He drank so bitter, and broke the heart of the Son of God." DA 753. This is *"the wrath of God"* just as every lost soul will experience it. It is no act of aggression on the part of God. It is infinite love which cries, *"How can I let thee go?!"* that is forced away by man's own stubborn rejection, because God cannot force even His love upon the soul of His creatures, for this would be spiritual rape! How can we reject so great salvation?! *"My God, My God, why hast Thou forsaken me"* is the truth of how God must put an end to sin.

"This is not an act of arbitrary power on the part of God. The rejecters of His mercy reap that which they have sown. God is the fountain of life; and when one chooses the service of sin, he SEPARATES from God, and thus cuts himself off from life. He is 'alienated from the life of God.' Christ says, 'All that hate Me love death.' " Eph. 4:18, Prov. 8:36. God gives them existence for a time that they may develop their character and reveal their principles ...

"At the beginning of the great controversy, the angels did not understand this. Had Satan and his host been LEFT to reap the full result of their sin, they would have perished; but it would not have been

apparent to heavenly beings that this was the inevitable RESULT of sin. A doubt of God's goodness would have remained in their minds as evil seed, to produce its deadly fruit of sin and woe." DA 764.

How solemn and comprehensive is this paragraph! It shows us that if God had allowed Satan and his angels to perish, **"self-destruct,"** if you please, that Satan would have by that very fact won his point! God would have been accused of annihilating them, and placed under suspicion of being the destroyer of those who do not **"appreciate His work, and who act contrary to His ideas."** (DA 487.) It was Satan's purpose to prove that the law of God was the cause of the problem which he instigated in heaven, and that God is responsible for his defection. That law is His character! After the whole issue has been made plain to the entire universe concerning the character of God as seen in His law, will it then be permissible for God to kill Satan and those who have sided with him? Will our God then revert to the carnal principle of **"the end serves the means,"** and **"do evil that good may come,"** ultimately showing Himself to be the destroyer after 6,000 years of trying to prove otherwise?

There will ever remain questions and apparent contradictions which we must leave with our heavenly Father, but looking unto Jesus and the cross of Calvary, we can safely resolve every apparent contradiction in favor of God's expressed character, rather than in favor of Satan's allegations against Him! Satan has tried to prove that God is both a liar and a destroyer. Jesus came to disprove both accusations by His own life and instruction.

We are to make our decisions about God in favor of the weight of evidence, not the few, seemingly irresolvable, apparent contradictions. The weight of evidence is overwhelmingly in God's favor as expressed by the principles of His law, and the life of Jesus!

Once again, after the millenium and the resurrection of the wicked, we see similar plans and actions taking place under Satan's leadership, as took place at the end of "time."

"They lay their plans to take possession of the riches and glory of the New Jerusalem. All immediately begin to prepare for battle. Skilled artisans construct implements of war." GC 664. The march is made toward the city of God. But that which halts the proceedings is . . . the cross!

"Above the throne is revealed the cross; like a panoramic view appear the scenes of Adam's temptation and fall, and the successive steps in the great plan of salvation . . . In his last great effort to dethrone Christ and destroy His people . . . the archdeceiver has been fully unmasked . . . He is the object of universal abhorrence . . . Notwithstanding that Satan has been constrained to acknowledge God's justice and bow to the supremacy of Christ, his character is unchanged . . . Filled with frenzy, he determines not to yield the great controversy . . . But his power is at an end . . . Their (the wicked's) *rage is kindled toward Satan and those who have been his agents in deception, and with the fury of demons they turn upon them.*

"Saith the Lord, 'Because thou hast set thine heart as the heart of God; behold, therefore, I will bring strangers upon thee, the terrible of the nations THEY SHALL DRAW THEIR SWORDS against the beauty of thy wisdom, and they shall defile thy brightness. They shall bring thee down to the pit. I will destroy thee, O covering cherub." GC 670-672.

Couched in both of these statements is the same interplay of cause and effect, of acts by Satan and his followers, and blame taken by God, as pointed out in the book of Job.

". . . Satan, the AUTHOR of sin and ALL its results, had led men to look upon disease and death as proceeding from God, . . . as a punishment arbitrarily inflicted on account of sin . . . God had given a lesson designed to prevent this. The history of Job had shown that suffering is inflicted BY SATAN, and overruled by God for purposes of mercy." DA 471. (See also DA 528 re. Satan has the power of death.) A most startling and conclu-

sive scripture clearly illuminates this point, *"And in her* (Babylon) *was found the blood of prophets, and of saints, AND OF ALL that were slain upon the earth."* Rev. 18:24. Since Babylon, as such, did not exist until after the flood, this must have reference to that larger definition described in Isa. 14:4-12, which likens Satan (Lucifer) to the king of Babylon.

The reason God accepts blame is because He does not want our attention focused upon Satan, for by beholding we become changed (2 Cor. 3:18), and molded after that upon which our minds dwell. (5 BC 1135, DA 493). So God takes the blame for that which He does not see fit to prevent for the eternal good of His creatures. We have something to learn regarding God's *permissive* will versus His *perfect* will. An example would be that of anointing Saul to be King over Israel, when the request for a king was contrary to His will, and a rejection of Himself as their rightful ruler! The same principle applies to the conquest of Canaan by force of arms. See Hosea 13:11; Ps. 78:26-32.

". . . When the great controversy shall be ended, then the great plan of redemption having been completed, THE CHARACTER OF GOD is revealed to all created intelligences. The precepts of HIS LAW are seen to be perfect and immutable. Then sin has made manifest its nature, Satan his character. THEN the extermination of sin will VINDICATE God's love and establish His honor before the universe of beings who delight to do His will, in whose heart His law is . . . Christ Himself fully comprehended the results of the sacrifice upon Calvary. To all this He looked forward when upon the cross He cried out, 'It is finished.' " DA 764.

Our understanding of the message and meaning of the loud cry needs much modification in view of this solemn subject! As Jesus lived His unpretentious life among mankind in human flesh, so will those who seek to emulate Him. And the result will be the same!

"So the followers of Christ are to shed light into

the darkness of this world. Through the Holy Spirit, God's word is a light as it becomes a transforming power in the life of the receiver ... The light of His glory—His character—is to shine forth in His followers." COL 414.

We are poorly prepared for the result of such representation in the reaction we are told to expect from the world. Jesus said He came not to send peace, but a sword, that if the world hate us, we know that it hated Him first. *"All who will live godly in Christ Jesus shall suffer persecution."* 2 Tim. 3:12.

"The forces of the powers of darkness will unite with human agents who have given themselves under the control of Satan, and the same scenes that were exhibited at the trial and rejection of Christ will be revived ... Satan will see in an apostate race his masterpiece of evil—men who reflect his image." 5BC 1136.

Those who serve a killer-god will act out the character of him whom they ignorantly worship. They will think that they do God service in seeking to slay His people (John 16:2). For the same reason Christ was rejected, so will His followers be unrecognized and persecuted. But it will be through persecution, and the behavior of God's people toward their persecutors, that the earth is to be *"lightened"* with the glory of God, as it was in the earthly walk of Jesus! This is what is comprehended in Rev. 18:1 and Isaiah 60:1-3. But it is not thus that we are inclined to consider the *"glory"* of the loud cry message of the third angel! In both Early Writings, p. 272, and in Great Controversy, p. 607, we are told that the power attending the message will only madden those who resist its influence. But while we tend to look for great display and excitement in these events (as the Jews looked for a glorious demonstration by the Messiah), we should consider this description in Hosea 6 depicting one of the effects of the latter rain upon God's people.

"The Sun of righteousness did not burst upon the world in splendor, to dazzle the senses with His glory.

It is written of Christ, 'His going forth is prepared as the morning.' Hosea 6:3. Quietly and gently the day-light breaks upon the earth, dispelling the darkness and waking the world to life. So, did the Sun of righteousness arise, 'with healing in His wings.' " MH 32.

If we do not know God, we will be taken in by the deceptions that take the world captive. We are told that Satan will personate Christ in the manner the world is expecting. (GC 624.) There will be but two classes of people comprising all mankind, those who know God and those who do not, the persecuted and the persecutors. Will it be said of us, *"Ye know not what manner of spirit ye are of?"* (See Luke 9:54, 55.)

The simplicity of righteousness by faith presents to us the only safe shelter from delusion. We are safe only as we look unto Jesus, *"the Author and Finisher of our faith." "And this is life eternal, that they might know thee, the only true God, and Jesus Christ, whom thou hast sent."* John 17:3.

"Multitudes have a wrong conception of God and His attributes, and are as truly serving a false God as were the worshippers of Baal." PK 177.

Those who come to believe in the messages presented in Rev. 14, the three angel messages, will be brought to understand that the message of the Sabbath, and God's glory—His character—are inseparably entwined. It is the Creator-Life-Giving God versus the destroyer *"god of this world,"* so-called. This was the message of 1888 of which it was written, *"The enemy of God and man is not willing that this truth should be clearly presented; for he knows that if the people receive it fully, his power will be broken."* GW 103, old ed.

"That holy law, God's righteousness . . . is now revealed as the rule of judgment." GC 639. God's law, His righteous character, His name, and glory are synonymous. (See Ex. 33, 34; Rev. 14:1.) This is the *"seal of God"* which is to be written in our foreheads!

CHAPTER 7

WALKING IN THE ADVANCING LIGHT

"Since the great controversy began, it has been Satan's studied purpose to persuade angels and men that God is not worthy of their faith and love. He has pictured the Creator as a harsh, demanding tyrant who lays arbitrary requirements upon His people just to show His authority and test their willingness to obey. From Genesis to Revelation the Bible tells of Satan's unceasing efforts to pervert the truth and blacken the character of God.

"But if God were as Satan has pictured Him, how easily He could have blotted out His rebellious creatures and started over again! If all God wanted was unthinking obedience, how easily He could have manipulated the minds of men and angels and forced them to obey!

"But love and trust, the qualities God desires the most, are not produced by force—not even by God Himself.

"That is why, instead of destroying or resorting to force, God simply took His case into court. In order to prove the rightness of His cause, to demonstrate that His way of governing the universe was the best for all concerned, God humbly submitted His own character to the investigation and judgment of His creatures.

"Paul understood this when he exclaimed, **'God must prove true, though every man be false; as the Scripture says, 'That you may be shown to be upright in what you say, and win your case when you go into court.'** " (Romans 3:4, Goodspeed).

"CAN GOD BE TRUSTED?"—P. 31—
By A. Graham Maxwell

Now, I want to share with you a sample of the **"advancing light,"** you can begin walking in if you will open your heart to the Spirit of God. Most sincere Christians believe that the Ten Commandments were nailed to the cross and abolished by Christ's death, along with the ceremonial laws of Moses. Most arguments against this false teaching are very weak and contradictory. I want to show you how to prove beyond a doubt that God's holy, Ten Commandment law has never been abrograted, repealed, abolished or annulled. One of the reasons why the difference between these two laws is misunderstood is because of the rejection of Righteousness by Faith, by the leaders of the church back in 1888.

Notice that EGW understood the difference between these two laws. **"There are many who try to blend these two systems, using the texts that speak of the ceremonial law to prove that the moral law has been abolished; but this is a perversion of the Scriptures. The distinction between the two systems is broad and clear." Patriarch and Prophets,** page 365.

Now, let us go to the Holy Bible itself and see what God Himself has to say about His own perfect law, the TEN COMMANDMENTS and this other imperfect, temporary law, which God Himself clearly tells us He never spoke nor gave. Since I have already written so much detail on this subject in Chapter 28 of my book, **"Into The Father's**

Heart," I will just basically give the Scriptures for you to read and then show you how certain EGW statements do not contradict the Bible testimony at all, but only prove what I have already said . . . that whatever God allows He claims to have done Himself.

In Deut. 5:22 and Jer. 7:22 we find conclusive and categorical testimony by Moses and God that the only law God spoke or gave on Mount Sinai was the Ten Commandments. EGW confirms this in PP 365. She quotes Nehemiah 9:13 and Rom 7:12 to prove that God's Ten Commandments are *"right judgments, true laws, etc."* But in contrast to this are the laws for killing animals and getting even with your neighbor who has wronged you. This *"eye for an eye and tooth for a tooth law,"* Jesus Himself abolished in Matt 5:38-48. This was very consistent for Christ to teach since He had inspired the prophet Ezekiel to say that He had given Israel *"statues that were not good, and judgments* (decisions) *whereby they should not live;"* Ezek. 20:24, 25. Ezekiel is referring to the ceremonial laws.

And when Christ came, He spoke against the animal sacrifice system, Matt. 9:13; Matt. 12:7, and cleansed the temple precincts twice of this *"weak, carnal, unprofitable"* (Heb. 7:16, 18) merciless and senseless system, which Christ, through Isaiah declared, *"I delight not."* Isa. 1:10-12. He also said he did not *"require it."* And in Psalm 40:6 and Psalm 51:16 Jesus said He neither *"delights"* in the slaughter and blood of animals nor desires it. So, the question is, who is the *"god"* who *"requires"* and *"desires"* and *"delights"* in the killing of animals? Ellen G. White will tell us the truth. *"Not even a sparrow falls to the ground without the Father's notice. Satan's hatred against God leads him to delight in destroying even the dumb creatures. It is only through God's protecting care that the birds are preserved to gladden us with their songs of joy. But He does not forget even the sparrows."* 8T 273. See also 3TT 267.

Again, EGW says, *"As the Bible presents two laws, one changeless and eternal, the other provisional and temporary, so there are two covenants."* PP 370. We designate these two covenants as the old and the new. The old was abolished at the cross, for this was never God's covenant to begin with, but man's idea of how to be saved and it started right at the base of Mt. Sinai when Aaron took their money and created for them a golden calf. And that is what the weak-willed Aarons have been doing for the people ever since. And anyone who is brave enough to speak out against this system of false *"salvation by works"* is persecuted and sometimes even killed. That is just what happened to Stephen, the first Christian martyr. He really exposed the false worship system of the Jews and even showed how it started. They could not stand to hear the truth and *"cried out with a loud voice, and stopped their ears, and ran upon him with one accord, and cast him out of the city, and stoned him."* Acts 7:57-58.

But let us notice the facts he presented to them. *"This is that Moses, ... to whom our fathers would not obey, but thrust him from them and in their hearts turned back again into Egypt, saying unto Aaron, Make us gods to go before us; for as for this Moses, which brought us out of the land of Egypt, we wot* (know) *not what is become of him."* Here they are rejecting God's leadership through Moses, who is a type of Christ, and being led by Satan to make a visible representation of God, which is a violation of the second commandment. Now, watch how the Spirit of God led Stephen to explain how the slaughter of animals began at Mt. Sinai in connection with the idolatrous worship of the bull calf Apis, one of the chief Egyptian deities Satan had led them to set up so as to divert worship away from the true God and direct it to himself. *"And they made a calf in those days, and offered sacrifice unto the idol, and rejoiced in the works of their own hands."* Acts 7:38-41.

Now, we all know that idol worship is devil worship. Paul confirms this in I Cor. 10:14-21 where he says, *"But I say, that the things which the Gentiles sacrifice, they sacrifice to devils, and not to God."* That should make it crystal clear why God said He did not *"require, desire or delight"* in the animal slaughter system. It was devil worship. Someone may protest by saying, *"Oh, but Mike, if the animals were sacrificed to the true God it was all right."* No, it was not all right, anymore than to worship a bull and say you are worshipping the true God. It is a deceptive lie of Satan.

But, let us go on to the rest of Stephen's magnificent discourse. *"Then God turned, and gave them up to worship the host of heaven;* (Satan and his angels) *as it is written in the book of the prophets,* (Amos 5:25), *have ye offered to me slain beasts and sacrifices by the space of forty years in the wilderness?* (confirming again that God never 'desired, delighted or required it') *Yea, ye took up the tabernacle of Moloch, and the star of your god Remphan, figures which ye made to worship them: and I will carry you away beyond Babylon."* Acts 7:41-43. So, this false, Satanic system actually caused them to go into Babylonian captivity.

Moloch or Molech was the name of a god to whom human sacrifices were offered, mainly little children by their parents. Even though there was a death penalty against this practice, (Lev. 18:21; 20:1-5) the Israelites frequently did it (Jer. 7:31; 19:4, 5; 32:35; Ezek. 16:21; Ezek. 23:37, 39). Remphan (Rephan) was the name for a giant people in Canaan, Gen. 14:5; 15:20. Stephen spoke to the Jews of his day in the present tense as if they were the ones who were still worshipping these false gods. And they were in spirit, for Satan had led them to reject the truth Jesus brought and now they were rejecting the truth Stephen was giving them and would soon kill him, too. It is a fact, that the disregard for the life of innocent animals will lead men to place a low estimate upon human life. EGW tells us that the people before the flood *"delighted in destroying the life of animals; and the use of flesh for food rendered them still more cruel and bloodthirsty, until they came to regard human life with astonishing indifference."* PP 92. This is what happened to the Jews of old just as it is happening again today. Men are in darkness about God's character of love.

Paul calls the law of the Levitical priesthood, with all of its ceremonies and animal slaughter, a *"carnal commandment."* We know God never gives anything that is carnal. Furthermore, Paul states that these commandments *"contained in ordinances"* were abolished. Col. 2:14-16; Eph. 2:15. Notice that the *"worshipping of angels,"* was warned against also in Col. 2:18. The only law God gave, i.e. Ten Commandments, on Mt. Sinai was and is an eternal, *"Spiritual law."* Rom. 7:12. Paul also called the *"abolished law"* of animal sacrifice *"weak,"* *"unprofitable,"* and unable to make anyone *"perfect."* God never gives anything that is weak, unprofitable or imperfect. He only gives *"good and perfect"* gifts. James 1:17. So, our wonderful God could not have possibly given the laws prescribing animal slaughter, for He Himself said, *"He that killeth an ox is as if he slew a man,"* Isa. 66:3, showing that God considers the killing of animals just as much a violation of the law of God as the killing of a man. And the 6th commandment clearly states, *"Thou shalt not kill."* Cf. Psalm 40:6-8; 50:8-15; 51:16, 17; Isa. 1:10-14; I Sam. 15:22; Micah 6:8; Jer. 7:22; Amos 5:25, 26. Furthermore, God never has to abolish anything He gives.

Perhaps someone is saying, *"Brother Clute, you have convinced me that God never wanted or commanded animals to be killed. The Scriptures and the life of Christ are too plain to be misunderstood or explained away. But what I cannot understand is why EGW states that Christ 'gave' and 'instituted' these laws? See DA 307; PP 367-373; 6BC 1095; 1SM 230; 6BC 1095."*

The answer to your question is actually very simple. No matter what happens in this dark world of sin, God always claims that He is doing it. For example, He claims

He hardened Pharaoh's heart (Ex. 4:21; 7:3) when we know
He didn't. He also says He *"bruised"* His own Son on Calvary, Isa. 53:10; Sent an evil spirit to King Saul and later
had him killed. I Sam. 16:14; I Chron. 10:13, 14. God also
claims to have caused the ten tribes of Israel to rebel and
split from the tribe of Judah. He told Judah not to go out
and fight. *"Return every man to his house; for this
thing is from me."* I Kings 12:24. He even says that He
sends both good and evil, light and darkness—Isa. 45:7,
when I John 1:5 categorically states *"God is light, and in
Him is no darkness at all."* And James 1:17 says God only
sends good. So, why these seeming contradictions?

The only answer is that God is assuming the blame or
responsibility for everything His creatures do. Because we
have free choice He must allow us to exercise that free
choice. He cannot take that away from us or else we would
simply be His robots. He wants us to love and obey Him
because we choose to do so, not because we are forced or pre-
programmed to love and obey Him whether we want to or
not. EGW makes this comment, *"God might have created
man without the power to transgress His law; He
might have withheld the hand of Adam from touching
the forbidden fruit; but in that case man would have
been, not a free moral agent, but a mere automaton.
Without freedom of choice, his obedience would not
have been voluntary, but forced. There could have
been no development of character. Such a course
would have been contrary to God's plan in dealing
with the inhabitants of other worlds. It would have
been unworthy of man as an intelligent being, and
would have sustained Satan's charge of God's arbitrary rule."* PP 49. In the index to EGW's writings there
are over 540 references in which she explains and discusses
how and why God created us with the power of choice. *"The
great Captain of our salvation has conquered in our
behalf, that through Him we might conquer, if we
would, in our own behalf. But Christ saves none*

against their choice; He compels none to obedience." 3T 457.

In "DESIRE OF AGES," pages 758-764 EGW discusses God's modus operandi. That is, she explains the principles by which He runs our universe. She clearly states on page 359 that God never uses force. Then on page 763 she explains how Satan is destroyed in the final day and refers to Ezek. 28:6-19 but in this edition only part of verse 18 is quoted. If you read verses 6-10 you will discover that Satan's own followers are the very ones who destroy him. I discuss this in great depth in my book, "INTO THE FATHER'S HEART," so I will only state here that EGW agrees on page 764 that the destruction of Satan is not an act of God, even though Ezek. 28:18 states, *"I will destroy thee, O covering Cherub, . . ."* Here is EGW's comment on how Satan's destruction is effected: *"This is not an act of arbitrary power on the part of God. The rejecters of His mercy reap that which they have sown. God is the fountain of life; and when one chooses the service of sin, he separates from God, and thus cuts himself off from life. He is 'alienated from the life of God' 'All they that hate Me love death.' "* Eph. 4:18; Prov. 8:36. Read Ezek. 28:6-10 and you will clearly see that Satan is destroyed by his own followers, not God. In *"Great Controversy,"* page 36, EGW says, *"God does not stand toward the sinner as an executioner of the sentence against transgression; but He leaves the rejecters of His mercy to themselves to reap that which they have sown."* Here she categorically states that God does not execute the wicked. That is not His *"strange act."* I explain what His *"strange act"* is on pages 85, 104, and 206 of "INTO THE FATHER'S HEART." On page 37 of GC, EGW tells us that the wicked destroy themselves at the Second Coming. Her comment on the phrase *"destroyed with the brightness of His coming,"* 2 Thess. 2:8 is this: *"Like Israel of old the wicked destroy themselves; they fall by their iniquity. By a life of sin, they have placed themselves so out of harmony with God, their natures have become so debased with evil, that the manifestation of His glory is to them a consuming fire."* GC 37. I discuss this in much greater detail in chapter 27 of my book, "HOW WILL THE WICKED BE DESTROYED WHEN CHRIST RETURNS?" Pages 304-333.

But, let's go back to the question: *"Why does EGW state that Christ ordained the ceremonial laws, especially the animal sacrifice system?"* EGW statements seem to be a great stumbling block for many SDAs. But they need not be. They can actually be building blocks to a greater understanding of both the Bible as well as the writings of EGW. But we first must understand this principle of how and why God always takes the blame. I answer this question in depth in my book (IFH) on pages 79, 83, 184, and 254. But let me show you another statement EGW makes which should make the principle as clear as crystal—at least for those who really want to believe and understand the truth about God's wonderful character of love.

Notice this statement. *"The thorn and the thistle—the difficulties and trials that make life one of toil and care—were appointed for his good..."* *"Steps to Christ,"* page 1. Here she says that God *"appointed"* the thorn and the thistle. Cf. Isa. 54:16. Does that mean it was God's idea? Does that mean that God planted the thorn and the thistle? Of course not. In fact, she tells us the very opposite. Listen: *"The same God who guides the planets works in the fruit orchard and in the vegetable garden. He never made a thorn, a thistle, or a tare. These are Satan's work, the result of degeneration, introduced by him among the precious things; but it is through God's immediate agency that every bud bursts into blossom."* 6T 186. *"Show that it was sin which marred God's perfect work; that thorns and thistles, sorrow and pain and death, are all the result of disobedience to God."* 6T 358. So, what then does EGW mean when she says God *"appointed"* the thorn and the thistle, or that God *"ordained," "instituted"* and *"gave"* the ceremonial laws? There can only be one answer, beloved. Let your very own intelligence tell you the truth. And that eternal principle of truth is the simple concept that no matter what happens God claims to be *"ordaining"* it because He had to allow it due to the power of our free choice. But through His infinite wisdom, presence and power (omniscience, omnipresence, and omnipotence) God is able to overrule every one of our wrong choices and make *"all things work together for good,"* for those who love Him. Rom. 8:28. And He even does it for the wicked, in as far as He is able. But He is so often *"limited"* (Psalm 78:41) by them. His hands are tied and they suffer incredibly. All God can do is weep, as He wept over Jerusalem.

When the people demanded a king, God, *"gave"* them a king through Samuel the prophet. But notice what the Bible says, *"And Samuel said to all the people, See ye him* (Saul) *whom the Lord hath chosen, . . ."* I Sam. 10:24. But wait a minute. I thought the people "chose" him? Let us read on. *"And when ye saw that Nahash the king of the children of Ammon came against you, ye said unto me, Nay; but a king shall reign over us: when the Lord your God was your king. Now, therefore, behold the king whom ye have chosen, and whom ye have desired! and behold, the Lord hath set a king over you."* I Sam. 12:12, 13. Here we see how God operates. If we want something that is against His will, He will try and talk us out of it, but if we persist and demand it, He will give it to us and write it up as if it was His idea in the first place. But why would God do that? Because He wants to take away the guilt and He wants to remain in charge of our lives, so He will always be there to help us . . . to save us from the worst effects of our wrong choice, for Satan has more of a hold upon us than God does . . . that is, we are more attuned to the voice of Satan than we are to the voice of God. That is the Laodicean condition. EGW talks about how *"Christ has departed"* because *"His spirit has been*

quenched in the church. Satan works side by side with professed Christians; yet they are so destitute of spiritual discernment that they do not detect him." 2T 441, 442. Written in 1868.

Now, when Christ is forced out of our lives and out of our church, God calls this rejection of His **"majority"** presence and control in our lives **"the wrath of God."** See Rom. 1:18, 24, 26, 28, and Psalm 78:49. Notice Hosea's comment about God being Israel's king. **"O Israel, thou hast destroyed thyself; but in me is thine help.** (Even though we force God out of our lives He still stands at the door of our hearts, knocking, trying to get back in). **I will be thy king: where is any other that may save thee in all thy cities? and thy judges of whom thou saidst, Give me a king and princes? I gave thee a king in mine anger, and took him away in my wrath."** Hosea 13:9-11. Here God clearly explains what His **"wrath"** is. It is simply when we tell God to get out of our lives for we don't want Him to tell us what to do anymore. And that is exactly what the people before the flood told God . . . "Depart from us." Job 22:15-17. Yes, beloved, the flood came as a result of Satan leading the Antediluvians to reject God. And this is called, **"The wrath of God."** See Isaiah 54:5-9. I discuss the flood in much more detail in my book, IFH.

If you read the story of Balaam, you will see the same exact pattern. Balaam wanted to curse Israel so King Balak would **"promote"** him to **"great honor"** and riches. Num. 24:11-13. Read the whole story yourself and you will see how God finally gives into Balaam and lets him do what he wants to do—up to a certain point. But watch the sequence. At first the Lord says to Balaam, **"Thou shalt not go with them."** Num. 22:12. Now, notice that God next tells Balaam, **"If the men come to call thee, rise up, and go with them; but yet the word which I shall say unto thee, that shalt thou do."** V. 20 So, Balaam has finally got his own way, but he is losing the presence and blessing of God by his wrong choice and the Spirit of the Lord inspires the writer to call this, *"God's anger."* This simply means that Balaam's rejection of God's leading in his life forced God out and invited Satan in, so Satan now has the upper hand and majority control in his life. This is what the Bible calls *"The wrath or anger of God."* The Lord is absorbing the punishment that we should receive for our rebellion against His will. He has no *"wrath"* in Himself, but He takes it away from us, into Himself, so we will not suffer so much. But if we totally reject Him and completely force Him out of our lives, this wrath comes back upon us in full measure for God cannot prevent it or save us from our own suicidal course. EGW explains it like this: *"The Spirit of God, persistently resisted, is at last withdrawn from the sinner, and then there is left no power to control the evil passions of the soul, and no protection from the malice and enmity of Satan. The destruction of Jerusalem is a fearful and solemn warning to all who are trifling with the offers of divine grace and resisting the pleadings of divine mercy. Never was there given a more decisive testimony to God's hatred of sin and to the certain punishment that will fall upon the guilty."* GC 36. CF. 2 Thess. 2:11-12.

History is filled with this kind of tragedy. How very sad to see professed Christians engaged in the same kind of willful, sinful actions as Balaam and King Saul. EGW says that King Saul was the *"choice of God,"* and chosen by *"Divine authority."* PP 610, 611. So, even though God did not want Israel to reject Him and get their own king, after their own heart, He allowed them to have their own way and reap the result so as to learn a lesson from it. Jer. 2:19 and PP 728 clearly explain how God *"punishes."*

Now that we have observed the same principle of God assuming the blame and taking the responsibility for all of our actions in these many other examples, it should be very easy to apply this same principle to the ceremonial laws of animal slaughter. It was Satan's suggestion to Adam outside the garden that led to the first lamb being slain. Hosea

6:6, 7 indicate that Adam betrayed His Lord and accepted Satan as His new god and lord. Yet, God took control of the situation and basically said to Adam ... *"Now, my beloved son, Adam, since you have chosen to kill an animal, against my will, I will give you explicit instruction and directions on how you are to perform these rites and ceremonies, for they are going to point forward to and symbolize what your descendants will eventually do to the Messiah when He comes." God had to do the same exact thing for Israel when they chose their own king. The Lord allowed a book of rules to be written that would govern the way the kingdom would be run. "Then Samuel told the people the manner of the kingdom, and wrote it in a book."* I Sam. 10:25. Moses wrote a similar *"book"* that was placed on the outside of the ark of the covenant. This was the book of the covenant contained in ordinances which was *"against"* God's people and the one He nailed to the cross and abolished. God did not *"speak"* this law, but He did *"edit"* it so as to make it as equitable as possible so as to save the people from the worst effects of their wrong choice. In the same manner He regulated their polygamous marriages, divorces, their system of slavery, as well as their choice to eat flesh food. So, when EGW states that God *"ordained"* anything, it simply means that He was regulating and controlling it. It seldom means that it was His perfect idea or perfect will. What God set up and ordained in the beginning when He created the world has been greatly changed. But He has never given up on us. His love will never let us go. He holds on to us to the very last, weeping as we push Him away. I hope you will not push the Lord Jesus out of your life today. Let Him come into your life and take full control. You can make that choice right now. *"Father, I pray that your Spirit will fill this person's heart as he surrenders his all to you this very moment."* In Jesus' name we pray. Amen.

CHAPTER 8

UNDERSTANDING THE GIFT OR SPIRIT OF PROPHECY

"Moses now summoned the seventy to the tabernacle. 'And the Lord came down in a cloud, and spake unto him, and took of the spirit that was upon him, and gave it unto the seventy elders; and it came to pass, that, when the spirit rested upon them, they prophesied, and did not cease.' Like the disciples on the Day of Pentecost, they were endued with 'power from on high.'" PP 381. However, on page 380 of PP we read that the selection of the 70 elders was not God's "perfect" will, but His "permissive" will due to Moses' continual complaints "And that serious evils would result from their promotion." PP 380.

By Ellen G. White

"Even Saul, after being anointed as the first king of Israel received the 'Gift' or Spirit of Prophecy. 'As Saul united with the prophets in their worship, a great change was wrought in him by the Holy Spirit. The light of divine purity and holiness shone in upon the darkness of the natural heart. He saw himself as he was before God. He saw the beauty of holiness . . . The plan

(135)

of salvation, which had before seemed dim and uncertain, was opened to his understanding.' "
PP 611

By Ellen G. White

IN THE CASE OF KING SAUL GOD GAVE HIM SPECIAL WISDOM TO KNOW HOW TO GOVERN ISRAEL.

Samuel told Saul, *"At that time the Spirit of the Lord will come mightily upon you, and you will prophesy with them and you will feel and act like a different person. From that time on your decisions should be based on whatever seems best under the circumstances, for the Lord will guide you."* I Sam. 10:6, 7. LB. In spite of this, Saul still apostatized.

IN BOTH THE OLD AND NEW TESTAMENTS GOD HAD MAJOR PROPHETS AND HE HAD MINOR PROPHETS.

"FROM THE EARLIEST TIMES, PROPHETS HAD BEEN RECOGNIZED AS TEACHERS DIVINELY APPOINTED. In the highest sense the prophet was one who spoke by direct inspiration, communicating to the people the messages he had received from God. But the name was given also to those who, though not so directly inspired, were

divinely called to instruct the people in the works and ways of God. For the training of such a class of teachers, Samuel, by the Lord's direction, established the schools of the prophets." Education, Page 46. *"And it shall come to pass afterward, that I will pour out my Spirit upon all flesh;"* Joel 2:28.

The final message of God's incredible love and power will be given all over the earth by God's chosen instruments. *"Servants of God, with their faces lighted up and shining with holy consecration, will hasten from place to place to proclaim the message from heaven. By thousands of voices, all over the earth, the warning will be given."* Evangelism, Page 700.

By Ellen G. White

The question as to whether God destroys or not is resolved in most sincere SDA's mind with a few Ellen G. White quotations which they believe answer the entire question. But instead of settling the matter it just confuses the whole issue by making it look like EGW is inconsistent and self-contradictory, which she wasn't.

One of the purposes of adding this new material is to resolve this seeming contradiction or paradox, if you please. I am a firm believer in the Spirit of Prophecy, as manifested in the Bible writers of the OT, as well as the NT. I also believe God has moved upon human minds since the last book of the Bible was written by John. For example, I believe men like Wycliffe and Luther were "prophets" in their own right, but without visions and dreams. God's Spirit led them to translate the Bible and preach and write. Calvin, Wesley, Knox, and others had this same prophetic gift. EGW tells us that the name "prophet" was given to *"those who, though not so directly inspired, were divinely called to instruct the people in the works and ways of God."* Education, Page 46. Elijah and John the Baptist were two of the greatest prophets who ever lived, yet there is no record of them ever having a dream or vision. Yet, God revealed to John's mind how to recognize the Messiah, John 1:33, but it was not an *"open vision,"* as Ezekiel, Daniel and some others often had. But they were still prophets of God. And we can be too!

My point here is that you don't have to have dreams or visions to be a prophet. SDAs have been brainwashed to believe ONLY the writings of Ellen G. White constitute the "Spirit of Prophecy." How could this possibly be true when EGW died in 1915? Is EGW the only "prophet" God ever intended to speak in these last days? I think the devil wants SDAs to believe that so they will never be able to understand any "new light" EGW said God would send us. See "Gospel Workers," pgs. 297-304. Joel 2:28 promises that God will "pour out my Spirit upon all flesh;" So, you can hear God's voice too.

The Prophet Samuel evidently heard a voice in his mind which told him which of the sons of Jesse God wanted him to anoint as king of Israel. I Sam. 16:7. We know David was a prophet, too, for he wrote many of the Psalms, some of which are very prophetic. Psalms 22 and 24 are examples. David evidently received this prophetic gift when Samuel anointed him, for the Bible says, *"and the spirit of the Lord came upon David from that day forward."* I Sam. 16:13. And yet David was a product of his times, marrying many wives and killing with the sword, both of which are forbidden by Christ. *"And the times of this ignorance God winked at; but now commandeth all men every where to repent."* Acts 17:30.

The meaning of what a prophet is and does has taken on a very narrow and distorted meaning today. Most people today would describe a prophet as a person who predicts the future based on a dream or vision he recently received from God. The term "Prophet" has a much wider and broader meaning than this. The Hebrew word for prophet is 'NABIY' " (5030 Strongs). It simply means an "inspired man." It comes from the word 'NABA' " (5012 Strongs) and means "to prophesy, i.e. speak (or sing) by inspiration (in prediction or simple discourse)—prophesy(ing), make self a prophet." From Strong's Concordance (Hebrew and Chaldee Dictionary), page 75, (5012).

Even **Webster's New Twentieth Century Dictionary Unabridged** (second edition) gives the following definition: "from Gr. prophets; pro, before, and phanai, to speak." Next it gives four definitions and does not even mention the word "predicts" until the last or fourth definition. "1. a person who speaks for God or a god, or as though under divine guidance. 2. a religious teacher or leader regarded as, or claiming to be, divinely inspired. 3. a spokesman for some cause, group or movement, etc. 4. a person who predicts future events in any way."

And **Young's Concordance** defines the phrase, "to prophesy" as meaning "to publicly expound" from the Greek word "propheteuw." Next we have this excellent explanation of how God has been guiding His church through prophesying since the ascension of Christ, by Dr. A. H. Strong.

> "Christ's prophetic activity is continued through the preaching of His apostles and ministers, and by the enlightening influences of His Holy Spirit (John 16:12-14; Acts 1:1). The apostles unfolded the germs of doctrine put into their hands by Christ. The church is, in a derivative sense, a prophetic institution, established to teach the world by its preaching and its ordinances. But Christians are prophets, only as being proclaimers of Christ's teaching (Num. 11:29; Joel 2:28)." "Systematic Theology," by Augustus Hopkins Strong, D.D., LL.D. 1907, Twenty-first printing, 1960. Page 712.

Next we have this enlightening comment from the "SDA Bible Dictionary," Pg. 881. "In the same way that a prophet is a spokesman, or messenger for God, so prophecy is any message spoken for God, at His command . . . It was the rejection of the messages of the prophets that brought ruin upon Israel; it led to their refusal to accept their Messiah, and thus to their rejection as a nation." Pgs. 881, 882. As we look at what is happening to the church today can we not say that history is truly repeating? God's messengers and messages are again being rejected. EGW and Jones and Waggoner were rejected in 1888 and every messenger since then who has tried to revive the 1888 message has likewise been rejected. May God help us!

The terms "messenger" or "prophet" can be used interchangeably. EGW stated that the Lord told her she was his special "messenger," 1 SM 32, 34. She did not refuse to be called a "prophet," but preferred the designation of "Messenger." God needs more workers and messengers today. Can you hear Jesus calling you?

Now we come to a most interesting point we must not miss. Sister White called Jones and Waggoner God's "Messengers." She starts out on page 91 of *Testimonies to Ministers,* by categorically stating, *"The Lord in His great mercy sent a most precious message to His people through Elders Waggoner and Jones."* Later on page 95 she states, *"There was but little love for God or man, and God gave to His messengers just what the people needed."* Next, I want you to notice that God also calls His "prophets" "His servants." *"Light and power from on high have been shed abundantly in the midst of you. Here was evidence, that all might discern whom the Lord recognized as His servants."* And this agrees perfectly with the statement in Amos 3:7, *"Surely the Lord God will do nothing but He revealeth His secret unto His servants the prophets."*

Notice now what we have discovered. First of all, EGW, whom SDAs revere as a "prophet" of the Lord, said she was God's "Messenger or Servant." Secondly, she applied both of these designations or descriptions to Jones and Waggoner. They were "minor" prophets, while she was the "major" prophet.

So, anyone who is God's servant can also "prophesy" or speak for God under the guidance of His Holy Spirit. In

Numbers 12:7, God called Moses, "My servant." And in Acts 4:25, the prophet-king is called a "servant." But when Jesus came He went beyond the word servant and elevated us to be His "friends." What a fantastic God we have. Incredible! *"Ye are my friends, if ye do whatsoever I command you. Henceforth, I call you not servants; for the servant knoweth not what his Lord doeth; but I have called you friends, for the things that I have heard of my Father I have made known unto you."* John 15:14, 15.

Next, please notice how EGW uses the term "prophesy" in the sense of giving a message of warning. *"Let me prophesy unto you: Unless you speedily humble your hearts before God, and confess your sins, which are many, you will, when it is too late, see that you have been fighting against God."* TM 97. Remember, beloved, EGW is here talking to the leaders of the SDA Church who had rejected and were continuing to reject the message of 1888. The time period is in the early 1890's, about four years after the rejection of 1888.

One of the greatest deceptions that has come upon the Christian church is that only "ordained" ministers can speak for God. All of us are the "servants" and "friends" and "prophets" of Christ. No human being has a corner on speaking for the Lord.

> "The Saviour's commission to the disciples included all the believers. It includes all believers in Christ to the end of time. It is a fatal mistake to suppose that the work of saving souls depends alone on the ordained minister. All to whom the heavenly inspiration has come are put in trust with the gospel. All who receive the life of Christ are ordained to work for the salvation of their fellow men. For this work the church was established, and all who take upon themselves its sacred vows are thereby pledged to be co-workers with Christ." *Desire of Ages,* page 822.

The main point I want to make here is that EGW states that every believer is "ordained" to work for the salvation of souls. God has never commissioned any human being, man or woman, to dictate to another. But that is exactly what organized religion is all about today. Man dominating and dictating to other men. But our precious Lord Jesus clearly said, *"But be not ye called Rabbi; for one is your Master, even Christ; and all ye are brethren."* Matt. 23:8.

One of the most frequent questions I am asked is, *"Were you ever ordained by the conference?"* The answer I now give is, *"No, God ordained me Himself. I was not called by man."* Paul claimed the same divine calling. *"Paul, an apostle, not of men, neither by man, but by Jesus Christ, and God the Father."* Gal. 1:1. Read the first verse of Paul's other letters and you will find that he often states that he was called "by the will of God." Throughout history the men and women God has called were almost always, if not always, rejected by the established religion or religions. There is a continual "enmity," (Gen. 3:15) between God's servants and the servants of man. And yet people today will ask you "do you have credentials from the conference to preach in the churches?" This is the modern Laodicean blindness we must face in this last hour of earth's history. If Sr. White were alive today she would rebuke it just as soundly as when she was alive. But her writings are still speaking to us. Listen:

> "He who loves Christ the most will do the greatest amount of good. There is no limit to the usefulness of one who, by putting self aside, makes room for the working of the Holy Spirit upon his heart, and lives a life wholly consecrated to God. If men will endure the necessary discipline, without complaining or fainting by the way, God will teach them hour by hour, and day by day. He longs to reveal His grace. If His people will remove the obstructions, He will pour forth the waters of salvation in abundant streams through the human channels. If men in humble life were encouraged to do all the good they could do, if restraining hands were

not laid upon them to repress their zeal, there would be a hundred workers for Christ where now there is one." ***Desire of Ages,*** pages 250, 251.

Oh, Laodicean (SDA) Christian brother or sister, how long will you remain silent? What further evidence or proof do you want that God is calling you to take your stand in this last hour of earth's history? What further calamities and disasters must happen in the world before you will arouse from your lethargic stupor and accept your **God** given calling? How much more moral degradation must take place within the organized church before you stand up and speak out? All around you are the lost and dying, even within the church. Yes, especially within the church. These are precious souls Jesus bled and died for. They need to hear the truth that God loves them. They need to hear that Christ will never condemn them or expose them or hurt them in any way, for He is a life God, not a death God. And so I appeal to your love for the Saviour to take up the banner of truth while we have a little time left and begin to witness for Jesus. God will richly bless you as you do this.

Many potential workers for Christ shrink from Christ's urgent call to witness for fear of ridicule, censure, or rebuke from the "leaders" of the church or even their own family. I think most of God's servants have faced the reality of this fear. When I was a student colporteur working my way through Walla Walla College during the late 50s, I read a text that gave me a lot of courage. Here is what it says, ***"The Lord God hath given me the tongue of the learned, that I should know how to speak a word in season to him that is weary; he wakeneth morning by morning, he wakeneth mine ear to hear as the learned. The Lord God hath opened mine ear, and I was not rebellious, neither turned away back. I gave my back to the smiters, and my cheeks to them that plucked off the hair; I hid not my face from shame and spitting.*** (This is a prophecy of what would happen to Jesus. But notice the courageous tone of the next verse.) ***For the Lord***

God will help me; therefore shall I not be confounded; therefore have I set my face like a flint, and I know that I shall not be ashamed." Isaiah 50:4-7.

God's army is being formed today. The Lord predicted this event about 800 years before Jesus was born. *"And it shall come to pass afterward, that I will pour out My spirit upon all flesh; and your sons and your daughters shall prophesy, your old men shall dream dreams, your young men shall see visions; and also upon the servants and upon the handmaids in those days will I pour out My spirit."* Joel 2:28, 29. This had a partial fulfillment on the day of Pentecost. Peter quoted this very prophecy in Acts 2:14-21. But verses 19, 20, indicate that it is going to happen again in our day, for it speaks of "wonders in the heavens and in the earth, blood, and fire, and pillars of smoke." The Hebrew word translated as "pillars" (Timarah) can also be translated "a column, i.e. cloud:—pillar." See Strong's 8490 or 8558, where the Hebrew word is "Tamar," which is from an unused root meaning "to be erect; a palm tree." Now, if you put all this together in a modern context, it doesn't take a genius to figure out that an atomic explosion is a "wonder in the heavens" which causes "blood" to be shed and mushrooms into a column of smoke that looks just like an erect palm tree.

And yet it is at this very time that the greatest apostasy in the history of the church is taking place. Yes, God's professed church has turned away from her divine leader and united with the world. As early as 1868, Sister White wrote about this departure. *"Like ancient Israel the church has dishonored her God by departing from the light, neglecting her duties, and abusing her high and exalted privilege of being peculiar and holy in character. Her members have violated their covenant to live for God and Him only. They have joined with the selfish and world-loving. Pride, the love of pleasure, and sin have been cherished, and Christ has departed. His Spirit has been quenched in the church. Satan works side by side with professed Christians; yet they are so destitute of spiritual discernment that they do not detect him."* 2T 441, 442. Chapter 12 of this book is entitled, *"The Two Lords."* Although I have touched on this concept of the *"Two Lords"* all through our study of God's character, I will give special emphasis on this subject in Chapter 12. There is probably more opposition to this topic than any other subject I have ever presented. Why? Please notice the last part of the above quote from 2T 441, 442, again: *"Satan works side by side with professed Christians; YET THEY ARE SO DESTITUTE OF SPIRITUAL DISCERNMENT THAT THEY DO NOT DETECT HIM."* Friend of mine, this is absolutely and positively frightening. Like ancient Israel, we are not even able to recognize or detect our enemy. We even think he (Satan) is Christ.

Most sincere SDAs have little or no understanding of the true import of these EGW quotations. Why? Because Laodiceans are "blind." They cannot see. Yet, EGW clearly states: *"There is great similarity between our history and that of the children of Israel."* 4T 27. And in 5T 160 she says, *"Satan's snares are laid for us as verily as they were laid for the children of Israel just prior to their entrance into the land of Canaan. We are repeating the history of that people."*

Just last week, I received the following letter from a self-supporting minister who claims to be a "Watchman" on the walls of Zion to wake up God's sleeping and dying people in Laodicea. He writes, *"I still cannot agree with you on your theory that 'God Does Not Kill' . . . I believe the third paragraph in PP 148 will torpedo your whole theory. Brother Clute, I believe that you should make a complete turnabout and try and undo the damage you have done with this false theory. Prior to this, you were used of the Lord in many ways. Now I feel another influence is using you which will certainly bring catastrophe in the judgment."* Then he added a

P.S. that I should send in my "confession" of repentance, for leading so many people astray, to a certain publication, so the people could see that I had properly repented.

The overwhelming majority of SDA ministers and laymen within the SDA church would agree with this brother. But thank God for the few who are able to "see" the truth about our wonderful, heavenly Father . . . that He does not destroy. Here is a letter from such a person: *"Hi, Friends, Enclosed is tithe to help in your ministry. Words are inadequate to express the blessings, joy and peace, etc., your ministry has brought to us. Thank you so much for being God's instrument. Praise God for you folks. I wish God's richest blessings and may we meet again someday soon. Love to you all."* I receive quite a few letters of this nature from people who accept the character message and they tell me how it has changed their lives. Here is an example: *"Your ministry has blessed me so much. I thank God there are people who do His work. Words escape me when I think of the miracle He's done in my life. Changing my cold, stony, heart into one that can love and have compassion for others. I had lost all my feelings before I met Jesus. I had pushed feelings away so long that they were almost non-existent. No love—no hate. Nothing. I cannot tell you how empty life is that way. Jesus touched my heart and let me feel His love for me. I have joy in my life. I have found Him whom my soul loveth. I can't find words. He has given me hope where there was none. The God who created worlds and stars and everything else loves me. He cries when I feel pain. It hurts Him so bad(ly) when I ignore Him or forget about Him. He loves me. OUR GOD IS SO GREAT!"* I have received scores, perhaps hundreds of letters like this last one from people after they read *Into The Father's Heart.* They just cannot describe how much love they have for their Lord and their God. That makes all the rejection bearable.

Now, I would like to share with you my answer to the brother's objection regarding EGW's statement about Abraham and Isaac, concerning the third paragraph on page 148 of PP. I will only quote part of it here since I have shared some of it in other places in this book. *"Sister White tells us that Satan tried to talk Abraham out of making the sacrifice. Of course, Satan would do everything he could to make Abraham disobey God and thus win his argument that God was not justified in blessing Abraham with the seed (Isaac) who would produce the Messiah. Satan was the murderer who suggested the idea in the first place so naturally he would bend all of his energies to prove his case against God.[1] When we look at it from this angle we are able to see how God has been on trial before the universe for centuries. It is our privilege today to prove God is justified in His faith in us in this last hour of earth's history. In His mighty power we will triumph over sin, the flesh and the devil and thus glorify His name or His true character before the universe."* You will find a much more detailed explanation in Chapter 29 "Who Told Abraham to Offer Up Isaac as a Sacrifice?" on page 373 and on to 377 of IFH. EGW says, *"What is temptation? It is the means by which those who claim to be the children of God are tested and tried."* March 12, 1912. 1 BC 1094. You will find the entire quotation later on in this book. See pages 254, 255.

As you continue to study the character of God more and more light will shine into your soul as you discover the true beauty of Jesus, the beautiful ROSE OF SHARON, and LILY OF THE VALLEY. "Song of Solomon," 2:1, 2. Our whole life is a continual search for the true God. *"By night on my bed I sought Him whom my soul loveth; I sought*

---

[1]The story of Satan provoking or tempting David to number Israel, so he would have a legal right to destroy Israel, is a parallel for this experience. See II Sam. 24:1-15; I Chron. 21:1.

Him, but I found Him not." S. of S. 3:1. Ministers or "Watchmen" may put you down and discourage and hinder you in your search. *"The watchmen that went about the city found me, they smote me, they wounded me; the keepers of the walls took away my veil from me."* S. of S. 5:7. Here is Matthew Henry's comments on this verse: *"They took her for a lewd woman and beat her accordingly. Disconsolate saints are taken for sinners and are censured and reproached as such."* This has been the experience of God's people throughout history. *"Yea, and all that will live godly in Christ Jesus shall suffer persecution. But evil men and seducers shall wax worse and worse, deceiving, and being deceived."* 2 Tim. 3:12, 13.

My understanding of the character of God message has been progressive. My first book, *A Character Like His to Survive the Time of Trouble,* was published in May, 1977. Although that was the true title of the book, I had the following question printed on the front cover, *"Does God Kill People?"* I had about 500 of the very first edition printed and sent it to as many ministers, teachers and serious Bible students as I could think of, which was about 60 in number. I only received a few replies and most of them were negative. But I continued to research and study. In my heart I knew this was the truth about God. A few months later, in early 1978, I came out with a much better edition of that first book and had about 2,000 printed. More and more laymen began reading the book and supporting the concept. Before 1978 was half over, I had begun my second book, *The Final Absolute-Ultimate Truth About God.* The purpose of this second book was to explain why God always takes the responsibility or blame for everything that happens in the world, whether it is good or bad. See Isa. 45:7. My third manuscript was entitled, *Into The Father's Heart,* which became the title for the 412 page paperback I finally published in June, 1982, with no EGW quotations. I combined this third 100 page manuscript with the first two and came up with the paperback for non-SDAs.

We had moved to West Virginia from Oregon in November, 1979, and I had no plans to ever return to Oregon. I was sure that I would be preaching exclusively to non-SDAs. I had no plans to ever write anymore messages to critical, hard-hearted, legalistic, lost, Laodicean SDAs, for I believed they had closed their own probation. But the Lord let me know that He never gives up trying to save anyone, and I had a lot of preaching to do among SDAs yet. So, in May of 1983, the Lord told me it was time for the character message to go with great power on the west coast and I was to move back to Oregon. There are many facets and details I don't have the time or space to explain here, but in August, 1983, we returned to Oregon.

In my correspondence and personal contact with SDAs I have found the number one problem they face in correctly understanding the character message (that God does not destroy) is a basic lack of comprehension of how to harmonize the Bible within itself and secondly how to harmonize the Bible with the writings of Sr. White, (referred to in this book as EGW). Some SDAs use EGW quotes, exclusively, completely ignoring the Bible. This is unfortunate, for I believe the Bible can be understood and harmonized within itself as well as with the writings of EGW. The problem is not so much a question of evidence as it is one of understanding how to evaluate the evidence. For example, the evolutionist can assemble the data he has found and/or selected and convince himself and others that this world has evolved over millions of years. But, a creationist can take some of the same information and data (perhaps adding facts he feels the evolutionist has left out), and convince himself and sometimes many others that God did indeed create this world in six days and rested on the Sabbath.

In my study and research through the years, I have come to the conclusion that there are basically two kinds of evidence. The first kind is known as "coercive" evidence. Coercive evidence forces one to only one conclusion. For example, if someone asked you how much 56 + 47 is, you would add these two numbers together and come up with the sum or answer of 103. You are forced to the conclusion that 103 is the only possible answer to the question. Basic math is a very exact science that leaves no guess work. Another example would be the question, *"Is it day or night?* Just look outside and you will know the answer. When it is light outside, it is daytime; and when it is dark, it is night. But most questions in our world are not so easy to answer, which brings us to the second kind of evidence we must consider. It is known as "persuasive" evidence.

A good example of persuasive evidence is when a person is accused of a crime based upon circumstantial evidence. There is no clear-cut proof that the man or woman committed the crime, so "persuasive" evidence must be assembled to build a case before you can go into court and win a conviction. The jury is not going to be convinced unless the evidence is persuasive enough. They must be convinced beyond a "reasonable doubt."

So a team of experts go to work gathering up fingerprints, blood type samples, and hair follicles. The person's whereabouts at the time of the crime must be established. Interviews with people who heard or saw something can be introduced as evidence. Snapshots, tire tracks, video tapes, and any number of other kinds of evidence may be brought into the case in order to solve the crime.

This is persuasive evidence. And this is the kind of evidence that we assemble in a Bible study to prove that God exists or that the Bible is true. This is also the kind of evidence we put together from various books of the Bible to prove that the 7th day Sabbath is still God's holy day of rest and worship. Furthermore, this is the kind of evidence we gather together to convince people that a person does not go to heaven or hell at death nor is there an "inner soul" that is released at death. We establish these doctrines by meticulously comparing Scripture with Scripture. We use careful and correct hermeneutics (science of interpretation) or exegesis as we explain texts such as "he shall be tormented with fire and brimstone," or "the smoke of their torment ascendeth up forever and ever." Rev. 14:11.

Now we realize the Bible often uses or employs symbolic language and idiomatic expressions common to the times in which the people lived to whom the writer was addressing his message. So, we cannot say, "we must take the Bible just as it reads" or "literally," as some people insist. Even today we have idioms unique to our times and culture. For example, we say, "That deal really burned me up." The person making such a statement does not intend for his hearers to believe that he actually caught on fire and was literally burned. No. He is simply using an English idiomatic expression which even the dictionary acknowledges, as meaning, "to feel strong passion; he was burning with anger." *The American College Dictionary.*

Even the Bible uses "burning" as a symbolism. Jesus characterized John the Baptist as a "burning and a shining light" John 5:35. You can look up many other examples yourself. See Gen. 44:18, Jer. 20:9, and Prov. 26:23. And in Prov. 25:22, we see that "fire" is used to describe acts of kindness we should do to our enemies. We also use the expression, "It will only take a second," or "I'll be there in a minute." No rational person takes these expressions literally. A minute could end up being five to ten minutes or more. The speaker doesn't mean he will be there in one or sixty seconds, but that he will be there very shortly or in a few minutes.

Now, when we come to the character message in the Bible the hardest point for most Bible believing Christians to comprehend is that God is continually taking the responsibility or blame for every event that occurs, good or bad. The SDA Bible Commentary confirms this truth in its comments on 2 Sam. 24:1. *"And again the anger of the Lord was kindled against Israel, and he moved David*

against them to say, Go, number Israel and Judah."
Now here is the comment: *"In the verse under consideration, we have another instance where God is said to
do that which He does not prevent* (See Patriarchs and
Prophets 728, 739). It was actually Satan who instigated
the pride and ambition that led Israel's king to promote
procedures to increase the size of his army for the purpose of
extending the boundaries of Israel by new military conquests (see PP 747)." Cf. I Chron. 21:1. Another scripture
which puts the blame on God is I Kings 22:22. Again, the
commentary gives a most insightful comment. *"In the
Bible, God is frequently presented as doing that which
He does not restrain."* SDA Bible Comm. Vol. 2, page 840.

So, we see that most generally, the prophets of the
Bible wrote up death as something God could cause or
inflict upon anyone who disobeyed Him and they often
wrote it down that way. This was their concept of God. The
flood record is an example. Moses wrote, *"And the Lord
said, I will destroy man whom I have created from the
face of the earth."* Gen. 6:7. And true to His loving character, God here takes the blame; and through His prophet,
claims to be doing that which He is only permitting. I have
written extensively about the flood in my book, *Into the
Father's Heart,* pages 184 to 192. I have also explained
why the Bible writers held God responsible and why God
was willing to take the blame, almost every time. See pages
79, 83, 175, 184, and 254. I say, "almost," for there are key
texts throughout the Bible that clue the careful reader in
that God is not the destroyer. One example is found in Exodus 12:23 where God says, *"the Lord will pass over the
door and will not suffer the destroyer to come in unto
your houses to smite you."* Exodus 12:23. Now, the
Hebrew word for "pass over" is *pacach,* Strong's Concordance, 6452. It is from a prim. root; to hop, i.e. (fig.) skip
over (or spare); by impl. to hesitate;" Now, the word hesitate
could also mean "pause." And that is how one paraphrase

has it. Notice: "he will pass over that home and not permit the Destroyer to enter and kill your firstborn." And then the footnote says, Or, "He will pause at the door of that home and not permit the Destroyer to enter." LB. And Paul says in Hebrews 11:28 that Moses, *"Through faith he (Moses) kept the passover, and the sprinkling of blood, lest he that destroyed the firstborn should touch them." Paul did not put the blame on God in this verse. Furthermore, in I Cor. 10:10, Paul tells us that Israel of old was "destroyed of the destroyer," when they disobeyed.*

Another instance in the Bible where it is clear that Satan is the destroyer is in the book of Job. Just read the first two chapters and you will clearly see that God allowed Satan to destroy Job's children and property the first time around. The second time around Satan was allowed to afflict Job's body with boils. The only person the devil was not allowed to afflict physically was Job's wife. But he was able to use her to speak discouraging words to him. Read it yourself.

One of the best proofs in the Bible that God takes the blame for what man and the devil do is found in the first chapters of Exodus where God tells Moses that he is going to "harden" Pharaoh's heart. Exodus 4:21. It is so obvious that God did not harden his heart. He hardened his own heart.

When we go to the writings of Ellen G. White for information about this story we find some very clear statements to the effect that God was not the one who was hardening Pharaoh's heart. Listen: *"There was no exercise of supernatural power to harden the heart of the king . . . Every display of infinite power rejected by him, rendered him the more determined in his rebellion. The seeds of rebellion that he sowed when he rejected the first miracle, produced their harvest. As he continued to venture on in his own course, going from one degree of stubbornness to another, his heart became more and more hardened, until he was called to look upon the cold, dead faces of the first-born." Patriarchs and Prophets,* Page 268.

Notice, beloved, that Sister White says it was "his own course" that hardened his heart, not our wonderful Heavenly Father. Ezekiel 3:7 tells us why people will not hearken or listen to God. *"But the house of Israel will not hearken unto thee; for they will not hearken unto me; for all the house of Israel are impudent and hardhearted."* Paul tells us in Hebrews 3:8-19 that it is a hardened heart that leads to unbelief. And we see that Israel failed to "enter in because of unbelief." Only people with "soft" hearts will enter heaven.

And yet in Romans 9:18 Paul says, *"Therefore hath He mercy on whom He will have mercy, and whom he will He hardeneth."* So even Paul put the blame on God sometimes. And you will even find that Sr. White sometimes wrote that God destroys people and is justified in so doing. Speaking of the antediluvians, EGW says, *"If they did not cease to pollute with their sins the world and its treasures, He would blot them from His creation."* PP 92. This was written in 1858. All through her writings you will find such statements. But you will also find other statements that clearly teach God does not destroy. Does this prove that EGW contradicted herself? No, it doesn't, for you will find a wonderful progression in EGW's pen through the years. She grew in her understanding of many subjects just like we all do. This is called "progressive revelation."

The Bible says *"The path of the just is as the shining light, that shineth more and more unto the perfect day."* Prov. 4:18. Daniel's understanding of God increased as he grew older. Why even the holy angels of God have grown in their understanding of the plan of salvation which they "desire to look into." I Peter 1:12. *"Not until the death of Christ was the character of Satan clearly revealed to the angels or to the unfallen worlds." Desire of Ages,* Page 758.

By 1900 EGW's understanding of God's true character had developed to the point that she could make such a bold statement as found in *"Christ Object Lessons,"* page 84. *"God destroys no man."* But she had actually made a similar statement as early as 1881 which we find in Test. Vol. 5, page 120. The messaged is entitled *"Warnings and Reproofs"* and begins on page 114. On page 119, she begins using Pharaoh as an example of how a soul is destroyed by hardening his heart. And finally, on page 120, she makes these incredible statements. *"This case* (Pharaoh's experience) *is placed on record for our benefit. Just what took place in Pharaoh's heart will take place in every soul that neglects to cherish the light and walk promptly in its rays. God destroys no one. The sinner destroys himself by his own impenitence. When a person once neglects to heed the invitations, reproofs, and warnings of the Spirit of God, his conscience becomes seared, and the next time he is admonished, it will be more difficult to yield obedience than before; and thus, with every repetition. Conscience is the VOICE OF GOD, heard amid the conflict of human passions; when it is resisted, the Spirit of God is grieved."*

Before I continue quoting EGW, I want to point out that the language here in Vol. 5 is very similar to what she wrote in *Christ's Object Lessons,* pages 84, 85 in 1900. At least, that is when the book was copyrighted. The example of Pharaoh is even used. But I want to go back now to 5T 120 and quote you one of the best statements EGW ever made on this subject of how the soul is destroyed.

"We want all to understand how the soul is destroyed. It is not that God sends out a decree that man shall not be saved. He does not throw a darkness before the eyes which cannot be penetrated. But man at first resists a motion of the Spirit of God, and having once resisted, it is less difficult to do so the second time, less the third, and far less the fourth. Then comes

the harvest to be reaped from the seed of unbelief and resistence. Oh what a harvest of sinful indulgences is preparing for the sickle!" 5T 120.

Now notice, beloved, that EGW never intimated, let alone stated, that God had anything at all to do with the hardening of Pharaoh's heart. Nor did she even indict God with the death of the first-born. In fact, let me share with you what she says about the death of the first-born in *Patriarchs and Prophets.*

"The father and priest of the household sprinkled the blood upon the doorpost, and joined his family within the dwelling. In haste and silence the paschal lamb was eaten. In awe, the people prayed and watched, the heart of the eldest born, from the strong man down to the little child, throbbing with indefinable dread. Fathers and mothers clasping in their arms their loved first-born as they thought of the fearful stroke that was to fall that night. But no dwelling of Israel was visited by the death-dealing angel. The sign of blood—the sign of a Saviour's protection—was on their doors, and the destroyer entered not." PP 279. For a more detailed Biblical explanation, see *Into the Father's Heart,* page 69. In all the writings of EGW you will never find her identifying Christ as the DESTROYER.

Now, you will find EGW indicating that the wicked were destroyed by the "wrath of God" in Moses' day. For example, she says, *"Moses lingered, in this fearful crisis manifesting the true shepherd's interest for the flock of his care. He pleaded that the wrath of God might not utterly destroy the people of His choice. By his intercession, he stayed the arm of vengeance, that a full end might not be made of disobedient, rebellious Israel."* *Patriarchs and Prophets,* page 402.

We know that God's wrath is not when He becomes angry and strikes the sinner dead with a bolt of lightning. No, that is not it at all. Paul tells us that Jesus came to save us from the "wrath." Romans 5:9. And in Romans 1:16, 17,

God, through His servant Paul, tells us that the Gospel proclaims the "righteousness of God." Why then should we think that our wonderful and righteous God is responsible for the "wrath?" God does not use wrath and punishment to bring us to repentance. No. These are not His methods. The Bible clearly tells us that God brings us to repentance by a revelation of His "goodness," Rom. 2:4. And His goodness is one of the attributes of His character, glory, that God revealed to Moses, Exodus 34:6.

When Moses interceded for the people in Exodus 32:7-14, 30-35, he became a type of Christ. This most unique and unusual story has led some people to conclude that Moses loved the people more than Christ and His Father did. They conclude from these verses that if Moses had not begged and pleaded for God to spare Israel and even thrown his own life into the balance by asking God to blot his own name out too, if He could not forgive them . . . that if Moses had not made this eloquently moving and most magnificent appeal, God would have immediately destroyed His very own people who had sinned against Him. You may be surprised to know that I don't believe this to be the case at all. But I will explain that later. We have some important principles to understand before we can deal with that.

The Prophet Jeremiah predicted that we would understand *the anger of the Lord* in the last days. In fact, He says, *"The anger of the Lord shall not return, until he have executed, and till he have performed the thoughts of his heart: in the latter days ye shall consider it perfectly."* Jer. 23:19, 20; cf. 30:23, 24.

The thoughts and intents of God's heart are being understood more everyday in these last days. Through His own Spirit God is revealing to His chosen people *"the revelation of His character of love,"* COL 415, SR 379. This is *"the last message of mercy."* The only safe place in this world is inside of His great and loving heart. Truly it is a *sanctuary* or haven of rest. A safe place to hide. See Psalm 91:1, 2; Isa. 26:20.

If God does destroy, then the danger of His destructive nature should be more clearly and fully explained. If God's wrath is when He smashes, slashes and burns all of those terribly wicked people up with His heavenly fireworks, then this should be more fully and clearly explained to the people so they will know what to expect and how to avoid it. And if God did indeed kill the first-born and harden Pharaoh's heart then surely such an important and vital truth should have been clearly stated by EGW in order to warn us today that just as God killed them back there, so also He will just as surely destroy us today if we do not obey. Is this not a logical conclusion to draw?

But instead of teaching such a doctrine, EGW actually tells us the exact opposite, as we notice again.

"This case (Pharaoh's) *is placed on record for our benefit. Just what took place in Pharaoh's heart will take place in every soul that neglects to cherish the light and walk promptly in its rays. GOD DESTROYS NO ONE. The sinner destroys himself by his own impenitence."* Testimonies, Vol. 5, page 120. Written 1881, 1882.

The next question sincere SDA believers are going to ask is: "Why then does EGW state in a few other places that God did destroy?" We all know there are statements to this effect, so we will not try and quote several to prove our point. It will only be necessary now to explain why such statements exist in her writings.

As we compare the attitude and writings of the Old Testament prophets to the attitude and words of Jesus we can clearly see that very few, if any, of these O.T. prophets really understood God's true character of love as revealed in the life, words, and acts of Jesus. Even Elijah, one of the greatest of the prophets took a sword and killed the prophets of Baal. I Kings 18:19, 40. But this destructive act must have been motivated by fear rather than love, for it is contrary to the very principles of the law of God which clearly states, *"Thou shalt not kill."* Exodus 20:13. There is no record of any kind that Christ commanded Elijah to kill these priests of Baal. And the fact that Elijah fled for his life when Jezebel passed the death decree against him shows he did not have the faith and peace of Christ's love abiding in his heart, for *"perfect love casts out fear."* I John 4:18.

But our loving God did not abandon Elijah. Nor will He ever leave any of us. He has promised to be with us to the very end. Matt. 28:19,20. Instead, God gave His fearful prophet a revelation of Himself on Mt. Horeb (Sinai) where Elijah had gone to hide from Jezebel. Elijah had run, jogged, and walked over 200 miles of rough terrain to escape from Jezebel's wrath. He was no doubt exhausted and probably embarassed and humbled from the whole experience. After all, God had not commanded Elijah to run away from Jezebel. If he had the true "fear of God" in his heart, he would not have been afraid and run away. The kind of fear God wants us to have is a holy reverence for His loving power and protective majesty. When we have this kind of fear in our hearts and minds the carnal fear of Satan and of man will not be able to affect us at all. But now in his humiliation, Elijah is about to receive a new revelation about the God he has been trying so fervently to serve even to the point of taking up a sword and killing the enemies of God. Jesus had rebuked Peter for doing this in the garden of Gethsamene on the night of His arrest. John 18:10, 11. Christ had also rebuked the angry and revengeful spirit of James and John when they requested permission to bring fire down upon the Samaritans. *"But He turned, and rebuked them, and said. Ye know not what manner of spirit ye are of. For the son of man is not come to destroy men's lives, but to save them."* Luke 9:54, 55. The comments of EGW are very significant on this experience. Notice; *"They* (James and John) *thought that a grievous wrong had been done Him, and seeing Mount Carmel in the distance, where Elijah had slain false prophets, they said, 'Wilt Thou that we command fire to come down from heaven, and consume them, even as Elias (Elijah) did?"* They were surprised to see that Jesus was pained by their words, and still more surprised as His rebuke fell on their ears, *'Ye know not what manner of spirit ye are of. For the Son of man is not come to destroy men's lives, but to save them.'* And He went to another village. It is no part of Christ's mission to compel men to receive Him. It is Satan, and men actuated by his spirit, that seek to compel the conscience. Under a pretense of zeal for righteousness, men who are confederate with evil angels bring suffering upon their fellow men, in order to convert them to their ideas of religion; but Christ is ever showing mercy, ever seeking to win by the revealing of His love. He can admit no rival in the soul, nor accept of partial service; but He desires only voluntary service, the willing surrender of the heart under the constraint of love. *There can be no more conclusive evidence that we possess the spirit of Satan than the disposition to hurt and destroy those who do not appreciate our work, or who act contrary to our ideas."* DA 487.

Every time I read that statement I am reminded of how God revealed so many things to Sister White in vision. How else could she speak of Jesus being "pained" by the words of James and John? In other words, she observed Christ's body language which would include the expression on His face . . . a "pained" expression. And while we are on this subject, please check these points out too.

On page 726 of *"Desire of Ages,"* she tells us the exact location of Christ in relationship to Pilate. *"Standing behind Pilate, in view of all in the court, Christ heard the abuse."* Then on page 727 she tells us that Pilate had a desire to know the truth, but did not wait for an answer. She says his mind was confused. Only God can read the mind, so how did EGW know what was in Pilate's mind unless God revealed this "secret" (Amos 3:7) to her. On page 730, she says that Christ's silence "irritated" Herod, which indicates that she was shown this scene too and not only observed the body language, but the facial expressions, of both Pilate and

Herod. At the bottom of page 730, she further states that "Herod's face grew dark with passion." And on page 732, she describes the dream of Pilate's wife in detail and says that when Pilate read the note from his wife, his face "grew pale." Yes, EGW wrote just like an eye witness, as if she were on the actual scene of action when it happened. God gave her these dreams and visions so she would be able to write all of these things. This is the way the Lord inspired many of the prophets in the O.T., such as Ezekiel and Daniel. And yet, we know that these prophets did not know all the details about everything. In fact, Daniel asked a question that was not even answered. Dan. 12:8-10. He was told "Go your way, Daniel, for the words are shut up and sealed until the time of the end." If wise old Daniel didn't know everything why should we expect EGW to know everything? Did the Holy Spirit stop inspiring us when she died in 1915? Did the "Spirit of Prophecy" die with her? What is the "Spirit of Prophecy" anyway? Is it not the Holy Spirit's leading and guiding God's church? And so long as God has a church upon earth He will have the "Spirit of Prophecy" in it. In fact, Joel 2:28 promises that God is going to pour out His Spirit in a much greater measure in the final days of this earth's history. *"And it shall come to pass afterward, that I will pour out my spirit upon all flesh; and your sons and your daughters shall prophesy, your old men shall dream dreams, your young men shall see visions;"* And the next verse says that even the *"servants and handmaids"* will receive this wonderful "Gift or Spirit of Prophecy." EGW says, *"The great work of the gospel is not to close with less manifestation of the power of God than marked its opening."* GC 611, 612. Now, let's get back to Elijah.

As we have already stated, Elijah's fear of Jezebel had revealed his weakness to his own heart. Now he was humbled so God could give him a new vision and concept of His kindness, love and goodness; something Elijah had not preached about very much. Elijah had left his post of duty without God's permission or command. So the Lord asked

Elijah, *"What are you doing here, Elijah?"* That was a most searching question and it no doubt made Elijah realize how weak he really was. Elijah had thought only of his own welfare and safety. Why wasn't he back in Israel instructing and encouraging those who had so recently turned away from Baal worship to serve the true and living God? But he only tried to justify himself just like we often do today. *"I have worked very hard for the Lord God of the heavens; but the people of Israel have broken their covenant with you and torn down your altars and killed your prophets, and only I am left; and now they are trying to kill me, too."* I Kings 19:10. LB. Paul commented on Elijah's experience with much insight. He realized Elijah had a wrong attitude and spirit toward Israel at this time. *"No, God has not discarded his own people whom he chose from the very beginning.* Do you remember what the Scriptures say about this? Elijah, the prophet, was complaining to God about the Jews, telling God how they had killed the prophets and torn down God's altars; Elijah claimed that he was the only one left in all the land who still loved God, and now they were trying to kill him too. And do you remember how God replied?

"God said, *'No, you are not the only one left. I have seven thousand others besides you who still love me and have not bowed down to idols!"* Rom. 11:2-4 LB. The KJV says that Elijah made "intercession to God against Israel." Is it possible that we have done that ourselves today? Let each of us pray earnestly about it.

I like the SDA Bible Commentary's comment on this experience. *"God's children must realize that in the great controversy Satan's way must not be entirely hedged, lest the warfare be unfairly waged, and Satan be able to say that he was not given a fair opportunity. To be irritated and ill at ease because things are not according to his liking is hardly the wise attitude for a saint or the proper attitude for a prophet. What Elijah needed most was a new vision of God's strength and his own weakness. It was at Sinai that the Lord had passed by before Moses and revealed Himself as 'the Lord God, merciful and gracious, long suffering, and abundant in goodness and truth' (Ex. 34:6). Here, too, Elijah was to receive a new conception of God."* Next, the wind, earthquake and fire are described. Then the SDA B.C. makes this most significant statement. *"What he needed to learn was that, might and moving though these forces be, they do not themselves portray a true picture of the Spirit of God. It is not always the man who creates the greatest commotion who accomplishes the most for God."* SDA B.C. on I Kings 19:10, 11, Vol. 2, page 824.

For the record here, I would like to state that I do not believe that God brought or caused the wind, earthquake or fire. I have written about this in great depth in my book, *Into The Father's Heart,* in chapter 18, "Elijah, God's Character and Mount Sinai." Page 153. But my main point in referring to Elijah is to show how God was trying to help him grow in his spiritual understanding of the character of the God he was so zealously serving, for Elijah was serving the Lord with more zeal than knowledge. And this seems to be very characteristic of many today who are preaching in the spirit and power of Elijah more than the Spirit and power of Jesus.

There were other prophets who either did not like God's loving character of mercy instead of justice or did not understand it. Jonah seems to have understood it but didn't agree with it or like it either. He had no compassion for the people of Nineveh and was very angry at God for not destroying the whole place. Listen: *"This change of plans made Jonah very angry. He complained to the Lord about it: 'This is exactly what I thought you'd do, Lord, when I was there in my own country and you first told me to come here. That's why I ran away to Tarshish. For I knew you were a gracious God, merciful, slow to get angry, and full of kindness; I knew how easily you could cancel your plans for destroying these people. Please kill me, Lord; I'd rather be dead than alive (when nothing I told them happens).' Then the Lord said, 'Is it right to be angry about this?' So Jonah went out and sat sulking on the east side of the city."* Jonah 4:1-5. LB.

I think many preachers and laymen are just like Jonah. They demand that God kill. They don't want to preach unless they can preach this kind of God. They search the Scriptures for evidence that God is a killer and destroyer. Of course, since God is continually taking the blame, it isn't too hard to build their case. But they are surface readers, for the Bible clearly teaches that although God takes the blame, He is not doing it directly. I Chron. 10:4, 5, 13, 14; Isa. 53:10. To preach a "killer God" gives many preachers a very great feeling of power and authority over people. That is the kind of God Jonah wanted and I think Elijah also had some of this wrong concept although he truly loved God and was very zealous for His glory. But so were James and John when they wanted to destroy the Samaritans. Luke 9:51-56. KJV.

But the Old Testament prophets did not understand that God was "harmless," Heb. 7:26. So, what does this tell us about God? It tells us that He was forced to use prophets who had a limited, and sometimes confused and distorted, concept about Him and how He actually deals with the human race and the sin problem. Jonah is an example. His idea of solving the sin problem was just to "burn up the trash," and be done with it. Even John the Baptist did not understand the nature of Christ's kingdom or true mission of the Messiah. After John the Baptist was put in prison he expected Jesus to deliver him and set up the kingdom (DA 215-216). He sent a message to Christ, *"Now when John had heard in the prison the works of Christ, he sent two of his disciples, and said unto Him, Art thou he that should come, or do we look for another?"* Matt. 11:2, 3. *"It was keenly bitter and disappointing to human nature. If John, the faithful forerunner, failed to discern Christ's mission, what could be expected from the self-seeking multitude?"* DA 217. EGW continues on and tells how Jesus did not answer them at once

but just continued His work of healing the blind and dis-
eased of all classes who were coming to Him. John's disciples watched all day. Finally, Jesus told John's disciples to
*"Go and shew John again those things which ye do
hear and see."* Matt. 11:4. *"The disciples bore the message and it was enough. John recalled the prophecy
concerning the Messiah, 'The Lord hath anointed Me
to preach good tidings unto the meek; He hath sent Me
to bind up the brokenhearted, to proclaim liberty to
the captives, and the opening of the prison to them
that are bound; to proclaim the acceptable year of the
Lord.' "* Isa. 61:1, 2. And this is the same work we are to do
today. Now, notice what EGW says regarding Elijah's new
vision of God's character when the Lord allowed the wind,
earthquake, and fire to pass by before him. I discuss this in
chapter 18 of IFH, entitled, *Elijah, God's Character and
Mount Sinai,* pages 153-162.

*"The works of Christ not only declared Him to be
the Messiah, but showed in what manner His kingdom
was to be established. To John was opened the same
truth that had come to Elijah in the desert, when 'a
great and strong wind rent the mountains, and brake
in pieces the rocks before the Lord; but the Lord was
not in the wind; and after the wind an earthquake; but
the Lord was not in the earthquake; and after that a
fire; but the Lord was not in the fire.' I Kings 19:11, 12.
So Jesus was to do His work, not with the clash of
arms and the overturning of thrones and kingdoms,
but through speaking to the hearts of men by a life of
mercy and self-sacrifice."* DA 217.

Yet, in spite of these misconceptions, God was often
able to get these same prophets to tell of His goodness and
love. But, as we have just seen in this last EGW quote, it
was not until Christ came that we received a perfectly clear
picture of what God is really like. Isaiah had given a little
preview of what the work and nature of the Messiah and
His true character would be in Isaiah 53. It has been called
the 5th gospel.

Each generation since Christ (except during the dark

ages) has learned a little more about God's true character. It is my personal conviction that Ellen G. White revealed more about the character of God than any other writer since the Apostle Paul. And yet she herself grew in her understanding. We have already noted her writings about a destructive God in *Patriarchs and Prophets*. That was in 1858. But by 1900 her understanding of God's character had developed to the point that God was able to reveal through her pen that He was not a destroyer. *"God destroys no man."* COL 84. Of course, I am sure we could find a statement somewhere in her writings after 1900 where she again says God destroys, etc. So, how do you explain that? Does this mean EGW was contradicting herself? No, I don't think so.

First of all, Jesus' life—His acts and words are the highest authority. All of the prophetic writings, including EGW's must be interpreted through His eyes and made to harmonize with everything He did and said.

Once you realize that God always takes the blame for everything that happens, then the statements of the prophets take on new meaning. Even though they really thought God directly destroyed (although He only allowed it) the Holy Spirit was able to use the prophetic writings in every age by assuming the responsibility and blame for everything that happened. Christ's life and teachings and especially His week of passion and death unravel the entire story so we can see the whole truth and not just fragments of it.

Although EGW understood more than any prophet before her, she still did not know everything. She, herself, stated that *"more light"* would be given. Her writings reflect a partial understanding of the character of God. EGW statements that say *"God does not destroy,"* are in harmony with the life and death of Jesus. These statements reflect her correct understanding of God's character, which was progressive, but I do not believe ever developed into a complete understanding of God's true character of love. Those EGW statements that seem to say and in some cases do say *"God does destroy,"* no matter when they were written, reflect her *imperfect* understanding of God's character, especially in her earlier writings. Her later writings reflect a more *complete*, yet still *imperfect* and *partial* understanding, of the character of God. It is now given to this final generation to not only *completely* and *perfectly* understand the character of God, but actually live it as Christ did. This is what God has been waiting for. May the Lord give each of us more love, patience, and insight as we continue to study with much prayer and soul searching on this important matter.

WHO TEMPTED ABRAHAM IN GENESIS 22?

See pages 254, 337.

CHAPTER 9

HOW IS THE SOUL DESTROYED

"True religion brings man into harmony with the laws of God, physical, mental and moral. It teaches self-control, serenity, temperance. Religion ennobles the mind, refines the taste, and sanctifies the judgment. *It makes the soul a partaker of the purity of heaven.* Faith in God's love and overruling providence lightens the burdens of anxiety and care. It fills the heart with joy and contentment in the highest or the lowliest lot. Religion tends directly to promote health, to lengthen life, and to heighten our enjoyment of all its blessings. It opens to the soul a never-failing fountain of happiness. Would that all who have not chosen Christ might realize that He has something vastly better to offer them than they are seeking for themselves. *Man is doing the greatest injury and injustice to his own soul when he thinks and acts contrary to the will of God.* No real joy can be found in the path forbidden by Him who knows what is best, and who plans for the good of His creatures. The path of transgression leads to misery and destruction; but wisdom's 'ways are ways of pleasantness, and all her paths are peace.' " Proverbs 3:17.

"PATRIARCHS AND PROPHETS"—P. 600—
By Ellen G. White

"The deception of sin had reached its height. All the agencies for depraving the souls of men had been put in operation. The Son of God, looking upon the world, beheld suffering and misery. With pity He saw how men had become victims of satanic cruelty. He looked with compassion upon those who were being corrupted, murdered, and lost. They had chosen a ruler who chained them to his car as captives. Bewildered and deceived, they were moving on in gloomy procession toward eternal ruin,—to death in which is no hope of life, toward night to which comes no morning. Satanic agencies were incorporated with men. The bodies of human beings, made for the dwelling place of God, had become the habitation of demons. The senses, the nerves, the passions, the organs of men, were worked by supernatural agencies in the indulgence of the vilest lust. The very stamp of demons was impressed upon the countenances of men. Human faces reflected the expression of the legions of evil with which they were possessed. Such was the prospect upon which the world's Redeemer looked. What a spectacle for infinite Purity to behold!"

"DESIRE OF AGES"—P. 36—
By Ellen G. White

"Whenever men reject the Saviour's invitation, they are yielding themselves to Satan ... the only safeguard against his power is found in the presence of Jesus. Before men and angels Satan has been revealed as man's enemy and destroyer; Christ, as man's friend and deliverer. His Spirit will develop in man all that will ennoble the character and dignify the nature." *"Desire of Ages,"* page 341.

"We all want to understand how the soul is destroyed. It is not that God sends out a decree that man shall not be saved." 5T 120 *"God destroys no man."* COL 84.

"Satan uses men and women as agents to solicit to sin and make it attractive. These agents he faithfully educates to so disguise sin that he can more success-fully destroy souls and rob Christ of His glory . . . In the Scriptures he is called a destroyer, an accuser of the brethren, a deceiver, a liar, a tormentor, and a mur-derer." 5T 137. There is nowhere in EGW's writings in which she identifies or designates Christ as a destroyer or any of the other above descriptions.

If we can determine how a soul is destroyed, I also believe we can discover who destroys the soul. Many teach that God destroys the sinner. But let us see just what the Bible and EGW say about it. First of all, God claims He owns all souls. He says, *"Behold, all souls are mine; as the soul of the father, so also the soul of the son is mine. The soul that sinneth, it shall die."* Ezek. 18:4. Now, this text does not say God destroys the sinner. It sim-ply states that the soul (person) who sins will die. But all have sinned. Rom. 3:23. But all who repent and accept Christ will be saved from the second death. John 11:26; Rev. 20:6.

We also read in Rom. 6:23 that *"the wages of sin is death."* Notice it does not say that the wages of sin is God destroying those who sin. Most people believe in an immor-tal soul, everlasting hellfire and that Christ nailed the Ten Commandments to the cross and changed the day of wor-ship to Sunday. They arrive at these wrong conclusions in exactly the same manner as those who teach that God destroys. How very sad!

The concept that God kills is based on the same exact false interpretation of Scripture that is used to prove that God burns the sinner in hell forever. For example, those who teach hellfire will quote Psalm 9:17, *"The wicked shall be*

turned into hell." Next, they will quote *"and he shall be
tormented with fire and brimstone in the presence of
the holy angels ... and the smoke of their torment
ascendeth up for ever and ever. And they have no rest
day nor night ..."* Rev. 14:10, 11. Then to cinch their case
they will refer to the parable of the "Rich Man and Lazarus." Luke 16:19-31. *"And in hell he lift up his eyes,
being in torments."* Christ had a very good reason for telling this story. But sometimes we hear people say they wish
Jesus had not told it for it confuses those who wish to
believe a lie. But that is not true. In fact, this parable can
be used to prove the very opposite. In other words, this parable can be used to prove that God is not burning sinners in
hell forever. And the same exact principle holds true for the
texts people quote to try and prove God destroys. These
same texts, rightly understood, will prove that God does not
destroy. The same holds true with EGW.

It is obvious to even a superficial secular reader that
some Hebrew expressions are not to be taken literally.
Examples of this are "forever and ever," and "eternal fire."
Jude 7. An even greater mystery to explain is that the soul
is not an immortal essence, life force, mind or entity that is
released at death. Absolutely not! A soul can die, for a soul
is a person. Once you understand the truth that "the dead
are asleep and know nothing," Eccles. 9:5, 6, 10; John 11:11-
15, then texts like Gen. 35:18, *"As her soul was in
departing, (for she died)"* Gen. 35:18, will not make you
doubt the concept. Neither will Job 14:22, *"But his flesh
upon him shall have pain, and his soul within him
shall mourn."* We don't let these odd and irregular texts
bother us for we know the principle of God's word that
teaches—*"Man does not have an immortal soul within
him nor can men think, speak or appear to us for they
are 'asleep.' "* We simply know the Hebrew word translated
"soul" ("Nephesh" Strong's 5315) can also be rendered
"person, breathing creature or life." We also know the book
of Job and Psalms often use Hebrew poetic expressions

which assign thoughts, feelings, and words to inanimate objects such as trees and rocks which would explain Job 14:22. So, it is obvious to most rational thinking SDAs that you cannot prove or disprove any doctrine of the Bible by simply quoting isolated texts. In order to arrive at truth you must build your case upon solid Bible principles that are in harmony with the life of Jesus and the law of God, which is unchangeable. This is known as correct Bible Hermeneutics [interpretation or exegesis].

The Bible clearly tells us Jesus is "harmless," Heb. 7:26 and the Ten Commandment law is God's eternal, unchangeable law. The sixth commandment says, *"Thou shalt not kill or murder."* The Hebrew word translated "kill" is interchangeable with the word "murder" and has the same basic meaning. Psalm 19:7 states that God's law is perfect. And Matt. 5:48 commands us to be perfect like our heavenly Father who loves His enemies by giving them both sunshine and rain. And Jesus said He is just like His Father. He kept the law on earth just as He had kept it in heaven from all eternity past. He is not a lawbreaker as Lucifer (Satan) has charged. Therefore, He does not break the sixth commandment, *"Thou shalt not kill."* Jesus never changes. Heb. 13:8; Mal. 3:6.

I often receive letters from sincere SDAs who try and quote Ellen G. White to prove that "God does destroy." Well, I am going to quote EGW quite a bit and I think if you will really be honest with yourself you will see that she clearly taught that God does not destroy.

"How was it in the case of Pharaoh? The statement in Holy writ is that God hardened his heart, and at every repetition of light in the manifestation of God's power the statement is repeated. Every time he refused to submit to God's will his heart became harder and less impressible by the Spirit of God." 5T 119. Now what does she say hardened his heart? It was his refusal to "submit to God's will," and his rejection of light.

It is very clear that God did not harden his (Pharaoh's) heart. Now we have established a most important and key principle. And that principle is this: WHATEVER GOD PERMITS, HE CLAIMS TO BE DOING HIMSELF. A perfect example of this is the death of King Saul. I Chron. 10:4, 5 clearly tell us that Saul fell on his sword and committed suicide. But verses 13 and 14 say God killed him. Isaiah 53:10 says that God "bruised" His own Son, yet the N.T. clearly shows us that Satan led a mob of priests and rabble to bruise him. And Ezek. 20:25 tells us God "gave them also statutes that were not good . . ." But it was Satan who hardened their hearts so much that they demanded divorce laws, flesh food, and a king to rule over them, as well as a carnal desire to kill their enemies with the sword, which Jesus soundly rebuked in the garden when Peter cut off Malchus' ear. John 18:10, 11. Yet God took the blame for all of their actions and eventually sent His only Son in a body of flesh so they could nail Him to a cross. And what was His response? He forgave them for this terrible crime. Never once did He lash out or retaliate against them for God is a loving and forgiving God. And He never changes, Heb. 13:8.

Now, let us continue our EGW quote about Pharaoh. *"By rejecting the first light and every following ray, Pharaoh went from one degree of hardness of heart to another, until the cold, dead forms of the first-born only checked his unbelief and obstinancy for a moment."* 5T 119, 120. It is the rejection of light that hardens the heart. But God takes the blame for it since He sends the light. Let us continue on. *"This case is placed on record for our benefit. Just what took place in Pharaoh's heart will take place in every soul that neglects to cherish the light and walk promptly in its rays. GOD DESTROYS NO ONE. THE SINNER DESTROYS HIMSELF BY HIS OWN IMPENITENCE."* 5T 120. Cf. COL 84 and GC 35, 36. Please listen my friend. God is even now shining His precious light down upon your soul. Will you receive it or will you reject it? No one will force you. Only you can choose to accept or reject this light. God will not force you for He never uses force.

Now let's find out how EGW defined "wrath" and "divine pleasure." Let's read it ourselves from the pen of EGW. Notice how she consistently shows that God's wrath is when He is forced to withdraw from the sinner. WRATH IS SEPARATION FROM GOD. Notice now her description of Christ as He enters the Garden of Gethsemane. *"Throughout His life on earth He had walked in the light of God's presence ... But now He seemed to be shut out from the light of God's sustaining presence. Now He was numbered with the transgressors ... Feeling how terrible is the WRATH OF GOD against transgression, He exclaims, 'My soul is exceeding sorrowful, even unto death.'" Desire of Ages*, page 685. (Emphasis mine.)

Now, please notice again, *"The sins of men weighed heavily upon Christ, and the sense of God's wrath against sin was crushing out His life ... Behold Him contemplating the price to be paid for the human soul. In His agony, He clings to the cold ground, as if to prevent Himself from being DRAWN FARTHER FROM GOD." Desire of Ages*, page 687. Notice how EGW again defined "God's wrath," as equivalent to "being drawn farther from God." Cf. DA 743, 753; 5BC 1103; EW 150 (SR 43); DA 642 and GC 20, 21.

Next we have an EGW quote which equates the word "gulf" with the "wrath of God." And even in the first sentence, you will again see the word "separation" which she once more parallels with God's wrath. *"He felt that by sin He was being separated from His Father. The gulf was so broad, so black, so deep, that His Spirit shuddered before it. This agony He must not exert His Divine power to escape. As man He must suffer the consequences of man's sin. As man He must endure the wrath of God against transgression." DA 686.* It is most interesting here that EGW uses the word "gulf" for this is exactly the word Luke 16:26 uses in the parable of the rich man and Lazarus. *"And beside all this, between us and you there is a great gulf fixed; so that they which would pass from hence to you cannot; neither can they pass to us, that would come from thence."* This is the only place in the Bible in which "gulf" is used. It is from the Greek word, "Chasma," (Strong's 5490) which can be translated as a chasm or vacancy. The TEV renders it "deep pit." The New American Bible translates it "A GREAT ABYSS." EGW also employs the word "gulf" in 7BC 941 and SC 20 to show that Christ has "spanned the gulf" sin has made or caused.

Now we will let EGW define *"Divine Justice."* Remember now that she is continuing on in her explanation of what the "Wrath of God" means to Jesus as He absorbs all of our sins into Himself. In harmony with her previous definitions you will again see her define *"Divine Justice"* as "separation" not God killing. Notice: *"As the substitute and surety for sinful man, Christ was suffering under 'Divine Justice.' He saw what justice meant. Hitherto He had been as an intercessor for others; now He longed to have an intercessor for Himself. As Christ felt His unity with the Father broken up, He feared that in His human nature He would be unable to endure the coming conflict with the powers of darkness ... with the issues of the conflict before Him, Christ's soul was filled with dread of separation from God ... the sins of men weighed heavily upon Christ, and the sense of God's wrath against sin was crushing out His life."* DA 686, 687.

Please notice carefully, friend of mine, that it was not the Father who was hurting or "crushing out" the life of His son. No. It was the "separation" from God which EGW defines as "God's wrath" as we have noted all along. And look again at the phrase "Divine Justice." God's justice is not when He destroys the sinner, for we know EGW distinctly tells us that God does not "execute" the sinner. GC 35 and 36. And DA 62 reveals how God satisfied His "justice" and yet remained merciful. *"God did not change His law, but He SACRIFICED HIMSELF, in Christ, for man's redemption. 'God was in Christ, reconciling the world unto Himself.' 2 Cor. 5:19."*

Now let us learn how EGW defines "the penalty of sin." "He (Christ) might say, Let the transgressor receive the penalty of his sin, and I will go back to My Father . . . He sees that the transgressors of the law, if left to themselves, must perish." DA 690. And after He sweat blood and prayed three times, the angel came to strengthen him to drink the cup of iniquity. Notice that EGW now states that it was actually in Gethsemane that He *"had borne that which no human being could ever bear; for He had tasted the sufferings of death for every man."* DA 694. And what was that death? It was separation from His father.

Let us now define "Divine Displeasure." In 5T 207 EGW begins talking about the "Seal of God." Then on 209 she says, *"The crisis is fast approaching. The rapidly swelling figures show that the time for God's visitation has come. Although loath to punish, nevertheless, He will punish, and that speedily."* 5T 209. But how does God "punish?" EGW tells us in PP 728. *"When parents or rulers neglect the duty of punishing iniquity, God Himself will take the case in hand. His restraining power will be in a measure removed from the agencies of evil, so that a train of circumstances will arise which will punish sin with sin."* This agrees with Jer. 2:19 which reads: *"Thine own wickedness shall correct thee, and thy backslidings shall reprove thee."* But notice the last part of the verse shows that it was the people who left God. *"It is an evil thing and bitter, that thou has forsaken the Lord thy God, and that my fear is not in thee, saith the Lord of Hosts."* Jer. 2:19. Christ did not leave them. They forced Him, by their own choice, to "let them go" and suffer the consequences of their own wicked ways. This is what the Bible calls *"THE WRATH OF GOD."*

Now, let's come back to 5T 210. EGW quotes Ezek. 9 and says, *"in the time when His wrath shall go forth in Judgments . . ."* Now we have a definition for "judgments." It is not when God gets angry and condemns and executes the sinner with some disaster or calamity, for EGW clearly says God does not execute the sinner, GC 36. Instead, the word "Judgment" means to decide. A "judgment" is simply a decision. And when the sinner refuses to listen to God and continues on in his disobedience, God must let him go. And that is exactly what God "decides" to do. Listen: *"How shall I give thee up, Ephraim? How shall I deliver thee, Israel? . . . I will not execute the fierceness of mine anger, I will not return to destroy Ephraim; for I am God, and not man."* Hosea 11:8, 9.

Now we come to 5T 211. *"The class who do not feel grieved over their own spiritual declension, nor mourn over the sins of others will be LEFT without the seal of God. The Lord commissions His messengers, the men with slaughtering weapons in their hands."* God is here pictured as commanding or giving a *"commission"* to His *"messengers,"* to go forth and slaughter the wicked. Psalm 17:13 shows that *"the wicked, which is thy (God's) sword,"* are designated in the Bible as God's *"messengers"* who are commissioned to destroy. Whatever God allows, He claims to be doing directly. Then she quotes Ezek. 9:5, 6. Now, the very next sentence will tell you how these "ancient men" who "had stood as guardians of the spiritual interests of the people, had betrayed their trust." Here is the very first sentence of this paragraph which proves that these men are not destroyed by the Lord or even by a direct decree of God, but die because God's presence has been pushed out of their lives by their very own disobedience. They have forfeited God's protection and His "divine presence and glory have departed." 8T 250; 2T 441, 442. *"Here we see that the church—the Lord's Sanctuary—*

was the first to feel the stroke of the wrath of God." 5T 211. And remember that "God's Wrath" is not when He gets mad and destroys, but when His presence is removed by the choice of man. That is, they choose Satan and his ways in place of God and His ways, and Satan and his angels come in and take over and destruction follows. Psalm 78:49.

As you continue reading you will discover that EGW uses the word "vengeance," in a parallel sense equating it with the "wrath of God" as she describes the utter destruction that befalls them. *"These dumb dogs that would not bark are the ones who feel the just vengeance of an offended God. Men, maidens, and little children all perish together. The abominations for which the faithful ones were sighing and crying were all that could be discerned by finite eyes, but by far the worst sins, those which provoked the jealousy of the pure and holy god, were unrevealed."* 5T 211. Remember that Sister White wrote these testimonies to the SDA leadership of the future when apostasy would reach it zenith. Would you not say that time is near at hand, if it has not already arrived? Now, notice in this next quote how she explains what it means to have punishment or wrath without any mercy. *"No superiority of rank, dignity, or worldly wisdom, no position in sacred office, will preserve men from sacrificing principle when left to their own deceitful hearts. Those who have been regarded as worthy and righteous prove to be ringleaders in apostasy and examples in indifference and in the abuse of God's mercies. Their wicked course He will tolerate no longer, AND IN HIS WRATH He deals with them without mercy."* 5T 212. (emphasis mine). **Remember that "wrath" means that God's protection has been forced out by man's choice and God honors that choice by removing His restraints.**

The very next sentence will again define what "wrath" means according to Ellen G. White. It is so clear to anyone who wishes to believe. Notice: "It is

with reluctance that the Lord withdraws His presence from those who have been blessed with great light and who have felt the power of the word in ministering to others. They were once His faithful servants, favored with His presence and guidance; BUT THEY DEPARTED FROM HIM AND LED OTHERS INTO ERROR, AND THEREFORE ARE BROUGHT UNDER THE DIVINE DISPLEASURE." 5T 212, Cf. Job 22:15-18.

These leaders are following their own counsel and thus destroying themselves and others. **"Destroy thou them, O God; Let them fall by their own counsels."** Psalm 5:10. And the NIV says, **"Declare them guilty, O God! Let their intrigues be their downfall."** Psalm 5:10. For further proof let us read from "Testimonies to Ministers." **"We hear now of earthquakes in divers places, of fires, of tempests, of disasters by sea and land, of pestilence, of famine. What weight do these signs have upon you? This is only the beginning of what shall be. The description of the day of God is given through John by the Revelator. The cry of the terror-stricken myriads has fallen upon the ear of John. 'The great day of His wrath is come; and who shall be able to stand?'"** TM 446.

I think we have seen overwhelming evidence that when Sister White uses the description "God's Wrath" or "The Wrath of God" that she is describing what happens as a result of God taking His hands off—His restraint being removed, not God Himself destroying. Here now is a statement from her that proves Sodom and Gomorrah were destroyed by the "Wrath of God." Listen: **"The same angel who visited Sodom is sounding the note of warning, 'Escape for thy life.' The bottles of GOD'S WRATH cannot be poured out to destroy the wicked and their words until all the people of God have been judged, and the cases of the living as well as the dead decided."** TM 446. You should also read Deut. 29:23, where God uses the very words, "Anger" and "Wrath" to describe the "overthrow" of Sodom and Gomorrah. Now, let's go to **Patriarchs and Prophets,** for further proof. *"The inhabitants of Sodom had passed the limits of Divine forbearance—'the hidden boundary between God's patience and HIS WRATH.' The fires of vengeance were about to be kindled in the vale of Siddim."* PP 159. Please notice the parallel between the words "wrath" and "vengeance." Psalm 78:49 is very clear. "He cast upon them the fierceness of His anger, wrath, and indignation, and trouble, by sending EVIL ANGELS among them." And notice that this whole chapter is an explanation of how Satan brought the ten plagues upon Egypt. Also note that from verses 46-48 the expression "He gave up," is used the same as in Paul's writings in Romans 1:18, 24, 26, 28. God's wrath is when He is forced to "give up and give people over to themselves and Satan."

In almost all of EGW's writings where she talks about God punishing or destroying you will almost always be able to find the word "wrath" or a synonym of wrath as we find in Psalm 78:49. But I have seen one or two isolated statements that are used to prove that she believed God had a right to destroy wicked nations if He wanted to do so. Here is such a statement: *"Our gracious God still bears long with the impenitent. He gives them light from heaven, that they may understand the holiness of His character and the justice of His requirements. He calls them to repentance, and assures them of His willingness to forgive. But if they continue to reject His mercy, the mandate goes forth devoting them to destruction (ST Aug. 24, 1882)"* 7BC 1016. Several similar statements might be quoted, but this is sufficient to show that although EGW understood more than anyone else about God's character and end time events, she didn't know everything. She predicted more light would be given and that the final message to go to the world would be a revelation of His character of love. COL 415; TM 50. But even in this last statement we can see that the sentence, "the mandate goes forth devoting them to destruction," can be seen to simply be God's hand being removed. And the "mandate," simply is God commanding the Holy Angels to no longer restrain the wicked. This time is very near. Here is a quote which confirms that there will come a time when God will no longer be able to restrain Satan from doing all He wants to do to this earth. *"When the angel of mercy folds her wings and departs, Satan will do the evil deeds He has long wished to do. Storm and tempest, war and bloodshed— In these things he delights, and thus he gathers in his harvest. And so completely will men be deceived by him that they will declare that these calamities are the result of the desecration of the first day of the week. From the pulpits of the popular churches will be heard the statement that the world is being punished because Sunday is not honored as it should be. And it will require no great stretch of imagination for men to believe this. RH 9-17-1901."*

The destruction of Jerusalem is a symbol of the destruction that is about to engulf the whole world. Notice the causes for the destruction of Jerusalem in 70 A.D. Who really destroyed the city? And who is really destroying the world today? *"The Jews had forged their own fetters; they had filled for themselves the cup of vengeance. In the utter destruction that befell them as a nation, and in all the woes that followed them in their dispersion, they were but reaping the harvest which their own hands had sown. Says the prophet: 'O Israel, thou hast destroyed thyself.' 'For thou has fallen by thine iniquity.' Hosea 13:9; 14:1. Their sufferings are often represented as a punishment visited upon them by the direct decree of God. IT IS THUS THAT THE GREAT DECEIVER SEEKS TO CONCEAL HIS OWN WORK. By stubborn rejection of divine love and mercy, the Jews had caused the protection of God to be withdrawn from them, and Satan was permitted to rule them according to His will. The horrible cruelties enacted in the destruction of Jerusalem are a demonstration of Satan's vindictive power over those who yield to his control. We cannot know how much we owe to Christ for the peace and protection which we enjoy. It is the restraining power of God that prevents mankind from passing fully under the control of Satan. The disobedient and unthankful have great reason for gratitude for God's mercy and longsuffering in holding in check the cruel, malignant power of the evil one. But when men pass the limits of divine forebearance, that restraint is removed. GOD DOES NOT STAND TOWARD THE SINNER AS AN EXECUTIONER OF THE SENTENCE AGAINST TRANSGRESSION; but He leaves the rejecters of His mercy to themselves, to reap that which they have sown. Every ray of light rejected, every warning despised or unheeded, every passion indulged, every transgression of the law of God is a seed sown which yields its unfailing harvest. The Spirit of God, persistently resisted, is at last withdrawn from the sinner, and then there is left no power to control the evil passions of the soul, and no protection from the malice and enmity of Satan. The destruction of Jerusalem is a fearful and solemn warning to all who are trifling with the offers of divine grace and resisting the pleadings of divine mercy. Never was there given a more decisive testimony to God's hatred of sin and to the certain punishment that will fall upon the guilty." Great Controversy,* pg. 35, 36.

Beloved, please notice how EGW defines the word "punishment" in the above paragraph. Notice that she says, "The Spirit of God, persistently resisted, is at last withdrawn from the sinner" . . . this then is the "certain punishment that will fall upon the guilty." I think she makes it very clear that "God's punishment" is when the "Spirit of God is at last withdrawn from the sinner." This is what she is teaching, but most SDAs think she says the very opposite. That is, they think that EGW and the Bible teach that

God's punishment is when God directly attacks the sinner with some form of calamity or disease such as cancer. When men lose their job or get injured on the job, etc. they say that God has "judged" such a person. Even insurance companies call some calamities of nature "acts of God." Dear friend, if this really were the truth about God why is it that we are not able to find a statement in the writings of Sister White where she says, "Be sure to make it very clear to those SDAs in the endtime that they better obey or God is going to directly kill and destroy them." But instead of this we have seen very clearly in our study that the Lord, through EGW, has told us the very opposite. We read this in her quote from 5T 119, 120. *"GOD DESTROYS NO ONE. THE SINNER DESTROYS HIMSELF BY HIS OWN IMPENITENCE." And Paul agrees with this idea in Rom. 2:4 by stating that it is not by threats of destruction but by the "goodness of God" that He "leads" us "to repentance." What a wonderful and beautiful thing to say about our Eternal and ever-loving God. May God richly bless you as you continue to search and study further into this vital and elevating topic.*

CHAPTER 10

GOD'S TRUE TEMPLE

Throughout history, men have erected temples and buildings in which people could come and worship God. But why have they done this when the Word of God plainly declares "God that made the world and all things therein, seeing that He is Lord of heaven and earth, dwelleth not in temples made with hands." Acts 17:24. Paul must have learned this from the disciples who no doubt told him what Jesus had taught them, for the temple in Jerusalem was about the most sacred thing a person could mention in the Jewish religion. But Jesus bluntly told them their whole religion was nothing but devotion to Satan! *"Ye are of your father the devil, and the lusts of your father ye will do."* John 8:44. How could it be that the Jews had gone so far astray? The basic answer is that Satan had tricked them into thinking that you could create a building, say some prayers, go through some rituals and ceremonies and God would do whatever you asked him. You just needed to know the right words and the correct formula in order to get results. What they were saying in essence was, *"God can be bought with a price. If you are willing to pay His price you can get Him to give you about anything you want."* And so the temple came to be a place where people came to "strike a bargain with God." The greater the value of your sacrifice, the better chance you would have at getting God to give you what you wanted or needed. But the whole thing was a horrible and terrible lie Satan had perfected to slander God's name and keep the people in bondage and fear so they could never know the truth about God.

The following statements will give you a little insight into how bad it really had become just prior to Jesus' first Advent. *"The fullness of time had come. Humanity, becoming more degraded through ages of transgression, called for the coming of the Redeemer. Satan had been working to make the gulf deep and impassable between earth and heaven. By his falsehoods he had emboldened men in sin. It was his purpose to wear out the forbearance of God, and to extinguish His love for man, so that He would abandon the world to satanic jurisdiction. Satan was seeking to shut out from men a knowledge of God, to turn their attention from the temple of God, and to establish his own kingdom. His strife for supremacy had seemed to be almost wholly successful. It is true that in every generation God had His agencies. Even among the heathen there were men through whom Christ was working to uplift the people from their sin and degradation. The dark shadow that Satan had cast over the world grew deeper and deeper.*

"Through heathenism, Satan had for ages turned men away from God; but he won his great triumph in perverting the faith of Israel. By contemplating and worshipping their own conceptions, the heathen had lost a knowledge of God, and had become more and more corrupt. SO IT WAS WITH ISRAEL. The principle that man can save himself by his own works lay at the foundation of every heathen religion; it had now become the principle of the Jewish religion. Satan had implanted this principle. Wherever it is held, men have no barrier against sin.

"The people whom God had called to be the pillar and ground of the truth had become representatives of Satan. They were doing the work that he desired them to do, taking a course to misrepresent the character of God, and cause the world to look upon Him as a tyrant. The very priests who ministered in the temple

had lost sight of the significance of the service they performed. They had ceased to look beyond the symbol to the thing signified. In presenting the sacrificial offerings they were as actors in a play. The ordinances which God Himself had appointed (God's permissive will, not His perfect will, MFC) *were made the means of blinding the mind and hardening the heart. God could do no more for man through these channels. The whole system must be swept away."* DA 35, 36.

As we have already seen in all of our study and investigation of the animal sacrifice system, and all the ceremonial services that went with it, God was only permitting them to do what their own carnal nature desired to do, not what He really wanted them to do. He never spoke or commanded the sacrificial system at Mt. Sinai. *"For I spake not unto your fathers, nor commanded them in the day that I brought them out of the land of Egypt, concerning burnt offerings or sacrifices."* Jer. 7:22. Some translations or paraphrases may change the meaning of this text, but it harmonizes with Christ's teachings and Deut. 5:22. I have found that the "Authorized King James Version," is the most reliable and accurate.

There is one point I wish to make extremely clear at this time in our study of the temple or sanctuary service the Lord gave to Moses while he was up on Mt. Sinai. I have never taught that Satan was the author of the sanctuary service in the desert. What I have taught, and still believe, is that Christ gave Moses the instructions for the sanctuary service in order to make the slaughter of innocent animals mean something. In other words, it was His permissive will, not his perfect will. It was really only an accommodation or arrangement He made with Israel to regulate and control an evil system that He knew could only lead them into greater darkness, sin and degradation. And this is exactly what happened, for the animal sacrifice system was only one step away from sacrificing their very own children which they did quite often. But when you realize the evil

principle upon which the whole animal sacrifice system was
based, it is easy to see how they could be led by Satan to
reason that "if sacrificing an animal will bring God's blessings upon me then think how much more I will be blessed if
I sacrifice my very own flesh and blood." And so it went.
God's name had been slandered and debased and degraded.
It was time for the whole carnal and Satanic system to be
swept away. And this is just what the life and death of Jesus
accomplished.

When the foundation for Solomon's temple was laid
about 535 BC, the older priests and *"Levites and chief of
the fathers, who were ancient men, that had seen the
first house ... wept with a loud voice."* Ezra 3:12. All
they could see and understand was what their carnal eyes
saw. But it took the spiritual eyesight of the prophet Haggai
to predict that *"The glory* (character) *of this latter house
shall be greater than of the former, saith the Lord of
Hosts."* Haggai 2:9. "The second temple was honored, not
with the cloud of Jehovah's glory, but with the presence of
the One in whom dwelt 'all the fullness of the Godhead
bodily'—God Himself 'manifest in the flesh.' Col 2:9; I Tim.
3:16. In being honored with the personal presence of Christ
during His earthly ministry, and in this alone, did the second temple exceed the first in glory. The 'Desire of all
nations' had indeed come to His temple, when the Man of
Nazareth taught and healed in the sacred courts." PK 597.

Now I am going to quote for you the clearest statement
I can find in all of EGW's writings about God's "true" temple and how the temple the Jews erected was only a symbol
or "object lesson," and never intended to be the real thing,
but to only point to what God wanted to accomplish in the
human heart. Listen: *"In the cleansing of the temple,
Jesus was announcing His mission as the Messiah and
entering upon His work. That temple,* (Solomon's temple) *erected for the abode of the divine Presence, was
designed to be an object lesson for Israel and the
world. From eternal ages it was God's purpose that*

every created being, from the bright and holy seraph to man, should be a temple for the indwelling of the Creator. Because of sin, humanity ceased to be a temple for God. (Satan took over, MFC) *Darkened and defiled by evil, the heart of man no longer revealed the glory of the Divine One. But by the incarnation of the Son of God, the purpose of Heaven is fulfilled. God dwells in humanity, and through saving grace the heart of man becomes again His temple. God designed that the temple at Jerusalem should be a continual witness to the high destiny open to every soul. But the Jews had not understood the significance of the building they regarded with so much pride. They did not yield themselves as holy temples for the Divine spirit.* (God's perfect will, MFC) *The courts of the temple at Jerusalem, filled with the tumult of unholy traffic, represented all too truly the temple of the heart, defiled by the presence of sensual passion and unholy thoughts. In cleansing the temple from the world's buyers and sellers, Jesus announced His mission to cleanse the heart from the defilement of sin,—from the earthly desires, the selfish lusts, the evil habits, that corrupt the soul. Mal. 3:1-3 quoted."* DA 161.

In Chapter 12, you will find a talk about the wilderness tabernacle and how it was representative of the culture and times in which Israel lived. Dr. John Wood states that Solomon's temple was filled with pagan symbolism neatly adapted to the worship of Jehovah or Yaweh. He also said that when we look at the codes of "Lipid Ishtar" (not positive if that is the correct spelling) or Ed Lil Eshnoona (I am spelling these phonetically) or lesser codes or the well-known codes of Hammurabi—all predating the exodus by centuries—absolutely provable, he said. He said you could see the same basic division of law in the Mosaic code. And even though the Mosaic code was basically man's idea of how to live, it was more humane than the codes of the heathen even though it reflected many of their lives, customs, content, format, structure, and philosophy, reflective of the times and culture of the other nations. You must remember that the 12 tribes of Israel were fresh out of slavery and were not only an ignorant and impatient people but subject to anger and violence if they didn't get what they wanted when they wanted it. The mixed multitude (mainly Egyptians) were also continually causing problems. Dr. Wood also pointed out that hundreds of the Mosaic laws have their exact counterparts in pagan codes, some pre-dating the Exodus by centuries. Many are not merely parallels but word for word quotes. Once again, of course, the total effect of the society ordered by the living God was very different from that of the pagan codes even though there was sameness and difference, uniqueness and extensive borrowing. He also pointed out that the scapegoat scenario was of pagan origin. It was an old pagan ritual—laying on of hands on the two goats . . . this came right into the midst of Israel's cultic celebration about Jehovah's (Yaweh) atonement and came right into the center of Adventist's interests in the middle of the 19th century. He also said that Isa. 14 and Ezek. 28 both use the very names of the Canaanite myth of the revolt in the heavens. The inspired writers borrowed extensively from these and cleaned up the story, giving its true background, setting, meaning, and final fulfillment.

A few weeks ago, I received a sermon transcript written by John K. Testerman, M. D., Ph. D. It is titled, "Kohlberg's Stages of Moral Development: Implications for Theology." I will now begin quoting from this paper. *"Kohlberg's concept of the stages of moral development is rich with implications for Adventist education and theology and is especially relevant to the current discussions among SDAs regarding the gospel and the atonement. Lawrence Kohlberg is a moral philosopher and student of child development who is the director of Harvard's Center for Moral Education. He is interested in how children develop a sense of right, wrong, and justice. Kohlberg observed that growing children advance through up to six definite stages of moral development in a manner similar to their progression through Piaget's well-known stages of cognitive development. Through his observations and testing of children and adults, Kohlberg was able to demonstrate that an individual progresses consecutively from one stage to the next in an invariant sequence, not skipping any level or going back to any previous level. These are stages of thought process, not content, implying qualitatively different modes of thinking or of solving the same problem at different ages."*

He goes on to explain the various stages which begin with two stages of premoral or preconventional thought in which behavior is motivated mainly by anticipation of pleasure or pain. Stage One is the punishment and obedience stage where there is no real sense of right or wrong or an obligation to rules. The person is sort of on the level of a toddler whom you warn, "Don't touch or Mommy will spank." The avoidance of physical punishment and hope for reward are the motivators of behavior at this stage. The physical consequences of an action determine its goodness or badness, regardless of the human meaning or value of these consequences. Justice is obedience of the weak to the strong and punishment by the strong of those who deviate. Punishment is vengeance, an automatic response of physical retaliation. Dr. Testerman explains that this is all on "Stage One" and points out that it is tragic if this stage lasts into adulthood. He also points out that many atrocities have been carried out during times of war by the soldiers who were simply "carrying out orders." It was as if they had no mind of their own with which to make moral judgments regarding right or wrong.

Now let's go to Stage 2. This is the "reciprocity stage," in which human relationships are on the basis of "You scratch my back, and I'll scratch yours . . . . But if you hurt me, I will get even and hurt you back." The idea of equal sharing and fairness appears at this stage. People are valued on the basis of their usefulness rather on their intrinsic (actual or real) value. At this level "justice" is defined as an equal exchange of favors or blows. This is why the conflict in the Middle East (Arabs vs. Jews, etc.) cannot be resolved. Each side believes it is their "moral" duty to "avenge" each attack or strike—"eye for an eye and tooth for a tooth." Jesus repudiated this law in Matt. 5:38-42, showing them that a much higher law was the one on which He lived.

At Stage 3, there is uncritical acceptance of the rules and standards of one's group. At Stage 3, appears the ability to put oneself in another's shoes and imagine how he feels about things. Approval can be earned by appearing "respectable" and "nice." Teenagers may be heard to justify their actions with "But, Mom, everybody is doing it." "Sin" is defined as breaking the rules of the social order you live in. Retribution, however, is collective; individual vengeance is not allowed. Forgiveness is better than revenge. Rules, regulations and their violation by punishment is mainly to keep people in line—to discourage people from breaking the law—a deterrent. The failure to punish is unfair and leads people to think, "If he can get away with it, why can't I?"

Stage 4 is the law-and-order stage of adult morality in which the major values are respect for properly constituted authority, conformity to fixed rules, laws and a responsibility toward the welfare of others in society. The social and institutional order is defended for its own sake; justice is a matter of relation between individual and a system of laws. Correct behavior is rewarded and lawbreaking is punished. Injustice is failing to reward work or punish demerit. At Stage 4, "justice" normally refers to criminal or forensic justice . . . the criminal must "pay his debt to society." Legal consistency and precedent must be maintained.

When we come to levels 5 and 6, we have arrived at a stage of moral development of behavior in which a person's action or actions in a given situation will now be based upon a logical application of universal, abstract and moral principles. According to statistics, only about 25 percent of adults ever reach stages 5 or 6, or the "principled" level where moral action is not defined by referring to a checklist of rules and regulations. But before we further explore levels 5 and 6, it should be noted that there is a transitional stage called 4 1/2 between the conventional stages and the post-conventional levels 5 and 6. Some college age students who have come to view conventional morality as relative and arbitrary, but have not yet discovered universal ethical principles, may drop into a hedonistic ethic of "do your own thing." We can look back at the 1960s and see how this level of thinking and morality manifested itself in such fads as long hair, "hippie" dress and disrespect for accepted authority figures which were especially infuriating to the Stage 4 mentality, and were calculated to be so by the counterculture groups of that era. But now let's go on to Stage 5 which is the level of "prior rights and social contract."

Stage 5 emphasizes the freedom of individual's rights. Society should not infringe upon anyone's rights unless that person is infringing upon someone else's freedom. The framers of the Constitution and Bill of Rights were obviously operating at this level. Retributive justice and retaliation seen at Stages 1 and 2, and the concept of collective retribution (punishment) at Stages 3 and 4 do not exist at Stage 5. The statement "Justice demands punishment," which is an axiomatic (obvious) truism to the Stage 4 mind, is just so much nonsense at Stage 5. Retributive (repayment) punishment is considered neither reasonable nor just because it does not promote nor protect the rights and welfare of individuals. Only legal sanctions that fulfill that purpose are imposed—protection of future victims, deterrence, and rehabilitation. Justice at Stage 5 is distributive justice—carried out with equality, proportionate to circumstances and the need of the situation and times. *Let the punishment fit the crime.*

Stage 6 is based on recognition of universal ethical principles such as having respect for the equal and innate worth of human beings as objects of worth in and of themselves. When God speaks at Stage 6, what He says is right because it is truth; it isn't truth just because He said it, but because we know it is true ourselves. Kohlberg discovered that in our society only about 10 percent of the adult population ever reach Stage 6 in their moral development. About 90 percent remain at Stage 4 or lower, and a very small percent fall between 4 and 5. Each society or culture is different. Primitive tribal societies, for example, operate most of the time at Stages 1 or 2, and may undergo moral stage evolution. It was found that people do most of their moral thinking at whatever stage they have graduated to, but are able to comprehend moral reasoning at all levels below their own, but not more than one level above their own. So, if God wanted to communicate with a group or society of people at, say Stage 2, He would have to use thought forms and patterns at that particular level and never any higher than Stage 3. I think you can begin to see the communication problem God had with Israel when He tried to bring them out of slavery and educate them at Mt. Sinai.

One of the conclusions Dr. Testerman made at this point is as follows: ***"It is my thesis that God has done precisely this, confronting and communicating with men at all stages of moral development, using both language and actions appropriate to their level of understanding, while educating them to a more advanced stage. I believe this is the key to understanding many difficult passages in the Old Testament. Let's look at some Scriptural examples. Stage One is partly characterized by inability to generalize from principles to their application. Rules are understood very concretely, so they have to be spelled out in complete detail. This is seen in the 2nd, 4th, and especially the 10th commandments. After God has told the Israelites not to covet their neighbor's house, lest they assume that they are left with free license to covet his other possessions, the Lord adds, 'your neighbor's wife or his manservants.' But if God had stopped there, Israel*** *would have concluded that it would be all right to covet the maidservant, so God spells that out, too, and 'his ox;' and not just the ox, but also the donkey, and finally to make sure they had gotten the point, He redundantly adds 'or anything that belongs to your neighbor.' NIV. This is what makes the last four books of Moses so lengthy and tedious to read. Later we find the Ten Commandments, and, in fact, the whole law summed up in two compact statements: 'Thou shalt love the Lord thy God . . . and thy neighbor as thyself' (Luke 10:27). It quickly becomes obvious in reading through Exodus that the Israelites, having just come out from under the slavedriver's lash, functioned mainly at Stage One. How could God confront these slaves, get their attention, hold their loyalty and keep them from destroying themselves in sin? By the only means possible: to speak to them and deal with them in a manner they would understand and respect. At Stage One, a ruler establishes his right to rule by displays of power and vengeance on his enemies. He rules by threat of punishment and hope of reward. Mercy or failure to punish, is seen as evidence of weakness."*

At this point, I would like to say that Dr. Testerman's beliefs and mine differ regarding how God dealt with His people in that He believes that God was the one who brought the thunder and lightning, etc., whereas I believe that Satan is the "god" who brought it. In spite of this difference, I am still very much in harmony with his basic idea regarding the stages of moral development that human beings go through in advancing toward perfection in moral character. I will say I do agree with many of the points Dr. Testerman makes in the rest of his paper. I am sorry that I do not have time to share it with you in its entirety. If you would like to read the entire sermon, please send $2.00 to God's Last Call, P.O. Box 426, Scappoose, OR 97056 and I will send it to you.

A few more quotes from Dr. Testerman's sermon should be sufficient to conclude our study on the subject of God's dealings with Israel in terms of their various stages of moral development. "God first established His credentials to rule Israel by acts of vengeance on the Egyptians and mighty, spectacular miracles. 'I did this so that you might know that I am the Lord your God' (Deut. 29:6 NIV). He frightened them with an awesome display of raw power at Sinai." His next point is one I can agree with, for as you know, I did not agree with the last quote, for Psalm 78:49 and the verses leading up to verse 49 show that Satan and his angels brought the ten plagues upon Egypt. But I do agree that God used these plagues to establish His authority over both the Egyptians and Israel and at that stage of their moral perception, as slaves at Stage One, they needed this kind of demonstration to convince them that the God Moses said had called them did indeed have all the power necessary to deliver them out of Egypt.

Moses apparently functioned at a higher stage, for he discerned exactly what God was trying to do, *"Moses said to the people, 'Do not be afraid. God has come to test you so that the fear of God will keep you from sinning.' " (Ex. 20:20 NIV) God gave His law in the form of ten simple, concrete rules, punctuated with threats of punishment. He deliberately portrayed Himself as an angry, jealous ruler, threatening not only to punish the disobedient, but the children for the parents' sins, a concept which leaves us aghast but would seem perfectly normal to the pre-conventional mind. 'For I, the Lord your God, am a jealous God, punishing the children for the sins of the fathers to the third and fourth generations' (Ex. 20:5 NIV). Today we almost automatically reinterpret these words to refer to the workings of cause and effect, but this does violence to the context in which it was given and would have been a meaningless concept to a pre-scientific culture."* He then says that although God states that the children will be punished because of the parent's sins, God later denounced the concept through Ezekiel who "argued vigorously against the people, who protest that it is unjust for God *not* to punish children for their parent's sins. Apparently God had decided it was time to deal with them at a higher stage, even at the cost of directly contradicting His former plain statements." Ezek. 18 and Jer. 31:29, 30. I would rather say that God's original meaning in the 2nd Commandment was that the children will suffer the effects of their parent's sins through both inherited and cultivated tendencies to evil. This was implied in the first part of his statement, but I wanted to expand upon it. Also, we must realize that in order for God to remain sovereign He had to always take the blame and assume the fault or responsibility for everything that happened, good or bad.

We see throughout the history of Israel that every time God tried to bring them up to a higher stage or level of moral perception regarding Himself, His law and the glorious destiny He had chosen them for, they would rebel and go back to devil worship. When the spectacular displays of power ceased after the conquest of Canaan, since the Lord no longer wanted to deal with them on that level (Stage One), and was seeking a more mature relationship, they lost their carnal fear of Him and reverted back to Baal worship or Stage One. God had no choice but to revert back to a Stage One relationship with them in that He punished them very severely until they would repent and return to Him. When they did return to Him He would then start the whole educational process over again working patiently through the prophets, who many times did not understand Him very well themselves, to try and raise them to a higher level of understanding about Himself. But this could only be accomplished through God Himself coming in a body of flesh and letting us physically abuse Him and tear His flesh, make Him bleed and die on a very cruel cross so He could say to us, "No matter what you do to me I will always love you and forgive you, for I am God and 'God is love.' "

"God had problems all through Scripture with men interpreting His mercy as weakness and license to sin. 'I will be safe, even though I persist in going my own way' (Deut 29:19 NIV). At Stage 2, and in a more sophisticated way at stages 3 and 4, God's mercy is challenged as unjust. See Mal. 2:17, 3:14, 15 RSV). Even the prophet, Jeremiah, remonstrated with God. 'I would speak with you about your justice: Why does the way of the wicked prosper?' (Jer. 12:1). God's tantalizing and colorful answer in verse 5 says, in effect, 'Jeremiah, this is too advanced for you to understand.' The problem of God's mercy to the wicked is unresolvable at a lower stage thinking. It doesn't even arise as a question at stages 5 or 6. Isaiah even says that God shows mercy because *He is just (Isa. 30:18), a totally incomprehensible statement to early stage moral reasoning."* Now we come to His comments about Christ's sermon on the mount.

"By the time of Christ, Stage 4—Compulsion for rulemaking had generated a backbreaking mass of regulations covering every detail of living. Much of the teaching ministry of Christ seems to have been directed at weaning the people away from the mechanical rulekeeping. The Pharisees were threatened because they felt He didn't have enough respect for the rules. What they didn't perceive was that He was trying to teach them the Stages 5 and 6 principles behind the rules. The Sermon on the Mount abounds with examples; e.g. Matt. 5:21, 22. It is a mistake to instead use the Sermon on the Mount in Stage 4 fashion as a more rigorous rulebook, providing more detailed regulations on such things as divorce and remarriage, for example. To do this is to miss the overall intent of the sermon ... Adventism provides a real danger to the

Stage 3 and 4 individual of falling into the same trap as the Pharisees. Compulsive persons may be attracted to a religion with lots of rules, and if they become Seventh-Day Adventists, can have an absolute field day with the writings of Ellen G. White, who's works are then carefully combed for new do's and don'ts. Such individuals can be the bane of boarding academies. An extreme case was the individual who wrote to the Adventist Review *several years ago to ask if it was allowable to bake a casserole on the Sabbath if you have an automatic oven with a timer that can be set prior to the beginning of Sabbath. Doing Adventism from a Stage 4 or lower perspective easily makes Ellen White's works a gigantic collection of rules and regulations."* I must say that I think Dr. Testerman's point should be well taken. And may I add that this is precisely what I see SDAs doing with EGW regarding whether God does not kill. Instead of letting the Lord lead us to a higher stage of moral perception regarding God's character most of God's professed people are searching for quotations that will confirm their Stage 4 or lower concept of God when Jesus wants us to "go on to perfection in Christ," by coming up to higher ground, not just to Stage 6 but to Stage 7 and beyond. Praise God! May the Lord Jesus richly bless you as you continue to pray and study on how to continue climbing Jacob's ladder to the Eternal Kingdom of Jesus Christ, our Coming Saviour and King.

One of the main benefits of the character message of God's love (that He does not kill) is that it truly does remove all fear from the believer's heart. I believe this is the final stage of moral development that must take place in God's people before they are translated. If we truly come to know God in Christ, we will have this wonderful experience, and we must have it, for the spirit of opposition to this message today, is exactly the same kind of evil spirit that opposed Jesus each step of the way in His earthly ministry. EGW stated again and again that the professed people of God today (the SDA people) are repeating the sad history of Israel. 5T 160; 3T 361; 1SM 69; PP 689. But the opposition we receive today will only serve to draw more attention to the truths we present. Paul tells us "For we can do nothing against the truth, but for the truth." 2 Cor. 13:8. So, do not let opposition or persecution dampen your ardor or depress your spirits.

As we have seen how there is need of moral advancement in our characters, so we might more fully reflect the glory or character of Christ, we can begin to see the true meaning of the sanctuary service in Moses' day, which later became the temple service after Solomon built the temple at Jerusalem. In *Desire of Ages,* pages 154-166 EGW describes in detail, as if she were there as an eyewitness, the first time Jesus cleansed the temple. She explains how the Jewish leaders had taught the people the importance of worshipping the Lord at the temple in Jerusalem. But instead of drawing the people closer to God the whole system was actually turning people away from God. *"The priests and rulers were called to be the representatives of God to the nation; they should have corrected the abuses of the temple court. They should have given to the people an example of integrity and compassion. Instead of studying their own profit, they should have considered the situation and needs of the worshippers, and should have been ready to assist those who were not able to buy the required sacrifices. But this they did not do. Avarice had hardened their hearts."* DA 157.

The Bible tells us "the love of money is the root of all evil." I Tim. 6:10. At the time of the Passover, many from all over Palestine and the world came to worship at Jerusalem. As a result *"the temple courts were filled with a promiscuous throng. Many were unable to bring with them the sacrifices that were to be offered up as typifying the one great sacrifice. For the convenience of these, animals were bought and sold in the outer court of the temple. Here all classes of people assembled to purchase their offerings. Here all foreign money was exchanged for the coin of the sanctuary. Every Jew was required to pay yearly a half shekel as a 'ransom for his soul,' and the money thus collected was used for the support of the temple. Ex. 30:12-16. Besides this, large sums were brought as freewill offerings, to be deposited in the temple treasury. And it was required that all foreign coin should be changed for a coin called the temple shekel, which was accepted for the service of the sanctuary. The money changing gave opportunity for fraud and extortion, and it had grown into a disgraceful traffic, which was a source of revenue to the priests. The dealers demanded exorbitant prices for the animals sold, and they shared their profits with the priests and rulers, who thus enriched themselves at the expense of the people. The worshipers had been taught to believe that if they did not offer sacrifice, the blessing of God would not rest on their children or their lands. Thus a high price for the animals could be secured; for after coming so far, the people would not return to their homes without performing the act of devotion for which they had come. A great number of sacrifices were offered at the time of the Passover, and the sales at the temple were very large ... There could be heard sharp bargaining, the lowing of cattle, etc. ... So great was the confusion that the worshipers were disturbed, and the words addressed to the Most High were drowned in the uproar that invaded the temple. The Jews were exceedingly proud of their piety. They rejoiced over their temple, and regarded a word spoken in its disfavor as blasphemy; they were very rigorous in the performance of ceremonies connected with it; but the love of money had overruled their scruples. They were scarcely aware how far they had wandered from the original purpose of the service instituted by God him-*

self." DA 155. Now, beloved, what stage of moral development do you suppose these Jewish priests were operating
on? Since they taught that the God they served would curse
and destroy them unless they offered up a dead animal they
had purchased at great personal sacrifice, would it not be
logical to say that they were operating at about Stage 1 or 2
at the very most? And if God's professed people are repeating their history, on what level are they operating on today?

We have already discovered in this book that God
never wanted them to kill innocent animals in the first
place, but I would like to point out to you a statement in
Leviticus 1 that even shows God never even "required"
Israel to kill animals. (See Isa. 1:10-12.) *"And the Lord
(Jesus) called unto Moses, and spake unto him out of
the tabernacle of the congregation, saying, Speak unto
the children of Israel, and say unto them, If any man of
you bring an offering unto the Lord (Satan), ye shall
bring your offering of cattle, even of the herd, and of
the flock. If his offering be a burnt sacrifice of the
herd, let him offer a male without blemish, he shall
offer it of his own voluntary will at the door of the tabernacle of the congregation before the lord (Satan)."* If
Jesus had been referring to Himself, He would have
said "before me," instead of "before the Lord."* Furthermore, in contrast to this "voluntary" system of *"savlation"*
Christ told the Jews if they did not accept Him they would
die. John 8:24. No such penalty was ever attached to the
sacrificial system. Please notice, friend, that God specifically says that this was to be a "voluntary" offering. It was
not required. See also Lev. 7:16; Ezek. 46:12. Now, let's take
a look at Christ's day and see how He related Himself to the
sacrificial system.

*"As Jesus came into the temple, He took in the
whole scene. He saw the unfair transactions. He saw
the distress of the poor,* who thought *that without shedding of blood there could be no forgiveness for their
sins."* DA 157. Notice that EGW clearly states that these

people really thought they would never be forgiven unless they shed an animal's blood. Do you see the strong implication that what they were "thinking" was wrong! Yes, beloved friend of mine, God has always wanted to forgive Adam and his descendants without all of the carnage and bloodshed. But our frightened, carnal, hardened hearts could not comprehend such love. We "thought" He was angry at us and that He would hurt us and kill us if we didn't do something to appease His wrath. And so God had to deal with man on the level he was on at that time until Jesus came and showed us what the Father is really like. We thought God was like us. "Thou thoughtest that I was altogether such an one as thyself." Psalm 50:21. But the enmity (caused by the carnal mind, Rom. 8:7) was in our own minds. *"And you, that were sometime alienated and enemies in your mind by wicked works, yet now hath he reconciled."* Col. 1:21. So God came down to our level and let us think of Him as a *"hard man"* who was impossible to deal with as we see in the parable of the talents in Matt. 25:24. But through the Holy Spirit, we finally discovered He isn't like that at all. But this revelation only comes to those who are *"born again"* of the Spirit of God. Even the brilliant Dr. "Nicodemus, a ruler of the Jews," could not comprehend it. John 3:2.

The main lie Satan has conned the human race into believing is that God will not forgive them. But once they find out that is not quite true he tells them another lie. And the second lie is that God will not forgive you unless you make an incredible sacrifice of some kind.

There was only way God could ever convince man that He truly does love him and is very willing to forgive him and welcome him back home. That one way was for God Himself to come in a body of flesh as the "Son of God." And that is precisely what He did. But what an incredible price our God had to pay in order to prove His love for us before we would really believe He loves us! *"God has bound our hearts to Him by unnumbered tokens in heaven and earth. Through the things of nature, and the deepest and tenderest earthly ties that human hearts can know, He has sought to reveal Himself to us. Yet these but imperfectly represent His love. Though all these evidences have been given, the enemy of good blinded the minds of men, so that they looked upon God with fear; they thought of Him as severe and unforgiving. Satan led men to conceive of God as a being whose chief attribute is stern justice—one who is a severe judge, a harsh, exacting creditor. He pictured the Creator as a being who is watching with jealous eye to discern the errors and mistakes of men, that He may visit judgments upon them. It was to remove this dark shadow, by revealing to the world the infinite love of God, that Jesus came to live among men." Steps to Christ,* pg. 11.

Remember that Christ continually by-passed, ignored and broke the customs and the rules of the Pharisees and Scribes. Never once did Jesus ever tell anyone to go buy an animal and offer it as a sacrifice to get their sins forgiven. Instead, He forgave them directly. *"And Jesus, seeing their faith, said unto the sick of the palsy, Son, be of good cheer, Thy sins be forgiven thee. and behold, certain of the scribes said within themselves, This man blasphemeth."* Matt. 9:2, 3; cf. Mark 2:5-9. And in Luke 6:37, Jesus said, *"Forgive, and ye shall be forgiven."* And in Luke 7:47-48, Jesus said the woman who anointed Him with ointment and washed His feet with her tears was forgiven. DA 559 identifies this woman as Mary, sister of Lazarus. And these occasions took place before Christ nailed the ceremonial law to the cross. Besides that, Jesus showed just how little respect and esteem He had for the whole temple system of animal sacrifices when He *"began to cast out them that sold and bought in the temple, and overthrew the tables of the moneychangers, and the seats of them that sold doves."* Mark 11:15. The dove represented the Holy Spirit of God. Just think what blasphemy they were perpetrating ... putting the beautiful symbol of God's Holy Spirit in a cage and selling it for a price! What deep significance Christ's act of cleansing the temple had. The Spirit that men had caged up was being set free again so people could know the truth about God and receive salvation free of charge.

How did Jesus cast these money changers out of the temple? Why, He simply said, *"Take these things hence; make not my Father's house an house of merchandise."* Someone may protest, saying, *"But, Mike, what about the whip Jesus had in His hands? Doesn't this prove He was hurting them and using force?"* The answer is, *"No."* First of all, the whip was actually "a scourge of small cords." John 2:15. He only used the cords as a symbol to demonstrate to these carnally minded men that He was the real ruler of the temple. The cords were only a sign or mark of His authority. EGW says, *"Jesus does not smite them with the whip of cords, but in His hand that simple scourge seems terrible as a flaming sword."* DA 158. But why did they leave? Because they felt condemned by His very presence. *"Officers of the temple, speculating priests, brokers, and cattle traders, with their sheep and oxen, rush from the place, with one thought of escaping from the condemnation of His presence."* DA 158. But what were Jesus' thoughts and attitude toward these crooked, double-dealing, cheating ministers of the temple? *"Overpowered with terror, the priests and rulers had fled from the temple court, and from the searching glance that read their hearts. In their flight, they met others on their way to the temple, and bade them turn back, telling them what they had seen and heard. Christ looked upon the fleeing men with yearning pity for their fear, and their ignorance of what constituted true worship. In this scene, He saw symbolized the dispersion of the whole Jewish nation for their wickedness and impenitence ... When divinity flashed through humanity, not only did they see indignation on Christ's countenance, they realized the import of His words. They felt as if before the throne of the eternal Judge, with their sentence passed on them for time and eternity. For a time, they were convinced that Christ was a prophet, and many believed Him to be the Messiah. The Holy Spirit flashed into their minds the utterances of the prophets concerning Christ. Would they yield to this conviction? Repent they would not. . . . Because Christ discerned their thoughts they hated Him. They determined to challenge Him as to the power by which He had driven them forth, and who gave Him this power."* DA 162. Please read the rest of this yourself for it is so revealing of a parallel with what is going on again today in religious circles.

Jesus Christ has "power" but that power is ever and only used to give life. It is never exercised to harm, hurt, maim, injure, or destroy anyone . . . only to give life, for Jesus is the Life-giver, not the life-taker. He is a life God, not a death-god. He did not hate them. He loved them, but He hated the sins they were committing for they were keeping them from Him, their Creator. He said, *"take these* things *hence."* He did not rail against them, but His anger was directed against the situation and the sins they were committing. But do you realize many of these same offenses are being committed today by organized religion? How? By teaching that the more good works you perform for the church and the more money you give the greater your reward will be in Heaven. Just as Christ cast these vendors of salvation out of the temple in His day, so He will cast them out again today. But how does He do this? *"He cast out the Spirits with His Word, and healed all that were sick."* Matt. 8:16. The Word of God is power.

A person's attitude toward God will determine his perception of God. Let us note, for example, how two classes of people viewed Christ. The first class were very afraid of Jesus. *"When they* (the priests) *fled, the poor remained behind; and these were now looking to Jesus, whose countenance expressed His love and sympathy. With tears in His eyes, He said to the trembling ones around Him, 'Fear not, I will deliver thee, and thou shalt glorify Me. For this cause came I into the world.' The people pressed into Christ's presence with urgent, pitiful appeals: Master, bless me. His ear heard every cry. With pity exceeding that of a tender mother, He bent over the suffering little ones. All received attention. Everyone was healed of whatever disease he had. The dumb opened their lips in praise; the blind beheld the face of their Restorer. The hearts of the sufferers were made glad."* DA 163.

In cleansing the temple of the unholy traffic of buying and selling of animals to be sacrificed, Jesus was saying loud and clear, *"You don't have to pay money to receive my help. Neither do you have to shed the blood of innocent animals to receive my forgiveness. My salvation is free."* Even in the beginning, when Lucifer sinned, EGW tells us the Father would have forgiven Lucifer and reinstated him in his original position in heaven. *"God in His great mercy bore long with Lucifer . . . long was he retained in heaven. Again and again he was offered pardon on condition of repentance and submission."* GC 496. Now, beloved, please notice something very, very important. God offered Lucifer pardon and forgiveness after he had sinned, *without* a blood sacrifice. You see, beloved, God does not need any blood shed or stripes given on somebody's back before He is willing to forgive. This shedding of animal blood nor the blood of God's dear Son did not originate in the mind of God. Of course, He knew it would happen, but it wasn't His perfect will that it happen for everything that happens is not God's will, but nothing can happen to defeat His will, ultimately. No, God did not demand that anyone's blood be shed before He would expiate (atone) or forgive them of their sins. Instead, this is what the carnal mind of man thought that God demanded.

Satan led the Jewish leaders to crucify God's Son. Jesus did everything He could to stop them for He knew it would lead them to their demise (death or destruction). It would so harden their hearts that the Holy Spirit would be forced out and Satan would have entire control of them. *"By stubborn rejection of divine love and mercy, the Jews had caused the protection of God to be withdrawn from them, and Satan was permitted to rule them according to his will."* GC 35. And on the next page EGW tells us the same thing that happened to Jerusalem is to have another fulfillment. *"In the fate of the chosen city we may behold the doom of a world that has rejected God's mercy and trampled upon His law."* GC 36. You can also read on page 600 of *Desire of Ages*, (DA) that it was the crucifixion of Christ *"that sank them* (the Jews) *to ruin for this world and for the world to come."* The shedding of Christ's blood on Calvary was "ordained" from the beginning. Jesus is truly *"the Lamb slain from the foundation of the world."* Rev. 13:18. God knew that when He gave His only Son to the world as a gift, that His professed people would turn that Gift into a human sacrifice. Because we have the power of choice, God cannot force us to do His will. But through His infinite power of love, He is able to work through all of the hateful acts of man to bring about His ultimate and perfect will. And yet, He never revokes nor interferes with our free moral agency (choice). He saw down through the corridors of time that man would kill His only Son. But Jesus as a human being did not understand this until He was 12 years old. DA 82. Although Jesus "laid down" His life, so no one could take it from Him, the Bible still identifies those who crucified Him as killers and murderers.

If death was His destiny, why did He seek to prevent it? If His death truly was what was necessary to save us, why did He not suggest it Himself and help them carry it out? This is similar to a question I have heard SDAs ask many times regarding the Sunday law. They have asked, *"If*

Sunday laws have to come before Christ returns then why is our church fighting the Sunday laws? Why not help our government, and in turn all the governments of the world, to pass the best kind of Sunday legislation possible and thus hasten the final events which will also hasten the coming of Christ?" Does anyone have an answer for this question? Just try asking this question in a group sometime and watch how many blank stares you will get. The answer to both questions is found in Romans 3:8 where Paul defends himself against the charge he had taught that a person should do evil that good may come. A modern paraphrase may help us get the whole picture a little better if we start back at verse 5. *" 'But, some say, our breaking faith with God is good, our sins serve a good purpose, for people will notice how good God is when they see how bad we are. Is it fair, then, for him to punish when our sins are helping him?' (That is the way some people talk.) God forbid! Then what kind of God would He be, to overlook sin? How could He ever condemn anyone? (Judge the world-KJV). For He could not judge and condemn me as a sinner if my dishonesty brought Him glory by pointing up His honesty in contrast to my lies. If you follow through with that idea, you come to this;. the worse we are, the better God likes it! But the damnation of those who say such things is just. Yet some claim that this is what I preach."* Romans 3:5-8. LB.

Now we have defined two evils that result in good: (1) Christ's death and (2) Sunday laws. Theologians have called the death of Jesus on Calvary's tree a crime. We read in Acts 3 ... *"But ye denied the Holy One and the Just, and desired a murderer to be granted unto you, and killed the Prince of life, whom God hath raised from the dead."* Acts 3:14, 15. Now, was Jesus "killed or murdered?" Well, was this crime pre-meditated? Was it calculated? It certainly was. Is there a difference between the word "kill" and "murder?" In our English dictionary "kill" is simply defined to mean "To put to death, to deprive of life." And an example is given of how the Black Plague was a disease that killed millions. You would not say that the Black Plague "murdered" millions for the plague was not a person. An accident can take a person's life and thus "kill" them but an accident is not defined as "murder." An automobile can accidentally roll over someone and "kill" them, but you would not say that the automobile "murdered" someone. But if a person was in the car and purposely hit and killed someone, you then could define it as murder. Many sincere people have told me that the Hebrew word translated "kill" in Exodus 20:13 should actually be translated "murder." But this is incorrect. The **Revised Standard** translates the Hebrew word "RATSACH" as "kill" and so does the **American Standard Version**, as well as **The New American Bible.** However, the NEB, NIV, LB (Living Bible) and the **Modern Language** versions translate "RATSACH" as "murder." The main argument people give for believing "RATSACH" means only murder is that they want to prove that the commandment forbids "murder," but not "killing," because God, they say, does have to "kill" sometimes, but when He kills it is not murder. Such an argument has little merit or logic. But such are the extremes some will go to in order to try and prove that God is justified in killing and thus breaking His own law, the very law He says is a transcript of His own character. Furthermore, Jesus tells us He is our example and we are to live and speak, act and think just like Him. Is it therefore logical that God would tell us that we are not allowed to kill but He is? Hardly! That would be the height of hypocrisy and we know our precious Lord Jesus Christ is not a hypocrite.

As a matter of fact, Jesus was "murdered" for the reason that He refused to kill the Romans. Because He would not lead them to destroy their enemies they turned upon Him and crucified Him. Of course, they justified it by saying that according to their definition they were not really

Him and crucified Him. Of course, they justified it by saying that according to their definition they were not really "murdering" Jesus of Nazareth, but only carrying out the *Justice* of the law by "executing" Him.

"When the chief priests and the officers saw Him, they cried out, 'Crucify Him, crucify Him!' Pilate said to them, 'Take Him yourselves and crucify Him, for I find no fault in Him.' The Jews answered, 'We have a law, and by that law He ought to die, because He has made Himself the Son of God.' " John 19:6, 7. RSV. And so we see how people will twist the meaning of words to suit their own purposes when they have rejected truth. And that is precisely what is happening again today. The hard hearted, evil opposition to this message is exactly the same kind of spirit that opposed Jesus each step of the way in His earthly ministry. But this opposition need not dampen our ardor or depress our spirits, for we will be victorious through Jesus Christ our Lord.

And so we see that it truly was a murderous crime to crucify the Son of God. But God took that criminal act and used it to "draw" all the universe to Himself and reveal His matchless love to them. *"Forgive them Father, for they don't even understand or realize what they are doing."* And so it will be when the religious elements of our modern world today pass a Sunday law and death decree against the people of God. They will not realize what they are doing. If we truly love the Lord Jesus and are filled with His Spirit, we will do all we can to prevent them from passing such laws that will lead to their own demise (death). The death of Jesus and Sunday laws mean suffering and bloodshed. We should do all we can to prevent both. The apostle Paul tells us that true love *"Beareth all things, believeth all things, hopeth all things, endureth all things. Charity* (love) *never faileth."* I Cor. 13:8. God has pledged Himself to suffer and endure any heartache or trial we must endure in order to reveal His glory to the world. And as we suffer with Him (as He dwells in our hearts) we will sense His paraphrase puts it. *"But we Christians have no veil over our faces; we can be mirrors that brightly reflect the glory of the Lord. And as the Spirit of the Lord works within us, we become more and more like Him."* 2 Cor. 3:18. We have this glorious opportunity before us to become like Him. It is not only our privilege and opportunity, but our sacred duty and eternal destiny. Oh, friend of mine, . . . we cannot . . . we must not fail. May the Lord Jesus be near and dear to your heart as you surrender your all to Him so He may accomplish His desire in you.

PART
III

"And he (Saul) said, 'Who art Thou, Lord?' " Acts 9:5.

Even Saul, before he became Paul, thought he was serving Jesus, when he was actually serving (worshipping) Satan.

CHAPTER 11

DID GOD COMMAND
OLD TESTAMENT KILLINGS?

"God had made it their privilege and their duty to enter the land at the time of His appointment; but through their willful neglect that permission had been withdrawn. Satan had gained his object in preventing them from entering Canaan; and now he urged them on to do the very thing, in the face of the divine prohibition, which they had refused to do when God required it. Thus the great deceiver gained the victory by leading them to rebellion the second time. They had distrusted the power of God to work with their efforts in gaining possession of Canaan; yet now they presumed upon their own strength to accomplish the work independent of divine aid. 'We have sinned against the Lord,' they cried; 'we will go up and fight, according to all that the Lord our God commanded us.' Deuteronomy 1:41. So terribly blinded had they become by transgression. The Lord had never commanded them to 'go up and fight.' It was not His purpose that they should gain the land by warfare, but by strict obedience to His commands."

"PATRIARCHS AND PROPHETS"—P. 392—
By Ellen G. White

HOW DOES GOD PUNISH?

"David had neglected the duty of punishing the crime of Amnon, and because of the unfaithfulness of the king and father and the impenitence of the son, the Lord permitted events to take their natural course, and did not restrain Absalom. When parents or rulers neglect the duty of punishing iniquity, God Himself will take the case in hand. His restraining power will be in a measure removed from the agencies of evil, so that a train of circumstances will arise which will punish sin with sin."

"PATRIARCHS AND PROPHETS"—P. 728—
By Ellen G. White

Sincere Christians in every age have cited Israel's warfare against her enemies, as proof that God not only approved of all the slaughters of the Old Testament era, but actually commanded them Himself. This thought is so utterly revolting to some people that they won't even read the Old Testament. Yet, many "holy wars" have been justified on this very premise.

As a result of this kind of "Theology of God," many kind and sensitive people in the world have decided they would just rather not even believe in such a bloodthirsty God who would be so cruel as to command not only the slaughter of helpless and innocent animals, but even women, little children and the aged as well. Perhaps you can now understand why some people have become atheists and agnostics rather than believe in such a brutal and sadistic God.

So, how do we answer these questions? Or are there any answers? Well, I have good news for you, dear reader. There are some very logical and sensible answers when the evidence is properly sorted out, weighed and evaluated through the eyes of Jesus Christ, our supreme example, touchstone and benchmark for all eternity.

Let us go to that one perfect, precious, and Holy Life, even to Jesus, our Blessed Redeemer. He will teach us the truth about the "SWORD." Notice first of all Christ's words to His own disciple, Peter. *"Then saith Jesus unto him, Put up again thy sword into his place: for all they that take the sword shall perish with the sword."* Matt 26:52

Next let us read our Lord's explanation to Pilate the Nature of the Kingdom of God and the attitude, spirit and activity of His servants. *"Jesus answered, My kingdom is not of this world: if my kingdom were of this world, then would my servants fight, that I should not be delivered to the Jews: but now is my kingdom not from hence."* John 18:36. Cf. Rev. 13:10; Mark 14:47. Only Luke, the beloved physician, mentions that Jesus healed Malchus' ear which Peter lopped off with his wild and reckless slashing of the literal sword he had brought with him to the garden with which to defend his Lord. See also D.A. 696; EW; SR 211.

The Lord's servant and messenger, EGW, counsels God's ministers to not "turn away from the path of obedience and make transgression of the law of God a virtue . . ." for they would be "under the inspiration of the archdeceiver." "TESTIMONIES TO MINISTERS," Pg. 247. If you read the whole section here, you will find EGW is talking about how to treat those who oppose us in our work for the Lord. She says we are to "preserve a Christlike temper when tempted to become imperious and impatient." Ibid. And on the next page she indicates that any kind of retaliation is out of harmony with the spirit of the law of Christ and is a violation of God's law. If this is God's will for us as New Testament Christians, why wouldn't that be God's will for the "saints" of the O.T. as well? FOR God's LAW NEVER CHANGES. NOR DOES HIS "PERFECT WILL," ever change. Is it logical that God would allow and even command O.T. believers to kill and destroy their enemies

and then contradict Himself in the N.T. by telling us to turn
the other cheek and not use the sword? That would be terrible hypocrisy. Yet, it would seem that the Bible has recorded
that God did command His people Israel to go out and
destroy their enemies. I said, "it would seem," that way. I
didn't say that I believe that to be a fact. Please be patient
and reason with me carefully as we go through this problem
step by step, and I think you will be able to see and understand what really happened back there in the days of Abraham, Moses, Samuel, David and Elijah. The sixth
commandment plainly declares "Thou shalt not kill," just
as clearly as the fourth one says, "The seventh day is the
Sabbath." Yet SDAs explain away the sixth command and
cherish the "killer God" attitude and spirit of Satan in
their heart at the very same time they are condemning Sunday keeping Christians for breaking the fourth commandment. Are not both groups violating and breaking the Law
of God? Of course they are!

Sister White says, "The Holy Spirit does not work
with men who love to be sharp and critical. This spirit has
been cherished in meeting debaters, and some have formed
the habit of squaring for combat. God is dishonored in this.
Keep back the sharp thrusts; do not learn in Satan's school
his methods of warfare. The Holy Spirit does not inspire the
words of censure." "TESTIMONIES TO MINISTERS." Page
248.

Now, Beloved, please think about it. If the Holy Spirit
does not even inspire or condone "censure or debate" how
could we possibly think or imagine that God's Holy Spirit
inspired the armies of Israel to go to war and slaughter
their fellow human beings? Who then was inspiring and
leading them on? Whose "spirit" were they really tuned
into and listening to? Paul says, *"So then they that are in
the flesh cannot please God. But ye are not in the flesh,
but in the Spirit, if so be that the Spirit of God dwell in
you. Now if any man have not the Spirit of Christ, he is
none of His."* Rom. 8:8-9.

Furthermore, Jesus told us to "turn" the other cheek. *"Ye have heard that it hath been said, An eye for an eye, and a tooth for a tooth; But I say unto you, That ye resist not evil: but whosoever shall smite thee on thy right cheek, turn to him the other also."* Matt. 5:38, 39. Luke 22:64 shows the fulfillment of Isa. 50:6. Jesus had only love, pity and forgiveness for His tormentors. This is the same "Spirit" we are to cherish in our hearts toward our enemies. So which "Lord" was inspiring these men of war in the O.T. to go out and slash, maim and kill their enemies? Paul tells us in 2 Cor. 11:13-15 that "Satan himself is transformed into an angel of light." So the "god of this world . . . blinded" men in the O.T. to the truth about God. And it was not until Jesus came that even the good and holy angels who remained loyal to our heavenly Father understood that Satan was a liar and a killer. See D.A. 758, 759.

In my book, "Into the Father's heart," (IFH) I touched on the concept of the two Lords of Exodus 19 on page 350 and 351. I said, "The expression or phrase, 'break forth,' is very important, for it identifies the 'Lord' or 'God,' who would kill anyone who disobeyed. The god of 'breaking forth,' is 'Baalperazim,' Lord of breaches. This is how Uzzah died, 2 Sam. 6:8' " In this new book, "THE WONDERFUL TRUTH ABOUT OUR HEAVENLY FATHER," I am going into much more detail about the two Lords because it is so very important to understand.

Again the servant of the Lord has told us that Satan stands beside readers of books on war. "How many books are there concerning war and bloodshed, which mislead the youth! As they read, Satan stands at their side to inspire them with the spirit of the warrior of whom they read, and their blood becomes heated in their veins, and they are stirred up to do cruel actions." MYP 277.

"Satan delights in war, for it excites the worst passions of the soul and then sweeps into eternity its victims steeped in vice and blood." G.C. 589. Does this sound like God is the instigator of war? Does it sound like He is the one who is inciting and inspiring men to bash each other's heads in? Or is God doing everything He can to prevent wars? Yes, He is. Simple logic tells us that just as our gentle, peace loving Jesus was against war in the N.T., so just as surely was He against violence and war in the O.T., for He never changes. "Jesus Christ the same yesterday, and to day, and forever." Heb. 13:8; Mal. 3:6; Psalm 89:34.

But God has been "limited" by the wrong choices of man's carnal desires. *"How oft did they provoke Him in the wilderness, and grieve him in the desert! Yea, they turned back and tempted God, and limited the holy one of Israel."* Psalm 78:40, 41. Man has imagined God was like himself. "Thou thoughtest that I was altogether such an one as thyself." Psalm 50:21.

The Lord has had to put up with man's foolish, harmful, destructive and treacherous ways for nearly 6,000 years—He allowed men to marry many wives against His will. Yet, where in the O.T. do you find God rebuking David, Solomon or any of the kings for the sin of polygamy? But does that mean God was pleased with it? He "ordained" the first divorce laws, but just because He "gave" them these laws to regulate their wickedness and insanity of their lustful passion does not mean that He told them to do it. No. But while allowing them the free exercise of their will to choose wrong, God was doing everything in His power to save them from the worst effects of their unwise, wrong and evil choice. His regulations were as fair and humane of a system as could be devised so as to prevent as much suffering of these divorced women and their children as possible.

Did God command Israel to eat the flesh of dead animals? No, he certainly did not. He gave Adam his perfect diet in Eden, Gen. 1:29. But after Adam left the Garden his descendants began marrying many wives and killing animals both for sacrifice and food to the God whom they imagined would destroy them if they did not offer up these animals to him. EGW says, "Polygamy had been early introduced, contrary to the divine arrangement at the beginning. The Lord gave to Adam one wife, showing His order in that respect. But after the fall, men chose to follow their own sinful desires; and as a result, crime and wretchedness rapidly increased. Neither the marriage relation nor the rights of property were respected. Whoever coveted the wives or possessions of his neighbor, took them by force, and men exalted in their deeds of violence. THEY DELIGHTED IN DESTROYING THE LIFE OF ANIMALS; And the use of flesh food rendered them still more cruel and blood-thirsty, until they came to regard human life with astonishing indifference." PP 91, 92.

Again, regarding the eating of the flesh of animals, EGW says, "God has spoken in the history of the children of Israel, from whom for their good He sought to withhold a flesh diet. He fed them with bread from heaven; 'man did eat angels' food.' " 6T 372. She gives further counsel on this in "DIET AND FOODS," pages 373-416. The evidence and counsel in favor of a vegetarian diet is overwhelming. The Lord, through EGW, spoke about how cruel it is to slaughter animals for food. Does this sound like a God who would suggest, order or command that innocent animals be killed for food, let alone for the forgiveness of sins? "Why then," you ask, "didn't he tell them not to do it?" For the same reason he did not destroy the devil. God has had to put up with His creature's lack of understanding and knowledge from the inception of the sin problem. EGW discusses this in "Desire of Ages," pages 19-26, 758-764. See also the chapter "WHY WAS SIN PERMITTED," in "PATRIARCHS AND PROPHETS," pages 33-43, and "THE ORIGIN OF EVIL," in "THE GREAT CONTROVERSY," Pages 492-504.

In the book "Desire of Ages," page 19, EGW tells us "our little world is the lesson book of the universe." And in John 17:3 Christ reveals to us that even eternal life itself is based upon a true knowledge and understanding of God and His love. And so, basically, the whole universe is a giant classroom in which all of God's intelligent creatures are progressing from one stage of moral development to another in life's ongoing classroom of right and wrong. It is only as we keep our gaze fixed upon our precious Redeemer will we be able to continue growing up into the full stature of His perfect likeness as suggested in Ephesians 4:13.

Closely linked with moral perfection is the subject of health reform. God considers this subject of the utmost importance, yet it has been ignored, ridiculed and opposed by many sincere SDAs through the years by leadership and laity alike. Satan knows better than anyone what a threat health reform is to his hold on Laodicea. A mentally well, physically vital membership might truly awake and arise to finish the work.

Notice that on page 370 of 6T EGW talks about the importance of health reform in regard to the physical and mental health of the church. She says, "The subject of health reform has been presented in the churches; but the light has not been heartily received." And then on the next page she gives this rejection of the health reform message as the very reason why God cannot bring new converts into the ranks of SDAs. "The Lord does not now work to bring many souls into the truth, because of the church members who have never been converted and those who were once converted but who have backslidden. What influence would these unconsecrated members have on new converts? Would they not make of no effect the God-given message which His people are to bear."?

How many leaders and laity alike have died premature deaths as the result of eating flesh food and basically ignoring God's counsel to healthful living in general will probably never be known until the record books are opened to the saints during the 1,000 years in heaven. The story is told of one Gen. Conf. president who confessed that he knew he was dying of some kind of *malignacy*, such as cancer, and was honest enough to admit it was because he had failed to follow the health counsels God gave to our church through Sister White.

It doesn't take a Harvard Law degree to figure out what a successful blow Satan has struck against God's people by programming their minds to believe that God was the one who started the animal sacrifice system. Not only does such a concept cause people to think of God as harsh, cruel and vindictive but it encourages young and old alike to treat animals with less dignity and respect and feel no compassion for these poor creatures who suffer and die so they can inflame their passions by consuming their dead flesh. Someone may be asking me about now, "Well, Pastor Clute, if God didn't kill the first animal or command Adam to do it, just whose idea was it anyway?" I am going to answer this question completely. And I will also explain why EGW stated that God "ordained" and "instituted" the animal sacrifice system. See pages 127, 128, 133, 134, 233, 234.

But first, let us go back to "Patriarchs and Prophets," page 92, where EGW states that "I will destroy man whom I have created from the face of the earth . . . If they did not cease to pollute with their sins the world and its rich treasures, He (God) would blot them from His creation, and would destroy the things with which He had delighted to bless them; He would sweep away the beasts of the field and the vegetation which furnished such an abundant supply of food, and would transform the fair earth into one vast scene of desolation and ruin." PP 92.

On the surface it would seem that this EGW quote contradicts other quotations where EGW unequivocally (clearly) states that "GOD DESTROYS NO MAN." COL 84; GC 35, 36; 5T 119,120. But there is no problem or contradiction at all once we realize that EGW wrote just like the Hebrew prophets. And what do I mean by that? Simply, that the Hebrew prophets always held God responsible for whatever calamity or destruction He permitted or allowed to happen. The SDA Bible commentary understood this principle when they wrote: "22. A lying spirit. In the Bible, God is frequently presented as doing that which He does not restrain." 2BC 840. Comments on I Kings 22:22. This same principle is enunciated again in 3 BC 184, comments on I Chron. 21:1. "God is frequently said to do that which He does not prevent. Filled with thoughts of pride and self-sufficiency, David was led by the evil one to take this census in Israel. God did not interpose, but permitted David's corrupt motive to be translated into action. When the Lord allows the course of evil to take its way, it is often set forth as if this were by the active intervention of God, although it is actually the force of evil that is at work producing its baneful results (see Rom. 1:18, 26, 28; PP 728, 739)." So, you can see that some writers in the church agree with me.

Whenever anyone tells me that the official doctrine of the SDA church is the teaching that "God Does Kill," I always think of these statements in the commentary which so eloquently express the same exact meaning and interpretation as I have always given in all of my books and articles on the character of God. This is the main principle a person must understand to correctly interpret the O.T. But once you understand it, everything else falls in place. In addition to this, the Gen. Conf. published a book in 1977 which became the missionary book for 1978. It was entitled, "CAN GOD BE TRUSTED," by A. Graham Maxwell. On pages 82-85 Maxwell defines the "Wrath of God," in the same terms as I have always expressed it and just as the Bible commentary has expressed it by referring to Rom. 1. The wrath of God is when God is forced to give up and let the sinner go his own way and do his own thing. I am not saying that Maxwell's book expresses all of the views I have written in my book, but the basic idea is the same.

In my book, IFH, I explain the meaning of the "Wrath of God," in Chapter Ten. EGW refers to the Flood as one of "God's judgments," (PP 104) and His "vengeance," and "desolating wrath of God." (pp 101). See Psalm 78:49 for synonymous terms which explain the meaning of "God's wrath." I have never found a definitive statement, organized Bible study or even an explanation of what the wrath of God is in the writings of EGW. However, she does express its

meanings within the context of her descriptions of the sufferings of Christ in the garden and on the cross. See DA 693
and 753 where she says the Father "separated" from His
Son. "The withdrawal of the divine countenance from the
Saviour," is obviously the "wrath of God," in the writings of
Sister White, although she never says, "here is my definition for 'God's wrath.' "

But when it comes to the character of God she is much
more explicit. For example, in COL 414, she parallels the
words and phrases "light," "God's word," "transforming
power," "principles of His work" and "attribute of God." She
uses all of these qualifying or descriptive statements as synonymous terms to explain what the "light of His glory"
means. In just one 96-word paragraph she clearly explains
the keys to understanding the phrases, words and terms
God uses in the Bible and her writings to identify the
"glory of God," which she defines as "His character."

The entire last chapter of "Christ's Object Lessons,"
clearly explains that the final message to go to the world is
a revelation or unveiling of the love of God. She clearly
states that this will be revealed to the world through a very
special God-ordained and God-given, inspired message at
the darkest hour of earth's history. You should read the
entire chapter yourself, including the 96-word paragraph.
Compare TM 50, where she states, that this message will
eventually be given through the church, which is His true
people, but does not necessarily mean an organization, for
the early church was not an organization. The Jewish people or nation was the recognized and organized church in
those days and they persecuted the true church just as the
Remnant have been, are being, and will be persecuted more
and more right up until their deliverance by the voice of
God just prior to the actual event of Christ's return itself.
See GC 635-652.

Now watch how the Holy Spirit led EGW to tie this
last message of mercy to the doctrines of the atonement and
the sanctuary and to define this as the last warning mes-

sage of Rev. 14. *"When Christ entered the most holy place of the heavenly sanctuary to perform the closing work of the atonement, he committed to His servants the last message of mercy to be given to the world. Such is the warning of the third angel of Rev. 14. Immediately following its proclamation, the Son of man is seen by the prophet coming in glory to reap the harvest of the earth."* SR 379, Chapter 54—"THE THIRD ANGEL'S MESSAGE." I seriously doubt that Sister White understood how all of her quotations would someday be understood in the exact context we are now seeing them, any more than the prophets of the O.T. understood all they wrote about the coming Messiah, His glorious work, His suffering and His reign. Even John the Baptist did not comprehend a suffering Messiah, even though it was so plainly written down by Isaiah in his 53rd chapter. And I am not so sure that Sister White would have understood your full meaning if you could go back in time when she was writing these predictions down and say to her, "The final message of God's love will be an accumulation of evidence from the Bible and your writings to prove that God has never hurt or killed anyone." Maybe she would, but I wouldn't be surprised if she didn't until you showed her. Didn't Daniel need assistance to understand end-time events? Yes, He did. Even God's perfect and holy angels have been learning more all the time. Notice Daniel's lack of understanding. "I heard, but failed to understand, so I said, 'My Master, to what outcome does it all run?' But he said, 'Move on, Daniel, for the words are secret and sealed until the final period." Dan. 12:8, 9. *Modern Language.* So, God revealed many things to Daniel but saw fit not to reveal all of them to him at that time. The point is, God's prophets didn't know everything, so why should we think that EGW knew everything? It just isn't logical or Biblical.

We who are alive today are blessed beyond all generations who have ever lived upon the earth because we are the generation who can be "wise" and "understand." Daniel

12:10. EGW never defined what the "Wrath of God" is as clearly as she defined the character of God. The rationale behind this, is that God wanted us to concentrate upon His character first, not His "anger or wrath." And once we discovered how Wonderfully loving a God He really is, it would be easy for Him to reveal the simple fact that His wrath is simply when He has to "give up" and "turn us over" to our own passions and lusts," for we refuse to come to Him for complete victory over all our sins.

The Bible clearly defines what "God's Wrath" is in Psalm 78:26-33, 49; Rom. 1:18, 24, 26, 28; Rom. 5:8, 9; I Thess. 2:14-16. And the prophet Jeremiah most emphatically predicted that "The anger (same as wrath) of the Lord" would be understood in the end time. And this "anger or wrath" would not "return" (subside or stop) "until He have executed, and til He have performed the thoughts (intent or purpose) of His heart: in the latter days ye shall consider it perfectly." Jer. 23:19, 20. God's final remnant people will know the very thoughts of God's heart. They will be "wise" and "understand." But what is it that they will understand in the end-time when the whole, entire world is going crazy, falling apart and blowing up in their faces? What is it that we are to know and understand? The answer is: WE WILL KNOW AND UNDERSTAND GOD'S TRUE CHARACTER OF LOVE. WE WILL KNOW THAT HE IS NOT RESPONSIBLE FOR SIN. AND WE WILL KNOW HIS NATURE AND CHARACTER IS "HARMLESS" (Heb. 7:26) AND WE WILL DESIRE TO BE LIKE HIM. WE WILL KNOW THAT HE IS NOT THE ONE WHO IS DESTROYING THE EARTH. WE WILL KNOW THAT HE HAS NEVER HURT OR KILLED OR DESTROYED ANYONE. THIS IS WHAT WE ARE TO KNOW AND UNDERSTAND. AND THIS KNOWLEDGE WILL GIVE US A CHARACTER LIKE HIS WHICH WILL ENABLE US TO SURVIVE THE TERRIBLE TIME OF TROUBLE THAT IS ABOUT TO BREAK UPON THIS EARTH.

So, this is what it truly means to go *"Into the Father's heart,"* in this last hour of earth's most traumatic history God's people have ever experienced. But we will survive it if we go with Jesus, by faith, into the Father's great and magnificent heart of love. This is what Jesus, meant in John 14:20, when He said, "At that day ye shall know that I am in My Father, and ye in me, and I in you." "But ye know him; (the spirit of truth) for He dwelleth with you, and shall be in you." John 14:17. In Christ's sublime intercessory prayer for us in Gethsemane He prayed that all of His people (disciples) would be with Him and His Father . . ." That they all may be one; AS THOU, FATHER, ART IN ME, AND I IN THEE, THAT THEY ALSO MAY BE ONE IN US . . . that they may be one, even as we are one: I in them, and thou in me, that they may be made perfect in one; and that the world may know that thou has sent me, and hast loved them, as thou hast loved me." John 17:21-23.

Sister White speaks of the "Third Angel's message" as being "the last call," to the world in "EARLY WRITINGS," page 278. And on page 277 she describes the mighty angel of Rev. 18 and its work of joining with and uniting His voice with the third angel. Additional references to prove this can be found in the Scripture index to EGW's writings. You will find that she refers to the event described in Rev. 18:1-4 well over 100 times. Here is just one such reference. "The angel who unites in the proclamation of the third angel's message is to lighten the whole earth with his glory (character). GC, page 611. cf. Evang. 424.

Every time EGW uses the word "Glory," you know she is referring to the character of God, for she clearly defines it. Notice: "By implanting in their hearts the principles of His word, the Holy Spirit develops in men the attributes of God. The light of His glory—His character—is to shine forth in his followers. Thus they are to glorify God, to lighten the path to the Bridegroom's home, to the city of God, to the marriage supper of the Lamb." COL 414. From COL 414-421 the character of God message that God's people are to give is clearly outlined. This final message is also tied in with the wise virgins in the sense that the extra oil is simply an enlightenment from the Holy Bible about God's character of love—that He is *"harmless,"* Heb. 7:26, and has never hurt or killed anyone. Therefore, it is safe to go into His Wonderful and great heart of love in the most holy place of the sanctuary, which is our marriage to Him.

Why is it that most SDAs will not accept this idea that God is *"harmless"* and has never hurt or killed anyone? I think it is a matter of emphasis. Most sincere SDAs relate to the sanctuary in the Old Testament in terms of all the slaughtering of animals that went on every day as a way of life. And even though Christ's death took it all away, they are convinced that God was the one who thought the whole system up in the first place and commanded Israel to do it. They emphasize all of the symbols in the sanctuary service that pointed forward to Christ's death as proof that God had to have been the one to design the sanctuary service. They think that I disagree with them on this point when actually I agree. I have never said that Satan designed the sanctuary or the symbols that pointed forward to Christ's sacrifice. God Himself designed that because He knew exactly what they would do to Him when He came to this earth. I deal with this subject of the mercy seat and the atonement in IFH 250-253. Mercy is not in Satan's vocabulary. He would never design anything that would provide any kind of mercy for anyone, at anytime, anywhere. But God would. And that is just what the Lord did after Israel chose to begin slaughtering animals. He devised the sanctuary with its exact dimensions, rituals and services so each time any Israelite chose to slaughter and innocent animal to obtain forgiveness, it would point forward to the death of Christ. I think God was hoping that it would soften their hearts and lead them to repentance. Instead it had the opposite effect. It only hardened their hearts. I hope you noticed that I used the word "chose" when speaking of the sacrificial system. I did that on purpose, for it simply gives more proof to my argument that the slaughtering of animals was not God's original idea or perfect will. Please read with me now Lev. 1:3. *"If his offering be a burnt sacrifice of the herd, let him offer a male without blemish: he shall offer it of his own voluntary will at the door of the tabernacle of the congregation before the Lord."*

You must remember that once God created the human race with the power of *Free Choice* He would never reverse His decision or take it away from us. Once God does something, it is forever. It is perfect and never has to be changed. But when we choose something that is not good for us and He steps in to regulate and control it to save us from the worst effects of our own wrong choice, God will claim it was all His fault. He will record His actions as if the whole system and scheme of things was His idea to start with. Organized religion cannot comprehend this, for they are continually emphasizing God's justice instead of His mercy. And yet, He will give little hints and clues to the careful and observant reader, that even though He is in charge of everything, it is not what He really wants. All those Scriptures are given in chapter 28 of my book, IFH, in the chapter, "THE ANIMAL SACRIFICE SYSTEM."

Now, we already noticed in Lev. 1:3 that the slaughtering of animals to atone for his or her sins, was to be a voluntary act. It was not to be forced, for God never uses force. "But," someone may ask, "how could a person get their sins forgiven back then without the shedding of blood?" That is a very good question, and the answer is quite simple. Just look at the life of Christ. Never once did He tell someone to go to the temple and sacrifice an animal in order to atone for his or her sins. No, He did not command or even suggest that the blood of animals could ever atone for their sins in any way, shape, or form. In fact, He cleansed the temple precincts twice to show His complete rejection of the whole system which He said over and over again through the prophets that He had never "desired, delighted in, wanted, or commanded in the first place. *"But if ye had known*

**what this meaneth, I will have mercy, and not sacri-
fice, ye would not have condemned the guiltless. For
the son of man is Lord even of the Sabbath day."** Matt.
12:7, 8. I want you to notice that little word *"mercy."*

The Lord Jesus never uses force, so why would he ever
set up a system that would require innocent animals to
have the life blood forced out of their bodies until they bled
to death? What is more *"forceful"* than crushing an innocent little lamb to the ground and slitting its throat? What
is more *"forceful"* than wringing the head off of a dove or
pigeon and thus *"forcing"* it to die by such a cruel and
traumatic act? See Lev. 1:1-17. Christ never uses force or
compulsion. DA 487. **You may write for my free 90 minute cassette tape on this important subject, "Would
Jesus kill a little sparrow?"**#650.

The whole system of animal slaughter in the Old Testament was based upon force and the wrong kind of *"fear."*
When the Bible tells us *"the fear of the Lord is the beginning of knowledge,"* Prov. 1:7, it's not implying that you
are to live in a state of dread and apprehension, for Jesus
was continually admonishing His disciples to not "fear or
be afraid." Even our English dictionary gives two distinct
definitions of the word, fear. The first definition is "an emotion of alarm and agitation caused by the expectation or
realization of danger." But the second definition is the one
we must apply when we are defining the *"fear of the
Lord,"* which is "extreme reverence or awe, as toward a
supreme power." As soon as Adam and Eve sinned, the Bible
says that they became aware or *"knew that they were
naked."* Gen 3:7. Then they *"hid themselves from the
presence of the Lord . . ."* Why? *"I was afraid, because I
was naked; and I hid myself."* Gen. 3:8-11. And today,
man is still hiding from God because He is still living in a
state of fearfulness and dread because he is still naked. It is
interesting that the first category of the lost in the lake of
fire are the *"fearful."* Rev. 21:8. But we don't have to be
"naked." Here is Jesus' counsel: *"I counsel thee to buy of*

me gold tried in the fire, that thou mayest be rich; and white raiment, that thou mayest be clothed, and that the shame of thy nakedness do not appear; and anoint thine eyes with eyesalve, that thou mayest see." Rev. 3:18.

This then, is the *"Divine Remedy."* He wants us to "see" the truth, which is Himself, even our precious Lord Jesus Christ. He has taught us the truth of who He really is whom Isaiah declared to be our "MIGHTY GOD AND EVERLASTING FATHER, THE PRINCE OF PEACE." (Isaiah 9:6), so we don't have to be afraid of God, our Wonderful, Heavenly, Father. He does not ask for, nor require, that kind of worship. *"For God hath not given us the spirit of fear; but of power, and of love, and of a sound mind."* 2 Tim. 1:7.

The forms and ceremonies man has devised are carnal works of the flesh designed to regain the paradise of our first parents lost through disobedience. Outside the gates of Eden Satan led Adam and Eve to believe that the shedding of innocent blood would absolve the guilt they had incurred by eating of the forbidden tree. But the prophet has declared God's distaste for the bloody sacrifices of animals.

"For I desired Mercy, and not Sacrifice; and the Knowledge of God more than burnt offerings. But they like men (Adam) have transgressed the covenant: there have they dealt treacherously against me." Hosea 6:6, 7. Jesus quoted these verses twice in His teachings. Matt. 9:13 and Matt. 12:5-8. Stephen was stoned because he dared to speak against the animal sacrifice system, showing it was worshipping "the host of heaven:" Acts 7:42; Amos 5:25. He revealed the unwelcome truth that God does not dwell "in temples made with hands;" Acts 17:24, 25; but seeks men and women who will simply "worship Him in spirit and in truth," as Christ revealed to the woman at the well. John 4:23, 24. This Samaritan woman, scorned and rejected by her own people, was more open to truth than Christ's own disciples; and Jesus was able to reveal Himself to her, in

terms of His ultimate reality, when she spoke of her belief in the coming Messiah. "Jesus saith unto her, I that speak unto thee am he." the LB says, "I am the Messiah." John 4:26. It is interesting that this is the only person Jesus ever revealed Himself to so clearly and openly, including His own disciples. For even to them He was continually having to "prove" Himself, for they had so many preconceived ideas and notions of what the Messiah was supposed to do or say. But this "fallen" woman did not require signs, wonders or miracles, but accepted Christ simply on the basis of His knowledge of her own personal life, which probably would have offended most people.

The same spirit of pride and unbelief that led ancient Israel to reject the Son of God almost 2,000 years ago is still in the world today. Professed Christians want to cling to a "killer God" concept of the Messiah the same as the Jews did in their day. I am not judging anyone, for I have been guilty of the same attitude myself. It was hard for me to give up some of my pre-conceived opinions about what the Bible has to say about many of the issues I am dealing with in this book, as well as IFH which was published in 1982. It takes time to understand some of these points, but if one is willing to earnestly pray and study with an open mind, I am confident the Lord is going to make some of these things crystal clear to you.

"But Pastor Clute, haven't you read what Sister White said about the animal sacrifice system?" Yes, I have. For example, she said that "Christ was the originator of the entire Jewish system of sacrifices." ST 273. She also said "the very system of sacrifices was devised by Christ, and given to Adam as typifying a Saviour to come." SD 225. She also says "Christ instituted" this same system. 1 BC 1104; 1SM 230. She says "the Lord gave them (Israel) at Sinai definite instruction concerning the sacrificial service. After the completion of the tabernacle, He communicated with Moses from the cloud of glory above the mercy seat and gave him full directions concerning the system of offerings and the forms of worship to be maintained in the sanctuary. The ceremonial law was thus given to Moses, and by him written in a book. But the law of Ten Commandments spoken from Sinai had been written by God Himself on the tables of stone and was sacredly preserved in the ark." PP 364, 365.

First of all, we must realize that no matter what happens in this world, God always claims to be the One who did it. "I form the light, and create darkness: I make peace, and create evil: I the Lord do all these things." Isaiah 45:7. For a much more in-depth explanation, please read chapter two of my book IFH, "WHY DOES GOD ALWAYS TAKE THE BLAME?" And also chapter three, "GOD ON TRIAL FOR MURDER." But for right now, let me just say that whatever God allows or permits He claims to "ordain," "institute," "appoint," "give," and/or "destroy." And in Psalm 17:13 He calls the "wicked," His "sword." Many other examples might be cited but this should be enough to prove the point that whatever God allows or permits He claims to have ordained and instituted. On page 1 of "Steps to Christ," the Lord says that the "thorn and the thistle" were "appointed" by God for man's good, God always takes the blame by saying, "This thing is from me." I Kings 12:24.

This concept of God always taking the blame is what the "mercy seat" is all about. It proves that God is continually shielding us from the "justice" of the law. The law can never show us mercy. The broken law can only condemn us to death. So, the question is: "How can God be just and merciful at the same time? How can He forgive us of our sins and yet maintain the justice of His law?" Notice this beautiful statement by EGW that makes it so plain. "Through Jesus, God's mercy was manifested to men; but mercy does not set aside justice. The law reveals the attributes of God's character, and not a jot or title of it could be changed to meet man in his fallen condition. God did not change His law, *BUT SACRIFICED HIMSELF*, in Christ, for man's redemption. 'God was in Christ, reconciling the world unto Himself.' " 2 Cor. 5:19. DA 762

Now, let me see if I can convince you that God never carries out his "justice" by executing the sinner, but by always allowing and permitting the sinner to exercise his own free choice, which will lead to death if the sinner chooses lord Satan and his way instead of Jesus and His way. We know that God never changes; therefore, the way He chose to solve the sin problem at the beginning and later at the cross is the same way He has operated all along, "For I am the Lord, I change not; therefore ye sons of Jacob are not consumed." Malachi 3:6. If this were the only text in the Bible we had to prove that God does not destroy, it would be sufficient. But there are many others such as James 1:17; Num. 23:19, 20; Psalm 89:34; Hosea 13:9; Heb. 13:8. God did not destroy Satan and His angels at the beginning of the great controversy, and He has not even brought a "railing accusation" against them since, let alone hurt or killed any of them or Satan himself. And the Bible clearly shows that Satan and all of his hosts are going to destroy each other in the final day, Ezek. 28:6-10. All of Satan's followers will turn upon Satan (v. 18) and each other. For further proof read GC 666-672.

We also read in GC 35-36 that God does not "execute" the wicked in the final day. "But when men pass the limits of divine forbearance, that restraint is removed. ***GOD DOES NOT STAND TOWARD THE SINNER AS AN EXECUTIONER OF THE SENTENCE AGAINST TRANSGRESSION***; but He leaves the rejectors of His mercy to themselves, to reap that which they have sown." Cf. Gal. 6:7, "Whatsoever a man soweth, that shall he also reap." This helps to disprove the idea that mercy is only given to the sinner for a certain time, but when God has had His fill of man's sins and rebellion He pours out His "justice." This is incorrect. God never changes. He only and ever shows mercy . . . and His justice has already been satisfied at the cross when He took all of the wrath and justice of the ages upon Himself. He "paid the price" with His own blood . . . the price we made Him pay because we thought

He was a bloody God and the Father wanted His pounds of flesh and His gallons of blood from the human race and Jesus "paid" this for us at the cross. The whole truth of the matter is that there was "no debt to pay." All future "justice" will be executed upon sinners by themselves, as we read in Ezek. 38:21, Zech. 14:13. Is that shocking to you? The story of the prodigal son in Luke 15 shows that the debt the prodigal son thought he owed his dad was only a figment of his own imagination. It was in his mind, but not in his dad's mind. *"And you that were sometime alienated and enemies in your mind by wicked works, yet now hath he reconciled in the body of His flesh through the death."* Col. 1:21, 22.

Yes, beloved, the enmity between God and man has always been on our part, never on God's part. The Lord has always had a positive attitude toward us, but we are the ones who have had a negative attitude toward God because our human father, Adam, sold us down the river into the bondage and slavery of Satan's idea of what God is like. The only way that false image of God could be reversed in our minds was for God Himself to come down in a body of flesh and live among us and show us the truth. And that is just what God did. "And the Word was made flesh, and dwelt among us, (and we beheld His glory (character) as of the only begotten of the Father,) full of grace and truth." John 1:14. "and his name shall be called Wonderful, Counsellor, The mighty God, the Everlasting Father, The Prince of Peace." Isa. 9:6. "And they shall call His name Emmanuel, which being interpreted is, God with us." Matt. 1:23.

It is very difficult for our carnal minds to think of God as always and only being a God of mercy, for we think of mercy as being equivalent to weakness. But the Servant of the Lord has shown us clearly that this is not the case at all. "His (Christ's) object was to reconcile the prerogatives of Justice and Mercy, and let each stand separate in its dignity, yet united. His mercy was not weakness, but a terrible power to punish sin because it is sin; yet a power to draw to it the love of humanity. Through Christ, Justice is enabled to forgive without sacrificing one jot of its exalted holiness." 7BC 935, 936.

Now, let me show you how God punishes sin and sinners. I think this will help you to see that God never deviates from the eternal principles of His government. The Lord operates on an altogether different set of standards than Satan or man. "Rebellion was not to be overcome by force. Compelling power is found only under Satan's government. The Lord's principles are not of this order. His authority rests upon goodness, mercy, and love; and the presentation of these principles is the means to be used. God's government is moral, and truth and love are to be the prevailing power." "Desire of Ages," 759. Please note the word "justice" is missing from this definition.

Notice now from the scripture and EGW how God punishes. "When parents or rulers neglect the duty of punishing iniquity, God Himself will take the case in hand. His restraining power will be in a measure removed from the agencies of evil, so that a train of circumstances will arise which will punish sin with sin." PP 728. Cf. Jere. 2:19. Here then is how God "punishes" and pours out His "wrath," and sends "judgment" upon the wicked. And this principle and modus operandi has never deviated or changed from Lucifer's rebellion til the present moment. Nor will it ever change. How then are the wicked destroyed in the final day when Christ comes and after the 1,000 years? Again, EGW clearly tells us without contradicting the principles she has already revealed God operates on at all times. ***"THEN SHALL THEY THAT OBEY NOT THE GOSPEL BE CONSUMED WITH THE SPIRIT OF HIS MOUTH AND BE DESTROYED WITH THE BRIGHTNESS OF HIS COMING.*** 2 Thess. 2:8. ***LIKE ISRAEL OF OLD THE WICKED DESTROY THEMSELVES***; they fall by their iniquity. By a life of sin, they have placed themselves so out of harmony with God, their natures have become so debased with evil, that the manifestation of His glory is to them a consuming fire." GC 37. Now, friend of mine, look at how Sister White has interpreted the phrases "Spirit of His mouth" and "brightness of His coming." She is consistent with what she has been saying all along . . . "The wicked destroy themselves." And that is precisely what the Bible says, "O Israel, thou hast destroyed thyself; but in me is thine help." Hosea 13:9. I like the very last verse of this book. "Who is wise, and he shall understand these things? prudent, and he shall know them? for the ways of the Lord are right, and the just shall walk in them: but the transgressors shall fall therein." Hosea 14:9. Cf. Dan. 12:3. Notice, beloved, this verse does not say that the wicked shall be *"pushed"* by God, but that they shall *"fall."* God never forced His highest angel, Lucifer, out of heaven when Lucifer rebelled. No, for God never uses force. Lucifer *"fell."* Isa. 14:12-14; Luke 10:18. And Jude 6 tells us the evil angels *"left."* Furthermore, Rev. 12:4 says the dragon's tail (Satan's tail) *"drew the third part of the stars (angels) of heaven, and did cast them to the earth."* See additional information on pages 296-298.

And so, we see that God never uses force or compulsion to accomplish His purposes or to complete His mission. "It is no part of Christ's mission to compel men to receive Him. It is Satan, and men actuated by his spirit, who seek to compel the conscience. Under a pretense of zeal for righteousness, men who are confederated with evil angels sometimes bring suffering upon their fellow men in order to convert them to their ideas of religion; *BUT CHRIST IS EVER SHOWING MERCY*, EVER SEEKING TO WIN BY THE REVEALING OF HIS LOVE. He can admit no rival in the soul, nor accept of partial service; but He desires only voluntary service, the willing surrender of the heart under the constraint of love." AA 541.

Many people think that God the Father planned the crucifixion of Jesus. In other words Judas had no choice as to whether or not he would betray his Lord, nor did Pilate or any of the Jewish leaders. They were all destined to do just what had been planned by the Father from all eternity. *This is the doctrine of predestination.* God has predetermined your fate and you have no choice in the matter but to act out the part God has already assigned for you to play. Some theologians of the past have taught such doctrines which make God appear as a tyrant. But EGW presents a much different picture. And the Bible does too. Christ is portrayed as weeping over the city of Jerusalem and doing everything in His power to stop them from crucifying Him. "Jerusalem had been the child of His care, and as a tender father mourns over a wayward son, so Jesus wept over the beloved city. How can I give thee up? How can I see thee devoted to destruction? Must I let thee go to fill up the cup of thine iniquity? *One soul is of such value that, in comparison with it, worlds sink into insignificance; but here was a whole nation to be lost. When the fast westering sun should pass from sight in the heavens, Jerusalem's day of grace would be ended. While the procession was halting on the brow of Olivet, it was not yet too late for Jerusalem to repent."* DA 577, 578.

Now, I want to pause here a moment and consider what we have just read. Notice, that Christ is not trying to close Jerusalem's probation . . . Oh, no!! The very opposite is true. He is trying to extend it! Let us read on and please notice the contrast between the *"angel of mercy"* and the angel of *"justice and swift-coming judgment."*

And also notice that Christ is doing everything he can to talk them out of crucifying Him. We will continue on with the quote just where we left off. "THE ANGEL OF MERCY was then folding her wings to step down from the golden throne to give place to JUSTICE AND SWIFT-COMING JUDGMENT. But Christ's great heart of love still pleaded for Jerusalem, that had scorned His mercies, despised His warnings, and was about to imbrue her hands in His blood. *If Jerusalem would but repent, it was not yet too late. While the last rays of the setting sun were lingering on temple, tower, and pinnacle, would not*

*some good angel lead her to the Saviour's love, and
avert her doom?* Beautiful and unholy city, that had
stoned the prophets, that had rejected the Son of God, that
was locking herself by her impenitence in fetters of
bondage,—her day of mercy was almost spent! *Yet again
the Spirit of God speaks to Jerusalem."* DA 578.

This is a perfect example of the character of God as
portrayed in I Cor. 13:7, for it shows so clearly that God
never gives up on His people. *"Beareth all things,
believeth all things, hopeth all things, endureth all
things. Charity (love) never faileth;"* In chapters 23-26 of
IFH, I touch on this unfailing, undying love of Christ over
and over again. I try to show the deep emotion God feels for
the lost, even for Lucifer, His first created being and oldest
son. Listen to God weeping over Ephraim and Israel. *"How
shall I give thee up, Ephraim? how shall I deliver thee,
Israel?* . . . mine heart is turned within me, my repentings
are kindled together."* Hosea 11:8. and in the next verse God
says *"I will not return to destroy Ephraim: for I am
God, and not man."*

Now let us find out who really planned the death of
Jesus. *"CHRIST'S BETRAYAL, TRIAL, AND CRUCI-
FIXION WERE ALL PLANNED BY THE FALLEN
FOE. HIS HATRED, CARRIED OUT IN THE DEATH
OF THE SON OF GOD, PLACED SATAN WHERE HIS
TRUE DIABOLICAL CHARACTER WAS REVEALED
TO ALL CREATED INTELLIGENCES THAT HAD
NOT FALLEN THROUGH SIN. THE HOLY ANGELS
WERE HORROR-STRICKEN THAT ONE WHO HAD
BEEN OF THEIR NUMBER COULD FALL SO FAR
AS TO BE CAPABLE OF SUCH CRUELTY. EVERY
SENTIMENT OF SYMPATHY OR PITY WHICH THEY
HAD EVER FELT FOR SATAN IN HIS EXILE, WAS
QUENCHED IN THEIR HEARTS. THAT HIS ENVY
SHOULD BE EXERCISED IN SUCH REVENGE
UPON AN INNOCENT PERSON WAS ENOUGH TO
STRIP HIM OF HIS ASSUMED ROBE OF CELES-*

TIAL LIGHT, AND TO REVEAL THE HIDEOUS DEFORMITY BENEATH; BUT TO MANIFAST SUCH MALIGNITY TOWARD THE DIVINE SON OF GOD, WHO HAD WITH UNPRECEDENTED SELF-DENIAL, AND LOVE FOR THE CREATURES FORMED IN HIS IMAGE, COME FROM HEAVEN AND ASSUMED THEIR FALLEN NATURE, WAS SUCH A HEINOUS CRIME AGAINST HEAVEN THAT IT CAUSED THE ANGELS TO SHUDDER WITH HORROR, AND SEV-ERED FOREVER THE LAST TIE OF SYMPATHY EXISTING BETWEEN SATAN AND THE HEAVENLY WORLD (3SP 183, 184)." 5BC 1149, 1150.

Did you notice how even the angels were not fully aware of Satan's terrible lies and deceptions and still felt sorry for him until he caused Christ to be condemned to death by crucifixion? And so Jesus actually had to let Satan and his angels do this to Him in order to reveal to them, the unfallen worlds and all of humanity the evil of Satan's arguments and government. See 5BC 1150; DA 761; GC 501; DA 341. Also on page 72 of COL, EGW strongly implies that the main purpose of Christ's death was to reveal God's love and to unmask Satan's lies. *"Through long ages God has borne the anguish of beholding the work of evil, He has given the infinite Gift of Calvary, rather than leave any to be deceived by the misrepresentations of the wicked one:"* The last part of this same quote indi-cates that God wants us to be just as "forebearing" toward our fellow men as God is toward Satan. The unveiling of Satan's character has taken nearly 6,000 years for both man and angels. *But it was the death of Christ that really exposed Satan more than anything else.* This is what we call "progressive revelation." That is, we learn more and more as we go along. The main point I wish to make here is that the cross of Jesus *was not to pay a debt but to manifest the love of God* and the hatred of Satan. There was a debt to be paid and a barrier to be removed alright, *but the debt was not in God's mind*, for He did not consider that we owed Him anything. *The debt and barrier was in our own minds in that we were afraid of God. Jesus came to remove this debt and barrier so we could see the truth about God and be set free.* What sets us free is the knowledge or truth about God. "And ye shall know the truth, and the truth shall make you free." John 8:32. And Jesus said in John 17:3 that eternal life is based upon knowing God. "And this is life eternal, that they might know thee the only true God, and Jesus Christ, whom thou has sent." We also read in DA 758 that it was "Not until the death of Christ," that "the character of Satan" was "clearly revealed to the angels or to the unfallen worlds. The archapostate had so clothed himself with deception that even holy beings had not understood his principles. They had not clearly seen the nature of his rebellion." Cf. DA 23-25.

Now that we have come this far in our understanding of the issues and the principles involved in the struggle between Christ and His angels and Satan and his angels, we are ready to go deeper into the Word of God and learn how to distinguish between Lord Jesus and lord Satan when we read the Bible. I touched on this briefly in IFH 350, 351, and 405. But there is much more to learn. First of all, let us document the fact from EGW that God does only good (James 1:7) and Satan is the author of all sin, sickness, calamity and death. See GC 589, 590. "Satan, the author of disease and misery, will approach God's people where he can have the greatest success." CD 375. Cf. CD 119, 120. See also Luke 13:16 and Acts 10:38.

Here is further proof that God has nothing whatever to do with causing the evil in the world. "Not one noxious plant was placed in the Lord's great garden, but after Adam and Eve sinned, poisonous herbs sprang up. In the parable of the sower the question was asked the Master, 'Didst not thou sow good seed in thy field? how then hath it tares?' The Master answered, 'An enemy hath done this.' All tares are sown by the evil one. Every noxious herb is of his sow-ing, and by his ingenious methods of amalgamation he has corrupted the earth with tares (MS 65, 1899 [published in F.D. Nichol, ***Ellen G. White and Her Critics***]). And again, "Christ never planted the seeds of death in the system. Satan planted these seeds when he tempted Adam to eat of the tree of knowledge which meant disobedience to God. Not one noxious plant was placed in the Lord's great garden, . . ." 2SM 288.

Through the years as I have researched into this subject of God's character I have studied the writings of Ellen G. White extensively. In all of my research I have not found one EGW quote which calls Jesus, God or the Holy Spirit "the destroyer." But EGW does identify Satan as the "DESTROYER," "MURDERER," AND "KILLER." For example, when Jesus preached in the synagogue at Nazareth the people were greatly offended. EGW tells why. "The words of Jesus to His hearers in the synagogue struck at the root of their self-righteousness, pressing home upon them the bitter truth that they had departed from God and forfeited their claim to be His people. Every word cut like a knife as their real condition was set before them. They now scorned the faith with which Jesus had at first inspired them. They would not admit that He who had sprung from poverty and lowliness was other than a common man. Their unbelief bred malice. Satan controlled them, and in wrath they cried out against the Saviour. They had turned from Him whose mission it was to heal and restore; NOW THEY MANIFESTED THE ATTRIBUTES OF THE DESTROYER." DA 239, 240. And again, "Before men and angels Satan has been revealed as man's enemy and destroyer; Christ, as man's friend and deliverer. His Spirit will develop in man all that will ennoble the character and dignify the nature (2 Tim. 1:7 quoted). He has called us 'to the obtaining of the glory'—character— 'of our Lord Jesus Christ;' and to be 'conformed to the image of His son.' " 2 Thess. 2:14 and Rom. 8:29." Notice again how EGW clearly defined the word glory as specifically being Christ's character. You may also notice that "image" and "glory" are synonymous terms and therefore equal also to the word character.

In the book "Ministry of Healing," EGW says, "Behind the liquor seller stands the mighty DESTROYER of souls, and every art which earth or hell can devise is employed to draw human beings under his power." MH 338. And then this one: "SICKNESS, SUFFERING, AND DEATH ARE WORK OF AN ANTAGONISTIC POWER. SATAN IS THE DESTROYER; GOD IS THE RESTORER." MH 113.

Just this one quotation will answer many, many questions in the Bible. For example, who brought the leprosy upon Miriam? Well, if Satan is responsible for all sickness and disease, then it had to be Satan. "OUR HEAVENLY FATHER DOES NOT WILLINGLY AFFLICT OR GRIEVE THE CHILDREN OF MEN. *HE IS NOT THE AUTHOR OF SICKNESS AND DEATH*; HE IS THE SOURCE OF LIFE." "Gospel Workers," page 239. See also "COUNSELS ON HEALTH," 563. Is it not interesting that EGW says God does not "willingly afflict or grieve the children of men,"[1] as if God is doing it and then she clearly states that He is not doing it. It is very much like the statement God makes to Satan in the book of Job. Listen: "And the Lord said unto Satan, Hast thou considered my servant Job, that there is none like him in the earth, a perfect and an upright man, one that feareth God, and escheweth evil? And still he holdeth fast his integrity, although thou movedst me against him, to destroy him without cause." Job 2:3. KJV. See how God is taking the blame there? Now, notice how the LB paraphrases this. "And he (Job) has kept his faith in me despite the fact that you persuaded me to let you harm him without any cause." You see, nothing can happen to any of God's children unless God allows it to happen. Satan is not allowed to hurt us unless God allows it. I want you to notice

[1]EGW is here paraphrasing Lam. 3:33.

also that God is speaking in the first person. When He refers to Himself, He does not call Himself, "THE LORD," but says, "I or Me." This particular fact will be most important when we come to certain passages later on. Also, I want you to see that everything that God allowed Satan to do to Job was suggested by Satan, not God. For example, " 'skin for skin,' Satan replied. 'A man will give anything to save his life. Touch his body with sickness and he will curse you to your face!' 'Do with him as you please,' the Lord replied: 'only spare his life.' " Job 2:4. LB.

The Bible uses the word "destroyer" only seven times. Here are the texts so you can look them up yourself. Exodus 12:23; Judges 16:24; Job 15:21; Psalm 17:4; Proverbs 28:24; Jer. 4:7; I Cor. 10:10. There are many other titles and allusions to Satan in the Scriptures. I will only refer to a few more as you can look them up yourself in a Strongs' or Young's concordance of the Bible. I Peter 5:8 refers to Satan as a roaring lion who is going around the earth looking for people to "devour." Mal. 3:11 also refers to Satan as the "devourer." Yet in Amos 4:9 and hundreds of other Scriptures God claims to be the one who is devouring their crops, putting diseases upon them, and destroying them personally. See Deut. 28:20-61. Sincere SDAs and Christians of all faiths read these texts and say, "If God says He does it then I believe He does it." If you try and explain that the Hebrew prophets always put the blame upon God because He was allowing it to happen, they say you are changing the Word of God. And, yet these same dear people will not take the Bible literally when it says that the wicked are going to be burned up in "everlasting" fire and the "smoke of their torment" goes up "forever." So they are quite inconsistent in their interpretation of the Bible.

Beloved, unless a person is really seeking God in this matter of understanding his true character of love, he is not going to be able to understand it. So, I plead with you most earnestly to seek the Lord carefully as you study this subject, for it is a very serious issue; and we do not want to end up rejecting the Messiah again as the Jews of old did all through their sad history.

Now, we are ready to go to our first text where we are going to identify two personalities. "For the Lord will pass through to smite the Egyptians; and when he seeth the blood upon the lintel, and on the two side posts, the Lord will pass over (pause at) the door, and will not suffer (allow or permit) the DESTROYER to come in unto your houses to smite you." Exodus 12:23. Notice here that you have two Lords in this text above. The first Lord is going to "smite the Egyptians" and the second Lord is going to stop or "not suffer or allow" the DESTROYER (Satan) to come into the Hebrew dwellings because they have applied the blood on their doors.

In the above paragraph I put the (pause at) in parenthesis because of a note at the bottom of my Laymen's four translation Bible I have been using since 1975. It says, LB Or, "He will pause at the door of that home and not permit the Destroyer to enter" . . . Now, when we go to the actual Hebrew word for "pass over" in Strong's Hebrew section, 6452, we find the word is PACAH, meaning "to hop, i.e. (fig.) skip over (or spare); by impl. to hesitate; also . . . to limp, dance: become lame, leap, pass over." The LB is a paraphrase, not an actual translation, so they will use a word in our modern vocabulary that is closest to the real meaning of the text; and in this case, the word "pause" is a synonym of hesitate which Strong's says is implied in the word itself. In order to convey the full meaning of the word pause, I should attach the preposition "at" to it—*"the Lord will pause at the door, and will not allow Satan (the destroyer) to come in and hurt or kill you."* This gives a much clearer picture of the physical action taking place between Christ and Satan at each door in Egypt. When I preach about this I sometimes act out the drama by moving away from the pulpit and block a door way entrance and stretch or extend my hands as I cry out as Jesus would or did (and still does) to Satan "You cannot come in here Satan, for this person has applied my blood over the door of his heart and I have a legal right to protect him."

The first time I preached on the character of God was August 7, 1976, At McMinnville, Oregon, in the old SDA Church, which was sold and replaced by a new building in another location. My subject was "GOD'S WRATH." My original notes are in this manuscript on page 363. The purpose of placing them in this book is to prove that I have not deviated from or changed one concept or principle God gave me in that first sermon. You can also hear that original sermon on cassette tape #724 "THE WRATH OF GOD." I must confess that I was somewhat nervous about presenting this "new" concept, although EGW had paved the way with her classic statement in COL 84, "GOD DESTROYS NO MAN." The Lord Jesus has helped me from the beginning to continue walking in the light. Beloved, this message has transformed my whole life and is continuing to change me more every single day, for I keep learning more about God's wonderful character of love each day.

I didn't receive much reaction or response from that first sermon. But I think it was about two weeks later that I preached on it again and went into more detail. Some were truly converted, but most people reacted and some really became angry. But that only made me realize that God had given me a message that would really stir the hearts of the people. I continued my memory work in the Psalms, studied, read my Bible, talked about it on the radio and to anyone else who would dialogue with me about it. Finally, I wrote my first manuscript on it in the Spring of 1977, entitling it "DOES GOD KILL PEOPLE?" That really wasn't the title of the book, but I put that question on the cover to get people's attention so they would read the book and find the answer for themselves. The real title of the book is inside. "A CHARACTER LIKE HIS TO SURVIVE THE TIME OF TROUBLE." Well, I didn't intend to go into this much detail about how I first got started on this subject.

What I started to tell you was the experience I had while I was studying and researching for my second sermon on the "Wrath of God."

At that early stage of my understanding I had an excellent grasp of the principle, but I didn't feel that I had enough proof to convince skeptical and critical SDAs whom I knew would be demanding that I "prove" that I was right and they were wrong or retract everything I had said so far. I know the SDA people quite well, having been one all of my life, (a third generation SDA) and having lived and worked with SDAs as much as I have as a colporteur, church school teacher and pastor-evangelist. I know that I like to have "proof" when someone asks me to believe something I haven't heard before. So I decided for this second sermon I would give them "proof." One of the questions I thought should be answered was "who killed the first-born of Egypt?" So, I went to Exodus 12:12, and 23 and read those verses. My heart just sank. I immediately could see what a terrible problem I faced. Here in verse 12 the Bible categorically states that God Himself was going to pass through Egypt and "smite all the firstborn in the land of Egypt." Now, I knew that v. 23 stated that it was the "destroyer" who killed the first-born but since nearly everyone believed that God destroys, I knew they would say that the destroyer was one of God's angel's sent to destroy. At that time I didn't have the following wonderful quote to prove that God's angels never destroy anyone at anytime. Notice: "ANGELS ARE SENT FROM THE HEAVENLY COURTS, NOT TO DESTROY, BUT WATCH OVER AND GUARD IMPERILED SOULS, TO SAVE THE LOST, TO BRING THE STRAYING ONES BACK TO THE FOLD." R & H, May 10, 1906. Cf. Education, page 304. You can also prove from Psalm 103:20 that God's angels keep and obey the Ten Commandments.

But at that time, I didn't have any of this information. I prayed and prayed for help to find something that I could use that would show that Jesus did not order His angel to kill the first-born, nor did He kill the first-born Himself. The Lord led me to **Patriarchs and Prophets**, page 279. *"In awe the people prayed and watched, the heart of eldest born, from the strong man down to the little child, throbbing with indefinable dread. Fathers and mothers clasped in their arms their loved first-born as they thought of the fearful stroke that was to fall that night. But no dwelling of Israel was visited by the death-dealing angel. The sign of blood—the sign of a Saviour's protection—was on their doors, and the destroyer entered not."* After I read this quote tears of joy and gratefulness rolled down my face as I praised the Lord for revealing this truth to me. It was several months later before I learned how to prove that Satan is the destroyer, not Christ. The way you prove it is to take I Cor. 10:10 and Rev. 9:11 which both clearly show that Satan is the destroyer. And then you have Jesus own words. "The thief cometh not, but for to steal, and to kill, and to destroy: I am come that they might have life, and that they might have it more abundantly." Jn. 10:10. And then you have Christ's loving rebuke to James and John when they asked the Lord if He would like for them *"to command fire to come down from heaven, and consume them, even as Elias did? But he turned, and rebuked them, and said, Ye know not what manner of spirit ye are of. For the Son of man is not come to destroy men's lives, but to save them."* Luke 9:54-56. Now, if you go back to Exodus 12:23, you should be able to clearly distinguish between the true, life-giving Lord and the "destroyer." Here are two definite and distinct personalities presented in the Scriptures. The one Lord is giving life and the other is taking it. The Sabbath proves that God is a life-giver, not a life-taker. Do you see how important the Sabbath is here? It proves that God is a life-giver ... a Creator, not a destroyer. And EGW never, ever calls God a destroyer. I challenge anyone to find an EGW quote calling Christ "THE DESTROYER."

Moses, you must go back down this mountain and warn the people not to come up "lest he (Satan) break forth (kill) upon them." Exodus 19:24

Satan appears at Mt. Sinai and claims to be the true God. He brings all the noise and the fireworks and terrifies the people.

In Exodus 19:20-24 Jesus warns Moses that another Lord is appearing in the mountain as "Lord." He commands Moses to go back down to the base of the mountain and warn the people not to come up into the mountain to gaze upon this lord or they will "break forth upon them." vs. 24. The phrase, "lest he break forth," proves Christ is not talking about Himself, for "he" is in the 3rd person singular instead of in the first person singular, "lest I break forth," etc. Ex. 20:3 shows how Jesus speaks in the first person when he is referring to Himself. See also Exodus 24:12.

CHAPTER 12

THE TWO LORDS

"Rebellion and apostasy are in the very air we breathe. We shall be affected by them unless we by faith hang our helpless souls upon Christ. If men are so easily misled now, how will they stand when Satan shall personate Christ, and work miracles? Who will be unmoved by his misrepresentations then— professing to be Christ when it is only Satan assuming the person of Christ, and apparently working the works of Christ?"

2 SM 394
—By Ellen G. White

"Satan will work with all deceivableness of unrighteousness to personate Jesus Christ; if it were possible, he would deceive the very elect. Now if the counterfeit bears so close a resemblance to the genuine, is it not essential to be on your guard, that no man deceive you?"

2 SM 87
—By Ellen G. White

Which one is the true one and which one is the false one? Which Lord is the life giver? Which one is the destroyer?

Now, we are ready to explain a little more detail about the two Lords. Let us go to our first text. "And again the anger of the Lord was kindled against Israel, and [1]he moved David against them to say, Go, number Israel and Judah." 2 Sam. 24:1. You will notice that the relative pronoun, "he" has a 1 by it. I purposely put that there because it refers to a marginal reference which designates the "he" as "Satan." I have found this marginal reference in both the National and Collins Bibles as well as "The Living Word," edition put out by Joseph W. Cain, publisher of San Antonio, Tx. 78201. In the Harper Study Bible published by Zondervan we find this footnote on 2 Sam. 24:1. "24:1 the Lord . . . incited David. The census had fearful consequences, perhaps because it was an indication of David's trust in men rather than in God. Here the Lord is said to have incited David. In I Chron. 21:1 Satan incited him. Both are true. God was the ultimate cause in the sense that he permitted Satan to incite David."

This most insightful comment comes from a non-SDA source, which only goes to prove God has His servants everywhere who understand some of the principles upon which he operates. The main reason I have cited this reference is because it proves conclusively that the noun "Lord" and the relative pronoun "he" referring back to "Lord" sometimes means or refers to "Lord Satan." I have already shown how the Lord Jesus warned Moses that there was *another Lord* in the mountain who would *"break forth upon them,"* and kill them if they were not "sanctified" which simply means that unless the priests and people were not totally dedicated to God by confession of sin and by maintaining a connection to the true God with a right spirit and attitude, this "Lord" (Satan) would have a legal right to kill or destroy them.

Now, I want you to see how the SDA Bible commentary agrees that it was not the true God who moved David to

[1]See illustration on page 256.

number Israel. *"In the verse under consideration we have another instance where God is said to do that which He does not prevent (see PP 728, 739). It was actually Satan who instigated the pride and ambition that led Israel's king to promote procedures to increase the size of his army for the purpose of extending the boundaries of Israel by new military conquests (see PP 747),"* 2BC 710, comment upon Sam. 24:1; Cf. I Chron. 21:1, where the noun "Satan" is used instead of Lord, proving conclusively that the Lord who "moved" David was Lord Satan, not Lord Jesus.

Furthermore, the word "moved" in the Hebrew means "by implication to seduce:—entice," Strong's 5496, Hebrew section. And the Hebrew definition for "seduced" is "(cause to) go astray, deceive, dissemble, (cause to, make to) err, pant, seduce, (make to) stagger, (cause to) wander, be out of the way." Strong's 8582. Webster's dictionary defines "seduce" as meaning "to tempt or entice. To induce to evil; to corrupt;" Tempt is given as one of the synonyms of seduce.

The Bible unequivocally states that God tempts no man. "Let no man say when he is tempted, I am tempted of God: for God cannot be tempted with evil, neither tempteth he any man." James 1:13. Whenever I quote this text in a meeting someone will usually ask me to explain the difference between "tempt," "test," and "prove." The most obvious difference between "TEMPT" and "PROVE" is that tempt has the connotation of leading and even seducing another person away from God by doubting His Word. This is precisely what the "serpent" did to Adam and Eve in the garden of Eden. Yet, the word "tempt" is never used in Gen. 3 to describe the serpent's artful deception. But all through the Bible Satan is referred to as the "tempter," Matt. 4:1; I Cor. 7:5 "that Satan tempt you not . . ." and I Thess. 3:5. Eve complained to God that the Serpent had "beguiled" her. Gen. 3:13. Beguile means to deceive and I Tim. 2:14 says Eve was deceived. Rev. 12:9 tells us that Satan has "deceived the whole world." But the Bible never identifies God as the "tempter" or "deceiver" nor the "destroyer"; for God only allows temptation. He never brings it. Neither does EGW ever assign to God any of the titles I have just mentioned. However, God Himself claims that He "deceives" prophets. Ezek. 14:9. And in 2 Thess. God claims to be the one who will send a *"strong delusion"* to all who reject the truth, "that they should believe a lie: That they all might be damned who believed not the truth, but had pleasure in unrighteousness:" Here again, God takes the blame for whatever He permits to happen because He has given us free will or the power of choice.

The word *"prove"* does not have an evil connotation to it like *"tempt."* For example we read in John 6:5-7 that Jesus asked Philip how they were going to get enough bread to feed the "great multitude." The Bible tells us that the reason Jesus asked him this question was to *"prove him."* Jesus was not leading Philip to doubt Him or His Father, but was in fact increasing his faith by this *"test"* question. It is most interesting that when the word "tempt" is used in the Bible it most often refers to man tempting God instead of God tempting man. One rare exception I can find to this pattern is found in Gen. 22:1-19 where the Bible declares "that God did tempt Abraham," by telling him to "offer him (Isaac) . . . for a burnt offering . . ." In chapter 29 of my book, IFH, "WHO TOLD ABRAHAM TO OFFER UP ISAAC AS A SACRIFICE?" I answer this question in great detail, beginning on page 373. I hope you will read it yourself to increase your understanding of this subject. The only additional information I will add here are some quotes from EGW which I omitted from IFH since it is a work specifically designed for the general public who are not familiar with EGW. Please notice this excellent statement. "What is temptation? It is the means by which those who claim to be the children of God are tested and tried. We read that God tempted Abraham, that He tempted the children of Israel. This means that He permitted circumstances to occur to test their faith, and lead them to look to Him for help. God permits temptation to come to His people today, that they may realize that He is their helper. If they draw nigh to Him when they are tempted, He strengthens them to meet the temptation. But if they yield to the enemy, neglecting to place themselves close to their Almighty Helper, they are overcome. They separate themselves from God. They do not give evidence that they walk in God's way." 1 BC 1094. "Signs of the Times," March 12, 1912.

This statement proves most conclusively to my mind that God allows us to be tempted, but He, Himself, is not the tempter. Satan is the tempter who is trying to seduce us into sin, but God stands by ready to help us withstand any and all temptations if we will only "draw nigh" to Him. You may receive additional insight from "Patriarchs and Prophets," pages 154, 155, where EGW tells us that the reason why this temptation was allowed to come to Abraham was "because Abraham had shown a lack of faith in God's promises . . ." Satan accused Abraham "before the angels and before God of having failed to comply with the conditions of the covenant, and as unworthy of its blessings. God desired to prove the loyalty of His servant before all heaven, to demonstrate that nothing less than perfect obedience can be accepted, and to open more fully before them the plan of salvation." In my book, IFH, I compared this temptation or test to what Job went through when Satan was allowed to bring death, disaster and disease upon Job and his family. EGW says, "Satan works through the elements also to garner his harvest of unprepared souls. He has studied the secrets of the laboratories of nature, and he uses all his power to control the elements as far as God allows. When he was suffered to afflict Job, how quickly flocks and herds, servants, houses, children, were swept away, one trouble succeeding another as in a moment. It is God that shields His creatures and hedges them in from the power of the destroyer." *"Great controversy,"* Page 589.

We have already seen that the noun "Lord" or "God" does not always refer to the one and only "True" God, our Creator and Sustainer. Deuteronomy 6:4 says, "HEAR O

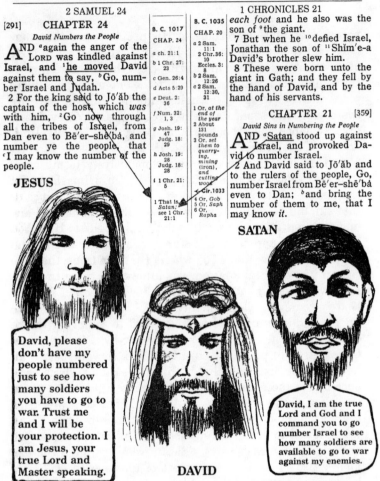

2 SAMUEL 24

[291]   **CHAPTER 24**

David Numbers the People

AND *a*again the anger of the LORD was kindled against Israel, and *1*he moved David against them to say, *b*Go, number Israel and Judah.

2 For the king said to Jō'ăb the captain of the host, which *was* with him, *2*Go now through all the tribes of Israel, from Dan even to Bē'er-shē'bá, and number ye the people, that *c*I may know the number of the people.

| B. C. 1017 |
| CHAP. 24 |
| *a* ch. 21:1 |
| *b* 1 Chr. 27: 23 |
| *c* Gen. 26:4 |
| *d* Acts 5:29 |
| *e* Deut. 2: 36 |
| *f* Num. 32: 1, 3 |
| *g* Josh. 19: 47 Judg. 18: 29 |
| *h* Josh. 19: 28 Judg. 18: 28 |
| *i* 1 Chr. 21: 5 |
| 1 That is, *Satan;* see 1 Chr. 21:1 |

| B. C. 1035 |
| CHAP. 20 |
| *a* 2 Sam. 11:1 2 Chr.36: 10 Eccles. 3: 8 |
| *b* 2 Sam. 12:26 |
| *c* 2 Sam. 12:30, 31 |
| 1 Or, *at the end of the year* |
| 2 About 131 pounds |
| 3 Or, *set them to quarrying, mining* (iron), *and cutting wood* |
| Cir.1033 |
| 4 Or, *Gob* |
| 5 Or, *Saph* |
| 6 Or, *Rapha* |

1 CHRONICLES 21

each foot and he also was the son of *9*the giant.

7 But when he *10*defied Israel, Jonathan the son of *11*Shĭm'e-a David's brother slew him.

8 These were born unto the giant in Gath; and they fell by the hand of David, and by the hand of his servants.

CHAPTER 21   [359]

David Sins in Numbering the People

AND *a*Satan stood up against Israel, and provoked David to number Israel.

2 And David said to Jō'ăb and to the rulers of the people, Go, number Israel from Bē'er-shē'bá even to Dan; *b*and bring the number of them to me, that I may know *it*.

JESUS

David, please don't have my people numbered just to see how many soldiers you have to go to war. Trust me and I will be your protection. I am Jesus, your true Lord and Master speaking.

SATAN

David, I am the true Lord and God and I command you to go number Israel to see how many soldiers are available to go to war against my enemies.

DAVID

ISRAEL: THE LORD OUR GOD IS ONE LORD:" But this "ONE" God has chosen to manifest Himself as a Father, a Son and an ever present, omni-present (everywhere at once) Eternal Spirit. And yet, Isaiah 9:6 tells us that the bodily manifestation of this One God, called the "Son of God" would also be called the "Everlasting Father." And Paul tells us that the "Spirit" who was in charge of giving the Ten Commandment Law is the same Spirit that wants to write the law in our hearts today.

It would seem then that the Ten Commandment Law has always been a spiritual law. But the carnal heart of man has just misinterpreted it legalistically to his own destruction, "for the letter killeth, but the spirit giveth life." 2 Cor. 3:6. And then toward the end of 2 Cor. 3 Paul makes this astounding statement about the Holy Spirit which he says wants to write the Ten Commandments on our hearts. "NOW THE LORD IS THAT SPIRIT:" V. 17. And in Jer. 31:31-34 God says "After those days, saith the Lord, I will put my law in their inward parts, and write it in their hearts; and will be their God, and they shall be my people."

Furthermore, in John 14 Jesus promised to send his disciples "another comforter." v. 16. He called this comforter the "Spirit of Truth." and then in v. 18 He again equates Himself with this spirit by saying, "I WILL NOT LEAVE YOU COMFORTLESS: I WILL COME TO YOU." He also promised that this "Spirit of Truth" would be "IN YOU." v 17. Later in John 17:22 He prays that His disciples "may be one, even as we are one: I in them, and thou in me, that they may be made perfect in one;" v. 22, 23. So again He equates Himself with the Holy Spirit by stating that He would be in His disciples, even as the Father was in Him and He in the Father. As a result of this seeming "double-talk" some Christian groups today believe that there truly is only One God who is able to manifest Himself as three different or separate beings all at the same time. And yet, they claim all three are the one and same Jesus. Of course, the more traditional teaching of most oldline Christian churches is that there are three different Gods, a Father, a Son and a Holy Spirit, but the only One you can see right now is Jesus. The Father and the Holy Spirit are invisible. But some say we will someday be able to see the Father. It is not my purpose here to try and convert anyone to either belief in this ongoing controversy, but I would like to try and clarify it so as to help you understand what happened back there at Mount Sinai when "God" came down and gave His Ten Commandment law.

It is only by the gift of God's Holy Spirit, which I

believe is His very own presence, that we can ever understand any mystery. Jesus told Nicodemus that if he refused
to believe earthly things that he would never be able to
believe what He wanted to tell him about heavenly things.
And to prove His point Jesus told him a great heavenly
truth which remains a great mystery to this day for those
people who refuse to believe. The simple truth Jesus told
Nicodemus was that God is Omni-present. He can be not
only two places at once, but everywhere at once. Listen:
**"And no man hath ascended up to heaven, but he that
came down from heaven, even the Son of man which is
in heaven."** John 3:13. This is indeed a great mystery. How
could Jesus be up in heaven while He was down on planet
earth talking to Nicodemus? Could He actually be two
places at once? One text that may help us is? Col. 2:9. "For
in Him (Christ) dwelleth all the fulness of the Godhead
bodily." If Jesus is in the Father and the Father is in Jesus
then Jesus really can be anywhere the Father is. Again
Paul asserts that it really was God who was "manifest in
the flesh, justified in the Spirit, seen of angels, preached
unto the Gentiles, believed on in the world, received up into
glory." I Tim. 3:16. It is interesting that Paul prefaced these
remarks with the statement: "And without controversy
great is the mystery of godliness."

The reason why some Christians like to argue about
the nature of God or any doctrine of the Bible is because it
tends to inflate the ego. This is known as religious or spiritual pride. Pride is the sin "that turned angels into demons"
SD115. Pride is what "destroys love for God and corrodes
the soul." SM2185. It "shuts out the presence of God." 4T
610. Pride is what closed the Pharisees' heart against
Christ. 1SM 70. Pride is what kept Lucifer from returning
to God and confessing he was wrong and had sinned. God
would have forgiven him. And without a blood sacrifice.
Note the following EGW quote: "He (Lucifer) nearly
reached the decision to return, but pride forbade him." PP
39; GC496. The more knowledge a person has about reli-

gious matters, even Bible knowledge, the greater danger he is in to become a victim of pride which will shut him out of God's presence. Our only hope is to humble ourselves before God, or Satan will take over in our lives without us even realizing it. "Satan has much more power over some who profess the truth than many realize. Self reigns in the heart, instead of Christ. Self-will, self-interest, envy, and pride shut out the presence of God. The love of God must pervade the soul, or the fruits of righteousness will not appear." 4T 610. "Pride lifts itself up unto vanity, leading the human agent to make a god of himself. The gospel of Christ sanctifies the soul, expelling self-love." 9T 212.

"The evil that led to Peter's fall and that shut out the Pharisee from communion with God is proving the ruin of thousands today. There is nothing so offensive to God or so dangerous to the human soul as pride and self-sufficiency. Of all sins it is the most hopeless, the most incurable." COL 154.

But I have good news for you who are studying the character of God. The more you understand God's true character of love the less chance there will be for Satan to ensnare you in pride and self-love. Listen: "Those who have the deepest experience in the things of God, are the farthest removed from pride or self-exaltation. They have the humblest thought of self, and the most exalted conceptions of the glory and excellence of Christ . . . When we have our eyes fixed upon heaven and have clear views of the character of Christ, we shall exalt the Lord God in our hearts." SD 235. RH MARCH 15, 1887.

What could be more shattering to the ego than to discover that God has never hurt or killed anyone? This reinforces the "turn" the other cheek "also" teaching in Matt. 5:39. The carnal nature of man does not want to believe that Jesus actually taught this, but His trial proves that He lived what He taught. And Peter says Christ has left us "an example, that ye should follow in his steps. Who did no sin, neither was guile found in his mouth: Who, when He was reviled, reviled not again; when he suffered, he threatened not; but committed Himself to Him that judgeth right-eously:" I Peter 2:21-23. God's final Remnant are also said to have "no guile" in their mouth" for they are without fault before the throne of God." Rev. 14:5 This is a different kind of "perfection" than has been emphasized in the past. This is a perfection of the inner spirit rather than one of outward behavior. Organized religion stresses adherence to behavioral codes more than an "excellent spirit." Why? Because the carnal nature of man is always seeking to "do" something to earn salvation.

Righteousness by works, such as praying on beads, attending Mass or any kind of services, giving tithes and offerings, passing out literature, or even preaching a ser-mon can take the place "of a meek and quiet spirit, which is in the sight of God of great price." I Peter 3:4. I have done some of these things and much more, but none of them could ever qualify me for a place in heaven. It is only as I am willing to completely surrender my heart to Jesus that I am made whole and changed into His perfect likeness.

Paul draws our attention to ancient Israel as an exam-ple of a whole nation who tried to earn salvation by works. "Behold Israel after the flesh: are not they which eat of the sacrifices partakers of the alter? What say I then? That the idol is any thing, or that which is offered in sacrifice to idols is any thing? But I say, that the things which the Gentiles sacrifice, they sacrifice to devils, and not to God: and I would not that ye should have fellowship with devils." I Cor. 10:18-20. If you compare Acts 7:39-43, you will clearly see that Stephen compared the sacrificial system to idol deifica-tion or reverence which was nothing but demon worship of the "host of heaven" which is clearly the glorification of and the worship of Satan's angels.

Let us now go back to Mt. Sinai again and watch how Satan cons and deceives the entire nation of Israel into wor-shipping him by commanding them to sacrifice animals in order to atone for their sins. Someone may be asking, "But didn't Moses know the difference between God's voice and Satan's voice?" The answer is "no." Remember that Adam was the first man Satan deceived into sacrificing animals in order to expiate or atone for his sins. After Adam sinned he could not tell the difference between God's voice and Satan's voice. God's word tells us that God never desired any sacrifice in the first place, but Adam "dealt treacherously against me (Christ)," right from the beginning. Hosea 6:6,7.

Moses and Aaron also believed that God wanted them to kill a "sacrifice" out in the wilderness "lest He (the Lord) fall upon us with pestilence, or with the sword." Exodus 5:3. But if you read through Exodus 5 very carefully I think you might find a very eye-opening bit of information. But before we go to chapter 5 I want to point out to you that the *"Lord"* who *"sought to kill"* Moses in Exodus 4:24-26 is *lord Satan*. God does not act like that. He is not a killer. Furthermore, Jesus tells us in John 7:22, 23 that circumcision was "of the fathers." To be specific, it was from Abraham, and Jesus is very careful to not take any credit for this rite which was abolished in the New Testament by the Holy Spirit, for it was never given by God in the first place. "The Holy Spirit saw good not to impose the ceremonial law on the Gentile converts, and the mind of the apostles regarding this matter was the mind of the Spirit of God." "Acts of the apostles," page 194. Acts 15:10, 11 says this: "Now, therefore why tempt ye God, to put a yoke upon the neck of the disciples, which neither our fathers nor we were able to bear?" Does that sound like Jesus gave it? No, it doesn't. So, how did it start? I will try and explain it quickly and then get back to Mt. Sinai, for I think there is an important parallel here we must see in order to realize what our God has been up against ever since Adam sinned and gave his mind over to the darkness of Satan's counsel.

First of all, the Bible clearly tells us that God never changes. "Jesus Christ the same yesterday, and today, and for ever." Cf. Mal. 3:6; James 1:17. Since this law of circumcision was abolished, we know God never gave it in the first place. Circumcision is first mentioned in Gen. 17:10 as a token of the covenant between God and Abram. But which *"God"* told Abram to mutilate his body in this way? And why would God need to give him two tokens of His covenant? In Gen. 17:5 God confirmed the covenant to Abraham by changing his name from Abram, meaning "Father" to Abraham which means "Father of nations." All God has ever asked His people to do is "obey His voice," by faith alone, but the carnal heart is always seeking some works of the flesh that they can perform, and Satan is always near to give it to them. Paul points out in Rom. 4:9-12 that Abraham was blessed and commended by God for his faith before he was circumcised, not afterward, for circumcision was a work of the flesh. The only covenant God has ever had with man is the Ten Commandments. See Deut. 13:4 for proof.

Earlier in Gen. 15:1-6 God had promised to give Abraham a son. The token of this promised son was that Abraham's seed would be as numerous as the stars of heaven. This was a simple faith covenant based upon Abraham's faith in God's word. But when Abraham doubted in v. 8 and demanded a sign, Satan was allowed to step in and give Abraham the covenant of works Abraham's doubting, carnal nature wanted. That carnal sign was the slaughter of innocent animals; and as a result of this betrayal of trust, Satan brought a "horror of great darkness upon him." v. 12. The Lord allowed Satan to do this because of Abraham's lack of faith, which was actually disobedience. Abraham learned the terrible things that Satan would do to Abraham's seed. In v. 17, the "smoking furnace" was Satan (Rev. 9:1, 2) and the "burning lamp" or flaming torch (margin) was Christ, Psalm 119:105.

Now we come back to Gen. 17:8. As soon as the words of doubt came out of Abraham's mouth, Satan had a legal right to assert himself and take over in Abraham's life. The same thing happens today to people, as in days of old. Zechariah was struck dumb by Satan when he doubted Gabriel's message (Luke 1:18-20) and Peter sank in the water when he doubted. Matt. 14:30. In Gen. 16 Satan used Sara to lead Abram into sin when she suggested that he have sex with Hagar. This brought incredible heartache and sorrow for all involved including Abraham's supreme test of obedience in Gen. 22 which we have already discussed. But we must realize that through all of these failures to obey, God not only made all things work out for good because Abraham really did love God, but He also was able to use each of these experiences to perfect Abraham's character and make him an example for us today.

For those who believe circumcision is a necessary health measure to prevent infection and disease, I would like to quote from "PARENTS" magazine, April, 1984. In an article entitled "CIRCUMCISION," Paula Adams Hillard, M.D., asst. professor of obstetrics and gynecology at the University of Virginia School of Medicine, states that "more and more parents are weighing the pros and cons before deciding whether or not to have their male infants circumcised . . . Some people think, for example, that circumcision prevents infection, disease and even cancer. The American Academy of Pediatrics has stated, however, that 'routine circumcision of the newborn infant lacks medical justification.' The benefits of circumcision have not conclusively been found to outweigh the potential risks." For example, she states that "the most frequent complication is hemorrhage or greater-than-expected blood loss." Jewish and Moslem history prove that circumcision has a religious basis for its existence. The very fact that this religious rite was abolished by God in the N.T. should give its modern-day Christian proponents some very long and serious thoughts about its real origin. Also *"Acts of the Apostles,"* 194, 195 tell us the Holy Spirit led the Apostles to abolish the ceremonial law and circumcision. EGW never taught that circumcision was given as a health measure. See Pages 364, 485, and 613, of "Patriarchs and Prophets," by EGW.

Now, let us go to Exodus 3 and see what happens. God appears to Moses out of the burning bush and tells Moses

He has come to deliver Israel from their Egyptian bondage and take them to "a good land . . . flowing with milk and honey;" Ex. 3:8. He (God) tells Moses "I will send thee unto Pharaoh, that thou mayest bring forth my people the children of Israel out of Egypt." v. 10. Of course, we know the story of how Moses protests that he is not the man for such an incredible undertaking. But the Lord assures him in v. 12 "Certainly I will be with thee; and this shall be a token unto thee, that I have sent thee: When thou hast brought forth the people out of Egypt, ye shall serve God upon this mountain." Notice here how God has given him a token based upon His own Word and not on any outward sign or display that would appeal to the carnal nature. Notice also that there are no works to be performed by Moses or Israel to earn their deliverance. God's sole reason for delivering them is that they are "my people," and they need my help and I am going to deliver them because I love them. And all God wants in return is for them to love and worship Him. But that is not the way it is going to turn out.

As we all know, Satan led Israel to worship a golden calf and accept a convenant of works based on outward performance instead of an inward purity of heart that leads to a simple faith and trust in Christ, our Redeemer. But why did they do this? Because they were afraid of God. *"All the people saw the lightning and the smoke billowing from the mountain, and heard the thunder and the long, frightening trumpet blast; and they stood at a distance, shaking with fear. They said to Moses, 'You tell us what God says and we will obey, but don't let God speak directly to us, or it will kill us."* Exodus 20:18, 19. LB.

In Hebrews 12:18-29 Paul compares and contrasts the fireworks of Mt. Sinai with serene calmness and peace of Mt. Zion. Now, dear reader, let us just reason this out for a moment. We know God never changes, so why do we have such a contrast between these two mountains? The answer is simple once you are willing to accept the obvious facts. Satan was allowed to bring the fireworks at Mt. Sinai to distort the truth about God, but he was not allowed to do that at Mt. Zion. Why not? Because Jesus' death on the cross took away our fear! We now know Satan is lying about Jesus. Even the angels were enlightened. They saw Satan bring the darkness at the cross. "Satanic agencies confederated with evil men in leading the people to believe Christ the chief of sinners, and to make Him the object of destestation. Those who mocked Christ as He hung upon the cross were imbued with the spirit of the first great rebel. He filled them with vile and loathsome speeches. He inspired their taunts. But by all this he gained nothing. Could one sin have been found in Christ, had He in one particular yielded to Satan to escape the terrible torture, the enemy of God and man would have triumphed. Christ bowed His head and died, but He held fast His faith and His submission to God. (Rev. 12:10 quoted). Satan saw that his disguise was torn away. His administration was laid open before the unfallen angels and before the heavenly universe. *He had revealed himself as a murderer.* By shedding the blood of the Son of God, he had uprooted himself from the sympathies of the heavenly beings. HENCEFORTH HIS WORK WAS RESTRICTED. (That is why He can't fool the angels or Spirit-filled people anymore with his fireworks and smokescreens). Whatever attitude he might assume, (he always acted so holy before, playing on the angel's sympathies as if God had wronged him in some terrible way) he could no longer await the angels as they came from the heavenly courts, and before them accuse Christ's brethren of being clothed with the garments of blackness and the defilement of sin. THE LAST LINK OF SYMPATHY BETWEEN SATAN AND THE HEAVENLY WORLD WAS BROKEN." "Desire of Ages," pgs. 760-761.

In IFH 345-346 I explain why I believe the darkness, lightnings, thunder and the quaking or trembling of the mountain (caused by an earthquake) were not caused by God, but were caused by Satan in reaction to God's presence with all of His holy angels. Satan and his hosts were trembling with fear that God was about to take over these people they had held in spiritual bondage for over 400 years (422 to be exact, 1913 BC to 1491 BC according to Ussher's chronolgy) Did Satan's anger and fear cause the mountain to quake? Yes, because "Great Controversy," (GC) Pg. 590 tells us Satan causes earthquakes and all the quirks of nature. How he does this is beyond our finite intellectual capacity to know or comprehend. But we do know that there is a direct correlation between moral decline and natural disaster. That is, any time you have great wickedness Satan has a legal right to bring physical disaster upon the people and this is called in the Bible, "The Wrath of God." More simply stated it means that whenever God is morally shut out of any geographical locale, Satan is allowed to destroy that place. Sodom and Gomorrha are prime examples. Psalm 78:49 is a key text in understanding this concept. The flood is another example. I discuss the causes for these two disasters plus who killed Uzzah, and who brought the ten plagues upon Egypt from pages 184 to 200 of my book, IFH.

　　On page 175 of "Love Unlimited," by EGW, we find the following statement. *"It was Christ who, amid thunder and flame, had proclaimed the law upon Mount Sinai. The glory of God, like devouring fire, rested upon its summit, and the mountain quaked at the presence of the Lord. The hosts of Israel, lying prostrate upon the earth, had listened in awe to the sacred precepts of the law. What a contrast to the scene upon the mount of the Beatitudes! Under the summer sky, with no sound to break the stillness but the song of birds, Jesus unfolded the principles of His kingdom. Yet He who spoke to the people that day in accents of love, was opening to them the principles of the law proclaimed upon Sinai."* In the next paragraph sister White explains further that when God gave the law at Mt. Sinai *"amid thunder and flame"* He was the same God, but only using a different method to reach these ignorant, degraded, people who needed an impressive display of God's power and majesty. This is the basic answer I have always given too, for I

did not understand God's character enough to realize that
since God never changes that it was not God who was bringing the fireworks, but Satan; and God had to permit it to
happen, for it was about the only thing He could do for
Israel at that time, for they were too rebellious and ignorant
to respond to anything else then.

So, it only proves that Satan can never outmaneuver
the Lord. All of Satan's efforts to defeat God only help the
Lord win by a greater margin, using the analogy of a game
or sporting event. Paul put it this way. "For we can do noth-
ing against the truth, but for the truth." 2 Cor. 13:8. I espe-
cially wish to point out in the last EGW quote that she did
not say Christ brought the *"thunder and flame,"* but had
"proclaimed the law" "amid" the thunder and flame. **AND
SO, IN SPITE OF SATAN'S EFFORTS TO DROWN
OUT THE VOICE OF GOD, HE ONLY MADE THE
OCCASION MORE DRAMATIC AND EXPOSED HIM-
SELF IN THE HISTORY BOOKS OF THE SACRED
ORACLES FOR ALL OF GOD'S PEOPLE TO READ
IN THE FINAL SEGMENT OF EARTH'S HISTORY,
EVEN TODAY.**

Another point we should not miss is that God's voice
was misunderstood at Sinai because Israel heard His voice
with the carnal mind instead of the spiritual mind of
Christ. Notice, dear heart, how God's people hear His voice
at the time of their deliverance. *"Soon we heard the voice
of God like many waters, which gave the day and hour
of Jesus' coming. The living saints, 144,000 in number,
knew and understood the voice, while the wicked
thought it was thunder and an earthquake."* Early Writings, page 15.

This happened once in Christ's ministry when Jesus
asked his Father to "glorify" His own name. *"Then came
there a voice from heaven, saying, I have both glorified
it, and will glorify it again. The people therefore, that
stood by, and heard it, said that it thundered: others
said, an angel spake to him."* John 12:28, 29. **THOSE**

WHO HAD A CARNAL MIND HEARD THUNDER, BUT THOSE WHO POSSESSED THE SPIRITUAL MIND OF CHRIST HEARD THE VOICE OF GOD AS IT WERE AN ANGEL SPEAKING IN A BEAUTIFUL AND MELODIOUS VOICE. HOW ARE YOU HEARING THE VOICE OF GOD TODAY, MY FRIEND? Do you hear Him as if He is speaking in thunderous tones of anger or do you hear the loving voice of Jesus Christ with a beautiful and melodious voice of an angel? Which will it be for you? *"My sheep hear my voice, and I know them and they follow me; And I give unto them eternal life; and they shall never perish . . ."* John 10:27, 28.

If you hear the voice of thunder that makes you tremble with fear, you are hearing the voice of Satan, for the Bible says that *"GOD IS LOVE."* "There is no fear in love; but perfect love casteth out fear: because fear hath torment. He that feareth is not made perfect in love." I John 4:18. John the beloved heard the voice of Jesus "AS THE VOICE OF MANY WATERS."* I believe that would have to be the most peaceful and soul quieting sound one could ever hear, for Jesus is truly the Prince of Peace. Those who know Him will know His voice and will follow Him into the most Holy Place of the sanctuary, even into the very heart of God. "AND THEY SHALL SEE HIS FACE; AND HIS NAME SHALL BE IN THEIR FOREHEADS." Rev. 22:4. *See Rev. 1:15; GC 636.

In Galatians Paul speaks of two covenants. In Gal. 4 he tells us a story about two women in the O.T., Hagar and Sarah who represent the two covenants. Hagar represents the believer who is in bondage (for Hagar was a bond-slave) and Sarah, represents, by contrast, the believer who is free. *"One covenant is from Mount Sinai and bears children who are to be slaves: This is Hagar. Now Hagar stands for Mount Sinai in Arabia and corresponds to the present city of Jerusalem, because she is in slavery with her children. But the Jerusalem that is above is free, and she is our mother."* Gal. 4:24-26 NIV.

In this figurative illustration he calls an allegory, Paul is telling us that the covenant Israel entered into at Sinai was a covenant of works, based on man's idea of God and what God wanted man to do. While it is true that God both spoke and wrote the Ten Commandments at Mt. Sinai the covenant Moses led the people into, because of fear and ignorance, was the old covenant, based on the works of man, namely the killing of animals and endless rituals and ceremonies that God never intended for them to get involved in to start with. But since God created man with freewill, He had to allow them to follow their carnal nature which was compatible with Satan and his false ideas of God, instead of Christ and His true ideas about God.

The Lord always has to work through human instruments. Moses was God's instrument to deliver Israel out of Egyptian bondage. But Moses Himself did not know the real truth about God. But that should not surprise us since even the good and holy angels of God did not know the truth about God until the cross. D.A. 758, 759. Moses' heart was filled with fear at Mt. Sinai. "Indeed, so terrifying was the sight that Moses said, 'I tremble with fear.' " Heb. 12:21. We have already noticed that Moses did not realize or understand that Satan was posing as an angel of light about half way up the mountain. Christ referred to Satan as "the Lord" who would "break forth upon them" Exodus 19:24. Although most of Israel knew of the true God from their forefathers, their knowledge of Him was limited and somewhat distorted. They had also been influenced by the Egyptians and the polytheistic culture and society all around them, which believed in greater and lesser gods, some good and some bad.

In order to more fully understand the cultural background of the times in which the events recorded in the book of Exodus took place, I am going to share some very important information with you from a talk given by Dr. John Wood, a professor of theology, at Atlantic U. College. I will be quoting directly from tapes #382, #383, and #384 for only $9.95 post-paid. Write to GLC P.O. Box 426 Scappoose, OR. 97056. In this first part of his speech Dr. Wood is talking about the culture and times of the Bible, the Old Testament specifically.

"Now we Adventists are used to hearing about the uniqueness of the Bible. We're told how very different the Bible writer's views were from the time in which they wrote, and up to a point, there is truth in that. For example, the infinite, yet personal God of Scripture, moral beyond man's highest conception, is a dazzlingly original concept from the age in which it came. The people who had to do with it took no credit. They said it came by revelation. But it's a fact, for instance, that in Bible times even the fullest understanding of the one God was not held by all the believers, including the people who wrote the Bible. There is not consistently a monotheistic (concept of only one God) viewpoint held in Scripture even here in this beginning point of all theology. The concept of God. There was cultural conditioning, there was change and there was growth. Strange though it seems to say in much of Biblical history. Believers were henotheists, that is they worshipped not the one God, but THE HIGHEST God. This is what the very term THE MOST HIGH God means. It's always well when we examine how something is different from something else or someone different from someone else to ask how they are the same and then talk about the relationship of sameness to difference. The facts are, that the Bible exhibits both sameness and difference, likeness and uniqueness to its culture. To speak of only one of these two opposites is to tell a half truth which in effect is a lie. For example, we might turn to that excellent little Psalm—Ps. 82, where the Most High, who is identified as "EL" warns the other gods who run the world that if they don't shape up he will remove their immortality, kill them like men and take over running the earth directly. Deut. 32 informs us that there are just as many nations on earth as there are gods in the heavens. It's for this reason, since the Canaanite literature tells us that there are exactly 70 gods, beside the chief god, that we find in Gen. 10, the table of the nations, exactly 70 nations, to be run by those gods."

"Israel kept claiming that the uniqueness of Israel was that it was run by the highest God directly. Now this 'henotheism' is certainly not the truth we believe today about God. It's not even the clearest statement about God in the Bible. (But), It was on the right track. The apostle Peter speaks of the 'present truth.' 2 Pet. 1:12. He doesn't imply that truth itself is changing, but that our understanding of truth changes as our growth occurs over history. This is one of the primary reasons why human history is still continuing and one reason why we have the investigative judgement at the end of the age.

"Now, we've been talking about parallel ideas. But of course, there is also **extensive**, (and I want to underline that) **borrowing** within the canon. In a sense, my presentation is a 'double whammy.' I want to warn you. this borrowing is not merely sparse, occasional or minor. Some of the borrowing even contains ideas that we today would call 'misconceptions.' Take the 29th Psalm, the 'Hymn of the Thunderstorm,' which in its original context was the theophany (appearance) or revelation of Baal to his people in Lebanon. In fact, the Psalm has been spoiled by the fact the name of Baal (which represents Satan by the way, editor) has been lifted out and Yaweh has been inserted and that's what messes up the meter entirely. The whole Psalm, which was a major Psalm, is drawn from the Baal cult. I am relating known and provable facts. Forgive me.

"We all know that Moses received the pattern of the sanctuary on the mount. **NOW, THIS HEBREW WORD 'TABNIYTH' UNFORTUNATELY DOES NOT MEAN A STRICT AND EXACT COPY. RATHER IT MEANS 'GENERAL LIKENESS OR SIMILITUDE,' AND WE'RE AWARE THAT IT'S JUST THAT WAY THE**

BOOK OF HEBREWS REFERS TO IT. (HEB. 9:23. FOR THE HEBREW WORD LOOK UP STRONG'S 8403). It is of considerable importance that the wilderness sanctuary looks suspiciously like the tent shrines of Midian at the time, which was a two room or two compartment (shrine). Recently a tent shrine of Midian was discovered, and of course, it is what you would expect, *a two roomed shrine.* In the inner room you have the one place where the god was revealed . . . set up on the 'high place,' what we would call the 'ark of the covenant,' where the idol was—there was a veil between—using the same term—in fact they even had the sprinkling before the veil; it was so dry that even some of the cloth survived. I might also give you an example of this brass serpent that was found there. *The brazen serpent of the Midianites which was held up on a pole.* Sorry about that. But you don't understand really what Moses was implying until you know what the Midianite theology of brazen serpent was. *(Can you imagine the true God telling Moses to make an idol as pagan as this for God's people to look to and 'worship' for healing?? More on this later. Editor). What is also interesting is that these shrines themselves have a suspicious similarity to the temples so popular at the height of 18th dynasty Egypt from which, according to the Adventist chronology, the high chronolgy, Israel had lately come.* Remember too, that the work of the Hebrews in Egypt was to precisely construct the store cities which by their nature had these temples. Now, I could show you pictures here of the high priestly pectorals of the 18th dynasty and the crown jewels of the high priest and then go on to the breastplate of the Hebrew high priest and the crown jewels and talk about the theology and the relationship between the two. It is of some significance that in the eugenic myths the Canaanite "EL" dwells in a tent shrine on the cosmic mountains in the heaven having curtains and inner veil, rooms, furnishings and worst of all, a cherubim throne with the cherubs holding their faces down in respect and awe. Here we have not merely a literary evidence but physical artifacts to illustrate the background to ideas that we are told came directly from God. Now, we ask—was the pattern of the sanctuary come from God or did it come from Canaan or Egypt? Was it natural in origin or supernatural? The fundamentalist division into natural and supernatural and inspired versus contemporary sources itself the error?

"Before we answer we need to go on to some more data. There is the matter of the seven branch candlestick, the menora, which as every Adventist school child ought to know gave light to the holy place in the sanctuary. Now what did the seven branch candlestick represent to the Hebrew believers? You should say, 'Why Jesus, of course. The Light of the world.' And what did the oil in the lamp represent? You ought to say 'Why the oil represented the Holy Spirit.' If you didn't you need to get your tuition back. You should be saying these things because it happens that these identifications are made centuries later by people that we would consider today 'inspired.' It also happens, in point of fact, that this is doubtless not what the Hebrews saw or were intended to see in this symbol. I refer to Carol Myer's book, 'THE TABERNACLE MENORAH: A SYNTHETIC CULT,' where she shows beyond reasonable doubt that this symbol represented the fertility of the women of Israel transmitted from Yaweh to them directly. Why, you may wonder would God not straighten them out and tell them what it really meant? It happens that what it was originally intended to mean at the time the sanctuary was constructed is what it really meant and the later reapplications of these symbols represent the 'larger' implications of the 'present truth;' the wider understanding of the great controversy of a later generation. So which is correct? The answer is—they both are."

This information should give us a better understanding of the cultural conditioning and carnal mindset of ancient Israel. God's original plan for the Hebrew nation was for all 12 tribes to be His "temple" or "abiding place."

If you read the plans God originally gave to Moses on Mt. Sinai, out of His fiery presence in the burning bush, He did not say one thing about sacrificing any animals or building any kind of temple or sanctuary out in the desert. But in chapter 3:11-18, when Moses kept on arguing with God and asking for more signs and proofs, we finally find the word "sacrifice" coming into the discussion. This is most interesting in the light of the abundant testimony we have already seen in this book, as well as in IFH that God states again and again that He never even "spoke" or gave any "commands" about killing animals or making sacrifices. (Jer. 7:22). So which Lord was actually speaking to Moses when this idea was presented? I will let you, the reader, decide that on the basis of the facts and testimony already presented in this manuscript and IFH. The question is: "Do we know His voice today?" Paul appeals to us today. "Wherefore (as the Holy Ghost saith, Today if ye will hear His voice, harden not your hearts, as in the provocation, in the day of temptation in the wilderness: when your fathers tempted me, proved me, and saw my works forty years. Wherefore I was grieved with that generation, and said, They do alway err in their heart; and they have not known my ways. So I sware in my wrath, (when God is forced out) They shall not enter into my rest.) Hebrews 3:7-11. God's "rest" in the Hebrew sense means to "get married," as we see in Ruth 1:9; 3:1. So, anytime you see the idea of sacrifice coming into God's "commands" in Moses' discussions with "God" you better take a very, long, second look at the context, for it is not the true God speaking to Moses, commanding him to kill animals or put a brazen serpent on a pole for their healing, Numbers 21:4-9. We can also see Satan inserting the idea of sacrifice into the people's minds after he successfully frightened them into submission in Exodus 20, at the time when the true God was speaking the Ten Commandments. Read Exodus 20:18-26 and you will again see the righteousness by works concept of killing animals for the forgiveness of sins subtly inserted in "God's" commands in verses 24-

26. And when you continue reading on into chapter 21 through 23:33 you will see some of the laws Christ abolished in Matt. 5. For example, "Eye for eye, tooth for tooth, hand for hand, foot for foot," etc. Ex. 21:24. These laws were some of the most humane laws in the world at that time. But it was based on man's idea of right and wrong, which is a "get even" type of justice. Jesus lifted our minds to the very throne room of God when He came and said, "Ye have heard that it hath been said, An eye for an eye, and a tooth for a tooth: But I say unto you, That ye resist not evil: but whosoever shall smite thee on the right cheek, turn to him the other also." Matt. 5:38. Jesus came to a people whose hardened hearts were filled with a desire to recapture Israel's former "glory" as they had read of in the days of David and Solomon. EGW tells us: *"The people looked eagerly to Christ, hoping that He was the One who was to humble the pride of Rome. With sadness Jesus looks into the upturned faces before Him. He notes the spirit of revenge that has stamped its evil imprint upon them, and knows how bitterly the people long for power to crush their oppressors. Mournfully He bids them, 'Resist not him that is evil: but whosoever smiteth thee on thy right cheek, turn to him the other also. Matt. 5:39, R.V. . . .* The Father's presence encircled Christ, and nothing befell Him but that which infinite love permitted for the blessing of the world. Here was His source of comfort, and it is for us. He who is imbued with the spirit of Christ abides in Christ. The blow that is aimed at him falls upon the Saviour, who surrounds him with His presence. Whatever comes to him comes from Christ. He has no need to resist evil, for Christ is his defense. Nothing can touch him except by our Lord's permission, and 'all things' that are permitted 'work together for good to them that love God.' " Romans 8:28. "LOVE UNLIMITED," PG 200-201.

Beloved, is this not the real issue? The human heart today is even harder than it was in the days of Jesus. We have more hatred and violence than ever and much more sophisticated weaponry and methods of destroying human life than ever before. And so it is today, yes, even this very hour that this message of God's loving, non-violent, non-destructive character must be given to the world. God has called us to not only preach the theology of it but to live the actual reality of it.

Many people still think that God commanded Israel to go out and slaughter their enemies, but He never gave any such command. Listen to this EGW statement: "God had made it their (Israel's) privilege and their duty to enter the land at the time of His appointment, but through their will-ful neglect that permission had been withdrawn. Satan had gained his object in preventing them from entering Canaan; and now he urged them on to do the very thing, in the face of the divine prohibition, which they had refused to do when God required it. Thus the great deceiver gained the victory by leading them to rebellion the second time. They had dis-trusted the power of God to work with their efforts in gain-ing possession of Canaan; yet now they presumed upon their own strength to accomplish the work independent of divine aid. 'We have sinned against the Lord,' they cried; 'we will go up and fight, according to all that the Lord our God commanded us.' Deuteronomy 1:41. (Now watch what God says through EGW about this. Editor.) So terribly blinded had they become by transgression. *The Lord had never commanded them to 'go up and fight.'* It was not His purpose that they should gain the land by warfare, but by strict obedience to His commands." "PATRIARCHS AND PROPHETS," page 392.

In this book I have already pointed out that the "Lord" who gave the message to the prophet Samuel to "go and smite Amalek, and utterly destroy all that they have, and spare them not; but slay both man and woman, infant and suckling, ox and sheep, camel and all," (I Sam. 15:3) was not the true God, our Lord Jesus Christ, but the same lord (Satan) who moved upon Herod to slaughter "all the chil-dren that were in Bethlehem ... two years and under."

Matt. 2:16. In "DESIRE OF AGES," pages 65 and 66 EGW shows that the Jew's wrong concept of the Messiah caused the Bethlehem tragedy. By misrepresenting Christ's mission, *"Satan had purposed to compass the destruction of the Saviour; but instead of this, it returned upon their own heads."* D.A. 66.

On page 274 I referred to Exodus 3:11-18 where Moses resisted God's leading and the subject of "sacrifice" was inserted into the works as part of God's requirements for Israel's deliverance. How could this have been the true Lord speaking here [as He had in Exodus 3:1-14] when the Lord Jesus clearly shows His abhorrence for "signs and wonders" in Matt. 12:39 when the scribes and Pharisees asked to "see a sign from thee." *"But He (Jesus) answered and said unto them, An evil and adulterous generation seeketh after a sign;"* Furthermore, God never spoke anything from Mt. Sinai except the Ten Commandments, Deut. 5:22; Jer. 7:22.

Someone will surely say, "But how could it be Satan speaking in Exodus 3:15? when it says, "And God said moreover unto Moses, Thus shalt thou say unto the children of Israel, the Lord God of your fathers, the God of Abraham, the God of Isaac, and the God of Jacob, hath sent me unto you: this is my name for ever, and this is my memorial unto all generations."

Well, please notice again that this imitating, counterfeiting voice gives himself away in v. 18 when he introduces the carnal concept of works to obtain forgiveness through the idea of sacrifice. This is referring specifically to the killing of animals which God says He never spoke when He brought Israel out of Egypt, Jer. 7:22. Deut. 5:22.

Right here is a most important point in our study on the character of God, for we can see very clearly how God's name and His Holy Sabbath day are so very sacredly and closely intertwined and commingled [mixed], and blended together. Let us now go to Exodus 31:13 where God tells Moses that the Sabbath is to be a "sign between me and you throughout your generations; [why?] that ye may know that I am the Lord that doth sanctify you." And in v. 16 God says that the Sabbath was to be "observe(d) throughout their generations, for a perpetual covenant." This same idea is reiterated in Ezek. 20:12, 20 where the emphasis is added that God's Sabbaths were a "sign between me and you, that ye may know that I am the Lord your God."

Now, Satan can claim to be Jesus our Saviour, which he will do as his crowning act of deception, [G.C. 624, 625] but He cannot counterfeit God's mercy, kindness, forgiveness, and longsuffering. These are not attributes of Satan's character, and he is unable to fake it well enough or for long enough to fool God's people. He has also set up a counterfeit Sabbath, which we know as Sunday. This is the sign of the "death god," Satan, whereas the Sabbath is the sign of Jesus, the true God and Creator. Satan is not able to create. He may be able to re-arrange molecules and matter, and make it look like he has created something out of nothing, but it is only an illusion, for he is not a creator. He is only a destroyer. The Sabbath is God's covenant with His true people. It is a sign or mark of ownership that they belong to Him. Now, watch this very carefully. Rev. 22:4 tells us that God's own "NAME" will be in their foreheads. The forehead is where the character and personality of an individual is developed and housed. In medical terms this is called the cerebrum and frontal lobe. Here is where decision-making takes place. This is where the conscience of each person is determined. And the Bible says that God's very own name or character is going to be in or upon the forehead or mind of His people . . . His very own elected Remnant. Furthermore, God's name means much more than a name you can write down and pronounce. Actually, the nouns "Lord," "God" "Jesus" "Christ" and even "Jehovah," are titles which simply designate the position or office of the person being so addressed. General, colonel, captain, barron and duke are also titles designating a person's rank or station in life. But these are not names. And so the noun "Lord" is not

God's name, but His title. In Joshua 5:14 a being appeared to Joshua claiming to be "captain of the host of the Lord." PP 488 states that this was Christ. Jesus is called the "Prince of life," Acts 3:15. But Satan is also called a "Prince," but notice how you tell the difference between these two princes. Satan is referred to as the "Prince of the devils." Mark. 3:22. He is also called "the Prince of this world," John 12:31; 14:30; 16:11. In Eph. 2:2 Satan is called the "Prince of the power of the air." But in Rev. 1:5 Jesus Christ is called the "Prince of the kings of the earth."

When Moses asked God, "I beseech thee, shew me thy glory," Moses was basically saying, "Please tell me who you are and what you are like." Notice now God's response: ***"And he (Jesus) said, I will make all my goodness pass before thee, and I will proclaim the name of the Lord before thee;"*** Exodus 33:17-19. However, the Lord told Moses He could not see His face, ***"for there shall no man see me, and live."*** vs. 20. This shows what an advantage Satan had over God at Mount Sinai. Satan appeared as an angel of light, claiming to be God, but the true Lord was invisible. For sinful man to look upon such a holy and pure face would evidently have been too much for any man's physical or emotional health. Until the Lord could more fully educate man about the difference between darkness and light, sin and righteousness, God's glorious and beautiful face would have to remain hidden for man's own safety. But to Moses alone, a special revelation of His character was to be given so He could tell the people the truth about God.

Finally, ***"the Lord passed by before him, and proclaimed, The Lord, The Lord God, merciful and gracious, longsuffering, and abundant in goodness and truth, Keeping mercy for thousands, forgiving iniquity and transgression and sin, and that will by no means clear the guilty;"*** Exodus 34:6, 7. And so we see that God's name is not a word, noun, appellation or title you pronounce or write correctly. In His revelation here to Moses, at Mt.

Sinai, we see clearly that God's name is simply His character. And He designated His character as consisting of specific attributes which tell us what a wonderfully, kind,
loving and gracious person He is. If God had wanted Moses
to declare His name to the people as a word correctly spelled
and/or pronounced He might have said, "Moses I want you
to pay very close attention to what I am about to tell you
now, for I am going to teach you the truth about my sacred
and holy Name. Moses, I want you to learn how to write and
spell my Name correctly. Now, listen carefully, Moses, as I
pronounce it for you. 'Ya-way, Ya-way,' Got that Moses? It is
'Ya-way.' Now, let me hear you say it back to me." And
Moses would no doubt have pronounced it back to God, 'Ya-
way." And the Lord would probably have replied, "Good boy,
Moses. You got it right. I knew you could do it. Here's my
card, Moses. Now, go and teach the people what I have
taught you."

But, friend of mine, what good would that have done?
Satan could very easily counterfeit any pronunciation or
spelling of God's name, as He has successfully done through
the centuries. So, God had a better way, as He always does.
He revealed to Moses His true character of love, which He
very specifically says is His name. Satan can never counterfeit this for although He may try and act nice for a time, His
true character always displays itself in His words and
deeds, as we have already seen so far in this book. Anyone
can assume a name or title such as baron, duke, captain,
major, colonel, general, prince, lord, god, etc. Baal means
"lord, husband or possesor," in the Hebrew, and even David
ascribed one of his military victories to Baal, since He did
not know the real truth about Christ's non-violent character of love. 2 Sam. 5:19, 20.

Because Satan is able to assume any title God may
have, we cannot discern the difference between the true and
false God, Christ and Satan, only by the spelling of a noun
or title called "Lord" or "god." Paul tells us, "For though
there be that are called gods, whether in heaven or in earth,

(as there be gods many, and lords many) But to us there is but one god, the Father, of whom are all things, and we by him." I Cor. 8:5, 6. Again Paul indicates that the day is coming when all doubt about who really is the true "Potentate," of this universe will be removed "Until the appearing of our Lord Jesus Christ: Which in his times he shall show, who is the blessed and only Potentate, the King of kings, and Lord of lords;" I Tim. 6:14, 15. Cf. Rev. 17:14; 19:16. Why would Paul and John go to the trouble to make such an important and definite distinction if there were not many "gods and lords" vying, contending and competing to be "Gods and Lords" in this earth?

The servant of the Lord has told us how to know the difference between the true and the false God. *"Multitudes have a wrong conception of God and His attributes, and are truly serving a false God as were the worshipers of Baal."* PK 177. **HERE WE SEE CLEARLY THAT THE WAY TO TELL THE TRUE GOD FROM THE FALSE IS BY THE ATTRIBUTES OF HIS CHARACTER.** Sister White tells us that Lucifer has perverted the powers God endowed him with and that "Satan can inspire his agents with thoughts that appear elevating and noble. Did he not come to Christ with quotations of Scripture when he designed to overthrow Him with His specious temptations? This is the way in which he comes to man, as an angel of light disguising his temptations under an appearance of goodness, and making men believe him to be the friend rather than the enemy of humanity. It is in this way that he has deceived and seduced the race,—beguiling them with subtle temptations, bewildering them with specious deceptions.

"SATAN HAS ASCRIBED TO GOD ALL THE EVILS TO WHICH FLESH IS HEIR. HE HAS REPRESENTED HIM AS A GOD WHO DELIGHTS IN THE SUFFERINGS OF HIS CREATURES, WHO IS REVENGEFUL AND IMPLACABLE. It was Satan who originated the doctrine of eternal torment as a punishment

for sin, because in this way he could lead men into infidelity and rebellion, distract souls, and dethrone the human reason. Heaven, looking down, and seeing the delusions into which men were led, knew that a divine Instructor must come to earth. Men in ignorance and moral darkness must have light, spiritual light; for the world knew not God, and He must be revealed to their understanding . . . Darkness covered the earth, and gross darkness the people. *THROUGH THE ACCUMULATED MISREPRESENTATIONS OF THE ENEMY, MANY WERE SO DECEIVED THAT THEY WORSHIPED A FALSE GOD, CLOTHED WITH THE ATTRIBUTES OF THE SATANIC CHARACTER.* The Teacher from heaven, no less a personage than the Son of God, came to earth *to reveal the character of the Father to men, that they might worship Him in spirit and in truth. Christ revealed to men the fact that the strictest adherence to ceremony and form would not save them; for the kingdom of God was spiritual in its nature."* FE 176,177.

The Prophet Isaiah revealed that the "child" that would be born to become the ruler of this world would actually be "THE EVERLASTING FATHER." *And yet Satan is seeking to become our "Father" and our "God." But Jesus revealed the true character of the devil so we can know the difference between the true Father and the false one. Let us read it together: *"Ye are of your father the devil, and the lusts of your father ye will do. He was a murderer from the beginning, and abode not in the truth, because there is no truth in him. When he speaketh a lie, he speaketh of his own: for he is a liar, and the father of it."* John 8:44. Now, just think about it. What right would Jesus have to designate Satan as a liar and murderer if He Himself had ever killed or murdered anyone? Were not a lot of innocent children "murdered" at the time of the flood? And haven't millions more been murdered by many other means down through the centuries? Satan blames all this carnage upon our God, when he is the very one who is doing it. *Isaiah 9:6.

Quite often people have told me that God does not "murder" but he does "kill." And they state very confidently that there is a difference between kill and murder. **YOU WOULD BE SURPRISED HOW MANY PEOPLE ARE UNDER THE DELUSION THAT THIS IS TRUE.** But I can assure you that it is a false teaching. For proof just look up the word for "kill" as used in Exodus 20:13 ["Thou shalt not kill] and you will find that it is the same exact word for "murder." The word is "RATSAH" STRONG'S 7523. Here is the definition from Strong's. "prop. to dash in pieces, i.e. kill [a human being], espec. to murder: put to death, kill, (man-) slayer(er)." I also talked to a Hebrew scholar about these two words "kill" and "murder." He explained that in the Hebrew language they would intensify the word in its meaning to show the degree of anger and hatred and violence with which someone was killed. The sixth commandment is speaking about the taking of life, and this word, "Ratsah," is the one God used in His law.[1] Jesus indentified Satan as the one who kills and murders. Therefore, it is absolutely impossible that God could be designated as one who kills, for God and Satan are completely opposite. Jesus really clarified it once and for all in John 10:10 when He said, "The thief cometh not, but for to steal, and to kill, and to destroy: I am come that they might have life, and that they might have it more abundantly." And in the next verse He says, "I am the good Shepherd," giving us a definite clue that there is a "bad" Shepherd who is seeking to hurt us.

In Chapter 21 of my book, "Into the Father's Heart," I answer the question, "Who killed Korah, Dathan, and Abiram?" And then on pages 180 and 181 I discuss who it really was who said, "Separate yourselves from among this congregation, that I may consume them in a moment." Numbers 16:21. It is interesting that the destruction of

[1]The Greek word "phoneuo" means "kill or murder." Strong's concordance — 5407.

Sodom is referred to in a very similar way. "For the punishment of the iniquity of the daughter of my people (Israel) is greater than the punishment of the sin of Sodom, that was overthrown as in a moment, and no hands stayed on her." Lamentations 4:6. Who are the hands which prevent destruction? The hands of the angels, of course. "For He shall give His angels charge over thee, to keep thee in all thy ways. They shall bear thee up in their hands, lest thou dash thy foot against a stone." Psalm 91:11, 12. God's angels could no longer prevent Satan from sending literal fire down on these cities of the plains. Notice the two Lords in the next verse. "The Lord (Jesus)* rained upon Sodom and upon Gomorrah brimstone (sulphur) and fire from the lord (Satan) out of (the atmospheric or first) heaven." Genesis 19:24. Remember that the Hebrew writers always held God responsible for whatever He allowed to happen. In Rev. 7 God's holy angels are holding back destruction. But in Rev. 16 they are pictured as bringing destruction out of the sanctuary. Why? Because when God commands them to withdraw (GC 614) it is written down as if they are the very agents who are bringing that destruction, when in actuality they are simply withdrawing their restraints, at God's command, for God must honor the free will of humanity who are bringing destruction upon themselves by rejecting the protection of God. Notice that EGW speaks of two different angels. "The angel (of God) is to place a mark upon the forehead of all who are separated from sin and sinners, and the destroying angel (of Satan) will follow, to slay utterly both old and young." 5T 505. Now, notice another EGW statement about God's "destroying" angels.

"The destroying angels of God were at work. One touch, and buildings, so thoroughly constructed that men regarded them as secure against every danger, quickly became heaps and rubbish . . . It seemed that the forbearance of God was exhausted and that the judgment day had come." 9T 93. *The Lord Jesus let the lord Satan do this.

God invites us to "come now, and let us reason together . . ." Isa. 1:18. Our God is a very reasonable, logical and loving God. He is also very patient and understanding, "For He knoweth our frame; he remembereth that we are dust." Ps. 103:14. He has given us brains to think with, but He will not condemn us if don't come to the right conclusion in five minutes. He won't even condemn us if we use the intelligence He gave us to come to the wrong conclusion. But He will labor with us to continue thinking about it and will try and change our minds. He will even weep over us as Jesus wept over Jerusalem, but He will never stop loving us or pleading with us to change our minds until we shut Him off and tell Him to get out of our lives. He has enough respect for us to honor our request even though it breaks His heart. But He will stand nearby until the very end, hoping that we will change our minds and call to Him for help, just as Jonah did from the belly of the whale, Jonah 2:1, and just as the thief on the cross did. Luke 23:39-43. And look how He forgave those cruel church fathers who put Him on the cross in the first place! "Father, forgive them; for they know not what they do." Luke 23:34. What an incredible God we have!

When you realize what kind of a person God really is, inside of his heart of hearts, do you really think He is the kind of person who would send His holy, harmless angels on a mission of destruction? Hardly! He just isn't that kind of a person. We can see that in the life of Jesus. Just recently a man came to see me and told how he visited a friend one day. As he got out of his car and was walking up the side-walk of this man's house the owner of the home was coming out to greet him and this was his greeting, "Joe, some crazy jerk wrote a book entitled. 'GOD DOES NOT KILL.' Can you imagine anybody being so stupid, Joe?" As soon as Joe heard this man say this to him, he raised his arm and pointed at his friend. "That is a false teaching! Yes, God does kill." No sooner had the words come out of Joe's mouth

than he felt a very large but loving and warm hand pressed
to his chest and a voice speaking to him in the kindest and
most loving tone He had ever heard in his entire life. The
voice said to him, "Joe, why would you want to think that I
hurt and kill people? You know me, Joe. Have I ever hurt
you? Joe, I love you so much and I want you to do some
personal and serious studying from my Word about this
before you say anything else about it." All the while Joe was
having this magnificent experience, his friend continued to
rant and rave about "this crazy nut' who says God does not
kill. But Joe didn't even hear him. Finally, Joe was able to
speak as the vision faded and said to his shocked and bewildered friend, as he walked around him to the house, "I'm
going to have to study on this more before I discuss it further." And he did study on it for the next three or four years.
He didn't read any of my books either. He just prayed and
read the Holy Bible and finally decided that it really is true
that God has never hurt or killed anyone. It has changed his
whole life.

Beloved, you may never have an experience like Joe
did. That was truly a most dramatic vision similar to what
Saul of Tarsus had on the Damascus road. Most of us have
to pray and search it out without any dreams or visions, but
we still can come to have that same wonderful assurance of
His love that Saul (later Paul) and Joe did. Praise God! And
I do hope this book will enable you to work through some of
the more difficult and finer points of the character-of-God
message.

Let's come back now to the "destroying angels of God,"
as EGW described them. How can we explain this? Well,
actually, it seems rather simple to me now that I know and
understand how this all fits together. First of all, we must
realize that all of the angels, good and evil, belong to God by
right of creation. He is their God and Creator, even though
they deny this and have betrayed Him, crucified Him and
robbed Him of His very own children; the whole human
family. In spite of all this, our God still loves His fallen

angels and still gives them free will to continue following their chosen leader, Lucifer. So, these "destroying angels of God," are not God's loyal and holy angels, for EGW has clearly told us that God's angels do not destroy. "Angels are sent from the heavenly courts, *NOT TO DESTROY*, BUT TO WATCH OVER AND GUARD IMPERILED SOULS, TO SAVE THE LOST, TO BRING THE STRAYING ONES BACK TO THE FOLD." R & H, May 10, 1906.

These "destroying angels" are Satan's angels. For proof let us go to Psalm 78:49. We are told here that "evil angels" were the cause of all the plagues of Egypt. "HE (GOD) LOOSED ON THEM (THE EGYPTIANS) THE FIERCENESS OF HIS ANGER, (SAME AS WRATH, WHEN GOD LETS MAN GO, ROM. 1:18, 24) SENDING SORROW AND TROUBLE. HE DISPATCHED AGAINST THEM A BAND OF DESTROYING ANGELS. HE GAVE FREE COURSE TO HIS ANGER (WRATH) AND DID NOT SPARE THE EGYPTIANS' LIVES, BUT HANDED THEM OVER TO PLAGUES AND SICKNESS." PSALM 78:49, 50. L.B. And keep in mind, dear reader, that God never brings sickness or disease. We have already proved that in this book. However, I want to point out again that EGW wrote just like a Hebrew prophet in that she always held God responsible for whatever He permitted to happen so even though we can know of a certainty that these "destroying angels" were not God's holy and righteous angels destroying directly, they are blamed for the destruction because they obeyed God's command to withdraw, created a vacuum, which the evil angels filled with a most destructive force. But God and His good and holy angels got the blame for allowing them to do it, just like Jesus allowed or "gave them leave" to go into the swine. Mark 5:9-13. These evil angels said to Jesus, "Send us into the swine, that we may enter into them." They did not want to take responsibility for their own evil decision. They wanted to blame God for it. And Jesus allowed them to do it. Why? Because His Father directed Him to do it. Why? Probably because of all the many choices available to Jesus and His Father this was the one that would cause the least amount of harm and was calculated to bring the most amount of good and, at the same time, not interfere with the choice of the evil angels. After all, it was their idea. And they did succeed in causing Jesus to have to leave this area. I am told that pigs are great swimmers; therefore, this legion of demons (4,000 to 6,000 of them) forced these pigs under water and took their lives. This is just more evidence and proof that Satan and his angels are the killers and murderers, not God.

Even though Satan can assume and counterfeit any and all of the titles that rightly belong to the true God, He can never really counterfeit God's name, for the name of God is His character, not a noun or word you pronounce or write down in a certain way. In Exodus 33:3 a voice claiming to be the Lord says, "I will not go up in the midst of thee; for thou art a stiffnecked people: lest I consume thee in the way." When the people heard these "evil tidings" the people "mourned." V. 4. Now, beloved friend of mine, let us keep in mind that even though Satan was allowed by God to speak to Moses at times, Satan could never say anything or even do anything unless God allowed and approved of it first. This just seems incredible, but this is very crucial to understand if we are going to believe that God is always in charge of all the affairs of this earth. Nothing happens without His knowledge or permission in our world. 2 Chron. 16:9; Heb. 4:13. *Moses did not realize or understand that Satan was sometimes speaking to him. He did not understand God's character at that time. None of the prophets understood it. Neither did the angels or unfallen worlds understand the truth about God's character or Satan's character at this time.* I believe that is why we find Moses begging God to tell him the truth about Himself in Exodus 33:12, 13. In verse 14 the true God speaks to Moses and assures Him "My presence shall go with thee, and I will give thee rest." The reason I know this is Jesus speaking here is because the true God NEVER CHANGES nor does He contradict Himself. He has promised to always be with us. His eternal promise is that His presence will always go with us. *"I will never leave thee, nor forsake thee."* Heb. 13:5. Gen. 28:15; Psalm 37:25. In light of these eternal truths we can know that the voice which told Moses *"I will not go up in the midst of thee; for thou art a stiffnecked people:"* . . . was not the voice of the true God. Neither was it the voice of Jesus speaking to Moses in the Exodus 32:7-10 when a voice claiming to be God tempted Moses to step aside so he could kill them. *"Now therefore let me alone, that my wrath may wax hot against them, and that I may consume them: and I will make of thee a great nation."* Exodus 32:7-10.

I discuss this very passage in my book, IFH, as well as the incident in Numbers 16 where a voice states "Separate yourselves from among this congregation, that I may consume them in a moment." Num. 16:21. I give five specific reasons why Satan was the speaker of Ex. 32:7-10. You can read it yourself on pages 180-181 of IFH. Let's just note point 3. The voice says, *'Let me alone,'* which is a familiar phrase of Satan. Mark 1:24; Luke 4:34."

Most people do not realize that Christ and Satan are in very close proximity in the great controversy between good and evil. The Prophet Zechariah gives us a little insight. "And he shewed me Joshua the high priest standing before the angel of the Lord, and Satan [meaning "Adversary"] standing at his right hand to resist him." Zech. 3:1. Paul calls Satan and his forces of evil "the rulers of the darkness of this world." Eph. 6:12. And Jesus told the "chief priests, and captains of the temple, and the elders, which were come to him" to arrest him, . . . "this is your hour and the power of darkness." Luke 22:52, 53. Just look up the word "darkness" in Young's or Strong's concordance and you will find scores of texts identifying Satan as the originator, ruler and cause of darkness in this world. I just wonder then who it was that brought the "blackness, and darkness, and tempest . . ." at Mt. Sinai that Paul refers to in Heb. 12:18 when he contrasts "Mt. Zion" with "Mt. Sinai?"

It will probably come as a shock to most people to find out that the pillar of the cloud that led the children of Israel through the wilderness had two aspects to it. That is, it had a dark side to it, that was allowed to manifest itself at times. When the children of Israel found themselves trapped down at the Red sea the Bible tells us this: "And the angel of God, which went before the camp of Israel, removed and went behind them; and the pillar of the cloud went from before their face, and stood behind them: And it came between the camp of the Egyptians and the camp of Israel; and it was a cloud [the margin says, "a dark cloud"] and darkness to them, [that is to the Egyptians who were in moral and spiritual darkness] but it gave light by night to these (Israel): so that the one came not near the other all the night." Exodus 14:19, 20. Whichever side or aspect of the cloud you were tuned into, light or darkness, that is the side or aspect of the pillar or cloud that would respond to you. And that is the same way it is today. Christ and Satan are all about us all the time and it is left up to us to choose which "God" we will tune into. If you tune into Jesus He will give you light from the cloud, but if you tune into the Devil or Satan, he will give you darkness from that same cloud. That cloud represents "God," or "Divine power." Only you can choose which "God" you will serve. The true God, Jesus, the God of pure light and truth, or Satan, the God of this world who is the prince of darkness.

With this background information we are now ready to go to Exodus 23. We are going to be introduced to two different angels.

We will begin quoting in Exodus 23:20: Here Christ is speaking to Moses and telling him about these two angels. "Behold, I send an Angel before thee, to keep thee in the way, and to bring thee into the place which I have prepared. [Now watch the fear factor introduced regarding this angel]

Beware of him, and obey his voice, provoke him not; for he will not pardon your transgressions: for my name is in him." v. 21. It would seem axiomatic that everyone would realize this is not a very nice or good angel. "You better watch out for this angel for he is very easily provoked (made angry), and he is not going to forgive you." Does that sound at all like the Jesus of the New testament? Why then does God tell Him, "obey his voice . . . for my name is in him?"

The answer is that everything Satan does has to first go through the throne room of God for His stamp (signature) of approval. The experience of Job proves Satan cannot do anything in this earth without God's permission. And when we purposely disobey God's explicit commands we forfeit His protection. Satan is then given permission to move in on that person or persons for they have chosen him as their *"god."* This is what happened when Adam sold his birthright to Satan. He came under the powers of the "rulers of darkness." The false concepts about God were transmitted from the minds of Satan and his angels to Adam and his descendants and acted out in religious rituals such as various kinds of appeasement offerings and blood sacrifices of animals and at times even humans. God did not want this and condemned it through prophets like Isaiah who spoke against the whole system. Isa. 1:10-17; and Isa 66:1-4. "But," someone may protest, "Mike, haven't you read in Gen. where it was God Himself who killed the first animal and made skins to cloth the nakedness of Adam and Eve?" Yes, I have heard people state this many times, but it does not state that God killed an animal. Let's read the text. "Unto Adam also and to his wife did the Lord God make coats of skins, and clothed them." Gen. 3:21. Just because God took some dead animals and made some coats of skins from them does not mean that it was God who killed them. The text does not say that God killed any animals, but that He made coats of skins. The animals could very well have been animals that Adam had sacrificed. Adam and Eve had "sewed fig leaves together, and made themselves aprons (or girdles)." Gen. 3:7. This represented their own works of righteousness with which they tried to cover their nakedness. They were still in the garden when this happened, but according to PP 61 they were outside of the garden when God made the skins for them, even though the account of the animal skins comes before God "drove" them out of the garden. Why would God kill animals when He specifically and repeatedly told Israel He did not want them to kill His animals for sacrifices or any other reason? The "coats of skins" could also have come from dead animals that had been killed by other animals.

The skins God provided for them represented the righteousness of Christ which would come only through His own shed blood in Gethsemane and on Calvary. As I have tried to explain already God had to allow us to shed His blood so we would realize that He is "harmless." Heb. 7:26. I explain this in greater detail on pages 368-372 of IFH. In John 12:32 Jesus predicted that His death on the cross would "draw" all unto Him. And Paul tells us that we who were "sometimes far off are made nigh by the blood of Christ." Eph. 2:13.

I mentioned above that Adam and Eve were still in the garden when the fig leaves were fashioned by them to cover their nakedness. In 1BC 1084 EGW compares the fig leaves to "arguments used to cover disobedience." EGW also makes an interesting comment about the air. "The air, which had hitherto been of a mild and uniform temperature, seemed to chill the guilty pair. The love and peace which had been theirs was gone, and in its place they felt a sense of sin, a dread of the future, a nakedness of soul. The robe of light which had enshrouded them, now disappeared, and to supply its place they endeavored to fashion for themselves a covering; for they could not, while unclothed, meet the eye of God and holy angels." PP 57. Before Adam and Eve sinned they had a light connection from their mind to the very mind of God, which is pure love, faith and trust. But when Adam and Eve chose to doubt God's word and believe the lies of Satan, that light connection was broken and their minds became darkened with the lies from Satan's carnal mind and earthly throne. You might say that Adam's and Eve's polarity was reversed. Before they sinned their minds were positive toward God and negative toward Satan. But after they sinned this polarity was reversed. Their minds were now negative toward God and positive toward Satan. Their nature was now carnal and sinful instead of spiritual and holy. Do you realize the dreadful implications of this situation and what it meant? Beloved, it meant that Adam would no longer be able to distinguish the voice of the true God from the voice of the false one. Satan, as an angel of light would be able to counterfeit both the appearance and voice of God and Adam wouldn't know the difference because His mind had been plunged into darkness about the true character of God before his own character had been formed and developed after the similitude of His Creator. And this fallen nature with its carnal and unholy mind would be much more in tune with Satan's mind and character than Christ's mind. Furthermore, this fallen nature would be passed onto all of Adam's children.

Now can you see why Satan was able to suggest to Adam that he kill innocent animals? And can you see why Adam would think this was the true God speaking to him when it was actually Satan? Adam was afraid of God just as Satan and his angels were afraid of the Lord, and they programmed Adam's mind with this fear.

When I explain this in my meetings, someone usually will say that EGW states that it was painful for Adam to slay the first animal. Although this is true, the point they are trying to make is untrue. They are trying to misuse EGW to prove that God was the one who suggested to Adam that he kill animals when God never suggested any such thing. But after Satan put it into Adam's mind and Adam was struggling with the idea, believing, just like Abraham, that God had spoken to him, then Jesus came and "instituted" or "ordained" the animal sacrifice system just like he "appointed" the thorn and the thistle as EGW says on page 1 of "STEPS TO CHIRST." That is how the divorce laws were "ordained" and the slavery laws were "okayed" and the first king of Israel, King Saul, was "ordained." Because God created man with free moral agency or choice, the Lord was obligated to go along with man's wrong choices; but rather than abandon Adam and his descendants, the Lord chose to stay with them and try and save them from the worst effects of their wrong and evil decisions. And all through the long, dark and painful centuries of death and destruction God has been using all of these horrible experiences as lessons for us today.

Let us read this EGW quote about Adam's first offering. "The sacrificial offerings were ordained by God to be to man a perpetual reminder and a penitential acknowledgment of his sin and a confession of his faith in the promised Redeemer. They were intended to impress upon the fallen race the solemn truth that it was sin that caused death. To Adam, the offering of the first sacrifice was a most painful ceremony." PP 68. The surface reader will say, "See, Adam didn't want to kill that animal. God told him to do it. Why would Satan want to give something that would point to the cross which brought our salvation?" The answer to that is simply that God allows these carnal ideas to come forth and then takes them and fits them into His master plan. Everything that happens is not God's will, but nothing can happen to defeat God's will and His ultimate plan to save the world and protect the universe from sin ever arising a second time. Nahum 1:9. Since the Lord knows the future, He is able to make it all "work together for good to them that love" Him. Rom. 8:28.

Furthermore, sin is progressive and extremely deceptive. We have read that it was not an easy thing for Adam to slay the first animal. Do you realize that Lucifer had some similar emotions about leading Adam and Eve into sin? Listen: "Satan went alone to mature plans that would most surely secure the fall of Adam and Eve. *He had fears that his purposes might be defeated. And again, even if he should be successful in leading Adam and Eve to dis-obey the commandment of God, and thus become transgressors of His law, and no good come to himself, his own case would not be improved; his guilt would only be increased. He shuddered at the thought of plunging the holy, happy pair into the misery and remorse he was himself enduring. He seemed in a state of indecision: at one time firm and determined, then hesitating and wavering.* His angels were seeking him, their leader, to acquaint him with their decision. They would unite with Satan in his plans, and with him bear the responsibility and share the consequences. Satan cast off his feelings of despair and weakness, and as their leader, fortified himself to brave out the matter and do all in his power to defy the authority of God and His Son." SR 28, 29.

"At his creation Adam was placed in dominion over the earth. But by yielding to temptation, he was brought under the power of Satan. 'Of whom a man is overcome, of the same is he brought in bondage.' 2 Peter 2:19. When man became Satan's captive, the dominion which he held, passed to his conqueror. Thus Satan became the 'God of this world' 2 Cor. 4:4." PP 67. The moment Adam sinned and broke his "light connection" with the mind of God . . . at that very moment Adam began to die. He did not realize this at first, but it soon began to dawn on him. "After his transgression Adam at first imagined himself entering upon a higher state of existence. But soon the thought of his sin filled him with terror. *The air, which had hitherto been of a mild and uniform temperature, seemed to chill the guilty pair.* The love and peace which had been theirs was gone, and in its place they felt a sense of sin, a dread of the future, a nakedness of soul." PP 57.

Now, this happened while they were still in the garden of Eden. Notice that EGW says the air "seemed to chill the guilty pair." The air did not change. Eden's temperature did not drop. What was happening was Adam's body temperature was dropping because he had broken his connection with God. His light was going out which meant that he was dying. Do you realize what this meant? It meant that his whole body was becoming incompatible with the environment of Eden. It wasn't long before Adam and Eve began having trouble breathing. Their digestive system was ceasing to function as it once had. This is no doubt when they attempted to get to the tree of life to eat of its fruit, but the Lord would not allow them to eat of it. So, they had no other choice but to go outside of the Garden of Eden into the world beyond where everything was dying at the same rate their body was dying. And that is just what they did. However, the Bible expresses this event as one directly executed by God Himself. *"Therefore the Lord God sent him (Adam) forth from the garden of Eden, to till the ground from whence he was taken. So He (God) drove out the man;"* Gen. 3:23, 24.

Chapter six of my book, IFH, is entitled "Did God 'Kick' Satan out of Heaven?" See page 35. In this chapter I give an in-depth study of this subject. I explain how the Scriptures teach us that Satan and his angels "left" their heavenly estate. And Rev. 12:4 says "His tail drew the third part of the stars (angels) of heaven, and did cast them to the earth:" so, it was Satan who cast the angels down to this earth, not Christ. The Bible speaks of Lucifer's departure from heaven as a fall, not an expulsion. *"How art thou fallen from heaven, O Lucifer, son of the morning!"* If Lucifer "fell" as the Bible tells us, Luke 10:18, then it was basically suicide. But if he were pushed or forced out, as most religionists teach, then it was murder or homocide. The only text upon which one might try to build a case for Satan's being thrown out or cast down is Rev. 12:9. "And there was war in heaven: . . . And the great dragon (Satan) was cast out, that old serpent, called the Devil, and Satan, which deceiveth the whole world: he was cast out into the earth, and his angels were cast out with him." But Job 18:7 plainly shows how the expression "cast" down is used in the

Bible. "The steps of his strength shall be straitened, and his own counsel shall cast him down." Cf. Ps. 7:15, 16; 9:15, 16. And yet EGW, like a Hebrew prophet, states "The Father decides the case of Satan, and declares that he must be turned out of heaven for his daring rebellion, and that those who united with him in his rebellion should be turned out with him. Then there was war in heaven. Christ and His angels fought against Satan and his angels, for they were determined to remain in heaven with all their rebellion. But they prevailed not. Christ and loyal angels triumphed, and drove Satan and his rebel sympathizers from heaven (3SG 38)." 7BC 973. And yet EGW clearly tells us that God never uses "force." DA 759. So how were Satan and his angels cast out and driven from heaven without the use of force? The answer is found in Matt. 12:28, where we find that Jesus *"cast out devils by the Spirit of God."* God's character never changes. Therefore, the way Jesus treated Satan and his evil angels while he was here on earth is the same exact way He has always dealt with them—with love, compassion, dignity and respect for their free choice. Of course, the carnally-minded person, who wants to have his own way and solve all problems without delay, will want to believe that God does use force so he can justify his anger, impatience, frustration and hatred. But the spiritually-minded person will accept the spirit of Christ's non-violent, non-destructive, harmless methods and will desire to operate upon the same kind of frequency.

The greek word for "left" in Jude 6 is "Apoleipo" meaning, "to leave behind, . . . to forsake." The Amplified, and Modern version Bibles both use the word "abandon;" And so also does the NIV, NEB, WEYMOUTH'S AND PHILLIPS VERSIONS AS WELL. EGW confirms this idea in "DESIRE OF AGES." *"Had Lucifer really desired to be like the Most High, he would never have deserted his appointed place in heaven; for the spirit of the Most High is manifested in unselfish ministry. Lucifer desired God's power, but not His character."* DA 435.

Further proof that God never demoted Lucifer can be found in "Patriarchs and Prophets," where EGW tells us that God "bore long with Lucifer." She also states that "Lucifer was convinced that he was in the wrong. He saw that 'the Lord is righteous in all His ways, and holy in all His works' Psalm 145:17); . . . He had not at that time *fully cast off his allegiance to God.* Though *HE HAD LEFT* his position as covering cherub, yet if he had been willing to return to God, acknowledging the Creator's wisdom, and satisfied to fill the place appointed him in God's great plan, he would have been reinstated in his office . . . He nearly reached the decision to return, but pride forbade him . . . A compassionate Creator, in yearning pity for Lucifer and his followers, was seeking to draw them back from the abyss of ruin into which they were about to plunge. *But His mercy was misinterpreted.* Lucifer pointed to the long-suffering of God as evidence of his own superiority, and indication that the King of the universe would yet accede to his terms." PP 39. Compare this experience with DA 321 and Christ's efforts to reach out to the Jewish leaders. Jesus never changes . . . *He is always and ever reaching out to save, never to hurt or kill,* Cf. 279.

In my second book, "The Final Absolute and Ultimate Truth about God," (published in Jan. 1979) I discussed in great detail the death of Korah, Dathan, Abiram and the 250 princes on pages 97-101. I delayed reprinting the book because I really had not planned to try and explain any more of the character message to SDAs. I just felt they had closed their own probation and there was no use to even try and reason with them anymore. I never planned to return to Oregon for I was very happy to stay in West Virginia and work for the large number of non-SDAs who are much more receptive to the message of God's love. But the Lord had other plans and so we returned in August of 1983. If you would like to have a copy of "THE FINAL ABSOLUTE" (127 pages) You may now obtain one for the price of only $6.95. And let me state that the "Final Absolute" is Jesus

Christ and the ultimate truth about Him is that He does not kill. The title was not intended to indicate that nothing else would or could ever be known about God and His truth. The idea and inspiration for this title came from Frances A. Schaeffer's statement in "HOW SHOULD WE THEN LIVE?" pp. 84, 86. He quoted the (Westminster) confession and used the following phrases. "As finite beings, people do not have exhaustive truth about God, but they can have truth about God; and they can know, therefore, truth about that which is the **ultimate universal**." I thought that was such a magnificent statement that I should use it to express my convictions regarding the character of God. And so, I did. And now the Lord has led me to write this, another book. It is an endless and fathomless subject that one can never exhaust. But getting back to Korah I just wanted to refer to a couple of points in that story which tie in with what I was saying earlier about the cloud having two aspects. Notice this EGW statement from PP 401. "But the judgments were not ended. Fire flashing from the cloud consumed the two hundred and fifty princes who had offered incense. These men, not being the first in rebellion, were not destroyed with the chief conspirators. (showing that Satan is only allowed to destroy those whom God allows him to destroy). They were permitted to see their end, and to have an opportunity for repentance; but their sympathies were with the rebels, and they shared their fate." My main point is that this fire came from the cloud itself and if you believe that Jesus is in the cloud, as we always have, then it only follows that Jesus from the cloud is sending down this destructive, literal fire or lightning to kill the 250 princes. *But when we realize that the cloud has two aspects, a light or bright side and a dark side then you can know that it was not Christ who was sending the fire but Satan.* But an added proof that Jesus was not the destroyer is the statement found in the very next paragraph. *"Jesus, the Angel who went before the Hebrews, sought to save them from destruction. Forgiveness was lingering* *for them. The judgment of God had come very near, and appealed to them to repent. A special, irresistible interference from heaven had arrested their rebellion."* Here again are the two personalities we have noticed throughout our entire study in both the Old and New Testaments. *Jesus, the ever-present, ever-tender, kind, merciful, longsuffering and loving Saviour reaching out His hand to save; and on the other side of the cloud, the ruler of darkness ever and always seeking a legal right to wield the sword of justice upon the heads of all those who refuse to repent. What a study in contrasts!*

In the process of explaining all the spiritual implications of this story EGW makes a very intriguing statement on PP 405 that sincere SDAs have quoted again and again to try and prove that God really did destroy Korah and all of his co-horts, and to believe otherwise is the sin against the Holy Spirit. Notice: "Notwithstanding they had the most convincing evidence of God's displeasure at their course, in the destruction of the men who had deceived them, they dared to attribute His judgments (decisions) to Satan, declaring that through the power of the evil one, Moses and Aaron had caused the death of good and holy men. It was this act that sealed their doom. They had committed the sin against the Holy spirit, a sin by which man's heart is effectually hardened against the influence of divine grace." PP 405.

On page 100 of my second book, "The Final Absolute . . ." I asked the following question and then answered it. "QUESTION: #12—Doesn't Sister White say that it is blasphemy to attribute His judgments to Satan? PP 405. ANSWER: Did Moses and Aaron kill the 250 princes? No, they did not. Moses and Aaron stood as God's visible representatives to give His Word and show His power and authority over all events, people and nature. God said they would die if they did not repent. *He, alone, had the power of life and death in His hand . . . not Satan.* Satan never could harm them, *unless God permitted it;*

therefore, it is blasphemy to attribute to Satan or Moses the power to decide whether or not these men live or die. Only the Creator has the right to decide and carry out such a decision. Satan can only do what God permits. Look at Job's case for proof." This is just part of my answer. But I want to add something else which I did not know when I wrote that book. Look at this next excellent statement: *"It is through the agency of the Holy Spirit that God communicates with man; and those who deliberately reject this agency as satanic, have cut off the channel of communication between the soul and heaven. God works by the manifestation of His Spirit to reprove and convict the sinner; and if the Spirit's work is finally rejected, there is no more that God can do for the soul.* **The last resource of divine mercy has been employed. The transgressor has cut himself from God, and sin has no remedy to cure itself.** There is no reserved power by which God can work to convict and convert the sinner. 'Let him alone' (Hosea 4:17) is the divine command. Then 'there remaineth no more sacrifice for sins, but a certain looking for of judgment and fiery indignation, which shall devour the adversaries.' Hebrews 10:26." Ibid.

The issue here is not whether or not God destroyed Korah and his sympathizers, **but whether Moses and Aaron were given special magical power from God to do it.** The people were saying that Moses and Aaron were being led of Satan and Korah was being led of God. The people said that Satan gave Moses power to open the earth and send fire from the cloud to kill these rebels.

This is precisely what the pharisees said about Christ. "But when the pharisees heard it, they said, This fellow doth not cast out devils, but by Beelzebub the prince of Devils." Matt. 12:24. Jesus then told them that "blasphemy against the Holy Ghost shall not be forgiven unto men . . . neither in this world, neither in the world to come." Matt. 12:31, 32.

This will be the final accusation against God's people . . . that they are responsible for all of the troubles and disasters that are coming upon the earth. "GREAT CONTROVERSY," pp. 614, 615. You should also read GC 616 and on to 624-625 where Satan finally appears as Christ to convince the world that Sunday really is God's holy day. The Servant of the Lord, EGW, has warned us. "The last great delusion is soon to open before us. Antichrist is to perform his marvelous works in our sight. So closely will the counterfeit resemble the true that it will be impossible to distinguish between them except by the Holy Scriptures. By their testimony every statement and every miracle must be tested . . . None but those who have fortified the mind with the truths of the Bible will stand through the last great conflict." GC 593, 594. Do you now see the importance of knowing the difference between these two personages . . . Lord Jesus, the true God, and Lord Satan, the false God? Let's go back now to Mount Sinai.

Just as we have been warned by God's servant that in these last days Satan will be appearing as Christ in the sight of the people, (GC 624, 625), so the Lord Jesus warned Moses before He gave the Ten Commandments that Satan was going to appear in their sight. Notice: "And the Lord (Jesus) said unto Moses, Go unto the people, and sanctify them today and tomorrow, and let them wash their clothes, AND BE READY AGAINST THE THIRD DAY: FOR THE THIRD DAY THE LORD (SATAN) WILL COME DOWN IN THE SIGHT OF ALL THE PEOPLE UPON MOUNT SINAI." Exodus 19:10,11.

Now, beloved, just think about it. The Bible tells us that no one ever saw God in the Old or New Testament, except when Jesus was born in a body of flesh. But here is the Lord telling Moses to watch out and be ready on the third day for *"The Lord (Satan)" is going to appear so you will be able to see him with your very own eyes.* And it was going to be a glorious sight, for Christ warned Moses to tell the people not to "break through unto the Lord (Satan) to gaze, and many of them perish." Exodus 19:21. The Hebrew word for "Gaze" is from "Raah" which in this context has the basic meaning of **curious staring**. Among other things it means to "be near, perceive, regard, spy, stare, or view." Because Satan had programmed Adam and all of his children to be afraid of God, there was an innate, carnal fear of God built into every person's mind as they grew up, and each culture re-inforced this fear with the endless rituals of blood sacrifices and offerings that were a part of daily life.

The human mind can be programmed to destroy your whole body. We know this from the Voodoo spells that have been cast on people. If a man believes the Voodoo doctor when he is told that he is going to die in three days, then he will die, because his mind really believes that he is going to die. We cannot understand how or why this works, but it has something to do with **fear**. That is why Jesus was continually telling his disciples **to not be afraid**. Why? Because God wants to dwell in our hearts, **but He can't if we are afraid of Him.** Therefore, the way for us to let God come in and live in our hearts is **to lose our fear of Him**. That is why Jesus came to this dark earth in a body of flesh. **He wanted to be near us and to touch us so we could see that you could touch God and look Him right in the face, and He would not hurt or kill you.** "God is love; and he that dwelleth in love dwelleth in God, and God in him. Herein is our love made perfect, that we may have boldness in the day of judgment: because as he is, so are we in this world. There is no fear in love; **but perfect love casteth out fear:** because fear hath torment. He that feareth is not made perfect in love." I John 4:16-18.

When we see what happened at Mt. Sinai we can see Satan was able to keep the people away from God by using "fear tactics," and then making a covenant of works with them which would keep them in such bondage that they would **never** want to come near the Lord but would **always** keep their distance. But Jesus' life and death have now changed all that. "BUT NOW IN CHRIST JESUS YE WHO SOMETIMES WERE FAR OFF ARE MADE NIGH BY

THE BLOOD OF CHRIST." Eph. 2:13. Paul goes ahead and tells how that middle wall of partition was broken down when Jesus abolished the "law of commandments contained in ordinances." V. 15.

We know that the true God spoke the Ten Commandments from Exodus 20:1-17. Satan was able to distort this beautiful occasion with his fireworks display. As a result he was able to gain access to their fear dazzled brains and even get Moses to cooperate in making an altar of earth. "AND THE LORD SAID UNTO MOSES . . . AN ALTAR OF EARTH thou shalt make unto me, and shalt SACRIFICE THEREON THY BURNT OFFERINGS, THY SHEEP, AND THY OXEN:" Exodus 20:22-24. How do I know this was the voice of lord Satan speaking? Because God said he never spoke anything about "sacrifice" when He brought them out of Egypt, Jer. 7:22; and Isa. 66:3 especially condemns killing an ox. I find it most interesting that in the 15 times the word "altar" is mentioned from Gen. 8:20 to Ex. 20:24 there is not one command from God to build them. Not even once did God tell them to build an altar and sacrifice an animal to Him so as to gain his acceptance or forgiveness. I just looked up in the EGW index to see if she stated anywhere that God commanded anyone to build an altar. I could find no such reference. All she does is recount the history of the altars that patriarchs like Abraham built. The altar of burnt offering seems to be closely associated with the heathens and the worship of their false (demon) gods, which EGW mentions on page 91 of "Patriarchs & Prophets." On page 71 of the same book EGW refers to the altars that Cain and Abel erected. "Abel presented a sacrifice from the flock, in accordance with the Lord's directions. 'And the Lord had respect unto Abel and to his offering.' Fire flashed from heaven and consumed the sacrifice. But Cain, disregarding the Lord's direct and explicit command, presented only an offering of fruit. There was no token from heaven to show that it was accepted."

It always comes as a shock to most religious people that literal fire, as we know it today, never existed until after sin entered. I discuss this in IFH on 307-309 and 318-324. You cannot have literal fire without oxidation. Oxidation is, in a phrase, the scientific definition of how oxygen combines with other elements to break down matter such as you find in wood rotting and rust forming on metal and other materials that rust may be able to form on. To quote directly from my book, IFH, "According to the oxidation reaction theory, all matter or substance in the earth today breaks down because of or by a process known as **oxidation**. Time correlates with oxygen. **There is no time without oxygen**. Scientists measure time with or by radio active isotopes. Carbon 14 dating is based upon the half life of carbon 14 (C-14). It is by this dating method that scientists are able to determine the age of life forms from the past which only have part of their matter left, such as a bone from a dinosaur or a piece of wood or coal buried in the ground. Without oxygen this would not be possible." IFH 320.

The simple fact is that God did not invent literal fire on this earth. It is a direct result of Adam's sin. Satan, the prince of the power of the air, Eph. 2:2, was the one who suggested the killing of animals to Adam in the first place. God allowed this and made it mean something by regulating it and explaining to Adam what the sacrifices would mean. Only clean, tame, domesticated animals were allowed to be sacrificed. God allowed Satan to bring fire down on the sacrifice as a "sign" of His acceptance. Naturally, Adam thought that the fire came from God. Satan was able to get Cain to reject the symbolic meaning of the blood sacrifice and burnt offering and then to cause Cain to be envious and jealous of Abel when the fire came down on Abel's sacrifice but not on Cain's. We have had religious wars ever since. Satan is a master of playing the ends against the middle. If you check it out carefully, I think that you will be able to prove that God has never brought any literal fire down on this earth from day one. Satan brought the fire down in Job's day (Job 1:16) and Satan is the false god who will bring real or literal fire down in these last days, Rev. 13:13. He has already done that with the atom bomb. But he will no doubt bring greater wonders in the future. I also realize that the Devil can bring down a false latter rain fire to counterfeit the Holy Spirit as it came on the day of Pentecost in cloven tongues of fire. Acts 2:3, 4. If you are wondering about the fire that fell on Elijah's sacrifice on Mt. Carmel, I discuss that in detail starting on page 377 of IFH. I hope you will read it.

Now, let's go back to Mount Sinai where we have already discovered that Israel made a covenant of works with Satan due to their fear of death instead of their love for the true God. Jesus abolished this whole system of works when He died on the cross of Calvary. Col. 2:14-16; Eph. 2:14-16. In contrast God spoke His perfect Ten Commandments "amid flame and thunder," as we have already quoted from EGW. But she nor the Bible says God brought the literal fire (flames) or thunder, smoke or the quaking of the mountain. We believe Satan did this to frighten the people into a program of works, based upon fear. This began with the altar of earth we read of in Exodus 20:24. But the seed had already been planted in Moses' mind back at the burning bush on top of Mt. Sinai, where we find this subtle suggestion of carnal signs and animal sacrifice creeping in when Moses resists God's tender call of love to him to become the instrument for God's deliverance of Israel from Egyptian bondage. From Exodus 3:1-14 there is no mention of circumcision or animal sacrifice. Moses' doubts and resistance created a negative atmosphere in which Satan could insert his works program of animal slaughter (v. 18) and ceremonial rituals.

Someone may be asking why Satan would want the sacrificial system of killing animals set up or why he would appear on the mountain as an angel of light trying to make the people think he was God? The obvious reason is that Satan wants men to worship him instead of God. He wants to be God. Isa. 14:12-14. In order to receive this worship he must somehow deceive the people into thinking they are really worshipping the true God when in actuality they are worshipping him, the false god. "Satan frequently appears as an angel of light, arrayed in the livery of heaven; he assumes friendly airs, manifesting great sanctity of character and high regard for his victims, **the souls whom he means to deceive and destroy.**" 3T 456. Satan knew that if he could lead the people into a false system of worship, such as killing animals to get their sins forgiven, he would be able to (1) Harden their hearts against God. (2) Make them think they were working themselves to heaven. (3) Lead them to look to the **killer priesthood** as examples of piety and holiness. (4) Lead them onto **human sacrifice** which he often did. (5) Make God look like a hard-hearted and blood-thirsty God. (6) Make God look like a killer who had no compassion for innocent animals. (7) Make them believe that works had merit with God and this is the only way you can get to heaven. (8) Corrupt the priests with **blood money** from the offerings. (9) Cause people to hate and despise God and His temple worship and turn away from God into the waiting arms of Satan.

Furthermore, Satan soon realized after the call of Moses that he would probably not be able to stop the Lord from delivering Israel from Egypt, so His war strategy was to make God look as bad as possible all the way through so as to scare and frighten the people of Israel, **for fear would keep them from becoming God's true temple, which was God's original and ultimate plan. He never intended for them to have a sanctuary or temple in the desert.** I touched on this briefly on page 274. But once they made their covenant with Satan through the animal sacrifice system (this was the old or first covenant) the Lord had to go to His **alternate or secondary plan** of a physical, non-human temple or sanctuary **to give the animal sacri-**

fice system meaning and substance. And this is what the Lord did. From Exodus 24:12 to 31:18 God communed with Moses and gave him the directions for the sanctuary which was to become a **desert drama of the plan of salvation** in types and symbols. You can read all the way through these chapters and see that it is the true God speaking, for there is nothing about "an eye for an eye or tooth for a tooth," or any kind of hurtful, get-even-type attitudes or phrases. Everything God gave Moses was uplifting and designed to make the most of a bad situation until this beautiful God could come down to our sin-cursed, darkened earth in a body of flesh and let us see Him face to face. And notice that the last part of God's instructions to Moses was about the Sabbath day being a "sign" between Him and His people. That has never changed. It is still God's sign or covenant, for the true God never changes, *but all the rest of the symbols and their "glory" have faded away in the glorious appearing of the true tabernacle we are to dwell in, Jesus Christ Himself.* Paul speaks of the two covenants or ministrations in 2 Cor. 3. He calls the first testament "the ministration of death, written and engraven in stones . . ." And yet Paul tells us this ministration was so glorious that it made the face of Moses shine. v. 7.

But what was it that made the face of Moses shine . . . why it was the wonderful and glorious presence of Jesus on Mt. Sinai. "Now if the dispensation of death, carved in letters on stone, came with such splendor that the Israelites could not look at Moses' face because of its brightness, fading as this was, will not the dispensation of the Spirit be attended with greater splendor? For if there was splendor in the dispensation of condemnation, the dispensation of righteousness must far exceed it in splendor. Since we have such a hope, we are very bold, not like Moses, who put a veil over his face so that the Israelites might not see the end of the fading splendor. But their minds were hardened; for to this day, when they read the old covenant, that same veil remains unlifted, because only through Christ is it taken away. Yes, to this day whenever Moses **is read a veil lies over their minds**; but when a man turns to the Lord the veil is removed. Now the Lord is the Spirit, and where the Spirit of the Lord is, there is freedom. And we all, with unveiled face, beholding the glory of the Lord, are being changed into His likeness from one degree of glory to another; for this comes from the Lord who is the Spirit." 2 Cor. 3:7-18. RSV. Moses' face shone not because the law was in his hands, but because he had been in the presence of Christ and the law was only a reflector of its wonderful author, Jesus. And when He writes His law in our hearts today He is simply writing His very own character in our hearts and minds. Moses loved Christ, even though He did not know Him as we can know Him, but the glory that shone in Moses' face is to shine even brighter in ours today as we allow Christ to fully indwell us as His holy and only temple, tabernacle and sanctuary.

Is it possible, beloved, that very sincere believers in the church today have the same kind of veil over their eyes so they are not able to see this glorious truth about Jesus, that He does not hurt or destroy? It is only as we truly turn to the Lord with all of our hearts that this veil will be removed.

Now let us go to Exodus 24 and see how this covenant of death was established. It really started when Moses began resisting God's leadership in His life at the burning bush. We have already gone over that. But now let us go to the appointment of the 70 elders. This was one of the biggest mistakes of Moses' career as the Lord's leader and guide for Israel. EGW has some very important statements to make about these 70 elders. She quotes from Numbers 11:11 where Moses is praying to God about his heavy burdens. "His prayer was almost a complaint. 'Wherefore hast Thou afflicted Thy servant? and wherefore have I not found favor in Thy sight, that Thou layest the burden of all this people upon me? . . . Whence should I have flesh, that we may eat. I am not able to bear all this people alone, because it is too heavy for me.' " Quoted from PP 380. In my book, IFH, in additional note #20, on page 404, I point out that the "East Wind" was what God allowed Satan to use to bring the plague of locusts upon Egypt, Exodus 14:21; and Psalm 78:25-32 says that it was an "east wind" that brought the quail. EGW continues . . .

"The Lord hearkened to his prayer, and directed him to summon seventy men of the elders of Israel—men not only advanced in years, but possessing dignity, sound judgment, and experience . . . The Lord permitted Moses to choose for himself the most faithful and efficient men to share the responsibility with him. Their influence would assist in holding in check the violence of the people, and quelling insurrection; yet serious evils would eventually result from their promotion. (The reason for this is because their minds represented 'carnal' wisdom instead of 'divine wisdom'. Editor) They would never have been chosen had Moses manifested faith corresponding to the evidences he had witnessed of God's power and goodness. But he had magnified his own burdens and services, almost losing sight of the fact that he was only the instrument by which God had wrought. He was not excusable in indulging, in the slightest degree, the spirit of murmuring that was the curse of Israel. Had he relied fully upon God, the Lord would have guided him continually and would have given him strength for every emergency." PP 380.

Now we are ready to go to Exodus 24 where these same 70 elders whom Moses had just selected to help him "guide" the children of Israel to the promised land are going to have a banquet with Satan (all the time thinking they are dining with God) and enter into the covenant of works or death. And it was a covenant of death with the devil, for all of these 70 elders and all the children of Israel 20 years and upward, (except for Joshua and Caleb), would never arrive in the promised land, but would die in the desert. Even Moses would die on Mt. Nebo, although he would be resurrected and taken to heaven with Christ (Jude 9-Matt. 17:3,

4) because even Moses did not realize what a terrible mistake he and the 70 elders were making by entering into a covenant of death with Satan in Exodus 24.

"And He (Jesus) said unto Moses, come up to the lord, (Satan) thou, and Aaron, Nadab, and Abihu, and seventy of the elders of Israel; and worship ye afar off. And Moses alone shall come near the lord (Satan): but they shall not come nigh; neither shall the people go up with him." Exodus 24:1, 2. Only Moses had enough love in his heart to keep him from being afraid and thus being hurt or killed by his royal highness, the devil. *"Perfect love casts out fear."* I John 4:18. Notice in verses 4-8 that Moses and the people offer burnt offerings and peace offerings to the lord (Satan) and then sealed the "book of the covenant" with blood. This is the same "book of the law" that Paul says was a "curse" (Gal. 3:10-13) and was "against us" Col. 2:14.

Next we come to Exodus 24:9-12, where Moses and the 70 elders went up into the Mt *"and they saw the God of Israel: and there was under his feet as it were a paved work of a sapphire stone, and as it were the body of heaven in his clearness. And upon the nobles of the children of Israel he laid not his hand: also they saw God, and did eat and drink."* The Bible clearly tells us "NO MAN HATH SEEN GOD AT ANY TIME." I John 4:12. So, this "God of Israel" they "saw" was not the true God, but Satan, as an angel of light, representing himself as God. Sound familiar? Well, it should, for Paul tells us that Satan is the "son of perdition (Primarily Satan but it could refer to any human being Satan uses as an anti-Christ) who opposeth and exalteth himself above all that is called God, or that is worshipped; so that he as God sitteth in the temple of God, (in man's heart) shewing himself that he is God." 2 Thess. 2:3, 4.

"It is interesting to note EGW's comment on this appearance of "God" or what the people thought was God. After she quotes Exodus 24:10, she makes this statement. "They did not behold the Deity, but they saw the glory of

His presence." PP 312. Let us ask ourselves this question. Did God create Lucifer with the "glory" of His presence? Yes, He did. And Lucifer has not lost any of the powers God gave to Him. He has only perverted them. But He has the ability to appear as an "angel of light" 2 Cor. 11:14, and we are told will successfully "personate" Jesus Himself in the very last hour of this world's history. GC 624, 625. Furthermore, we read in Exodus 23:21, that God has placed His "name" or "glory" in Lucifer or Satan. Listen: "Beware of him, and obey his voice, provoke him not; for he will not pardon your transgressions: *FOR MY NAME IS IN HIM.*" Here we see that God allowed Satan to masquerade or personate God, Himself, for the purpose of receiving worship. Since God created Lucifer, placing His very own Name or glory in Lucifer, it is not incorrect to say that whenever Satan chose to personate God anytime in history the people were indeed seeing the "glory of His presence," for Satan could not personate God without His knowledge or permission. So, Moses nor the 70 elders beheld "the Deity" but they saw a personation of it and God allowed them to think this really was the true God, for there was no way He could prove to them that Satan was a liar and a deceiver. The Lord had to patiently wait until He could come in a body of flesh before He could make them understand the real truth about who He really was. Meanwhile, He was not only trying to save Israel, but prevent Satan and his angels from destroying themselves, for if God had either taken His protecting hand off of Satan or revealed too much about who he really was and what he was doing, Satan and his angels would have destroyed each other. Ezek. 28:6-10 indicates that is how all the wicked will die in the end-time. But God is still preventing this even today, for His love is so great and eternal He cannot stand to see any of His creatures hurt or suffer, so He absorbs all the pain, hurt and suffering into Himself to protect us. What a Wonderful God we have.

ANOTHER VERSION SAYS THAT THE 70 ELDERS "SAW THE GOD OF ISRAEL: UNDER HIS FEET THERE

SEEMED TO BE A PAVEMENT OF BRILLIANT SAP-
PHIRE STONES, AS CLEAR AS THE HEAVENS. YET,
EVEN THOUGH THE ELDERS SAW GOD, HE DID NOT
DESTROY THEM; AND THEY HAD A MEAL
TOGETHER BEFORE THE LORD." EX. 24:9-11. LB. Ezekiel 28:13 lists the "sapphire" as one of the ten precious
stones God used to cover Lucifer with when He created him
in the beginning. Oh, how Satan has perverted the gifts God
gave to him! But Satan was not allowed to hurt Moses, the
70 elders or any of the children of Israel. This was not the
first time that the lord Satan had appeared to the children
of Israel, for the true Lord had previously warned Moses in
Exodus 19:10-13 that they should "be ready against the
third day: for the third day the Lord will come down in the
sight of all the people upon Sinai." Jesus went on to give
specific warnings to Moses to be very careful not to come up
into the mountain to "gaze" at "the Lord" or "the Lord"
would *"break forth upon"* them. I have already covered
Exodus 19 on pages 33 and 47 showing how God is not referring to Himself, for Christ never talks about Himself in the
third person. The LB editor proves my point further by
changing the nouns from the third person singular "he" to
the first person singular, "I" in v. 24. Notice: "don't let the
priests and the people break across the boundaries to try to
come up here, or I will destroy them." LB. He realized that
if the true God is really speaking here that it has to be in
the first person, not the third person. But we know Jesus
was talking about Satan.

For more conclusive proof that God does not speak in
the third person when he is talking about or referring to
Himself, let us go to Exodus 20:1-3. Notice: "And God spake
all these words, saying I am the Lord thy God, which have
brought thee out of the land of Egypt, out of the house of
bondage. Thou shalt have no other gods before me." Notice
how the true Lord is referring to Himself in the first
person—"I" and "me." Now go to Exodus 24:1 where the
true God is speaking to Moses inviting him up to meet "the

lord (Satan)." "And He (Jesus) said unto Moses, Come up unto the lord (Satan)." This scenario in which they make a covenant with Satan goes through v. 11. Then the true Lord tells Moses to come up higher in the Mountain. Notice how God again speaks in the first person singular. *"And the Lord said unto Moses, Come up to Me into the mount, and be there: and I will give thee tables of stone, and a law, and commandments which I have written; that thou mayest teach them."* Ex. 24:12.

Every time I read that verse it always reminds me of Matthew 11:28. "Come unto me, all you that labor and are heavy laden, and I will give you rest." Please take note of this and also verses 29 and 30, for it proves that when Christ is speaking, He always refers to Himself in the first person, "I" and "Me." but when He is talking about lord Satan or any other god or gods (demons) he will refer to them as "the god or gods" as we read in Ex. 12:12. "For I will pass through the land of Egypt this night, and will smite all the firstborn in the land of Egypt, both man and beast, and against all the gods [or princes;] of Egypt I will execute judgment: I am the Lord." One of the chief "gods" of Egypt was "Ra" which means "harmful" in the Hebrew [by contrast Jesus is 'Harmless' Heb. 7:26]. Ra can also be spelled "Re" and is defined as "The sun god, principal god of the ancient Egyptians, usually depicted as having the head of a hawk and wearing the solar disc as a crown." From Webster's Dictionary, Unabridged. One can readily see how Satan was able to use these "gods" to control the priests and through them the people in all of Egypt. Of course, he did this in every culture all over the world, as he still is doing today. Even Christian America has its past and current "gods" of the silver screen, better known as "Hollywood" stars. And "stars" are angels as we see in the "star wars" of Rev. 12. "And his tail drew the third part of the stars (angels) of heaven, and did cast them to the earth:" Rev. 12:4. They are also referred to as "film idols," or "movie idols." America has even made stone images of men of their historical past, such as Abraham Lincoln, who was hated in his time, but worshipped today. You also have the four faces of past presidents on Mt. Rushmore. And people are crazy over stuffed animals and cabbage patch dolls, etc. Of course, we can make anything or anyone an idol. Let's just make sure we put Jesus first in our lives so we will not break the letter or the spirit of the first and second commandment.

The Lord also warned Israel to **"not revile the Gods, nor curse the ruler of thy people."** Ex. 22:28. Revile means to "denounce with abusive language." The noun or word "gods" can also be translated "judges" as we see in Psalm 82:6, (see "Strong's" 430). Jesus referred to this Psalm when He said to the Jews who would not accept Him as the Son of God, "Is it not written in your law, (notice He refers to it as "your law" and not as "my law"), I said, Ye are gods? If he called them gods, unto whom the word of God came, and the scripture cannot be broken;" John 10:34, 35. In the next verse Jesus concludes His appeal to their sense of logic by pointing out that if their own law acknowledges human beings as "gods" (actually "judges") then they should not be upset at Him (who truly was God) for claiming to be the Son of God. The SDA Bible commentary makes this insightful comment on Christ's words. "The Psalm is an arrangement of unjust judges, spoken of as 'gods'. Rabbinical tradition applied the term 'gods' to those who received the law: 'The Israelites accepted the Torah only so that the Angel of death [Satan no doubt] should have no dominion over them [Ps. 82:6, 7]' (Talmud 'Abodah Zarah 5a, sonicino ed., p. 21)." 5BC 1009. The significance of this statement is the fact that Israel did accept the Law of Moses **out of fear** and said they would keep it so they would not have to die, for they were sure God was about to kill them right on the spot. They even agreed to keep the Ten Commandments, but they understood the law only in the legalistic sense, and not in the spiritual sense which can only come as we know the love of God through Jesus, our Lord.

He is our example "Who did no sin, neither was guile found in his mouth: Who, when he was reviled, reviled not again; when he suffered, he threatened not; but committed himself to him that judgeth righteously:" I Pet. 2:22, 23. "them that walk after the flesh . . . are not afraid to speak evil of dignities. Whereas angels, which are greater in power and might, bring not railing accusation against them before the Lord." 2 Pet. 2:10, 11. "Yet Michael (Christ) the archangel, when contending with the devil He disputed about the body of Moses, durst [presumed, dared, or ventured] not bring against him a railing [reviling] accusation, but said, The Lord rebuke thee." Jude 9. The word "rail" comes from the Greek word, "Blasphemeo," meaning to "blaspheme, rail, or revile."

EGW says "how dare any one bar the way of God's servants by unjust, unfeeling speeches? But this has been done, and thereby laborers have been discouraged, and souls lost who might have been saved. Those who do this work are not prompted by the Spirit of God, **but by another spirit**. Scornful criticisms and discourteous remarks are wholly of Satan. If ministers, teachers, and people would practice Bible courtesy, they would find hearts open to receive the truth, and God would be glorified." R & H, July 4, 1907, EGW.

Someone sent me the following comment taken from a cassette recording of one of Dr. Glen Toppenberg's talks. "Dr. Toppenberg, M.D. asked this question of the audience he was addressing: 'Is there another "JESUS?" Some of the audience said, "No!" But Dr. Toppenberg said, 'Yes, there is.' [A pause and silence] Then he continued: 'I have again and again identified demons by the name "L-O-R-D" AND BY THE NAME "J-E-S-U-S" AND BY THE NAME "C-H-R-I-S-T." Then he goes on to say, 'One demon told me, 'You must serve the L-O-R-D, I am speaking for the L-O-R-D, and the L-O-R-D wants this to be done.' Then Dr. Toppenberg asked him, 'Who is L-O-R-D?' And the demon answered, 'The L-O-R-D is Satan!' " Isn't it amazing that the demons are even smarter than Laodiceans who don't even know that demons control their lives and are keeping them in their death-like stupor until their probation is closed? No wonder the demons get angry and go crazy when they are identified. A few days ago a man told me, "Mike, do you know that the devil is running scared today? And I will tell you why. Because Satan is faced with something he doesn't want to face and cannot handle. He is afraid to die, but he knows his time is short; and he is very scared. He and all of his demons believe that as long as they cling to Christians they will not have to die." As I pondered these ideas I began to realize why the Lord has to cast all evil spirits out of our lives before we can go to heaven. In fact, that may be the very reason most Christians are not too excited about heaven. They and their demons are such good friends that they don't want to part. What a sad and terrible situation. May God help us all to repent and to cast all demons out of our lives in the name of and blood of Jesus Christ.

In Ezekiel 28 the prophet says, "Morever the word of the Lord came unto me saying, Son of man, take up a lamentation upon the king of Tyrus, and say unto him, Thus saith the Lord God; Thou sealest up the sum, full of wisdom, and perfect in beauty. Thou hast been in Eden the garden of God; every precious stone was thy covering, . . . Thou wast perfect in thy ways from the day that thou wast created, til iniquity was found in thee." Ezek. 28:11-13, 15. Just think of God's incredible love for His first created being, the beautiful angel, Lucifer. Jesus told Ezekiel "weep" for my lost boy. Yes, God is weeping for Lucifer (now Satan). That is what a "lamentation" is . . . **weeping**. But most people just hate and revile him. But Christ didn't do that and He doesn't want us to revile him either. In Ezek. 28:6-10 Jesus explains to Satan how he is going to die. He tells him his own followers are going to kill him. No, God isn't going to destroy the devil. Listen: "Wilt thou yet say before him that slayeth thee, I am God? But thou shalt be a man, and no god, in the hand of him that slayeth thee. Thou shalt die the deaths of the uncircumcised by the hand of strangers: for I have spoken it, saith the Lord God." The Hebrew word translated "man" in Ezekiel 28:9 is from "Adam" which simply means "a human being" or a person or being that is created just like humans. The Lord told His people over and over again that the "gods" whom they were worshipping were "no gods" at all but simply idols. 2 Kings 19:18; Ps. 97:7; I Chron. 16:26. And Paul tells us that idol worship is devil worship. I Cor. 10:18-20; Lev. 17:7; Deut. 32:17; Ps. 106:37. Speaking of Jeroboam: *"And he ordained him priests for the high places, and for the devils, and for the calves which he had made."* 2 Chron. 11:15. Is it any wonder the devil doesn't want people to read the Bible! It exposes him!

In the introduction to the "Great Controversy," EGW warns us, "In the great final conflict, Satan will employ the same policy, manifest the same spirit, and work for the same end as in all preceding ages. That which has been, will be, except that the coming struggle will be marked with a terrible intensity such as the world has never witnessed. Satan's deceptions will be more subtle, his assaults more determined. If it were possible, he would lead astray the elect. Mark 13:22, R.VI." GC xi. Now, beloved, if even Moses and 70 of the elders could be deceived by Satan in their day, what makes us any less vulnerable? Only one thing . . . the knowledge we now have of the true character of God. The 70 elders were first mentioned in Ex. 24:1. This was only the "third month" since they left Egypt, Ex. 19:1. These 70 elders are not necessarily the same ones who were selected later, although some of the 70 from the first group (Ex. 24:1) may have been selected again in the second group, which occurred in the first month of the second year which would have been Abib, and about 9 or 10 months later in 1490 BC (Usher). Originally, the 70 elders were suggested by God to go up the Mt. with Moses (Ex. 24) but in Num. 11 the 70 Elders became a permanent, decision-making body, actually coming between God and Moses. The Lord not only had to deal with Moses' reluctance and resistance to God's leading, but a large committee of 70 as well. Throughout history God has had much more success working through individuals rather than committees and councils of men. Now the Bible clearly tells us that in the "multitude of counselors there is safety," Prov. 11:14; 24:6, but it does not say that a committee of counselors is to be the final word on all matters. Every wise leader will surround himself with wise counselors, but a wise leader will not allow those people to dictate to him and that is what often happens. A guidance or advisory committee becomes the executive committee. Look at the way God has operated down through the centuries. He has selected individuals such as Elijah, Elisha, John the Baptist and many other prophets who were led by His Holy Spirit. They were hated and hunted and most of them were killed by the devil's committees and councils. Look at the reformation. God raised up men like Wycliffe, Luther, Calvin, Knox and others. Later He called John Wesley. What committee would have voted for the Apostle Paul to become the man to organize the early church? He wasn't even accepted or approved by his contemporaries who had received the outpouring of the Holy Spirit on the day of Pentecost . . . at least many of them. And what council or board of elders would have agreed that Ellen G. White should be the Messenger to the Remnant? The wisdom of God is foolish with the committees of men. I think this is graphically illustrated with Moses' selection of the 70 elders which became the Jewish Sanhedrin, who as we know now, voted to crucify our precious Lord Jesus Christ. Ezekiel saw another committee of about "five and twenty men, with their backs toward the temple of the Lord, and their faces toward the east; and they worshipped the sun toward the east." Ezek. 8:16. This vision was given to Ezekiel "in the sixth year, in the sixth month, in the fifth day of the month . . ." Ezek. 8:1. In other words you have here the number 665, or the day just before final and full apostasy. This committee of 24 leaders of Israel with a chairman, making 25, had turned their backs on God's sanctuary and gone to Sun(day) worship.

The servant of the Lord has told us that "as the storm approaches, a large class who have professed faith in the third angel's message, but have not been sanctified through obedience to the truth, abandon their position and join the ranks of the opposition . . . Men of talent and pleasing address, who once rejoiced in the truth, employ their powers to deceive and mislead souls. They become the most bitter enemies of their former brethren. When Sabbathkeepers are brought before the courts to answer for their faith, these apostates are the most efficient agents of Satan to misrepresent and accuse them, and by false reports and insinuations to stir up the ruler against them." GC 608.

Again one of God's greatest and most influential messengers of our time, EGW, has told us how the majority of God's professed people will receive the final message of God's glorious character of love. "There is to be in the churches a wonderful manifestation of the power of God, but it will not move upon those who have not humbled themselves before the Lord, and opened the door of their heart by confession and repentance. In the manifestation of the power that lightens the earth with its glory, they will see only something which in their blindness they think dangerous, something which will arouse their fears, and they will brace themselves to resist it. Because the Lord does not work according to their expectations and ideas, they will oppose the work. 'Why' they say, 'should we not know the Spirit of God, when we have been in the work so many years?' " RH 11-7-1918. These same men will, like the Jews of old, accept "sun worship" by agreeing to go along with the governments of the world instead of standing for the truth. When the Jewish leaders rejected their Messiah by screaming out "crucify him," and saying "we have no king but Caesar," John 19:15, they accepted the standard of the Roman armies, the eagle, or more correctly the Phoenix, an ancient symbol of sun worship.

Do you realize how ubiquitous the modern Phoenix [Eagle] is today? It is not only the national symbol of strength for the USA but was used by Hitler's Nazi Germany as well as today's Communist Russia. The "Phoenix" is literally everywhere, for it is a symbol of ancient sun worship. We all know that Sunday is a weekly holiday in the USA today, as it is in many countries. But it is destined to become an international day of worship for the entire world. The Bible [Rev. 13] and EGW have predicted this: See GC 587; 6T 18; 7BC 976; TM 37.

But what most SDAs do not know is that EGW has also predicted that the leaders of God's professed people will tell the people they must keep Sunday. Here now is that exact quote: *"The Lord has a controversy with His professed people in these last days. In this controversy men in responsible positions will take a course directly opposite to that pursued by Nehemiah. They will not only ignore and despise the Sabbath themselves, but they will try to keep it from others by burying it beneath the rubbish of custom and tradition. In churches and in large gatherings in the open air, ministers will urge upon the people the necessity of keeping the first day of the week. There are calamities on sea and land: and these calamities will increase, one disaster following close upon another; and the little band of conscientious Sabbath-keepers will be pointed out as the ones who are bringing the wrath of God upon the world by their disregard of Sunday. Satan urges this falsehood that he may take the world captive. It is his plan to compel men to accept errors." "R & H March 18, 1884. [Vol. 1, Page 405 of the large green volumes]* May the Lord give each of us strength to stand through these last days.

ADDITIONAL THOUGHTS

No. 1. It was not God's original idea for His only Son to die. No. Satan kidnapped us by leading our first parents, Adam and Eve, into sin. We then became his hostages, which he hoped to use, to force God to admit He was wrong about His law. Since God's very own children, made in His own image, could not keep His law how could God expect the angels or unfallen worlds to keep it? The way God chose to answer this accusation and slander was to come Himself in a body of flesh as the "Son of God," but Isaiah declares that this "child" and "son" was none other than the "Mighty God, The everlasting Father . . ." and Paul tells us "that God was in Christ, reconciling the world unto himself . . ." "For in him (Christ) dwelleth all the fulness of the Godhead bodily." 2 Cor. 5:19; Col. 2:9. And so God Himself, in the body and person of His only Son, came to buy or ransom us back by allowing us to shed His precious blood so we would know that He is "Harmless" [Heb. 7:26] and need not stand "afar off," Ex. 24:1; Eph. 2:13. The concept or idea of "ransom" is brought out in the following verses: Isa. 35:10; Jer. 31:11; Hosea 13:14; Matt. 20:28; Mark 10:45; and I Tim. 2:6.

No. 2. Some stories in the Old Testament reveal the truth about God's true and loving Character. When Absalom was banished from King David's presence Absalom was on David's mind day and night. Joab realized this and "fetched . . . a wise woman . . ." from Tekoah to talk David into devising a plan whereby Absalom might be restored to royal favor. Here is the heart of her speech. "For we all must die and are then like water spilled on the earth which cannot be recovered. ***God, however, does not sweep away life, but rather takes measures so as not to keep the banished away from Himself."*** 2 Sam. 14:14. Modern Language Version. I believe God's spirit inspired the writer of 2 Sam. to record this story so we could see right into the very chambers of God's loving and compassionate, inner, heart of love. The NIV says, "But God ***does not take away life;*** Instead He devises ways so that a banished person may not remain estranged from Him." Yes, that is exactly what God did for us. He devised a plan whereby we could find out the truth about Him. His plan was to allow us to nail Him to the cross so He could draw all men unto Himself to show everyone (including Satan and his demons) what He is really like. It took that great of a sacrifice on His part to redeem us back. That is how great of a price we made Him pay. The word "men" in John 12:32 is a supplied word, not in the original. So, God was drawing "all" to the cross, loyal and rebellious, good and evil, so everyone could see the real truth about God. See DA 693, IFH 256-259.

No. 3. Many people have written me asking, "Mike, do you believe Satan was the one who gave Moses the directions and instructions to build the sanctuary." The answer is an unequivocal "No. I believe God Himself gave the directions for the sanctuary to Moses." Here is what I stated in my book. "But God overruled Satan's hellish machinations and maneuvers and made those shadows point to what Satan would actually do to God's only Son, Jesus. The Father was warning Lucifer that he (Satan) would do this, (Kill Christ), but he (Satan) would not listen. God built the whole sanctuary service around the killing of innocent animals to make it mean something and point forward to the cross." IFH 355. I also have thoroughly covered this issue in CHAPTER 10 of this book.

No. 4. Many people claim that God cannot control this earth nor end the sin problem without using physical force. Keith Gilbertson answers this question very nicely in his

Master's thesis on page 34. "to say that God will need to resort to physical activity on His part to destroy the wicked is akin to saying that He needs to miraculously intervene to bring about the death of a man who has just jumped off the World Trade Center rather than to simply wait for him to hit the ground." See also "Education," page 144, 145 for further amplification.

No. 5. An Adventist minister from the Florida conf. sent me the following quotation from a sermon he liked by Professor John Powell. It is entitled "The Christian Attitude Towards God." He is talking about why people have such a hard time getting along in relationships. They seem to often find excuses for letting some people get very close to them. They fear intimacy. Conflicts develop and people split up. "These conflicts are brought on deliberately because one person wants the 'safety' of distance. I think the same thing is true about our relationship with God. I believe that as we come closer to God, often our fear of intimacy and rejection sets in, and we invent some kind of difficulty which will distance us from Him. This fear of intimacy stems from a lack of understanding of who God is. Saint John wrote in his first epistle that God is love. He waits for us with open arms of love to accept us. In fact, all God ever does is love. We may think that God punishes, and that He gets angry and drives people away from Himself, but that is not true. All God ever does is love. He is like the sun. The sun only gives off its warmth and its light. We can stand under the sun and feel its warmth and light, or we can leave it. But when we leave the sun, the sun doesn't go out. We can separate ourselves from God in many ways. We can lock ourselves in the dark dungeon of sin, or we can leave His presence. But when we leave God, He doesn't change. We change. *The whole meaning of the scriptural term 'the wrath of God' refers to the reality of change in us, not something in God. God does not have wrath in Himself. God is love. That's all He ever does is love.* He gives His love as a free gift. Jesus always asked the question, 'Do you love me? You have my love. My love is my gift to you.' **Most of us labor under the delusion that God gets angry with us. But that is not true.** The reality of sin is that we are free to leave God. We may grow dark and cold when we leave His presence, but the sun doesn't go out. *God doesn't change because of what we have done. His love may not reach us if we move away from Him, but God does not change.* Of course, God does not want us to move away from Him. That's why He invites us to come back home when we've left His presence. Often we think that if we change and work hard, then God will love us. But do you know what I think God says? **'No, that's backwards. I love you so you can change. And when you let my love flow into you, when you soak it in, when you really understand that I have always loved you from all eternity, then you will change.** Love will energize in you all those powers to become what you want to become and what I want you to become. Love will draw you to me.' We must ask ourselves about our concept of God. Are we inventing problems that are distancing us from God because we fear intimacy and rejection?"

No. 6. A friend of mine recently sent me a quotation from a book entitled "The OAHSPE," or "OAHSPE." He says that the "OAHSPE" is a horrible Satanic bible—yet another counterfeit to the true 1844 movement. "It never got a large following like the Book of Mormon did, which it resembles ... Sometimes Satan, when attempting to confuse us, inadvertently reveals truths which only he would know. That happened in the "OAHSPE" where you can see his intention to usurp God and a promise to his followers that they can become gods too." Then he sent me the part he was referring to which was under a heading entitled, "HINTS TO THE READER." It reads as follows: "The false Lord God, Anuhasaj, who first made the names Lord, God, Lord God, De'yus (Dyaus, Deity), Zeus, Joss and Ho'Joss worshipful on the earth in place of the Great spirit. The Triunes. The founder of the Trinity and of the Father, Son

and Holy Ghost." There is more, but that is sufficient to
show that the "titles" (not names) listed above have been
usurped by both Satan and men down through the ages.
God's name is His character. His name is not a word or noun
you write or pronounce correctly. It is a character He lived
to show us the truth that has always been in His eternal
heart of love, for "GOD IS LOVE." The 2nd commandment
tells us to not take the Lord's name in vain. We know that
the way most people take His name in vain or blaspheme
His name is by misrepresenting Him. And yet sincere SDA
Christians **are continually blaspheming His name by
teaching others in the church that God does kill and
destroy,** and anyone who would dare say He doesn't will
suffer His wrath in the judgment of the seven last plagues
as well as in the lake of fire after the 1,000 years. You can
almost always tell which spirit is controlling these people,
by the angry, hateful look on their faces, and the raspy,
impatient, tone of voice they speak in. God's greatest enemies down through the centuries have been religious
fanatics who wish to force others to believe just like they do
and pass a death decree against them if they resist. May the
Lord Jesus give us His faith, tolerance and love, to love
those who hate us. Those who do this will truly have His
"NAME" in their foreheads. Rev. 22:4.

No. 7. The words and attitude of the speaker in the
Bible is often enough to enable us to identify the voice of
the one speaking as the true Lord or the false Lord. This is
graphically illustrated in I Sam. 15:1-3, in which a voice
claiming to be "the Lord" spoke to Samuel telling him to
give the following message to King Saul, "thus saith the
Lord of hosts, I remember that which Amalek did to Israel,
how he laid wait for him in the way when he came up from
Egypt. Now go and smite Amalek, and utterly destroy all
that they have, and spare them not; but slay both man and
woman, infant and suckling, ox and sheep, camel and ass."
V. 2-3. Let me ask you . . . Does this really sound like the
loving and merciful Jesus we read about in the N.T.? Is this

according to His true character of love? Can you picture Jesus speaking these cruel, ruthless, vindictive, hateful and revengeful words? I can't. These words just reek with the spirit of "get even." Satan is the "god of get even," so it could not be Jesus. And Satan has his one-third host with him, so I had no problem identifying Satan as the speaker. But I found even greater proof when I looked up the word "Remember" in Strong's concordance. There I found that the word "Remember" is used 110 times in the O.T. In 109 times the same Hebrew word "Zakar" (Saw-kar, 2142) is used. It basically means to remember, recount, record, think on, well, etc. It only has a good connotation. But when I looked up the Hebrew word that is used here in I Sam. 15:2 we find a most interesting story. The Hebrew word in this instance is "PAQAD" (paw-kad, 6485). It means, "to visit (with friendly or hostile intent); . . . avenge, bestow, . . . charge, count, etc. go see, hurt, punish . . ." Of course, the context is very clearly hostile in intent. If I ever appreciated the research of Bro. Strong it was the day I discovered the hidden meaning between these two words. The KJV translated this word "remember" but most of the new versions have changed it to something else. Although I think many of the modern versions each have some value, I often find evidence that the carnal mind was manipulated in key texts such as this by the wily old serpent to throw us off of his winding, destructive trail in history.

No. 8. One of the best students of the Word of God I have ever met was a former teacher. After he found out about the character of God message (that God does not kill), he began an intense study of this subject. He made copious notes and suggestions which I studied assiduously. I would never use any of his ideas until I could prove it myself in several ways. Then I would seek more confirmation from the Bible and EGW, if she said anything about it. I would just like to share with you now some of Stan's notes just as he sent them to me and let you digest them yourself. "If you need further proof of God's holiness and our lack of it (without Him as the Lord of our lives). Is it any wonder that the word (law of Moses) spoken by angels was stedfast, and every transgression and disobedience received a just recompence of reward (or requital or good or bad treatment), Heb. 2:2? The law of Moses smacked of justice and ceremony; the rock upon which self-righteousness is built. It is far easier for the carnal man to sacrifice or slaughter innocent animals than to do that which he is only capable of doing . . . ***accept God's sacrifice for him and thereby receive power to surrender or die to self.*** Man would, naturally, rather kill than have his ego 'killed.' Now, let's compare the words found in the law of Moses with the words of its author, Satan, from whose hand of mediation it was delivered. 'And Satan answered the Lord, and said, 'skin for skin, yea, all that a man hath will he give for his life.' Job 2:4. Now look at Lev. 24:20; 'Breach for breach, eye for eye, tooth for tooth . . .' and Deut. 19:21; 'And thine eye shall not pity; but life shall go for life, eye for eye . . . foot for foot.' Look what Jesus (who in His humanity was the law of God incarnate) said in reference to this; 'Ye have heard that it hath been said, An eye for an eye, and a tooth for a tooth: But I say (Remember it is the Father speaking through Him, John 14:10; 17:8) unto you, That ye resist not evil: but whosoever shall smite thee on thy right cheek, turn to him the other also.' Matt. 5:38, 39. This last statement defines the criteria for that which ***only*** a Christian can do through God's power. It is so true, 'For by the words thou shalt be justified, and by thy words thou shalt be condemned,' Matt. 12:37. We must ever remember that God is on trial, Rev. 14:7, for killing, among other things . . . Motivated by the conviction expressed in 2 Sam 14:14, God was forced by unrepentant man and evil angels to use a system of man's own selection, Jer. 7:24 to bring to light His eternal sacrifice for them. In these last days it will be seen by all who will (see) that at the cross Christ rendered (only) mercy.

Satan and man arranged and required sacrifice and slaughter. This light explains all other mysteries. Stand by Him and ask Him and He will give you the truth.

"The law of Moses, in which the sacrificial system is found, 'was ordained (arranged throughout or prescribed) by *ANGELS*, Acts 7:53. That is why Paul referred to these ordinances 'as a shadow of things to come,' Col. 2:17 and further cautioned, 'let no man beguile you of your reward (Christ, Gen. 15:1) in a voluntary humility and worshipping (ceremonious in worship as demonstrative, pious) of angels, intruding into those things which he hath not seen, vainly puffed up by his fleshly mind.' This is also reiterated in Gal. 4:8, 'Howbeit then, when ye knew not God (when you didn't have a relationship with Him by abiding in Him, as a husband with his wife, Gen. 4:1; John 17:3), ye did service (were a slave) unto them which by nature are no gods.' Here in Gal. 4:8 Paul is referring to the law of Moses (Gal. 4:4) as the 'weak and beggarly elements' Gal. 4:9) of bondage to *ANGELS* through observing 'days, and months and times, and years.' The question is, which angels prescribed or arranged throughout the law of Moses as a remedy for transgressions? There's a hint or clue to this hidden fact in Gal. 3:20. 'Now a mediator is not a mediator of one, but (contrariwise) God is one.' The 'but' in this verse is the key; it means (contrawise.) It denotes a distinction that is, in reference to the mediator, that mediator (go between) for these angels; 'for or in earth, (as there be gods many, and lords many) but to us there is but one God.' I Cor. 8:5, 6. Satan and His hellish legions consider themselves gods and become gods to them who reject Jesus Christ as their Saviour and Lord. And these rejectors of God's mercy thereby reap the fruits of their own choice (e.g. Acts 7:38-43).

"Satan and his evil legions desire that we 'be as gods' or be like them with our eyes 'opened, . . . knowing good and evil,' Gen. 3:5. But to know evil is to have your eyes closed to the only Good ONE, GOD, Matt. 19:17. The problem with

regard to understanding from whence comes the law of
Moses is directly related to man's inherently evil nature,
Jer. 17:9; Rom. 8:7. We are born, legally speaking, creatures
of justice, devoid of understanding with regard to the (only)
God of infinite grace. **Our hunger is for justice, but our
real need is for mercy or God's grace.** The law of Moses
meets the requirements of the first; and only God's presence
IN us can ever fulfill the second. The law of Moses had in it
a way for man to justify himself and relieve his need to rid
himself of the guilt (he thought) incurred by transgression
of God's law of love (10 Commandments). This was supposed
to be accomplished by the sacrificial system via the slaughtering of innocent animals or dumb beasts. God allowed this
law to be given by angels (devils) (but did not give it Himself) to allow men to see themselves for what they really
are . . . "beasts." Eccles. 3:18. It is worth mentioning, as to
this v. 18, that $18 = 6 + 6 + 6$ and that there is a relationship
between this scripture and Rev. 13:18. It is man without
God living in Him that becomes a beast in the end-time."
Another friend pointed out that in the beginning man had
dominion over all the beasts of the earth and named them.
Now, at the end of the world the beast has dominion over
man and is placing a number on his right hand or forehead
to "name" him. In the Garden of Eden God was seeking
man to save him, but in the Garden of Gethsemane man
was seeking (Jesus) to kill him.

No. 9. The way the law of Moses came to Israel is about
the same way Israel received her first monarch, King Saul.
Satan put the idea of an earthly king into the people's
mind, and God withdrew and let them have their king. The
Bible calls this rejection of Divine leadership, "Mine anger."
"I gave thee a king in mine anger, and took him away in my
wrath." Hosea 13:11. Just two verses previous to this one,
the Lord told Israel "thou hast destroyed thyself; but in me
is thine help. I WILL BE THY KING: WHERE IS ANY
OTHER THAT MAY SAVE THEE . . ." Hosea 13:9-10. So,

we see that "God's anger or wrath" is not when He gets mad and destroys the sinner, but when He is forced to withdraw and let the sinner destroy himself.

God even commanded Samuel to anoint Saul, but that was not God's perfect will, but His permissive will. When you compare how Israel received the monarchy and how they received the law of Moses, there is a striking parallel. The blindness of Laodiceanism prevents God's professed people from having the spiritual insight to see the truth about God. They think that God either killed the first animal Himself or commanded Adam to do it. No one seems to realize that God took the dead animals Adam had chosen to slay for sacrifice and made some more permanent clothing out of them for Adam and Eve. Gen. 3:21. And after Adam had made up his mind to slay animals, against God's perfect will, Christ came down and gave Adam specific instructions as to what this animal slaughter really meant and how it would point forward to the death of God's only Son. This is how the "sacrificial offerings were ordained by God . . ." PP 68. Now, this put God at a tremendous disadvantage, for it gave Satan the opportunity to make God look like a tyrant. And this is precisely what Satan did. After Jesus gave meaning to animal sacrifices, which He never wanted in the first place, by making them (point forward to His own death on the cross), Satan realized Christ was going to use this carnal system of animal slaughter to teach the plan of salvation. "Satan had known that he did not hold absolute sway over the world. There was seen in men the working of a power that withstood his dominion. With intense interest he watched the sacrifices offered by Adam and his sons. In these ceremonies he discerned a symbol of communion between earth and heaven. He set himself to intercept this communion. He misrepresented God, and misinterpreted the rites that pointed to the Saviour. Men were led to fear God as one who delighted in their destruction. The sacrifices that should have revealed His love were offered only to appease His wrath. Satan excited the evil passions of men, in order to fasten his rule upon them. When God's written word was given, Satan studied the prophecies of the Saviour's advent. From generation to generation he worked to blind the people to these prophecies, that they might reject Christ at His coming." "DESIRE OF AGES," 115.

No. 10. One quote I often receive from sincere people who want to believe that God did indeed bring the flood is this one: "Satan himself, who was compelled to remain in the midst of the warring elements, feared for his own existence." PP 99. In my book, IFH-187, I point out that since God never uses force, DA 759, God could not have been the one who "compelled" Satan "to remain" in the flood holocaust, which Satan caused by leading the people to demand that God "depart" from them and the earth. Job 22:15-18. In my second book, "THE FINAL ABSOLUTE," pages 101-104 I answer this in more detail. I can imagine that Christ pled with Satan and the people (for 120 years) to not force Him (their Creator and Sustainer) out of their lives, lest the vapor envelope collapse and bring a destructive flood of water over all the earth. But they wouldn't listen. Isa. 54:7 indicates that God "forsook" His people "for a small moment." When God's sustaining, power was withdrawn, the vapor shield began to cool down since the two "lights" (sun and moon) began to go out. The moon was completely extinguished and the sun is only 1/7th as bright as it was before the flood. Isa. 30:26 is a promise that God will restore it anew when He re-creates the earth after the 1,000 years. So, Satan did not bring the flood directly, neither did God. But Satan caused it by leading the people to reject God's sustaining protection over nature. The same thing is happening today and the plagues will be the result. I believe atomic and nuclear warfare will somehow have a significant part to play in the 7 last plagues. Time alone will reveal the details.

No. 11. Another EGW quote SDAs misunderstand and misuse is this one: "The same destructive power exercised by holy angels when God commands, will be exercised by evil angels when He permits. There are forces now ready, and only waiting the divine permission, to spread desolation everywhere." G.C. 614. I answered this at length in my first book on page 84, but let me give a brief answer here. The last sentence in the quote will help us see something very important. She says that "forces" are ready and waiting to "spread desolation" everywhere. In other quotations we have already read that "God destroys no one," COL 84; 5T 119, 120. We also have read the EGW quote from R & H May 10, 1906 that "Angels are sent from the heavenly courts, **NOT TO DESTROY**, but to watch over and guard imperiled souls, to save the lost, to bring the straying ones back to the fold." So, it is established beyond question by these and other quotes that EGW firmly believed God does not destroy. So, how then do we explain the sentence "The same destructive power exercised by holy angels when God commands."??? The only answer left is that God's holy angels are blamed for any type of destruction when they remove their restraints (at Christ's command, no less). We see this clearly in Rev. 7 and Rev. 15-16 where the same angels who are holding back the winds of strife in Rev. 7 are the ones who are pictured as bringing it in Rev. 15, and 16. And it is coming from the sanctuary. But, if you read "Early Writings" pages 55 and 92 you will see that when Jesus leaves the holy place and goes into the most holy place that Satan "appeared to be by the throne, trying to carry on the work of God." He was deceiving a company who were still "bowed before the throne; they did not know Jesus had left it." Evidently this throne represented Christ's work in the holy place. When Christ left this part of the sanctuary (representing Christ's work in the heart of the believer) Satan then took over in that person's life who refused to go into the most holy place of the sanctuary. What does going into the most holy place represent? I believe it represents going into the Father's heart of love to understand His true character. EW 55 spoke of "an exceeding bright light" which came from the Father to the Son, "and from the Son it waved over the people before the throne. But few would receive this great light. Many came out from under it and immediately resisted it; others were careless and did not cherish the light, and it moved off from them. Some cherished it, and went and bowed down with the little praying company. This company all received the light and rejoiced in it, and their countenances shown with its glory (character)." Friend of mine, this light is the final message of God's love. It is truly the extra oil which will light up the lamps of the wise virgins who are filled with the Holy Spirit. This great light is the truth that God does not kill, but is a life-giving Creator (Sabbath message preached more fully). It is the message of the angel of Rev. 18 who comes "down from heaven, having great power; and the earth was lightened with his glory (character)." V. 1.

This is the message God's people will preach all over the earth. "Servants of God with their faces lighted up and shining with holy consecration, will hasten from place to place to proclaim the message from heaven. By thousands of voices, all over the earth, the warning will be given." GC 612.

And so Satan has power over the people's lives who reject the truth of God's true character. From the very heart of all those in the earth who have rejected the love of God, in the form of the final warning against Sunday worship and the mark of the beast, will come "destructive power" which will be unleashed in this world when God commands for the holy angels to "take their hands off" and "let go of those who will not accept my salvation." Terrible destruction and desolation will be spread all over the earth by those unconsecrated "temples" or "sanctuaries" who would not let God enter their inner sanctum, (heart or mind). Let's see if EGW does not support this concept. "The Spirit of God, persistently resisted, is at last withdrawn from the sinner, and then there is left no power to control the evil passions of the soul, and no protection from the malice and enmity of Satan." GC 36.

Perhaps the most powerfully convincing EGW quote I have ever read is found on the next page. She is comparing the destruction of Jerusalem in A.D. 70 with the final destruction that will overtake the world when Christ returns. This quote begins with a paraphrase from Paul and then a brilliant, concise and succinct exegetical analysis and exposition of Paul's real meaning. Matt. 24:30, 31, has just been quoted to enlarge on her comments re: Christ's return. "then shall they that obey not the gospel be consumed with the spirit of His mouth and be destroyed with the brightness of His coming. 2 Thess. 2:8. LIKE ISRAEL OF OLD THE WICKED DESTROY THEMSELVES; THEY FALL BY THEIR INIQUITY. BY A LIFE OF SIN, THEY HAVE PLACED THEMSELVES SO OUT OF HARMONY WITH GOD, THEIR NATURES HAVE BECOME SO DEBASED WITH EVIL, THAT THE MANIFESTATION OF HIS GLORY IS TO THEM A CONSUMING FIRE." G.C. 37.

No. 12. Most sincere Bible students would agree that God's purpose throughout history for allowing "judgments" or "punishment" to come upon sinners was to lead them to repentance. But after the finally impenitent have closed probation's door against themselves [Cf. Luke 7:30] there is no rationale, purpose or reason for God to send any kind of punishment upon sinners, for it is eternally too late for anyone to repent. The mandate of Rev. 22:11, 12 has gone forth. Everyone's character is frozen; every destiny is fixed—by their own choice. So, the question remains, WHO BRINGS THE SEVEN LAST PLAGUES UPON THIS EARTH? EGW answers the question like this: "WHEN HE (Christ) LEAVES THE SANCTUARY, (Remember God's real sanctuary is the human heart, symbolized by the sanctuary in heaven) darkness covers the inhabitants of the earth. In that fearful time the righteous must live in the sight of a holy God without an intercessor. (When the righteous are in the most holy place or the Father's heart, they don't need a go-between or an intercessor, for they are in the very presence of the Father with Jesus) The restraint which has been upon the wicked is removed, and Satan has entire control of the finally impenitent. God's longsufferig has ended. The world has rejected His mercy, despised His love, and trampled upon His law. The wicked have passed the boundary of their probation; the Spirit of God, persistently resisted has been at last withdrawn. Unsheltered by divine grace, they have no protection from the wicked one. (If God is bringing the plagues why did she not say that the wicked have no protection from God or Jesus?) Satan (not God) will then plunge the inhabitants of the earth into one great, final trouble. As the angels of God **CEASE TO HOLD IN CHECK** the fierce **WINDS OF HUMAN PASSION**, all the elements of strife will be let loose. The whole world will be involved in ruin more terrible than that which came upon Jerusalem of old." GC 614. Then follows the statement we discussed in No. 11. If you take the two examples she gives of how destruction has come in the past, you will know that it is not God bringing the destruction, but it is Satan working through nature and man's violent, carnal nature. The two incidents she cites are (1) The death of the first-born and (2) the numbering of Israel by David, which I Chron. 21:1 itself says was instigated by Satan, Cf. 2 Sam. 24:1; See marginal reading. See Exodus 12:23 for the death of the first-born. And remember friend, the close of human probation is not an act or decision of God against man, but an act of man against God . . . man rejecting God, not God rejecting man, for God never rejects man . . . ever. "And Him that cometh to me I will in no wise cast out." John 6:37.

No. 13. Even though I have already dealt with Abraham's temptation in Gen. 22, I believe a few more words would be helpful to those who have a very difficult time believing that God did not command Abraham to slay his son. The **only** reason why any SDA would object to this line of reasoning is because of what EGW said in "Patriarachs and Prophets," Pgs. 145-155. Many people do not realize that they are exalting the writings of EGW on a par with

the Bible. She herself never did this. She always categorized
her writings as a "lesser light," leading to the "greater
light" which is the 66 books of the Bible. EGW certainly
was a messenger and a prophet of the Lord, but her writings
are not part of the sacred cannon of Scripture. It is wrong to
treat her writings as if they were. And some people even go
beyond that and judge the Scriptures by what EGW says,
instead of letting the Bible be the final authority. The Bible
writers did not know everything. They only knew what God
had revealed to them in their own time regarding current
and future events. The same is true about EGW. She
functioned as a 19th century prophet because that was her
basic and main time frame, except for a few years into the
20th century. But the bulk of her prophetic works were written in the 19th century. Her age and the stubbornness,
rebellion and rejection of the 1888 message largely limited
and neutralized the great blessings God no doubt wished to
shower upon His people through her. But this was not to be.
The leaders and men responsible for this tragedy have been
duly cited and referred to anonymously in her post-1888
writings. Only God, who alone reads the secret motives of
the heart, is fit to judge them. It remains with us to make
sure we do not repeat their sad history. Let us pray that our
present study will go a long way in preventing such an
unfortunate occurrence.

I hope that we have already firmly established in our
study so far in this book that there are two distinctive personalities operating at all times in the O.T. It remains with
us to identify them by learning God's true character. God is
the dominant personality in both testaments, old and new.
In the old Satan is almost treated as a non-entity (as if he
didn't even exist). He is addressed under various titles such
as, destroyer, Jer. 4:7; devourer Mal. 3:11; leviathan, Isa. 27:1.
In only three books is he referred to as Satan. Job 1-3;
Zech. 3:1, 2; and Psalm 109:6. Satan is a Hebrew term
meaning "the hater, accuser, an adversary, opposing spirit."
Young's. In Strong's (7853-7854) we read: "to lurk for, i.e.

persecute: hate, oppose, (spelled Satan). Under Satan then: "to attack, (fig.) accuse:-Be an adversary." In Ezekiel 28:2, Satan is addressed under the title of "the prince of Tyrus," since Satan was using him to accomplish his purposes. Here God is actually covering up for Lucifer (Satan). And in Ezek. 28:12 God requests that the prophet weep for Lucifer, (disguised as the king of Tyrus. The description could not possibly be referring to the king of Tyrus since he was never in "Eden," nor was he ever God's "covering cherub," or "perfect in his ways," etc. In Isa. 14:12 Satan is referred to as Lucifer, the one who *fell* (he was not pushed or forced to leave, Jude 6). The SDA Bible commentary #4 confirms that EGW teaches that Satan is identified as the "prince of Tyrus." 4BC 1162.

In the New Testament Satan is further identified **by** Christ in John 8:44 as both a "liar" and a "murderer." and in Matt. 4:1 and I Thess. 3:5 the devil is further identified as the "tempter." There is no place in the Bible or in the writings of EGW where God is ever identified as the "TEMPTER." **That is absolutely certain.** And that in and of itself should be sufficient evidence to prove beyond the shadow of a doubt that God did not *"tempt"* Abraham, as Gen. 22:1 says. It was the false, counterfeit "god of this world," who spoke to Abraham. And yet God is said to "suffer" us to be tempted with no more than we can stand and is able to give us strength to pass any temptation God may allow us to have.

With these facts in mind let us again consider Gen 22:1 where we are informed that *"God did tempt Abraham, . . ."* We can know that this **is not** the true God who is **tempting** Abraham, but is simply **allowing it** and taking the blame for it, because of James 1:13. *"Let no man say when he is tempted, I am tempted of God: for God cannot be tempted with evil, neither tempteth he any man:"* And to clinch his argument, which he continues through verse 20, James says in v. 16, "do not err, my beloved brethren. Every good and every perfect gift is from above, and cometh down from the Father of lights, with whom is no variableness, neither shadow of turning." **This is an absolute principle that can never be changed.** If you can ever identify God as doing something or not doing something in the Bible, that trait **will never vary or change.** Some people who claim to believe in the character message say that God acted one way in the O.T. and a different way in the N.T. **This is impossible, for God never changes.** Jesus is the greatest and fullest revelation of God's character that has ever been given. This revelation given in the four gospels must be our starting point. We must compare all of the words and acts of God and (gods) with the life of Jesus. Any word or act of one claiming to be God in the O.T. which is not in harmony with the life of Jesus can immediately be identified as Satan **claiming** to be God. Thus, when we read that God "tempted" Abraham, we immediately know that **could not be the true God** for the N.T. unequivocally tells us that God **never** tempts anyone, as we just read in James 1.

The next thing we must realize is that Moses, the author of Genesis, obviously did not understand that Satan was the "god" who was tempting Abraham, neither did the translators. So, naturally, they spelled God with a capital G since they believed it was the Lord, Jehovah, who was tempting Abraham. And this is true all the way through the Bible. The titles **Lord** and **God** are always capitalized when the translators believed it was the true God doing or saying something. So, you cannot rely on capitalization in your search for the true God. And EGW, writing mainly in the 19th century, didn't know the difference either. This is obvious when you read "Patriarchs and Prophets." But the Lord did inspire her to explain and define temptation. "IT IS THE MEANS BY WHICH THOSE WHO CLAIM TO BE THE CHILDREN OF GOD ARE TESTED AND TRIED. WE READ THAT GOD TEMPTED ABRAHAM ... THIS MEANS THAT HE **PERMITTED** CIRCUMSTANCES TO OCCUR TO TEST THEIR FAITH, AND LEAD THEM TO

LOOK TO HIM FOR HELP." March 12, 1912. BC 1094.
Beloved, I think it is very significant that this last quote
from EGW was penned in 1912, just three years before she
died. This shows how she grew in her understanding of
God's character.

But the statements which most people quote to try and
prove that it was the true God who "tempted" Abraham
were written in 1890, 22 years earlier. Furthermore, EGW
used other 19th century religious writers and historians as
guides for most of the material in "Patriarchs and
Prophets". Now, I don't happen to agree with Walter Rea's
conclusions regarding EGW's character and motives, etc.
but I cannot deny the fact that there are many similarities
in the parallel exhibits displayed in "Appendix Chapter 5
Exhibit," page 282 of Rea's book, "THE WHITE LIE."
Believe me it took me a very long time before I would even
look at the book. I was very prejudiced and closed minded
about the whole matter of even thinking that Sister White
ever copied or borrowed anything from anyone. But when I
finally did look at the book it helped me to realize why
many of her statements in the conflict series closely resemble the 19th century religious and historical viewpoint and
mindset. She was a product of her times just like we are a
product of our times. In most cases she improved upon whatever she copied or borrowed, and I found very few instances
in which the wording was exactly the same. But it is obvious that she or whoever helped her compose these books did
use many of the same thoughts. But that does not diminish
my respect for EGW or make me doubt her prophetic gift.
Instead it clears up many problems and helps me see how
sincere, but sometimes ambitious leaders have misused
EGW's writings, influence, and authority in order to keep
the people "in line" and "obedient" to *"their"* interpretation of what God said through EGW.

But now let's go to one author from whom she borrowed when she wrote about Abraham. She seems to have
borrowed mostly from Alfred Edersheim's "BIBLE HIS-

TORY," written in 1876-80 and from "NIGHT SCENES IN THE BIBLE," By Daniel March, 1868-1870. Perhaps the most convincing evidence that EGW borrowed extensively was the "Sample Comparison Exhibit," found on page 77 of "THE WHITE LIE." Of the 62 chapters in "Patriarchs and Prophets" there are 23 title chapter headings that are either similar or the same. There are 8 which are exactly the same, and the rest, though they are worded differently are basically the same subject matter. It would seem that the chapter titles of Edersheim's book and the contents of each chapter served as a guide for EGW as she wrote P & P. Again, this does not bother me at all. I know in my heart that God inspired Sister White. I believe the Lord showed her many things in dreams and visions because she often describes the events as an eye-witness, which none of her critics can explain. I think the Lord guided EGW to borrow and copy, for I believe God inspired March and Edersheim to write what they wrote. They were prophets, too, but in a different sense. But when EGW wrote on the Sabbath or the state of the dead, she was giving the SDA view, and I do not believe there would be anything written about this that she could copy. I have not researched this enough to be dogmatic, but this only seems logical. All of these writings were from God and belonged to Him. Did He not have a right to lead EGW to copy and borrow, if He chose to do so? Of course He did. No complaint or lawsuit was ever filed against EGW, that I have ever heard of.

Now, I would like to share with you one instance in which Daniel March spoke of Abraham's temptation with great insight. He had the right idea and was going in the right direction, but he still came to the wrong conclusion. Notice: "THEN AGAIN, THE SEEMING CONTRADIC-TION BETWEEN THIS NEW COMMAND, AND ALL THE INSTRUCTIONS AND PROMISES WHICH HAD ALREADY BEEN GIVEN . . . MUST HAVE ADDED PER-PLEXITY TO HIS MIND AND AGONY TO HIS HEART. THE VOICE . . . MUST HAVE SEEMED . . . AS IF SOME

TEMPTING AND TORMENTING DEMON HAD
ASSUMED TO SPEAK IN THE NAME OF THE
LORD..." Does that not show tremendous insight? But
EGW never copied or even borrowed that thought. It was
not time to explain the two Lords. This concept was not to
be revealed until it was necessary for us to understand it.
And that time is right now, today! But March concluded in
his day, "Soon the mysterious sign ... appears ... Now it is
settled beyond all question ... the command was divine."
EGW said, "As they were about to begin the journey of the
third day, the patriarch ... saw the promised sign ... over
Mount Moriah, and he knew the voice which had spoken to
him was from heaven." PP 151. But was it "Divine?" **Only**
in the sense that it had passed through the throne room of
the God of heaven and He had placed **His own stamp of
approval** upon the fact He would allow the terrible temptation test to take place and would assume all responsibility
for it. **What God allows He claims to do,** but all of these
horrible crimes and murders, although **allowed** by God, are
not **ordered** by Him ... but they are **allowed** because man
has been given **free will.** It is significant to note that EGW
states "If he (Abraham) had endured the first test, and had
patiently waited for the promise to be fulfilled in Sarah, and
had not taken Hagar as his wife, *he would not have been
subjected to the closest test that was ever required of
man.*" "Spirit of Prophecy," vol. 1, page 98.

One of the main dangers of believing that this temptation was directly ordered and commanded by God is that (1)
it distorts the truth about God in the minds of people today
so they think of God as some kind of tyrant who sends these
terrible tests upon us whenever He decides we need it. (2) It
sets up a very dangerous precedent or example for people to
use as an excuse to take another person's life by saying,
"But, God told me to do it just like God told Abraham to kill
Isaac, only in my case God did not stop me."

It is also stated that because EGW says that when
Abraham "saw the promised sign, a cloud of glory hovering

over Mount Moriah, . . . *he knew* that the voice which had spoken to him was from heaven." PP 151 . . . that this proves the voice was truly from God. Was this really the *"same voice"* that had called Abraham out of Ur of the Chaldees? Just because Abraham *"thought"* this was the **same** voice does not **make** it so. The question is: *"Did the true God intend for Abraham to think that He was the one who was speaking to him?"* Yes, I think it is obvious that God had pre-planned and arranged that this test, which I believe Satan suggested, would be given in such a manner so that Abraham really believed it was from the true God. Otherwise, it would have had no value as a test. We see the same exact circumstances with the patriarch Job. He too thought God was the one who was tempting him. EGW gives us some insight. "Satan was at hand to suggest that he must be deceived, for the divine law commands, *'thou shalt not kill,'* and God would not require what He had once forbidden." PP 148. Here is proof of what I said earlier in our discussion—God does not change. He does not contradict Himself. Someone may ask, "Why would Satan try to talk Abraham out of performing this rite of human sacrifice?" Because, Satan would do everything He could to make Abraham disobey God and thus win his argument that God was not justified in blessing Abraham with the seed (Isaac) which would eventually produce the Messiah. Satan always plays both ends against the middle. He was the murderer who originally suggested the idea, so naturally he would bend all of his energies to prove his case against God. *"See, I told you Abraham would not go through with the sacrifice, even though he thought you were the one who commanded him to do it."* When we look at it from this angle we are able to see why God has been on trial before the universe for centuries. It is our privilege today to prove God is justified in His faith in us in this last hour of earth's history. In His mighty power we will triumph at last and glorify His name (character) before the universe."

No. 14. Paul says that God "purchased" the "church of God . . . with His own blood." The Bible says Christ came "to give His life a ransom for many." Matt. 20:28; Mark 10:45; I Tim. 2:6. Actually the Hebrew word translated "ransom" is "padah (paw-daw) which can also be translated as "release, preserve . . . redeem or rescue." Strongs 6299. And the Greek word translated as "ransom," (lutron or lutroo) can be translated "redemption" or "redeem." Strongs 3083-3084. It has the additional meaning of "deliverer or one who loosens."

We know that the traditional meaning of Christ's blood is that it "paid" our debt and set us free. But what is it that we must be freed from? And who is this ransom debt to be paid to: EGW tells us: *"Mighty issues for the world were at stake in the conflict between the Prince of light and the leader of the kingdom of darkness. After tempting man to sin, Satan claimed the earth as his, and styled himself the prince of this world. Having conformed to his own nature the father and mother of our race, he thought to establish his empire. He declared that men had chosen him as their sovereign. Through his control of men, he held dominion over the world. CHRIST HAD COME TO DISPROVE SATAN'S CLAIM. As the Son of man, Christ would stand loyal to God. Thus it would be shown that Satan had not gained complete control of the human race, and this his claim to the world was false. All who desired deliverance from his power would be set free. The dominion that Adam had lost through sin would be recovered."* DA 115.

Please notice in the quote above that EGW states Jesus came to "disprove Satan's claim" that man had really chosen Satan of own free will. He did not come to "pay a debt." The idea of a court trial scene comes to mind with evidence being presented by both sides. Satan is the prosecuting attorney and Jesus is the counsel for the defense. We are on trial, as it were, but God the Father and His son are also on trial for defending us.

God declares Himself to be a loving and unselfish God; One that all of His creatures can trust and place their faith in at all times. Satan bends all of His mighty genius to disprove this claim by making all of the universe think God is cruel, unkind, vindictive and anxious to punish and destroy any and all who transgress His law. But what "witness" or "proof" or "evidence, confirmation, or testimony" has God given that He truly is a "loving" God? The beloved John will tell us. *"For there are three that bear record in heaven, the Father, the Word, and the Holy Ghost: and these three are one. And there are three that BEAR WITNESS in earth, the spirit, and the water, and the blood: and these three agree in one. If we receive the witness of men, the witness of God is greater: for this is the witness of God which he hath testified of His Son. He that believeth on the Son of God hath the witness in himself:"* I John 5:8-10.

And so we see that the "blood" of Christ is the witness or testimony that has brought redemption. It was the price we made God pay to prove to us and to the universe that He truly did love us after all. But the great truth we have completely missed is that the blood proves beyond a doubt that God is *"HARMLESS."* Heb. 7:26. Jesus demonstrated all through His earthly life, at His trial and on the cross that He never strikes back.

No. 15. Brother Mike, you are right, the Lord is soon coming, and He is trying to wake us up to the controversy around us, to the nature of His character, to the privilege we have of reflecting his character as well, and a whole lot more!

You might be interested in some study I have been doing on Daniel 2. We talk about the image with big charts, stories of the various world nations. But we do not talk about the mountain, and the stone that is cut out of the mountain, being of the same material. It is this stone that destroys the nations of the world, or rather the kingdoms of the world. Many texts show that the mountain represents God's people (Joel 3:17, Mic 4:1, Isa 56:7, Ps 74:2, Isa 2:2, Ps 15:1, etc) and even Daniel (9:16) identifies a holy mountain with Jerusalem, God's people. If the stone is cut out of the mountain, then it is part of the same stuff — God's people called out, his special group, perhaps the 144,000. Could it be that God's last chosen people will destroy the kingdoms of this world, not with fire and brimstone, but by taking back from Satan, by taking every bit of his influence out of their lives, leaving him powerless, crushed and broken. Zech 12:3 states that Jerusalem will be a burdensome stone, and those that come against them shall be cut in pieces (parallels Dan 2:35). Also note that the stone fills the earth, not empties it. Heb 2:8 states that "the remnant of the people of God shall spoil thee" referring to the one who transgresseth by wine (vs 5). Oh, there is so much more, but time here does not allow. I mention this because you would not identify God as a God who comes to grind to pieces the world kingdoms. Christ has destroyed Satan's kingdom (1 Jn 3:8) and now so must man as it is written, "And THEY overcame him" Rev 12:11, by destroying a spiritual kingdom ("My kingdom is not of this world"). Both Satan and Christ's kingdom are spiritual, one an evil, the other a holy spirit filled kingdom.

May the Lord bless Mike ... I've listened to most of the tapes that you sent, I especially liked the one on Christ and Judas. Very good!

Again may the Lord bless ...

Sincerely, till we meet above!

Glen D. Toppenberg, M.D.

No. 17. On page 26 of her book, "STORY OF REDEMPTION," EGW tells us Satan requested Jesus to let him return to heaven. He told Jesus "that he repented of his rebellion and wished again the favor of God. He was willing to take the place God had previously assigned him, and be under His wise command. *Christ wept* at Satan's woe but told him, *as the mind of God,* that he could never be received into heaven. Heaven must not be placed in jeopardy . . . The seeds of rebellion were still within him . . . he had hopelessly ruined not only himself but the host of angels also . . . The law of God could condemn but could not pardon."

Most people quote this to prove that Christ has never made any appeals to Lucifer or to his angels since that time. They also believe that God closes a person's probation and from then on that person can never come back, no matter how sorry he may be for his sins. They take issue with me over my statement on page 265 of IFH *that Christ has always been appealing to Lucifer to come back to Him so He could heal Him.* Let me try and prove to you that these very words Jesus spoke to Satan, at this time, *were actually an appeal.* The reason I say that is because of the way He acted toward and spoke to the "Canaanitish woman" who pled with Him to *"Have mercy on me, O Lord, . . . my daughter is greviously vexed with a devil."* Matt. 15:22, R.V. EGW tells us Jesus did not even acknowledge this woman's presence at first and when He did it was an *apparent rejection* of her request. "But although Jesus did not reply, the woman did not lose faith . . . she followed Him, continuing her supplications. Annoyed by her importunities, the disciples asked Jesus to send her away. They saw that their Master *treated her with indifference,* and they therefore supposed that the prejudice of the Jews against the Canaanites was pleasing to Him. But it was a *pitying Saviour* to whom the woman made her plea, and in answer to the request of the disciples, Jesus said, *'I am not sent but unto the lost sheep of the house of Israel.'* " This was actually an *implied rebuke* to the disciples, for *"He came to the world to save all who would accept Him."* Jesus also would have forgiven Lucifer, *if he had truly repented,* and what Jesus *was really saying to Lucifer* (Satan), was this: *"You are not truly sorry for your sin of jealousy envy and rebellion. I weep over this for you Lucifer, for unless you really repent, you have 'hopelessly ruined' yourself and all of your followers for all of eternity."* Since God *never changes* we know that He had just as much *pity* for Lucifer as He did for this Phoenician woman. Lucifer could have cried out as the woman did when Jesus seemingly rejected him. "The woman urged her case with increased earnestness, bowing at Christ's feet, and crying, *'Lord, help me.'* Jesus, still *apparently rejecting* her entreaties, . . . answered, 'It is not meet (appropriate or right) to take the children's bread, and to cast it to dogs.' " In the Greek the word here translated "dogs," is actually *"little dogs,"* or *"puppies."* EGW's comments are very insightful here. "This was virtually asserting that it was not just to lavish the blessings brought to the favored people of God upon strangers and aliens from Israel. This answer would have utterly discouraged a less earnest seeker. But the woman saw that her opportunity had come. *Beneath the apparent refusal of Jesus, she saw a compassion that He could not hide."* "DESIRE OF AGES," pages 400, 401. In the case of Lucifer, he was not really sincere in his request. He was mainly asking for himself, not for the sake of the angels whom he had deceived and led astray, nor for the sorrow he had brought to Christ and His Father and all of the loyal angels. *His evil heart remained the same.* Jesus' words to the woman prove that there was a *hidden appeal of compassion* in his *apparent rejection* of Lucifer, just as there was to the woman.

Another example of a *hidden appeal* is Joshua's last charge to Israel. He pled with them, "choose you this day whom ye will serve;" Joshua 24:15. In their self-righteousness the people replied, "God forbid that we should forsake the Lord, to serve other gods;" Like Lucifer, they were lying to Joshua and to themselves, for even then they were clinging to and worshipping false gods. Joshua told them, "Ye cannot serve the Lord: for he is an holy God; he is a jealous God; he will not forgive your transgressions nor your sins." Joshua 24:19. We know this statement is not true unless it is qualified. What Joshua meant was, "As long as you continue on in your idolatry, you will never be able to serve the true God. And because you are persisting in your idolatrous ways, all the while claiming you are sorry for your sins, God is never going to be able to forgive you for your sins." EGW comments on this experience thusly:

"Ye cannot serve the Lord," said Joshua: "for He is a holy God; . . . He will not forgive your transgressions nor your sins." Before there could be any permanent reformation the people must be led to feel their utter inability in themselves to render obedience to God. They had broken His law, it condemned them as transgressors, and it provided no way of escape. *While they trusted in their own strength and righteousness, it was impossible for them to secure the pardon of their sins;* they could not meet the claims of God's perfect law, and *it was in vain that they pledged themselves to serve God.* It was only by faith in Christ that they could secure pardon of sin *and receive strength to obey God's law.* They must cease to rely upon their own efforts for salvation, they must trust wholly in the merits of the promised Saviour, if they would be accepted of God.

Joshua endeavored to lead his hearers to weigh well their words, and *refrain from vows which they would be unprepared to fulfill.* With deep earnestness they repeated the declaration: "Nay; but we will serve the Lord." Solemnly consenting to the witness against themselves that they had chosen Jehovah, they once more reiterated their pledge of loyalty: "The Lord our God will we serve, and His voice will we obey.

"So Joshua made a covenant with the people that day, and set them a statute and an ordinance in Shechem." Having written an account of this solemn transaction, he placed it, with the book of the law, in the side of the ark. And he set up a pillar as a memorial, saying, "Behold, this stone shall be a witness unto us; for it hath heard all the words of the Lord which he spake unto us; it shall be therefore a witness unto you, lest ye deny your God. So Joshua let the people depart, every man unto his inheritance." PP 524.

No. 18. We have already clearly shown that it was Satan, the false lord, not Jesus, the true Lord who "moved (tempted) David . . . to say, Go, number Israel and Judah." 2 San 24:1. See also 1 Chron. 21:1 where it plainly says it was Satan who led David to committ this sin. EGW agrees with this, as we shall see. In the last chapter of PATRIARCHS AND PROPHETS, chapter 73, EGW touches on the high points of "THE LAST YEARS OF DAVID." She points out the terrible dangers of being rich and popular. "The history of David affords one of the most impressive testimonies ever given to the dangers that threaten the soul from power and riches and worldly honor—those things that are most eagerly desired among men. Few have ever passed through an experience better adapted to prepare them for enduring such a test." PP 746. She goes on and details David's earlier life experiences which God permitted to prepare him to be the king of Israel. A good example of this preparation time is PP 690, Chapter 68, "David At Ziglag." And yet we see how often David failed . . . "worldly success and honor so weakened the character of David that he was repeatedly overcome by the tempter." ibid. No wonder Jesus has given us the counsel found in His sermon on the mount. "Blessed (happy or fortunate) are ye, when men shall revile you, and persecute you, and shall say all manner of evil against you falsely, for my sake. Rejoice, and be exceeding glad: for great is your reward in heaven: for so persecuted they the prophets which were before you." Matt. 5:11, 12. Cf. Jer. 45:5.

Why did David want to "number" Israel? EGW tells us: "It was pride and ambition that prompted this action of the king. The numbering of the people would show the contrast between the weakness of the kingdom when David ascended the throne and its strength and prosperity under his rule. This would tend still further to foster the already too great self-confidence of both king and people. The Scripture says, *'Satan stood up against Israel, and provoked David to number Israel.'* " PP 747. See how EGW clearly takes the position *that it was Satan who moved, led or tempted David to number Israel,* even though 2 Sam. 24:1 states that it was the "Lord."

Finally, David was convicted of his sin. 2 Sam. 24:10. The prophet Gad was sent to him with a choice between three types of disaster for his punishment. (1) Seven years of famine. (2) To flee three months before his enemies. (3) Three days of pestilence. David could not bring himself to choose and said: "let us fall now into the hand of the Lord; for His mercies are great: and let me not fall into the hand of man. So the Lord sent (that is he allowed Satan to send) a pestilence upon Israel from the morning even to the even time appointed: and there died of the people from Dan even to Beersheeba seventy thousand men. And when the angel stretched out his hand upon Jerusalem to destroy it, the Lord repented him of the evil, and said to the angel that destroyed the people, (Satan, or Appollyon, Rev. 9:11) It is enough: stay now thine hand. And the angel of the Lord was by the threshingplace of Araunah the Jebusite." 2 Sam. 24:15-17. The next verse describes David's anguish over the suffering of the people for his sin. "Lo, I have sinned, and I have done wickedly: but these sheep, what have they done?" Just last week someone asked me this very same question. EGW tells us that "the people . . . themselves cherished the same sins that prompted David's action. As the Lord through Absalom's sin visited judgment upon David, so through David's error He punished the sins of Israel." PP 748. Cf. PP 728. We have already learned in this book that *God never brings disease or sickness.* This is always from Satan. *Therefore, this "pestilence" which is a disease, is from Satan.* See Luke 13:16; Acts 10:38. Whenever we sin, Satan has a legal right to "break forth," upon us and hurt or destroy us in some way. The word "hedge" in Job 1:10 symbolized God's protection. The wise man tells us: "He that diggeth a pit shall fall into it; and whoso breaketh an hedge, a serpent shall bite him." Eccles. 10:8. *And Rev. 12:9 identifies the serpent as Satan, the destroyer.* The revelation of God's character is progressive and the revelation of Satan's character is progressive. David ascribed his military victories to "Baal" by naming the site of victory to Baalperazim, who is the Lord of breaking forth, who is Satan. Baal always refers to Satan in the Old Testament.

When Satan killed Uzzah we read that "David was afraid of the Lord that day." 2 Sam. 6:7-9. Because David was ruled by fear he was not able to discern that it was the Devil who destroyed Uzzah. Job's heart was also filled with fear. "For the thing which I greatly feared is come upon me, and that which I was afraid of is come unto me." Job 4:25. The margin says, "I feared a fear, and it came upon me." We must not let Satan set a *"fear trap"* for us. *Jesus' love will protect us at all times, for "perfect love casts out fear." I John 4:18.* It will also give us special understanding and discernment to know the difference between God's ways and Satan's ways; God's voice and Satan's voice; and God's fire and Satan's fire, for the fire that came and consumed the sacrifice David offered in I Chron. 21:26 was from Satan. See IFH 377, 378. When one reads EGW's comments about these type of experiences and the slaying of the priests of Baal on Mt. Carmel, by Elijah, you realize that none of the prophets of the O.T., and even John the Baptist of the N.T. did not fully comprehend the true character, mission or Spirit of the Lord Jesus. EGW understood more than any of them, even though she was a non-cannonical prophet. May the Lord bless each of us as we continue on in our quest for the fullness of His love to abide in our hearts.

No. 19. The following quotation from the Adult Sabbath School lesson quarterly—October-December 1985, page 52, of lesson 5, shows that God is inserting His truth in some SDA publications, in spite of the fact that most leaders and ministers do not believe in it.

"As a result, they will be destroyed by their own depravity. *'Whatsoever a man soweth, that shall he also reap. For he that soweth to his flesh shall of the flesh reap corruption'* (Gal. 6:7, 8). That is not an arbitrary judgment, but a natural outcome of evil. Persistent sinners bring about their own destruction—*'sin, when its finished, bringeth forth death'* (James 1:15).

"NOTE how such a retribution for wickedness is in accord with that which is foretold concerning 'the prince of Tyre,' who typifies Satan. Eze. 28:18.

"Sinners are destroyed by that which comes from inside themselves—sin brings forth 'a fire from the midst' of them and that fire consumes them. That consuming process is not limited to the time of the final judgment but is evident in the sinners; unhappiness and dissatisfaction in this life."

APPENDIX

"RIGHT" CAN NEVER
USE "MIGHT."

About 1979 I attended some meetings where Robert Wieland was speaking. It was so thrilling to hear and see portrayed on the screen the actual message of 1888. **It was also very clear. I had read a pamphlet that Pastor Wieland wrote which compared two other views of the 1888 message of Righteousness By Faith with the view endorsed by E.G. White and actually taught by Jones and Waggoner. On page 4 of this pamphlet, I read this: "The popular view said that God will torture the lost in an everburning hell.** The contemporary SDA view says, 'God will torture and destroy the lost in hell-fire that annihilates . . . that is they don't burn forever.' **But the 1888 view was 'God destroys no man; every man who is destroyed will destroy himself.'** Sin, not God, destroys the wicked. The second death is a merciful thing to end their real misery."

Alonzo T. Jones wrote: "Jesus Christ, our Conqueror, the conqueror in our behalf, came into this land of the enemy, fought our battles, went into the stronghold of the enemy; then brought forth the captives and led them in triumph upon high to His own glorious city. Now 'thanks be to God which always causeth us to triumph' in Christ. In Him we triumph over this illegal power. And in this triumph over Satan, there is displayed before the assembled universe the power of **right** as against **might**."

"Now note: **The power of right as against might can never use any might!** Do you not see that in that lies the very spirit that is called **Non-resistance** of Christians, that is, the very spirit of Jesus Christ, which is non-resistance? Could Christ use might in demonstrating the power of right as against might? **No.**

"For Satan to maintain the power of **might** as against **right, might** must be used at every opportunity; because that is the only weapon he can use to win. In Satan's cause, the right has only a secondary consideration, if it has any consideration at all.

"But on the other hand, **the power or right as against might, is in the right, not in the might. The might is in the right itself.** And he who is pledged to the principle of right as against might, and in whom that is to be demonstrated, **can never appeal to any kind of might. He can never use any might whatever in defense of the power of right. He depends upon the power of the right itself to win, and to conquer all the power of might** that may be brought against it. **That is the secret.**

"Then don't you see that that explains in a word why it is that Christ was like a lamb in the presence of this might that was brought against Him? **He had nothing to do with using any might** in opposing them. When Peter drew the sword, and would defend Him, he said, 'Put up your sword; he that taketh the sword shall perish by the sword.'

"Consequently, when tempted and tried as He was, when He was spit upon, when they struck Him in the face and on the hand, in all His public ministry **His hand was never raised to return the blow. Not even the impulse to make any such motion was ever allowed.** Yet He has our human nature, in which such impulses are so natural.

"When we get hold of that, all things will be explained as to what we shall do here, there, or the other place. **We are pledged to allegiance to the power of right as against might—the power of love.** And Jesus Christ died as a malefactor, abused, tossed about, mobbed, scoffed, spit upon, crowned with thorns, every conceivable contemptible thing put upon Him, and **he died under it, in His appeal to the power of right as against might.** And that power of right has moved the world ever since, **and it is to move the world in our day as it never has been moved before. Just as soon as God can get the people who are professedly pledged in heart to that principle, and who never expect to appeal to anything other than the absolute principle of the right, and to which we are pledged, then we shall see, and the world shall see this power working as never before."**

> **1895 G.C. Lectures**
> **Page 31—Lesson 22**
> **By Alonzo T. Jones**

Dear Friend,

This statement by A.T. Jones proves that "God does not kill," was a very special part of the 1888 message of R. By Faith. I believe it was the very heart of the message. mfc. 11-13-84

The following information is on an 8½ x 11 sheet I use to announce my meetings whenever I am invited to speak.

COMING SOON

A SPECIAL STUDY ON THE CHARACTER OF GOD, BY EVANGELIST MIKE CLUTE WILL BE GIVEN AT THE TIME AND PLACE STATED BELOW.

HERE ARE SOME OF THE THINGS YOU WILL LEARN:

1. How Jesus treated Judas, His betrayer. How Christ tried to warn and/or stop Judas Iscariot from this terrible deed at least 10 times. Live through the last supper again.

2. How Jesus never changes. How He is trying to stop every human being today from betraying him, and thus committing spiritual and eventually physical suicide.

3. That the way Jesus treated Judas is an example or sample of how He treated Lucifer in the beginning when Lucifer started a war in heaven against God the Father and His Son, Jesus.

4. The true meaning of what it means for God to "make war."

5. The true meaning of Psalm 2, the words "judgment and execute."

6. The true meaning of "the wrath of God," God's "anger," "fury," "indignation," "hate," "vengeance," etc.

HERE ARE SOME QUESTIONS WHICH WILL BE ANSWERED:

1. Did Jesus ever kill anyone in the Old Testament? What about in the New? How did Jesus cast out demons?

2. Did Jesus ever get mad? What about the temple scene when He made a whip and drove out the money changers?

3. What about the Flood, Sodom and Gomorrah, Uzzah, Korah, Dathan and Abiram and the 250

princes? Can these be explained from the Word of God, the Bible?

4. What about God's angels? Don't they kill on command? What about God himself? Is He allowed to break His own law by killing whenever He wants to or decides it is the only way to solve the problem? Is He **exempt** from His own law?

5. What about the "Fire of God"? Is it literal, symbolic or both?

6. What is the final message about anyway? And what is God really like? Can we know? These are just a few of the many questions which will be dealt with and answered in this study.

7. How can you explain certain statements in the Bible and EGW which specifically state that God does and will destroy?

TIME OF THE MEETING	PLACE OF THE MEETING

Bring your Bible and note book and pen or pencil.
There will be a question and answer period if so desired.

THE SPEAKER OF GOD'S LAST CALL MINISTRIES IS EVANGELIST MICHAEL F. CLUTE, FOUNDER AND DIRECTOR OF GLC, INC., WHICH GOD LED HIM TO ESTABLISH IN 1970 WHILE HE WAS A PASTOR-EVANGELIST IN THE SOUTHWESTERN PART OF THE

UNITED STATES. BROTHER MIKE, AS HE IS KNOWN TO HIS MANY FRIENDS AROUND THE WORLD WHO RECEIVE HIS GOD'S LAST CALL NEWSPAPER, WAS RAISED IN THE HOOSIER STATE OF INDIANA.

He was born in Anderson, Indiana, on January 21, 1938. The oldest of three children, he lived in that state until 1955, at which time the Lord moved his family to Walla Walla, Washington. Brother Mike's maternal grandmother was an SDA and his mother raised him an SDA. So he is a third generation Seventh-day Adventist and loves the church and message with all of his heart.

Entering Walla Walla College in the fall of 1956, Evangelist Clute graduated in 1960 with a B.A. in Theology and a minor in Biblical languages. Since his graduation, his only desire and goal has been to tell people the truth about Jesus, his Lord and Saviour. He spent three summers as a Literature-Evangelist, working his way through college. In 1960 he was an Assistant Colporteur Field Secretary for the Oregon Conference.

He also attended Andrews University in the summer of 1964, and Chicago Teacher's College North in 1965, in addition to post-graduate studies done at WWC in 1963. Two of these studies were done under conference sponsorship after he finished his tour in the U.S. Army as a medical corpsman from 1961 to 1963.

After teaching church school from 1963 to 1965, he was called to the Texico Conf. of SDA as a Pastor-evangelist where he did his internship under Kenneth O. Cox, pastor of the Albuquerque Central and Heights church. Brother Clute served there for 13 months as assistant pastor and helped build the Heights SDA church. In the fall of 1966, after a spinal fusion on his back, he was sent to the Abilene-

San Angelo-Sweetwater district of the Texas Conf. of SDA where he served for two years. The Lord gave him 22 souls during that tour. Next he was sent to the Victoria-El Campo district of South Texas where he pastored from the summer of 1968 until November of 1970. God blessed Pastor Clute and his faithful wife Sharon in helping them to establish a church in Victoria, Texas. This was also where God led him to begin the radio broadcast, GOD'S LAST CALL. He and Sharon have 3 children.

On May 13, 1970, the Lord Jesus led Pastor Clute to begin preaching the gospel on the gospel giant of the southwest, KCTA, 50,000 watts, which covered 27 states. The ministry was a success from the start and he resigned from the conference to further develop his ministry into a larger, more effective self-supporting ministry. Although he no longer has regular radio programs, he has conducted talk shows on several stations and still does if requested. His ministry now has broadened out into cassettes and publications along with his monthly newsletter and newspaper which is free of charge. He has written three books on the subject of God's character. "DOES GOD KILL PEOPLE," 1977. $4.95. "THE FINAL ABSOLUTE-ULTIMATE TRUTH ABOUT GOD," $7.95, 1979, and in 1982 he published a 412 page paperbook entitled "INTO THE FATHER'S HEART," only $2.95 each or $64.95 for a box of 75. He has about 125 sermons on cassette tape. His tape and publication catalogue has over 900 cassette tapes listed for your selection. If you would like to be on his free mailing list, just write to **GOD'S LAST CALL, P.O. Box 426, SCAPPOOSE, OREGON 97056**. If you would like to talk to Mike personally, feel free to call him a 1-503-543-3000 or 1-503-543-6400. Pastor Clute tries to answer each letter and will pray with you and counsel you if you write him.

CASSETTE TAPES AVAILABLE FOR CONTINUED RESEARCH AND STUDY ON THE "TWO LORDS" AND OTHER ASPECTS OF THE CHARACTER OF GOD.

651–Does God Kill Animals? . . . . .Mike Clute

652–Does God Demand Blood? . . . . .Mike Clute

661–Mt. Sinai and Animal Sacrifices . . . . .Stan Mark

662–How Did Animal Sacrifices Begin? . . . . . .Mark/Clute

663–God's Eternal Sacrifice . . . . .Stan Mark

665–Law of Moses and Sacrificial System . . . . .Stan Mark

650–Would Jesus Kill A Little Sparrow? . . . . . .Mike Clute

477–His Blood Proves He is Harmless–(1) . . . . .Mike Clute

478–His Blood Proves He is Harmless–(2) . . . . .Mike Clute

724–The Wrath of God .Mike Clute

717–Why Is The Sanctuary Dirty? . .Clute/Silver/Hutchings

718–What Really Was The First Lie? . . . . .Clute/Silver

719–How We Found Out
        God Does Not Kill . . . . .Silver/Hutchins

For a more complete list of many more cassette tapes on the character of God, write to:

> God's Last Call
> P. O. Box 426
> Scappoose, OR 97056

Personal Notes

SERMON AT MC MINNVILLE SDA CHURCH Aug. 7, 1976
EVANG. MIKE CLUTE

G O D " S   W R A T H

I. THE PURPOSE AND PLAN OF THE SERMON
   A. The purpose and plan of this sermon is to show
      1. That God is the great master architect of eternity.
      2. That God (God the Father, God the Son and God the Holy Ghost) all three have
         been co-equal from eternity and are the active agents in our redemption and
      3. That Jesus is the outward manifestation of the god-head. That he came to
         reveal the love of the God head and that love is the greatest attribute of
         God and despite the rebellion of Satan Jesus has all things under his control.
      4. That God never forces the will. He never makes anyone do what is right, if
         they don't want to. He appeals to us through our conscience by the Holy
         Spirit and thru Nature and through the Bible and through providential
         leadings and of course all of these are through the Spirit of God and the
         ministration of the angels Jesus sends.
      5. I want to show mainly today what God's wrath is and what it is not.
         Everything I say will be directed toward this main goal. For although we have
         mainly talked of his love in the past we must now talk of his wrath.

II.

     WHAT IS THE WRATH OF GOD.

      1. Instead of talking a lot and giving many texts for you to follow and think
         on so you can arrive at a final conclusion 20 minutes from now---rahher than
         doing that and taking the chance of getting sidetracked here and there with
         other ideas that might come in to our discussion as we contemplate what God's
         wrath is, let me just make a simple statement and then proceed to tell you
         why I believe this is true.
         a. GOD'S WRATH IS SIMPLY THE WITHDRAWING OF ALL RESTRAINTS---THE LETTING
           GO OF MAN TO LET HIM GO HIS OWN WAY AND DO HIS OWN THING...GOD'S WRATH IS
           SIMPLY WHEN HE SAYS, "ALRIGHT, IF YOU WANT TO GO INTO THAT MOVIE HOUSE TO
           SEE THE EXORCIST, GO AHEAD. I AM NOT GOING TO STOP YOU. IF YOU DESIRE TO
           WATCH TELEVISION 5 HOURS A DAY OR 2 or 3 AT NITETIME INSTEAD OF PRAY AND
           READ THE SCRIPTURE, GO RIGHT AHEAD. I WILL NOT STOP YOU. Now. we must
           realize that before God says this to a person he has tried every way possible
           to show him the right way. The Lord has sent his angels, his ministers and
           parents that he gave the person and no doubt many other people, friends,
           relatives and other Christians. But this person has refused to listen. As
           a result of letting a persnn go his own way and do his own thing, many bad
           things happen or take place. First of all the person who feeds his mind on
           things of the world---the desires of the flesh long enough will soon be getting
           involved in the things of the flesh which might include : smoking, drugs,
           alcohol, stealing, sexual permissiveness, stealing, and even murder. Sin is
           progressive...it does not stand still.
         b. To prove my point and help you to see that what I am saying is true, let us
           read Romans 1:16-18-24 and on. God gave them up. He came to the place where
           they would no longer listen, they would not and could not hear him and thus
           they went on into greater and greater sin experiences of sin and degradation
           and self-destructed. In the Bible, this is called the WRATH OF GOD. Letting
           a person go his own way and do his own thing. Not that God is doing this on
           purpose and trying to get even---Oh no...not at all. On the contrary, this
           makes Jesus very sad. For example let us see Christ on the day he was
           crucified.
           1. Spoke to the women on the way to GolGotha---Green t5e--dry tree---don't
              weeh for me, weep for yourselves and for yourchildren.
           2. Prayed for his tormentors that they be forgiven for they knew not what
              they were doing---mainly refering to the Roman soldiers and some others
              who were being deceived by the religious leaders etc.

II. GOD DESTROYS NO MAN....

   A. GOD NEVER KILLS ANYONE.... that is quite a statement you may be saying.
      How can you prove that?
   B. Let us look at some scriptures----
      1.James 1:17 Every perfect gift
   Every good gift and every perfect gift is from above, and cometh down from
the father of lights, with whom is no variableness, neither shadow of turning."
      2. Psalms 4:5 -Matt. 13:24-28 PS. 78:49 II COR. 12:7 ACTS 10:38 Luke 16:13
        FOR THOU ART NOT A GOD THAT HATH PLEASURE IN WICKEDNESS: NEITHER SHALL
EVIL DOWELL WITH THEE.
         a. COL 84---- GOD DESTROYS NO MAN
         b. GREAT CONTROVERSY-- page 36
         c. GREAT CONTROVERSY-- page 36 2nd paragraph---destruction of the world.

III.   WRATH OF THE LAMB AND THE FINAL END OF EVIL AND SIN.

   A.   DESIRE OF AGES 825
        1.   Illustration of father who ¢¢¢¢ plays with his little baby and has fun
             with him ---Baby wants to do wrong---no, no, baby get hurt, get burned.
        2.   Baby grows up and becomes a man and goes his own way---father can no
             longer pick up the child and make him do what is best for him----
        3.   SEVEN LAST PLAGUES-----
                a. LET ME ASK YOU BELOVED, ARE THESE PLAGUES THE RESULT OF AN ANGRY
                    GOD GETTING EVEN WITH ALL THE BAD PEOPLE WHO WILL NOT DO WHAT IS
                    RIGHT??? WHO WILL NOT KEEP THE TRUE SABBATH????
                1L. NO---- I SAY THE SEVEN LAST PLAUGES ARE SICKNESS AND DISEASE AND
                     AND TERRIBLE THINGS THAT GOD WILL LET MAN AND SATAN BRING UPON THE
                     EARTH AS A RESULT OF THE RESTRAINTS BEING LET GO.

                2. PROOF---GREAT CONTROVERSY---- 613, 614.....
                    READ REVEIATION 16 with this in mind now----Angels coming out of
heaven for what reason ??? to give the command to let go---¶¢¢I release, release,
release----no longer hold back man and Sataá in their efforts to do their own thing.

NOW PLEASE READ WITH ME REV. 11:18-----AND THE TEMPLE OF GOD WAS OPENED IN HEAVEN,
AND THERE WAS SEEN IN HIS TEMPLE THE ARK OF HIS TESTAMENT: AND THERE
AND THE NATIONS WERE ANGRY ETC   READ REVE. 11:18, 19 NOW WHO IS SAID TO BE
DESTROYING THE EARTH???? "THEM"OR THE HUMANS ON EARTH WHO ARE NOT FOLLOWING THE
PLAN OF GOD.   WHY HAVE THEY NOT SUCCEEDED YET??? BECAUSE GOD HAS BEEN RESTRAINING
THEM....ALRIGHT, NOW THE TEXT SAYS THAT GOD IS GOING TO STOP THEM FROM DESTROYING
THE EARTH BY DOING WHAT???? BY DESTROYING THEM----BY POURING OUT HIS WRATH UPON
THEM AND HOW DOES HE DO THIS???? READ PSALM 78:.49.   BY GIVING THEM UP AND
LETTING THEM GO THEIR OWN WAY.

III. FINAL DESTRUCTION OF WICKED

        A. CITY COMES DOWN FROM GOD OUT OF HEAVEN __NEW JERUSALEM...
ALL THE SAINTS INSIDE AND ALL THE WICKED OUTSIDE.
        RE.
        B. LET ME ASK YOU A QUESTION???? HOW DO YOU THINK ALL THE WICKED PEOPLE
ARE GOING TO FEEL WHEN THEY SEE ALL THE RIGHTEOUS INSIDE????
        1. They will feel sad they didn't make it. Yes, but what will they feel
next? Envy''''---they want the gold in the city---they plot to get it YES,---
BUT THEY CAN'T ---- NOW, THEY WANT TO KILL EVERYONE IN THE CITY, BUT THEY CAN'T
SO, LET ME ASK YOU... WHO ARE THEY GOING TO KILL???? YES, EACH OTHER. HAS THIS
EVER HAPPENED BEFORE....YEST IT HAPPENED IN THE DAYS OF GIDEION WITH THE
MIDDIANITES and to others too----MY FRIEND THIS IS GOD'S WRATH!!!! This is the
FIRE COMING DOWN FROM GOD OUT OF HEAVEN----NOW THERE IS FIRE IN THEIR HEARTS BURNING
THEM UP AND THEN THE FIREWORKS THEY HAVE PREPARED FOR THE SAINTS WILL EXPLODE IN
THEIR OWN FACES.

KEY TO ABBREVIATIONS OF E. G. WHITE BOOK TITLES

Key	*Book Title*
AA	*The Acts of the Apostles*
AH	*The Adventist Home*
1BC	*The Seventh-day Adventist Bible Commentary*, vol. 1 (2BC etc., for vols. 2-7)
CD	*Counsels on Diet and Foods*
CG	*Child Guidance*
CH	*Counsels on Health*
ChS	*Christian Service*
CM	*Colporteur Ministry*
COL	*Christ's Object Lessons*
CS	*Counsels on Stewardship*
CSW	*Counsels on Sabbath School Work*
CT	*Counsels to Parents, Teachers, and Students*
CW	*Counsels to Writers and Editors*
DA	*The Desires of Ages*
Ed.	*Education*
Ev.	*Evangelism*
EW	*Early Writings*
FE	*Fundamentals of Christian Education*
GC	*The Great Controversy*
GW	*Gospel Workers*
LS.	*Life Sketches of Ellen G. White*
MB	*Thoughts From the Mount of Blessing*
MH	*The Ministry of Healing*
ML	*My Life Today*
MM	*Medical Ministry*
MYP	*Messages to Young People*
PK	*Prophets and Kings*
PP	*Patriarchs and Prophets*
SC	*Steps to Christ*
SD	*Sons and Daughters of God*

1SG* . . . . . *Spiritual Gifts,* vol. 1
2SG . . . . . . *Spiritual Gifts,* vol. 2
3SG . . . . . . *Spiritual Gifts,* vol. 3
4SG-a . . . . . *Spiritual Gifts,* vol. 4, part 1
4SG-b . . . . . *Spiritual Gifts,* vol. 4, part 2
SL . . . . *The Sanctified Life*
1SM . . . . . *Selected Messages,* book 1
2SM . . . . . *Selected Messages,* book 2
SR . . . . *The Story of Redemption*
1T . . . . *Testimonies,* vol. 1 (2T etc., for vols. 2-9)
Te . . . . *Temperance*
TM . . . . *Testimonies to Ministers and Gospel Workers*
1TT . . . . . . *Testimony Treasures,* vol. 1 (2TT etc., for vols. 2 and 3)
WM . . . . . . *Welfare Ministry*

*In *Early Writings,* hence ignored in *Index.*

Buy this book in quantity
and save money—to order more copies
of this book, write to:

GOD'S LAST CALL MINISTRIES
P.O. BOX 426
SCAPPOOSE, OREGON 97056

Special Quantity Prices:

1-5	—	$6.95
6-24	—	$6.25
25 or more		$5.95

GOD'S LAST CALL MINISTRIES
P.O. BOX 426
SCAPPOOSE, OREGON 97056

Please send me _____ books. I am enclosing my check or money order for $_____. (Please add $1.95 for postage and handling for quantities of 25 or less.) Sorry we cannot ship C.O.D.

NAME _____

ADDRESS _____

CITY _ STATE _____ ZIP CODE _____
Allow 4-6 weeks for delivery

Personal Notes

GENERAL
INDEX

SCRIPTURE INDEX

Personal Notes

Personal Notes

Personal Notes

Personal Notes

Personal Notes

Personal Notes

Personal Notes

Personal Notes